ROMANTIC COMMUNIST

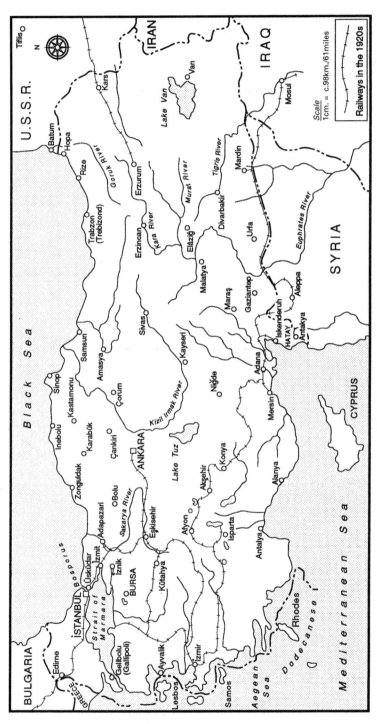

THE TURKISH REPUBLIC

SAIME GÖKSU
EDWARD TIMMS

Romantic
Communist

The Life and Work of
Nazım Hikmet

ST. MARTIN'S PRESS, NEW YORK

ROMANTIC COMMUNIST

St Martin's Press, Scholarly and Reference Division,
175 Fifth Avenue, New York, N.Y. 10010

First published in the United States of America in 1999

Printed in Malaysia

ISBN 0-312-22247-5

Library of Congress Cataloging-in-Publication Data

Göksu, Saime.
    Romantic communist : the life and work of Nazim Hikmet / Saime
Göksu, Edward Timms.
    p.   cm.
    Includes bibliographical references (p.   ) and index.
    ISBN 0-312-22247-5 (cloth)
    1. Nazim Hikmet. 1902-1963—Criticism and interpretation.
I. Timms, Edward. II. Title.
PL248.H45Z655   1999
894'.3513—dc21   98-51918
                                                                CIP

CONTENTS

ILLUSTRATIONS

vii

Sources of Illustrations

Permission to reproduce illustrations from the following sources is gratefully acknowledged:

Abidin and Güzin Dino (18, 32); Akşam Matbuası, Izmir (10a); Aziz Nesin Vakfı, Istanbul (5, 20, 26, 28b, 30a, 30b); Broy Yayınları, Istanbul (9); Bulgaristan Komunist Partisi Yayınları, Sophia (19); Cahit Uçuk (12a); Hungarian Press Archive (27); Ibrahim Balaban (15b, 21a, 21b); İletişim Yayınları, Istanbul (2); Iskusstvo Press, Moscow (29a, 29b, 29c); *Jane's Fighting Ships* (13); Joyce Lussu (31); Kıymet Coşkun (Fotoğraflarla Nazım Hikmet) (1, 17a, 24, 25, 28a); Memet Fuat (10b, 11, 14a, 14b); Münevver Andaç (22); Müzehher Va-Nu (4); Nazım Hikmet Vakfı, Istanbul (8, 16); *Sebilüreşad* magazine, Istanbul (23); Semiha Berksoy (12b); Toker Yayınları, Istanbul (7); University Library, Uppsala (6); *Vatan* newspaper, Istanbul (17b); Weidenfeld & Nicolson, London (3).

Authors' Note and Acknowledgements

This biography of the Turkish poet Nazım Hikmet portrays a writer who combined political courage with artistic creativity, even in the conditions of a prison. Born in Salonika in 1902, he was descended from a cosmopolitan Ottoman family. It was the turmoil of the First World War and the Allied occupation of Istanbul that inspired him to start writing poetry. After escaping to Ankara at the age of nineteen to join the anti-imperialist resistance, he was advised by Mustafa Kemal (Atatürk) to write 'poetry with a purpose', but it was in Moscow during the 1920s that he found his mission, drawing inspiration from the artistic experiments of Mayakovsky and Meyerhold as well as the political vision of Lenin. Returning to Istanbul in 1928, he became the charismatic leader of the Turkish avant-garde, publishing an exhilarating series of poems, polemics and plays. He was not only a communist committed to revolution, but a romantic who was passionately in love: with his country and his people, with nature, and with the women to whom he dedicates his finest poetry. Repeatedly arrested for his political beliefs, he was sentenced in 1938 to twenty-eight years' imprisonment on the trumped-up charge of organizing a revolt in the armed forces. His epic poem *Human Landscapes* was written during a ten-year period in Bursa prison.

An international campaign centred in Paris helped to secure Nazım's release under an amnesty in 1950, but the anti-communist climate of the Cold War led him to fear further imprisonment, and he fled to the Soviet Union in 1951. During the following decade he used his literary prestige to campaign against the spread of nuclear weapons, sharing a platform with Sartre, Picasso, Neruda, Ehrenburg and Aragon. In exile he remained remarkably creative, becoming involved in the theatre and broadcasting and entering into further relationships which find their echo in poignant lyrics and love letters, as well as political poetry of great imaginative power. His work, though banned in Turkey, was translated into many other languages. Approaching the age of sixty, he fell in love and married again, but his health had been undermined by the years in prison, and his late poetry is permeated by intimations of death. He died in Moscow in June 1963.

The career of Nazım Hikmet forms a microcosm of twentieth-century politics. He was a Turkish patriot who campaigned for international solidarity, and a poet of aristocratic temperament committed to the working class. Neither threats nor promises could induce him to renounce his political ideals and join the Kemalist establishment, and he paid for his beliefs by spending many long years in prison. If in exile he became the poet laureate of the Soviet-backed peace movement, this reflected a lifelong commitment to internationalism. His satire on Stalinism, *Ivan Ivanovich*, which was banned by the Soviet authorities, led Stalin's daughter Svetlana Alliluyeva to identify him with 'romantic communism'. His poetry celebrates the vitality of struggle rather than the authority of any system, and his writings retain their own vitality precisely because they challenge the historical determinism of his day, keeping the spirit of communism alive for future generations. 'He says his head accepts the historical, social and economic conditions, but his heart still burns', his critics would sneer, 'Well, just look at that Marxist!' The poet responded by insisting that a Marxist is not a 'mechanical man', but a 'social human being with flesh and blood, nerves, head and heart'. Communism, thus construed, is a commitment to an ideal future lived out under the all too real constraints of the present. The adventures inspired by this ideal are necessarily at odds with the frailty of its protagonists and the constraints of their historical situation.

This English literary biography of a passionately Turkish poet is the work of two authors of contrasting temperament: a therapist with a flair for human relationships and a historian fascinated by the power of ideas. The experience of co-authorship has confirmed the enrichment to be gained from self-immersion in another culture. Almost every sentence has been talked through between them during ten years of intensive collaboration, as the demand for a clear chronology and rigorous narrative structure came into conflict with the need to respect emotional ambiguities and artistic nuances. The aim is to avoid the idealization which has impaired some previous accounts, while at the same time doing justice to a life transfigured by poetic and political vision. The literature about Nazım Hikmet abounds in legends, and previous biographers have understandably become confused about the sequence of events.

In the present study a systematic attempt has been made to check every incident against a plausible source and obtain confirmation through personal interviews. However, there are inevitably omissions and errors which will have to be remedied by further research.

The origins of this book may be traced back to the experiences of a schoolgirl growing up in the Turkey of the the 1940s, when Nazım and most of his comrades were in prison and their work was banned. Saime's father served as health officer in Malatya, a provincial town in central Anatolia, and one of his duties was to ensure that adequate standards of hygiene were maintained in the local prison. This provided an opportunity to make contact with Kemal Tahir, a political prisoner who was one of Nazım's closest friends. In his novel *Kadınlar Koğuşu* (The Women's Block), which he began in Malatya prison, Tahir pays tribute to the helpfulness of Ibrahim the health officer, who has 'nothing to lose but his chains'. The writings of Turkish communists circulated secretly during this period, and Saime was reprimanded by one of her teachers when she ventured to recite a subversive poem in class. For almost a generation the radical tradition of Turkish writing was suppressed, and it was not till the early 1960s that a collected edition of Nazım's writings appeared, published by a Turkish-language press in Sofia. When Saime came to study in England, this edition rekindled her enthusiasm for Nazım's work, and it was during long discussions with Edward Timms that this biography was conceived.

The book could not have been written without the help of many people who knew Nazım well and have generously shared their memories of his life and times. Special thanks are due to members of the poet's family: his stepson Memet Fuat; his sister Samiye Yaltırım and half-sister Fatma Melda Kalyoncu; his cousin Ayşe Baştımar; his widow Vera Tulyakova Hikmet; and Münevver Andaç, the mother of his child. In a further series of interviews and conversations we received valuable guidance from Niyazi Berkes, Nermin Menemencioğlu, Refik Erduran, Halet Çambel, Nail Çakırhan, Ibrahim Balaban, Kemal Sülker, Aydın Aydemir, Güzin Dino and her husband Abidin, Müzehher Vala Nurettin, Kıymet and Atilla Coşkun, Cahit Uçuk, Semiha Berksoy, Mehmet Bozışık, Mehmet Ali Aybar, Mehmet Ali Sebük, Mustafa Ekmekci, Leman Karaosmanoğlu, Bilal Şen, Vedat Günyol, Vedat Türkali, Rady Fish and his family, Vera Feonova, Katerina Kobalatze,

xii   *Authors' Note and Acknowledgements*

György Somlyó, Itsvan Kúnos, Yılmaz Gülen, Gün Benderli, Yıldız Sertel and Rasih Nuri Ileri. A number of others have answered our queries by correspondence and helped to obtain illustrations and other source-material, including the Nazım Hikmet Vakfı in Istanbul, Joyce Lussu, Ilona Sármány-Parsons, Tofik Melikov, Şükrü Göksu (photographer), Ülkü Özen and Emrecan Özen. Thanks are also due to relatives and friends who provided hospitality on our visits to Turkey.

We are grateful to those who have read our manuscript and made many helpful criticisms, including Talat Halman, Celia Kerslake, Andrew Mango and Gündüz Vassaf; and to friends who have commented on specific chapters, including Robin Milner-Gulland, Ritchie Robertson, John Ramsay, Brian Easlea and Yeter Göksu. Our debt to previous scholars, especially the late Kemal Sülker, will be evident from the Bibliography, which also lists the archives which have generously faciltiated our research. Ali Nesin was particularly helpful in allowing free access to the archive established by his father, Aziz Nesin, at the 'Children's Paradise' in Çatalca. During a week's stay Saime particularly appreciated the welcome she received from the children and the staff.

We would like to acknowledge a grant from the British Academy, which supported a research trip to Moscow. Nazım's literary executor, Memet Fuat, has been particularly generous in answering our questions and allowing us to quote from his edition of the collected works. We would also like to thank those who have given permission to quote their translations of Nazım's poetry: Randy Blasing and Mutlu Konuk; Richard McKane; and Taner Baybars. We hope that this biography will whet the reader's appetite to read more of Nazım's poetry, currently available in English in two volumes published by Persea Press: *Poems of Nazım Hikmet* and *Human Landscapes: An Epic Novel in Verse*, both translated by Randy Blasing and Mutlu Konuk.

We are delighted that the poet Yevgeny Yevtushenko, who knew Nazım personally in the 1950s, has written a Preface for this book. Finally, we would like to record our appreciation for illuminating discussions with our son Yusuf, in whom the spirit of revolutionary socialism lives on.

March 1999   S. G.
                                                 E. T.

Preface

Great Actor – Pity about the Play!

by Yevgeny Yevtushenko

How communism murdered communism

There are many examples of major twentieth-century figures in the arts who were convinced communists for at least part of their lives: Mayakovsky, Picasso, Greene, Orwell, Neruda, Kobo, Pasolini, Eluard, and finally the great Turkish poet Nazm Hikmet – the subject of this first comprehensive biography. Why should this have been so? It would be easiest of all to dismiss the phenomenon with a haughty shrug of the shoulders and the contemptuous response 'Propaganda'. It was all more complicated than that. Official communist propaganda was essentially too primitive to win over so many hearts. People could hardly become seriously enamoured of such *bon mots* as Lenin's 'Communism equals Soviet power plus electrification', or Stalin's 'The teaching of Lenin is invincible because it is true', or Brezhnev's 'Economics must be economical'.

The greatest propaganda for communism was none other than the capitalist system with its genuine exploitativeness (no mere invention of the communists), with its crises, its unemployment, its venal politicking and the most barbarous of its forms of expression: imperialism, racism and finally fascism. The 'spectre of communism', rather poetically conjured up by Marx and Engels in the *Communist Manifesto*, self-confidently promised to get rid of all this; its authors can scarcely have suspected that communist exploitativeness and even communist imperialism could also exist, while the Gulag Archipelago could scarcely have figured in their worst nightmares. But their fine and, alas, unwise idea contained within it the lethal seed of perfectionism, out of which sprouted the forcible 'perfectionising of the people', which required the setting-up of those merciless organs of power, the Cheka, GPU,

NKVD and KGB. The spectre, formerly amiable, changed its skeleton into a governmental structure and became as alarming as if it were a Cyclops with the single eye of a single permitted ideology. It is significant that the writer Zamyatin – a citizen of Russia, the country where communism (so long awaited by the workers and leftist intelligentsia throughout the world) first turned from a spectre unto reality – wrote the first diatribe against barrack-room communism at a time when George Orwell (who later continued Zamyatin's work) was still full of youthful communist illusions. The International Brigade in Spain, made up mostly of idealists, began to fall apart together with its illusions when sectarian folly in the shape of fanatics like Marti, or the cynical Stalinist agents described by Hemingway, started to take over.

The Second World War nurtured the second wave of pro-communist illusions. The italian *Unità* journalist Augusto Pancaldi told me that he had joined the Party after reading Arthur Koestler's *Darkness at Noon* towards the end of the 1930s and deciding it was a fascist-inspired anti-Soviet work. But together with euphoria, victory brought mutual fear between the former allies, who were now enemies, and again illusions collapsed. The Cold War induced paranoia on both sides of the so-called ideological front. The resulting witch-hunt was shameful both in the Soviet Union and the United States, though with the difference that McCarthyism seemed relatively modest in comparison with the scale and harshness of what went on in the land of the hideously fleshed-out 'spectre of communism'. More and more people in the West, as they beheld the spectre that not long before had looked like their salvation, became disillusioned and fearful.

But there was a Third World too where the tyranny of powerlessness and hunger was so terrible, and the spectre of communism so distant, that the latter appeared as the one and only hope of all disenfranchised people of the world. Such a land was Turkey, where the poet Nazım Hikmet had languished for many years in prison before and during the Cold War. As idealistic communists like him became ever fewer, they came to look like mammoths spared from extinction by some miracle. During the following decades the Pasternak affair, the crushing of the Hungarian uprising, the crackdown on abstract artists, the invasion of Czechoslovakia and finally the Afghan war did away with such idealism. But it remains as an inalienable part of history: it has its noble knights, for whom the communist ideal was a romantic a symbol as Dulcinea was for Don Quixote. This romanticism ended tragically: perhaps with a bullet in the back of the head or with prison-camp, perhaps with full-scale disillusionment and then suicide (physical or moral), perhaps through saving one's skin by betraying friends, perhaps through absurdly nurturing past illusions by shutting one's eyes to the present.

In 1980 I had a call from my old friend Warren Beatty, notable as an actor and yet more notable as seducer of famous actresses, who told me he was making a film of John Reid's *Ten Days that Shook the World* and offered me the part of Trotsky. 'Have you ever seen a photograph of Trotsky?', I asked him. A negative grunt came out of the telephone, and I cheekily guessed that the great seducer simply hadn't had the time for little details like that.

'Trotsky is not important. I just want to put you in the film.... Think of a part for yourself.'

'Ok', I agreed, 'send the script along.'

'What script?' said Warren in native amazement. 'I'm my own boss. Every day I get new ideas....'

Warren did not manage to tempt me into a part. I suggested the Polish writer Jerzy Kosinski for the role of Trotsky: unlike me, he at least bore a distant resemblance to the theorist of permanent revolution. But when I watched this inevitably simplistic, even though talented film, I was forcibly struck by its documentary section at the beginning: a series of interviews with a small number of elderly Americans who had miraculously survived history as idealistic communists. I was endlessly sorry for them since they were the most pure-hearted people, betrayed by their own illusions.

Of course, there were communist spies during the Cold War. Were there no anti-communist spies as well? Or is everyone else allowed to spy except the Russians? Some were lured by money; others, however, by ideology. Nothing can be more villainous than a romantic bribe. Communism offered the greatest of temptations – social justice. The tragedy of the idealistic communists was that when their idea materialised in its Stalinist form, it turned out to be a bloodstained caricature of a dream. The dream had been violated by cynics. Communism had killed communism.

Warren Beatty filmed *Reds* virtually without a script. Basically, history itself is just such an improvisatory film-director; in history, just as in a theatre, one can sometimes act one's role brilliantly even in a bad play. Nazım Hikmet played just such an inspirational part in the spectacle of communism, so poorly directed by history and thus doomed to an unhappy ending.

The arrival of an idealist in a land of cynicism

When a nineteen-year-old redheaded Turk with cornflower-blue Russian eyes first reached Soviet Russia in 1921, he came to a place of idealism, even if already blood-spattered by the Civil War. Chagall was still painting the decor for propaganda spectacles; avantgardists like Malevich, Rodchenko, Lerionov, Goncherova, Filonov, Falk and Lentulov were on exhibition; Mayakovsky was thundering forth in all arenas like a versifying Eiffel Tower and putting out agitational posters with pictures of round-bellied bourgeois spitted on the merciless bayonet of Revolution; Eisenstein in *Battleship Potemkin* set a pram-wheel in motion on the Odessa steps that has bounced down staircases in a multitude of films ever since; Isadora Duncan danced for Red Army men, trying not to notice the husks of sunflower-seeds sticking to her bare feet; Meyerhold staged his explosive productions without guessing that before long he – the great theatre director of the Revolution – would be beaten with rubber hosepipes in the blood-smeared cellars of the Lubyanka, since the country had room for only one great director of the Revolution: Stalin himself. But this Soviet Thermidor still lay in the future.

As a young man Nazım found himself amidst the convulsive post- revolutionary artistic renaissance that made haste to flower, sensing instinctively the tragic brevity of its blossoming. A hungry Revolution, which also managed to be generous to talent, splashed out on screens, stages, gallery walls and journal pages an abundance of new names – each more talented than the last. It was the pre-Prison-Camp Renaissance. Its energy was so great that it gave world art an impulse that determined its course for many years. It was the same as happened with the cosmos: Russians were the first to make space flights, but could not manage to be first on the moon.

When Nazım returned to Russia through Romania after a twenty-three year absence, his experience was that of an idealist coming to a place of cynicism. What had extracted him from

behind bars was a political campaign in his defence run mostly
by French leftists, but also by some Soviet writers. As a nineteen-
year-old poet myself at the time, I too published ringing rhetorical
poems dedicated to Nazım, and now lo and behold: this legendary
person was at last coming to live with us in Moscow! While still
behind bars he had written a heartfelt ode to Stalin as victor over
Hitler; but he hadn't yet guessed (or perhaps he feared to guess)
that there was another personality living within Stalin: the ex-
ecutioner not only of so-called 'enemies of the revolution' but
of the Revolution itself. The country of Nazım Hikmet's dream
did not exist: he had come to a very different land. It was 1951.
Stalin's ultimate paranoia was beginning, and was to end with
the arrest of his own doctors.

The euphoria brought about by Nazım's return was superim-
posed on this paranoia. When asked in Romania whom he would
like to see again, he joyously exclaimed 'Kolya Ekk'. The film
director Nikolai Ekk was a friend from his youth. In 1931 he
had filmed the famous *Ticket to Life* about homeless children whom
the Soviet authorities were engaged in 'remodelling', to use the
expression of the time. In 1932, at the first Venice International
Film Festival, Ekk had been voted Best Director in a poll of
spectators. But times were changing. Soviet power was intruding
not only on the ideology but on the style of art, treating even
formal experiments as a deviation from the newly-invented 'Socialist
Realism'. The boisterous experimentalism of the 1920s and 1930s
gave way to a communist provincial Hollywood. Ekk was no
longer needed and became all but unemployed; he began drinking.
In 1951 he was practically pulled out of a ditch, smelling like an
old dog, to meet Nazım; they washed him down, freshened him
up as far as possible, pinned a copy of his medal (which he had
either lost or pawned for booze) on his lapel, shoved a bunch
of roses into his hastily-manicured hands, pushed him into a big
black car and drove him off to meet the famous Turkish peace
campaigner.

Nazım greeted his old comrade and asked – quite against the
expectations of his entourage from the KGB and Writers' Union
– 'What are you doing for us in the cinema nowadays, Kolya?'
A panic-stricken silence ensued. One of the cultural bosses began
making desperate gestures to Ekk from behind Nazım's back,
rolling his eyes and waving his arms as if to say: 'For goodness

sake tell him something, *anything*....' Ekk realised that this was his unique opportunity and shuddered like a cavalry charger being hitched up to a dung-cart.

'For some reason, Nazım, I've been attracted to the circus recently. I want to do a water-based spectacular!' he answered, triumphantly resurrecting a semi-intoxicated idea which had long ago been 'spiked' in some office; he grabbed the nearest cultural bureaucrat by the shirtfront and whispered: 'Now you can't get out of sending along a contract....' But in spite of Nazım's support, they still eventually managed to 'get out of it', since Ekk put forward a science-fiction style project which would have required the Central Market building on Tsvetnoy Boulevard to be totally demolished and artificial hills erected in its place, with water on the scale of Niagara cascading down them.

Soon after his arrival, Nazım was due to be received by Stalin. Before this meeting Nazım, a long-time man of the theatre, hungry to experience the Moscow stage he had once worshipped, eagerly sought out plays by the heirs of Meyerhold, the director he had so admired. But what were these heirs like? In those days the stage was dominated by Surov and Sofronov, both Stalin Prize winners, authors of dozens of current plays. It later emerged that Surov himself didn't actually write his plays: for this purpose he hired what he called 'niggers', that is to say Jewish writers whom he himself had forced out of the Writers' Union. Sofronov, author of some fairly good wartime songs, did write his own plays, but only in the limited time available from his work of unmasking 'cosmopolitans', so he could scarcely manage to polish up his masterpieces. Theatre was dominated by the 'theory of non-conflict', which held that there could be no conflict between good and bad in the happy life of the Soviet People – only conflict between the good and the outstanding. Such was the emasculated drama that Nazım could watch in 1951.

A banquet for the so-called 'creative intelligentsia' was held in honour of Nazım one evening after the theatres had finished. It was hosted by Yury Zavadsky, a talented but thoroughly cynical director with the manners of a former aristocrat turned *maître d'hotel*. He made a long welcoming speech consisting of phrases as polished as he was; meanwhile Kolya Ekk, washed and clothed by the Soviet powers-that-be, yet still with an ineradicable doggy smell, sat at the banqueting table and, nervous in case he should

be summarily removed, kept accidentally knocking over glasses
of top-quality Armenian brandy.

Nazım patiently heard out the compliments flying in his direction; but when the time came to make a speech in response, his
face hardened and his eyes took on a metallic glint. 'Brothers',
said he in his guttural Russian, 'when I was in solitary confinement,
I think I got through only by dreaming of the Moscow theatres.
I dreamt of Meyerhold and Mayakovsky.... It was street-revolution
that had turned into stage-revolution. And what have I seen in
the Moscow theatres now? I've seen a petty-bourgeois tasteless
art that somehow manages to call itself realism – socialist realism
into the bargain. As well as that, I've seen any amount of servility
on the stage – and off-stage, too. How can servility be revolutionary?
In a few days I have to meet Comrade Stalin, whom I deeply
admire. But I'm going to talk with him frankly, as one communist
with another, and tell him he ought to arrange for those endless
portraits and statues to be taken away: it's all so vulgar....'

A deathly silence descended – the only sound was of Kolya
Ekk slurping brandy. Some of the guests began trying to tiptoe
out of the room so that with any luck they might not be counted
as witnesses of this unimaginably daring speech. Quietly, so that
only those sitting beside him could hear, Kolya muttered: 'Nazım
wouldn't talk like that if he did a stretch in one of our prisons
instead of a Turkish one....' In an attempt to relieve the atmosphere
of shock, Zavadsky raised a glass of champagne in his trembling,
manicured fingers with the words: 'My dear Nazım! I'm sure
Comrade Stalin doesn't like some of his portraits either. But there
aren't enough Rembrandts or Repins to fix his image properly.
You can't imagine that Comrade Stalin would forbid the people
to love Comrade Stalin! Let's drink a toast to Comrade Stalin!
To Communist Number One!'

'What, you mean it's not only the communists in prison who
have numbers?' asked Nazım. Evidently, Kolya Ekk or another
of his old friends had already enlightened him as to where so
many of his teachers had vanished to. The remark was made
quietly. But those who needed to hear it did so.

Next day Nazım was informed that the intended meeting had
been indefinitely postponed since Comrade Stalin was extremely
busy.

The penitent driver goes down on his knees

Early in the morning I get a telephone call: a familiar guttural voice speaks in a unique and bewitching accent. 'How are you doing, brother? Do you need my money? No? What a pity. I've just had a cash advance which is much too big for me. Here – don't you know any good people who are short of money at the moment?' (unimaginable nowadays that such a call should come from anybody).

Nazım loved and supported young artists who had no official recognition; he was one of the first to buy work from the still little-known Oleg Tselkov, to whom he gave the job of doing the sets for his play *Sword of Damocles* at the Satire Theatre. Oleg recently told me how, about 1955, they once sat together on the bank of the Moscow-Volga canal at Tushino, and Nazım ironically shifted his eyes to indicate two shadowy figures looming at a polite distance. 'Who are those men?', asked Tselkov, not understanding. Nazım shrugged his shoulders: 'They're following, brother....' 'What, following *you*? A Peace Prize winner? Why?', asked the astonished Tselkov. 'One's following so that nobody annoys me. The other's following so that I don't annoy anyone else.... That's the way it is, brother!'

The same year, Nazım invited the artist Yuri Vasilyev and me to Peredelkino for a couple of days. That was his form of hospitality: he would unplug the telephones and devote all his time to one or two guests. We sat around all day on Turkish cushions and our conversation wandered unhurriedly, like the steam rising from the Turkish tea which he served in bulbous glasses set in silver holders; meanwhile Yuri Vasilyev was just as unhurriedly decorating the inside of the door, while history, unpredictable in its cruel haste, rushed headlong on its way on the far side of the door.

But history itself opened up that door, which was too weak to withstand its pressure. History burst in on us in the form of a drunken elderly man with drifting eyes as blue as Hikmet's. Taking not the slightest notice of the two of us, this person looked at Nazım alone, lowered his gaze, tore off his sodden imitation-fur hat with its remarkably phony violet-coloured trim and suddenly collapsed on to his knees.

'For Christ's sake forgive me, Nazım – relieve me of my sin.... I've something I must tell you.' Violet tears trickled from his hat to the floor. Nazım hauled him up: 'Up you get, brother – you don't have to say a thing.' 'No, I'm certainly going to tell you. I've been carrying it around with me for so many years and I can't stand it any more.' Tripping over his words, the newcomer told the story that was tormenting him.

In 1951 Nazım had an official car with a driver put at his sole disposal. The newcomer was that very driver. They became friends, and Nazım had once even been invited to his home. In 1952 the driver had been summoned to the Lubyanka. He was shocked to see Beria himself appear in front of him.

'Do you know who it is you're driving around?', Beria asked him. 'A Peace Prize winner...a Turkish communist...a great poet...a friend of the Soviet Union...', answered the bewildered driver. 'He's not a friend of the Soviet Union but an enemy,' muttered Beria, 'an experienced enemy who has put on the mask of a revolutionary. He wants to kill Comrade Stalin. But we can't arrest him – he's too famous; besides, he's Turkish. You must help us remove him. How tricky would it be for a good professional driver to stage a realistic-looking accident? We'd have one spy fewer!'

'I can't believe it,' said the driver. 'He's like a father to me.' 'We each only have one father,' said Beria darkly. Next day the driver was called into the Lubyanka again and his agreement was demanded. The driver was given a beating, but he refused to agree. Then his wife was brought into the office, and after that some hardened criminals. 'These nice boys haven't tried out any female flesh for years,' said the policeman, eloquently looking first at them and then at the driver's wife. The driver got the message and agreed.

Several times he was alerted that the accident was to take place the following day, but for one reason or another it would be postponed at the last minute. Then Stalin died, and Beria was shot. Nazım got a car of his own and no longer needed the official one. His driver went off to drive a taxi – anything to get away from the government that had nearly made him into a murderer. But his guilt towards Nazım burned on inside him, tormented him and gave him no peace: so now he had come to repent.

During this story, which made my blood run cold, I looked at Nazım rather than at the driver. He had the self-control of the real conspirator: not a muscle of his face moved. Or had he maybe guessed it all before? 'Lift the sin off my soul,' begged the driver again. 'There's no sin involved,' replied Nazım. 'Better have a drink of vodka. My doctors have told me not to, but I reckon I can take a little with the right person. And you, brother, are an honest man. How are your wife and children getting on? I remember her very well. She made nice cherry pastries when I came and visited you.... Incidentally, did you know that the Russian word for cherry, *vishnya*, comes from Turkish?' None of us had known that.

Universal passport

I believe that a few high United Nations officials hold a 'universal passport', although I have never seen one. But Nazım belonged to the class of people whose whole life, rather than their official duties, earned them a passport of this kind.

The authorities in his own country did all they could to ensure that Nazım was forgotten, but they did not succeed. When I first visited Turkey in 1986, not one of his volumes was on display at the book market in Ankara, and the Turkish schoolteachers and pupils whom I questioned had never heard his name. But the young Turkish poet Özdemir Ince gave me his photo, which had hung like a little icon in his home. I put this portrait above my writing desk at Peredelkino on a faded wooden post labelled B-13 with a tangle of barbed wire from a Kolmya prison camp. That was the end-point of the illusions of many idealists of the same species to which Nazım belonged. Turkish prison bars saved him from Soviet ones, and if he had not returned home by the beginning of the 1930s he would not have survived 1937. Beyond the limit of that year he would have been as unimaginable as Meyerhold or Mayakovsky. He was a reminder of so many un-realised revolutionary illusions, a uniquely entrancing living anachronism from the romantic period of the 1920s and a belated tragic witness to the epoch of the Great Betrayal of Hopes.

He did not behave in the Soviet Union like a foreigner; in contrast to many of our cowardly fellow-countrymen he spoke out boldly on any topic, criticised the authorities, and defended talented people who were being persecuted. This irritated the bosses. His satire on Soviet bureaucracy, the play *Ivan Ivanovich*, was eventually banned. They threw at him the accusation that as a foreigner he had no right to poke his nose into our internal affairs, but he considered that humanity had no 'internal affairs', and he was right. He had to move to Poland; when he returned, he managed to obtain a Soviet passport. I remember an evening devoted to his work, at which after official congratulations on becoming a Soviet citizen he held aloft his new passport and cheerfully, proudly announced that not a single Ivan Ivanovich would be able to reproach him now for being a foreigner who had no business to be 'poking his nose in'.

Eventually his heart, worn out by prison life, let him down. One day he went out as usual to get the Moscow morning papers and died as he got back home, clutching them to his chest – as if they represented the whole planet with its many hopes, whether disappointed already or still confident of realisation.

Wherever they are, people like Nazım are never foreigners: their heart becomes their universal passport. The role Nazım played in history was foreordained for him. Only such a foreordained role can be acted out with genius.

February 1998   YEVGENY YEVTUSHENKO
                                  (translated by Robin Milner-Gulland)

Guide to Turkish Spelling and Pronunciation

For almost all Turkish words and proper names, this book uses the modern Turkish spelling. However a small number of proper names have been simplified, including Nazım, Celal and Melahat, which in Turkish publications are written as Nâzım, Celâl and Melâhat (the *â* has the effect of softening and lengthening the vowel).

In the Turkish alphabet there are 29 characters. Apart from *â*, there are six other characters which do not exist in English:

ç pronounced as in *ch*urch
ğ like *gh* in English fri*gh*tened, the *ğ* is not itself voiced but has the effect of lengthening the preceding vowel
ı as in Nazım, sounded like the second vowel in lov*a*ble
ö as in French '*seul*'
ş is the equivalent of *sh* in short
ü as in French '*lu*mière'

1

The Young Patriot
1902-1920

'I never returned to the city of my birth,' Nazım recalled in a late poem (A 7, 99).[1] The place where he was born, on 15 January 1902, was the troubled city of Salonika, the westernmost outpost of the Ottoman Empire, where his father served as a government official. Its geographical position, as well as its cosmopolitan population, made Salonika particularly accessible to Western ideas, and it is no coincidence that it was also the birthplace of Mustafa Kemal (Atatürk), founder of the Turkish Republic. It was through Salonika that revolutionary ideas began to enter the Ottoman Empire, and in 1908 the city provided the base from which the Young Turks made their bid for power, challenging the authority of the despotic Sultan Abdul Hamid. The new government sent the Sultan into exile, replacing him with the more malleable Sultan Mehmed Reşad. But far from bringing stability, the change of regime exacerbated the weaknesses of the system. Even the seizure of power in January 1913 by Enver Pasha, the most hawkish of the Young Turks, could not prevent further reverses. Military defeat in the Balkans forced the Ottomans to renounce almost all their European territories, and Salonika was ceded to Greece.

Pashas and poets

Nazım, originally named Mehmet Nazım, grew up amid this turmoil. He came from a cosmopolitan family which formed part of the Ottoman ruling class, since his mother Celile was partly

---

[1] For an explanation of the system of abbreviations and references used in this book, see page 352.

of Polish, partly of Huguenot descent, and both her grandfathers
were men of great distinction. Her mother's father was Mehmet
Ali Pasha, who had begun life under the name Karl Detroit as
a member of a Hugenot community in Brandenburg. The career
of this remarkable man is recalled in a memoir by Theodor Heuss,
first President of the Federal Republic of Germany. Born in 1827,
he was brought up in an orphanage before becoming cabin-boy
on a ship sailing from Hamburg to Istanbul. There the adventurous
youth swam ashore, landing by chance in the park of the Ottoman
Foreign Minister, Ali Pasha, who became his protector. After
converting to Islam and adopting the name Mehmet Ali, he made
his career in the Ottoman army, winning honours in the campaigns
against Russia and rising to the rank of Field Marshal. At the
Berlin Congress of 1878 he acted as representative of the Sublime
Porte, negotiating under the auspices of Bismarck for the best
possible peace settlement with Russia. During the congress his
gift for languages and his wide-ranging literary interests won him
many admirers. Later that same year, however, he was sent to
quell a revolt in Albania, only to meet his death at the hands of
the insurgents (Heuss, 246-59).

The second of Nazım's distinguished great-grandfathers was
Constantine Borzenski, a Polish aristocrat who was forced into
exile after the revolution of 1848. He escaped to Istanbul with
other Polish and Hungarian radicals and converted to Islam, changing his name to Mustafa Celalettin Pasha. Later he made his
reputation not only as an Ottoman military commander, but also
as a historian, cartographer and linguist. In his book *Les Turcs
anciens et modernes* (1869) he emphasized the links between Turkey
and Europe, arguing in favour of a westernization of the Ottoman
Empire. Nazım was proud of the radical tradition associated with
his Polish ancestry. 'Whenever there was a struggle for freedom',
he wrote in a late poem, 'wasn't there a Pole in the front line?'
(A 6, 31). Towards the end of his life, after being forced into
exile and deprived of his Turkish nationality, he himself became
a Polish citizen, adopting the name Hikmet-Borzenski.

Constantine's son, Enver Celalettin Pasha, was also a linguist,
with progressive views on education, and he set up a school in
the Istanbul suburb of Erenköy. It was from his marriage to Leyla
Hanım, the daughter of Mehmet Ali Pasha, that in 1879 Nazım's
mother Celile was born. As a young woman she had consented

to an arranged marriage with Hikmet Bey, but she was an un-
conventional person, determined not to be trapped by domesticity.
By the age of fifteen she was already showing talent as a painter,
and she developed into a liberated woman who participated in
mixed social gatherings without wearing the customary veil. In
her late thirties she became increasingly dissatisfied with her marriage, feeling that her artistic talents were being frustrated. She
had a good knowledge of French and enjoyed reading poetry,
especially the work of Lamartine, and she encouraged her son's
interest in literature and painting. Reading the novels of Jules
Verne, the young Nazım was inspired by fantasies of exotic travel,
and towards the end of his life he recalled he had longed to be
a postman, driving a dog-sled across the ice in the Arctic twilight
to deliver mail to remote communities (A 6, 36). He began drawing
pictures of postmen whenever he had a spare moment. Despite
family tensions, Nazım remained strongly attached to his mother,
who was to provide him with invaluable moral support later in
life.

Nazım's father Hikmet Bey, who was born in Istanbul in 1876,
came from a more traditional background. His father, Nazım
Pasha, had been a leading figure in the Ottoman civil service.
The name Nazım Hikmet, which was later adopted by the poet,
thus incorporated both his father's and his grandfather's name.
Hikmet Bey studied at Galatasaray High School, where he learned
to speak French. He was working for the Foreign Ministry in
Salonika when his mother, Samiye Hanım, chose the talented
Celile as his bride. Salonika was already a hotbed of political
intrigue, and when he returned to Istanbul, Hikmet Bey was
detained for twenty days and interrogated about alleged subversive
activities. In 1905, when Nazım was three years old, his father
was obliged to resign from the foreign service, and the family
moved to Aleppo to live with Nazım Pasha. There Hikmet Bey
invested his money in an unsuccessful project to grow birch trees.
It was not only the saplings that wilted in the heat of Aleppo;
Nazım's baby brother, Ali Ibrahim, also succumbed to the effects
of the arduous climate. When Nazım Pasha was transferred to a
new post, Hikmet Bey decided to return to Istanbul, and it was
here in April 1907, at their home in Kadıköy, that Nazım's sister
Samiye was born, a lively playmate who was to prove his lifelong
ally. In Istanbul, Hikmet Bey attempted to start a new business,

this time a dairy farm, but he was easily distracted and soon began to fritter away his money on foreign travel. After visiting Paris with a theatre group, he lost interest in the business and was declared bankrupt. However, the success of the Young Turks brought a change in his fortunes. In 1909 he was appointed as translator in the press department of the Foreign Ministry, even doing a short spell of duty at the Turkish consulate in Hamburg in 1918. On his return to Istanbul after the defeat of the Central Powers, he resigned from the foreign service and became managing director of a publishing firm which produced the magazine *Alemdar* (Standard Bearer). During the final phase of his chequered career, he became manager of a cinema, and so remained till his death in March 1932.

Through his family heritage the young poet found himself poised between the old world and the new, the cinematic culture of modernity and the mystical traditions of Islam. For his most important role model was not his father but his grandfather, Nazım Pasha, an Ottoman administrator with mystical tendencies. Born in Istanbul on 29 August 1840, Nazım Pasha had become a friend of the three great liberal poets Namık Kemal, Ziya Pasha and Mithat Pasha during the 1870s. He was thus associated with the movement for cultural renewal which was to sow the seeds of revolution. Unlike the poets, whose radical writings earned them many years in exile, Nazım Pasha managed to combine a progressive outlook with a successful career. Initially he worked with Mithat Pasha at the Ministry of Justice, but in 1877, when Mithat Pasha was exiled, Nazım Pasha was transferred to a provincial position in Adana. After a series of further appointments came his posting to Aleppo in 1905, after which he was moved in 1908 to Konya, the centre of the Mevlevi sect. When the children visited him in Konya, a photograph was taken of Samiye perched on grandfather's chair with the seven-year-old Nazım standing proudly beside her (Fig. 1). In 1909 Nazım Pasha was offered yet a further posting, to Sivas, but decided it was time to retire. However, in 1912 he was dispatched to Salonika as governor for what proved to be the final year before the city was ceded to the Greeks. During his last thirteen years he lived in retirement with his family in Istanbul, writing his reminiscences, and he died on 17 December 1926.

In his grandson's eyes the most exciting thing about Nazım

1. Nazım with his sister Samiye during a visit to Konya.

Pasha was his poetic bent. For the Pasha was a Mevlevi – a follower of the poet Mevlana Celalettin Rumi, whose mystical quatrains, written in Persian in the thirteenth century, express a pervasive sense of the divine. In younger days the Pasha had himself written books about the Ottoman education system, as well as poems in the Sufi tradition. His literary and philosophical interests made a deep impression on his grandson, and during the Pasha's retirement the two developed a close rapport, even attending open-air rituals together under the stars: 'My grandfather used to take me to his Mevlevi ceremonies. There would be thirty to fifty people, meeting in the dark, carrying small lights in their hands, praying and singing. I didn't understand much, but I was able to whirl faster than any of them' (Babayev, 29-30). The Pasha introduced his grandson to the Sufi ideals of freedom, spirituality and love, and Nazım's poetic impulse may have been shaped by Rumi's meditations with their sensitivity to the deeper meaning of everyday life. The day he finished primary school, he received from his grandfather a leather-bound writing book embellished with a Mevlevi inscription in Persian. This was intended not only for copying out his favourite verses, but also for writing poems of his own. Poetry recitations were another feature of family life, and since Turkish is permeated by the principle of vowel harmony, Nazım's ear became attuned to the melodic cadences of his own language.

The cry of my country

After attending primary school in Göztepe, Nazım followed in his father's footsteps as a pupil at Galatasaray, a prestigious fee-paying school where he too began to learn French, but in 1913, after his grandfather had retired, the family ran into financial difficulties, and Nazım was transferred to the state school in Nişantaşı. His schooldays coincided with a period of political upheaval. In August 1913 the Treaty of Bucharest forced the Ottomans to renounce their territory in Europe except for a small area of Thrace. It was partly in the hope of regaining these territories that in October 1914 the Young Turk government entered the First World War on the German side. It also felt threatened by Tsarist Russia, which demanded control of the Bosphorus, but war with Russia meant that massive forces had to be deployed to defend Turkey's eastern frontier. In the ensuing battles there were thousands of casualties, and many soldiers froze to death in the Caucasus. The Ottoman Empire was fighting a war on several fronts, since its forces were also engaging the British in Mesopotamia and Palestine, while in April 1915 the Allies landed in Gallipoli in an attempt to gain control of the Dardanelles. Here the Turkish resistance, led by Mustafa Kemal, proved too strong, and in December the Allies withdrew with heavy losses. Winston Churchill, instigator of the Gallipoli campaign, was so compromised by this fiasco that he resigned from the cabinet.

These events elicited a vigorous response from the aspiring poet. One of his earliest poems, 'The Cry of My Country', was

written at the age of eleven, a year before the outbreak of the
First World War:

> It was a misty morning still
> everywhere covered in smoke
> a distant voice is heard: help help!
> Hearken to the cry of your country,
> hear it and tell your conscience
> the torn heart of your country
> is counting on you.
>   ('Feryad-ı Vatan', 3 July 1913, A 8, 9)

The 'torn heart of the country' alludes to the division of Thrace
in 1913 and the ceding of Salonika to Greece. Another poem
'To My Country!' ('Vatana!'), dated 8 March 1915, captured the
patriotic spirit of the time so successfully that it won a school
prize. It takes the form of a dialogue between a mother and her
son, who follows his mother's exhortation to 'say farewell to your
betrothed' and 'sacrifice your blood for your country' (A 8, 13).
On 7 May 1915, a few days after the Allied landing in the Dar-
denelles, Nazım wrote an even more patriotic poem, 'Corporal
Mehmet!', which concludes with the stirring lines: 'Once more
Turkish ships / Will sail across the seas / [...] Once more the
history of the Turks / Will be written on gold-illuminated pages'
('Mehmet Çavuşa!', A 8, 12). The Turkish casualties included
one of Celile's brothers, Mehmet Ali, commemorated in several
poems dedicated 'To My Uncle' ('Dayıma', A 8, 15-17). In this
atmosphere of euphoria, Nazım could hardly wait to become
involved, and his patriotic verses won him his opportunity. The
Chief of Naval Staff, Cemal Bey, a friend of his father, happened
to hear a reading of one of them entitled 'A Naval Man Speaks'
('Bir Bahriyelinin Ağzından', A 8, 9), and was so impressed that
he persuaded Nazım's family to register him at the age of fifteen
as a cadet at the Naval College at Heybeliada, an island near
Istanbul in the Sea of Marmara.

The final years of the Ottomans form one of the strangest
interludes in modern history. When Sultan Mehmed Reşad died
in July 1918, he was succeeded by his younger brother Mehmed
Vahdettin, who was known for his sympathies with Britain and
France. This may explain why defeat of the Ottoman Empire
did not lead to the immediate deposition of the dynasty. It was
the Young Turk leaders who were held responsible for the crimes

of the Ottoman regime, including the Armenian massacres. The
armistice signed at Mudros on 30 October 1918 by Rauf Bey,
Minister of the Navy, and General Calthorpe on behalf of victorious
Allies, left the old order intact. However, this treaty allowed the
Allies the right to occupy the capital and its hinterland along the
Sea of Marmara to the Dardanelles. By November Istanbul was
controlled by foreign troops. Worse still, on 15 May 1919, Izmir
(Smyrna) was occupied by the Greeks with the support of the
Allies. The future of Turkey seemed to lie in the hands of occupying
powers intent on dividing it and sharing the spoils among themselves. It was at this juncture that Mustafa Kemal, realizing the
hopelessness of the situation in Istanbul, set out for Anatolia,
landing at Samsun on 19 May 1919. His orders from the Ottoman
government were to supervise the disbanding of the remaining
Turkish forces. Instead, he set about the task of organizing political
and military resistance, setting up a Turkish National Assembly
in Ankara in April 1920.

For patriots in Istanbul there seemed no alternative to a regime
under foreign control, perhaps in the form of a British protectorate.
At first the Allies did not officially occupy the city, and in theory
the Ottoman government was still in control, but the reality was
very different. The Greeks swaggered through the streets, flaunting
the blue-and-white flag and expecting the Turks to salute it. For
the Western Allies, still smarting from defeat at Gallipoli, November
1918 was the moment of triumph:

With formal pomp and ceremony Admiral Calthorpe led a sixteen-mile
convoy of British and other allied warships through the Dardanelles and
into the Bosphorus. Here they anchored off the Golden Horn, so closely
congested that the water could scarcely been seen between the decks. It
was another black day for the Turks when General Francet d'Esperey made
a triumphant entry into the city at the head of his troops, riding without
reins on a white horse, and thus aspiring to lay the spectre of Fatih, the
Moslem Conqueror of Byzantium, who had done the same (Kinross,
134-5).

This spectacle was designed to humiliate the Turks, whose sufferings
are memorably recalled by a young woman journalist, Sabiha
Sertel, who was an eye-witness:

In the harbour the enemy ships were flying all the different flags, while
Turkish soldiers were arriving from Yemen and other fronts in cartloads,
looking worn out. Haydarpasha station was full of people looking for their

loved ones. The ones returning seemed as young as children, not knowing why or for whom they had been fighting in the Arabian desert. [...] In this adventurism, nobody knows how many died, were wounded or went missing. Nobody knows how many died within our own country from hunger and disease. Nobody dares to question these things. Everybody is anxious about the future of the country (Sertel S, 9-10).

The leaders of the Young Turks, Talat, Celal and Enver Pasha, had escaped across the Black Sea on a German gunboat to avoid the consequences of their crimes. Public opinion was divided about the future of the country. Some newspapers supported the foreign occupation, condemning the Young Turks for having entered the war on the wrong side. Grand Vizier Damat Ferit was even prepared to leave the city in the hands of the British. The United States attracted support among Turkish intellectuals, who were so impressed by the principles of democracy and self-determination enshrined in President Wilson's Fourteen Points that they formed a society to promote Wilsonian principles. Influential writers like Halide Edib, Ahmet Emin Yalman and Adnan Adıvar hoped that the United States would prevent the country from being partitioned by the victorious British, French, Italians and Greeks. In June 1919 a group called the 'National Front' was formed to co-ordinate resistance against the occupying powers, and some intellectuals rallied around the journal *Büyük Mecmua* (Grand Magazine), which Sabiha Sertel edited with her husband Zekeriya. Despite the censorship, this journal became a forum for impassioned debate about the future of the Empire. The different factions, united only in their hostility to the occupying powers, ranged from Ottoman loyalists and religious fundamentalists to militant pan-Turanists dreaming of an alliance with the Turkic-speaking peoples of Central Asia. Despite the humiliations of defeat and occupation, there were also more positive developments. For the first time women were admitted to classes at the university and entered public life.

Halide Edib was one of the leaders of the patriotic resistance, addressing the crowds at open-air public meetings (Fig. 2). The impact which she made during a demonstration in May 1919, organized in protest against the occupation of Izmir by the Greeks, is recalled by Sabiha Sertel:

Sultan Ahmet Square was filled with tens of thousands of people spilling into the side streets. It was impossible to get to the square. The balconies,

2. Halide Edib addressing a protest meeting in Istanbul.

windows, even the roofs of the houses were full. On the trees people looked like leaves [...] Halide Edib was on the rostrum, in her black veil, standing proud. Above the platform there was a black flag, and below the star and crescent moon it read 'Either freedom or death'. On another banner it said 'Wilson's Fourteen Points', while another, which stretched the whole distance between the minarets of Sultan Ahmet and Aya Sophia, said 'Izmir is ours'. As Halide Hanım spoke, one could hear people sobbing. Imams from the minarets were chanting from time to time, and 200,000 people's voices prayed as one voice. Halide Edib offered people her commitment: 'I am going to fight until my people regain their freedom', and this powerful commitment coming from the voice of 200,000 people travelled like waves above the people's heads through the streets. This was the enthusiasm of a nation dedicated to fighting for national liberation (Sertel S, 27-8).

There was a series of such demonstrations in Istanbul, one of which, on 13 January 1920, was attended by Nazım in the company of his friend Vala Nurettin (Va-Nu).

Va-Nu, too, was an aspiring poet, and their friendship is vividly recalled in a memoir written many years later. Born in Salonika in 1901, he was a year older than Nazım, and at the age of five he attended a boarding school in Salonika, before transferring at the age of eleven to Galatasaray where he and Nazım first met. However, his father Nurettin Bey died that same year, at the age of forty-two, leaving no pension for his wife and four children; therefore, like Nazım, Va-Nu had to leave school early, and the plight of the family worsened during the war, when they lived on meagre rations from the soup kitchen. At the age of sixteen, however, Va-Nu won a scholarship offered by the Itibari-milli Bank and was sent to study in Vienna. On his return he began to work for the bank, and since he also had contacts in publishing, he was well placed to promote Nazım's poetry, as well as sharing his passion for politics.

'When we listened to Halide Edib', Va-Nu recalls, 'we were high with excitement.' The impression which Nazım made on his friends at this time is described in another passage:

His hair was like a flame and with his high sideboards he was an impressive sight in streets of Istanbul, slim, 1.80 metres tall. [...] When walking with a group, or with one other person, he would always walk half a step ahead of everyone else. He would turn halfway round and step in front of you talk to you, looking straight into your face. In order to convince you he would cut you short and shout aloud and shake his fist and talk and talk (Va-Nu, 38-40).

In practice, Nazım's sphere of action was constrained by the fact that he was still a naval cadet, based on the training ship *Hamidiye*. There were further humiliating developments, including the official occupation of Istanbul by the Allies on 16 March 1920. Military courts were established, and officials who supported the resistance were dismissed, imprisoned or exiled. The press was strictly censored, and patriotic journalists like Ahmet Emin Yalman were deported to Malta.

The impending partitioning of the Ottoman Empire provoked Nazım to write a poem entitled 'Hostage of the Forty Thieves', published in August 1920 ('Kırk Haramilerin Esiri', A 8, 71). In this allegory the thieves cut off the arm of their hostage, but their victim seizes the axe and fights back. By implication Nazım is encouraging people to join the liberation movement in Anatolia. There are Islamic religious undertones in another poem which describes the poet's feelings on seeing the Greek flag flying from a mosque: 'I became devoted to my belief like an anguished child' ('Ağa Camii', A 8, 115). Nazım's patriotism is reflected in his fascination with a further episode, recorded by Va-Nu:

He kept repeating the story of a dreadnought that had been hit by a torpedo and turned on its side. In order to stop it from sinking, it needed to have water pumped into another section of the boat. But the door of this section was broken and it could only be closed from inside. A young officer went inside and closed the door, which meant that he was drowned as the section was filled with water. While telling the story Nazım's blue eyes would shine with excitement. [...] 'I wish I also was a hero like that officer who drowned in order to save the dreadnought', he would say, taking off his fez and throwing it on the ground (Va-Nu, 39).

For the young patriot it was becoming intolerable to serve in a defeated navy which was effectively under foreign control.

Separation and departure

These humiliations were all the harder to endure because they coincided with the disintegration of Nazım's family. The tensions between Celile and Hikmet Bey led in 1919 to the irretrievable breakdown of their marriage. Nazım found the situation so painful that he wrote a letter to his mother begging them not to separate (Aydemir, 1986a, 34). He must have been aware of his father's infidelities, but it was the rumours about his mother's relationship with the poet Yahya Kemal that caused him most concern. This relationship lasted from 1916 till 1919. They had first met at a gathering of the Bektashi sect, where the ceremony involved chanting, drinking and dancing. Yahya Kemal was fascinated to meet such a liberated woman, but his consciousness of his position at an institute of higher education led him to shy away from marriage. When Nazım's parents were divorced, Celile moved to Paris to study painting, while Hikmet Bey took a second wife, Cavide Hanım, a woman twenty-four years younger than himself by whom he had a son, Metin, and a daughter, Fatma Melda. The effect of their mother's absence on Nazım and his sister Samiye is reflected in the poem 'From My Torments', written in 1919: 'Her eyes brimming with tears / why does my sister hug the empty chair / every night at suppertime? / It is "always her face" we have in mind' ('Acılarımdan', A 8, 38).

These tensions were exacerbated by bouts of ill-health, which eventually led to Nazım's discharge from the navy under circumstances which have never been fully explained. He developed pleurisy in October 1917 after being locked up in the college prison for several hours for disobeying the rules. The illness recurred in 1919, when he was serving as a trainee on the Peyki Şevket torpedo boat, and the seventeen-year-old was sent home on sick leave. Nazım's father took him to see Dr Hakkı Şinasi Pasha, the director of the military hospital and a family friend. The young man was admitted to hospital for two months, after which he spent a further two months recuperating at home. It is unclear whether Nazım was finally discharged from the navy because of ill-health or as the result of some disciplinary offence. This is one of many points where fact becomes interwoven with fantasy, particularly in accounts written by communists. The German novelist Anna Seghers, in a tribute written to mark Nazım's sixtieth birthday, implausibly claims that he took part in a 'revolutionary sailors movement' (Seghers, 260). But Nazım's own recollections, recorded by his friend Ekber Babayev in the 1950s, suggest that the causes were more complex:

We were enraged by the occupation of Istanbul. There were a few officers who had been to Germany and were telling us about the German revolution and the mutiny in the German navy. At the same time we were hearing the news from Anatolia, where Mustafa Kemal was organizing the army against the occupying forces. One day we decided not to attend classes. Somebody found a record of the Marseillaise, which we listened to all day long. We demanded to be allowed to join Kemal, but when the commander came in to ask us what we were protesting about, we said that we did not have knives and forks. He sent us to town to get them. A few days later, some of us were discharged from the college, supposedly on grounds of ill-health (Babayev, 26).

Given the poet's patriotism, one can readily believe that by 1919 he was longing to leave the navy and join the struggle against the occupying powers. The official report merely records that he was discharged from the navy because of his failure to report for duty after a long absence due to illness. This document is dated 17 May 1921, almost five months after Nazım had left for Anatolia (Sülker 1, 52).

Meanwhile Nazım was becoming increasingly productive as a poet. His first published poem, entitled 'Are They Still Weeping Among the Cypresses?', appeared in the journal *Yeni Mecmua* in September 1918 over the name Mehmet Nazım ('Hala Servilerde Ağlıyorlar mı?', A 8, 65). It expresses the sadness of lovers whose feelings reverberate beyond the grave: 'Are they still weeping among the cypresses?' Va-Nu recalls that Nazım's mother showed this poem to her admirer Yahya Kemal, who had it published – after making several changes. The young poet also had his first experience of falling in love. According to Va-Nu, his first love was Sabiha, the daughter of a governor, for whom he wrote a poem called 'The Woman with Black Eyes' (Va-Nu, 35). He also formed a more enduring relationship with a girl called Nüzhet, whom he first met in Nişantaşı in 1915 when she was fifteen. Nüzhet, who had been orphaned at the age of eleven, was being brought up by her elder sister and her brother-in-law Muhiddin Birgen, a journalist who worked for the newspaper *Tanin*, which supported Enver Pasha's Committee of Union and Progress.

Poems by Nazım appeared both in Va-Nu's series of 'Books' and in various magazines, including *Alemdar*. The editor Yusuf Ziya, who believed that the resistance movement was doomed, endorsed the British occupation of Istanbul, hoping that by this means the unity of the Ottoman Empire might be preserved. To attract younger readers, he launched a literary supplement, and it was here that a series of Nazım's poems appeared between August and December 1920. In a more resolute poem he ironizes conventional images such as 'My heart is like a butterfly' by proclaiming 'My heart is an eagle' (*Alemdar*, 25 September 1920). He even won a prize with a poem called 'One Minute', which explores the theme of suicide (Sülker 1976, 315). The poet resolves to take his life by leaping into the sea, but starts shivering so uncontrollably at the moment when he has to jump that he changes his mind. There is even more self-irony in the poem 'Her Shadow', dedicated to Suat Derviş, an aspiring poet later to become a successful novelist. When the poet took a fancy to her, she simply ignored him, so he resolved his dilemma with the defiant gesture: 'I jumped on her shadow' ('Gölgesi', A 8, 102).

From September 1920 onwards, further poems appeared in the almanack *Ümid* ('Hope'), with romantic illustrations to enhance the Ottoman typography. They included a text written jointly by Nazım and Va-Nu called 'A Tale for Our Children' ('Çocuklarımıza Masal'). At first sight this appears to be a mystical tale about a saint living in a holy castle, but a further meaning becomes apparent after five men who desecrate the sanctity of the castle are crushed by falling masonry. The poem uses religious motifs to emphasize the need to resist the five imperial powers on Turkish soil (Sadi,

94-6). A similar allegorical technique is used in Nazım's first play, *Ocakbaşı* (By the Fireside, A 10, 6-33). Here the motif of unrequited love, apparently inspired by Nazım's infatuation with an Armenian actress, can also be interpreted as a parody on the decaying Ottoman Empire (A 21, 264). These early writings earned him a precocious reputation. The programme for a concert of classical Turkish music at the Apollon Theatre on 19 November 1920 records that 'Nazım Hikmet' recited some of his poems (Coşkun K 1990, 26).

In the short space of two years Nazım experienced a series of separations – from the navy, from his family, and finally from Istanbul. However, he was able to endure these losses through the strength of the friendships he formed. When he left for Anatolia at the end of 1920, he was accompanied by Va-Nu and two other young poets. The decision to leave was precipitated by an encounter with a soldier from the army of occupation: 'When we were walking towards Dalyan from Fuat Pasha Street', Va-Nu recalls, 'a whip cracked in front of our faces. It was a sergeant, two metres tall, with a prostitute on his arm, who was threatening us, claiming that we were looking at his woman. We were lucky to escape unhurt' (Va-Nu, 41). Many intellectuals had already left for Ankara, among them the journalist Yunus Nadi, who had started a nationalist newspaper called *Anadoluda Yeni Gün* ('New Day in Anatolia'). On 30 March 1920 Nadi was joined by the Halide Edib and her husband Adnan Adıvar, who managed to leave for Ankara by train just one day before the British occupation forces took control of the railway. In April they had a meeting with Mustafa Kemal and drew up a list of those who should be invited to join them. However, it was not till November 1920 that a message reached Istanbul inviting Nazım, Va-Nu and a number of other young writers to join the Kemalist cause. To facilitate their escape, they obtained identity cards with false names and occupations: Va-Nu was described as an egg merchant. Nazım arrived wearing a grey raincoat with a velvet collar and a fez without a tassel (Va-Nu, 45-7). Rather than discuss his impending departure with his family, he had left a farewell poem on his father's desk, calling on Turkish youth to commit themselves to action ('Gençlik', A 8, 62). The two friends spent their final day in a hotel, and on 1 January 1921 they slipped down to Sirkeci to board a battered coaster laden with bales of cotton. The name of the boat was *Yeni Dünya* – 'The New World'.

2

The New World
1921

The train journey from Istanbul to Ankara lasts ten hours, but in 1921 the railway was controlled by the occupying powers, so the two friends had to sail along the Black Sea coast before striking south across the mountains of Anatolia. The first stage of their journey, from Istanbul to Inebolu, involved a voyage of about 500 kilometers. Nazım and Va-Nu were accompanied by two other poets, Yusuf Ziya (later to assume the surname Ortaç) and Faruk Nafiz (Çamlıbel). As the 'New World' slipped its moorings at Sirkeci, at the mouth of the Golden Horn, there were moments of great anxiety, and it was only after they had safely passed the watch-tower on the Bosphorus that they came out of their hiding places among the bales of cotton. There were many other passengers travelling under assumed names, including students and soldiers eager to support the campaign for national liberation. Va-Nu has left a vivid account of the reception they received at their first port of call:

When we arrived in Zonguldak, we were welcomed by boats decorated with flags. The young residents of the town boarded our ship, and enquired about us, the four modern poets. They took us ashore in their boats and entertained us in a restaurant [...] We read poetry and we drank rakı, even though this was illegal in those days (Va-Nu, 55-6).

Despite stormy weather, they continued their journey to Inebolu, although the waves rose so high that it needed all the boatmen's skill to transfer them safely to shore. At Inebolu there were police checks on all arrivals from Istanbul and departures to Ankara, and they had to obtain travel permits before they could set out across Anatolia.

The long march through Anatolia

In January 1921 Inebolu was teeming with people waiting for permission to go to Ankara, including Turkish students who had been deported from Germany for their involvement in the Spartacus movement in Berlin. The German Spartacus revolt, led by Karl Liebknecht and Rosa Luxemburg, had been defeated in January 1919, but its revolutionary ideas inspired a group of young Turkish students in Berlin. When they were deported to Turkey, they decided to support the Kemalist movement in Anatolia. Through this group Nazım and Va-Nu were introduced to the ideas of Marx and Lenin, Liebknecht and Kautsky, and the heroic life of Rosa Luxemburg. Sitting in the hotel, they began to grapple with the concepts of class struggle and proletarian revolution, becoming eager participants in an informal seminar on Marxism. After two weeks the news arrived that only Nazım and Va-Nu had permission to travel to Anatolia. Yusuf Ziya was to remain behind, since his journal *Alemdar* had supported the occupation, while Faruk Nafiz was regarded with suspicion because he had received a prize from the Young Turk government. Nazım and Va-Nu received not only travel permits but also a useful sum of money to cover expenses, sent at the suggestion of Halide Edib. Since Nazım was notoriously impractical about money, he entrusted his share to Va-Nu. The Spartacus group had already left, just as the snows were falling over Anatolia (Va-Nu, 56-67). Two young poets were so eager that they could not wait for transport to be arranged. There was – and indeed still is – no railway connection between Inebolu and Ankara; the distance is over 300 kilometers, but this did not dampen their spirits. Joining a group of half-a-dozen other young people, they decided to walk. They faced a formidable journey, since there were snow drifts in the mountain passes and at certain points the road to Ankara rises to a height of almost 2,000 metres. To prepare for the long march, they bought warm woollen socks, heavy-duty boots, overcoats, gloves, scarves and kalpaks – fur-hats in the Russian style. The kalpak had been adopted by Mustafa Kemal as one of the emblems of the Turkish revolution, and was proudly displayed in a group photograph taken at the congress held in Sivas in September 1919 to organize national resistance (Fig. 3). Through him it became one of the emblems of the new Turkey, displacing the fez which he regarded as the

3. Mustafa Kemal at the Sivas Congress, wearing a kalpak.

4. Nazım and Va-Nu, dressed for the long march to Ankara.

outworn symbol of the Ottoman era. The clothing chosen by
Nazım and Va-Nu was also defiantly modern, combining European
elegance with Russian panache, as can be seen from the photograph
taken at Kastamonu during the first stage of their long march
(Fig. 4).

Since there was no motor transport, the poets hired a horse.
Its owner agreed to take their bags as far as Kastamonu, a journey
of 85 kilometers over a precipitous mountain pass. They loaded
their belongings into saddlebags and walked ahead of the horse,
taking it in turns to clear a path. As the snow crunched beneath
their boots, they recited poems to sustain their spirits, including
an exuberant 'Marching Song': 'Burning on our forehead is the
crown of youth, / we care not for fatigue' ('Yol Türküsü', A 8,
110). The track was so steep that it took them eight hours to
cover 30 kilometers, before reaching a village where they could
stop for the night. Over the next three days they met villagers
who had no education and little knowledge of life outside their
own communities: thus for the first time the young idealists from
Istanbul were confronted with the life of impoverished Anatolian
peasants. Some of the people were so severely malnourished that
their bodies were misshapen, but even their extreme poverty did
not lessen their hospitality. This first-hand experience, enhanced
by the critical awareness they had gained through the Spartacus
group, marked a decisive stage in their political education. At
one point they met a luxurious carriage drawn by three horses,
carrying an Ottoman government official to the coast. This encounter inspired Nazım to write the poem 'Barefoot', contrasting
the needs of the peasantry with the privileges of the élite
('Yalınayak', A 1, 102). Wading through slush and snow, they
took six full days to cover the 100 kilometers from Kastamonu
to Çankırı, where they were once again shocked by the locality's
poverty and backwardness. Here they rested for two days, taking
advantage of the fact that they had caught up with the Spartacus
group to continue their discussions. Three days later, weary from
a trek that had taken almost a fortnight, they finally arrived in
Ankara.

Ankara: 'poetry with a purpose'

Ankara was a city searching for a new identity. Its geographical

position, at the head of the railway network but out of range of
the imperialist powers, made it the ideal base for Kemal's resistance
movement, but in the early 1920s it was still a dilapidated provincial
town. Having recently been badly damaged by fire, it was poorly
equipped to provide accommodation for Kemal's staff and his
numerous supporters. The celebrated Stone Lodge (Taşhan) Inn
in the Ulus district was reserved for important visitors, but the
new arrivals soon met kindred spirits at the Swan Café (Kuğulu
Kahve), where they would sit for hours, endlessly discussing literature and politics. Ankara offered other diversions, including performances of Shakespeare's *Othello* and *The Merchant of Venice* by
a group of travelling players under an actor-director named Kamil.
The plays were staged in a converted barn lit only by oil lamps,
but this production seems none the less to have recaptured something of the primitive vigour of the Elizabethan theatre. This was
Nazım's first experience of Shakespeare on stage and he felt ex-
hilarated by it. He went to see *The Merchant* several times and
later recorded that it was Kamil in the role of Othello who
opened his eyes to the significance of Shakespeare (A 21, 265).

   During the spring of 1921 two topics dominated the political
horizon: the military campaign against the Greeks in western
Anatolia and the victories of the Bolsheviks in Russia. During
the First World War, Ottoman Turkey and Tsarist Russia had
been implacable enemies. But amid the revolutionary turmoil of
the immediate post-war period, Lenin and Kemal became allies
in the struggle against imperialism. Soon after his arrival in Ankara,
Kemal put out the first feelers to Moscow, realizing that the two
governments had much to gain from an alliance. As early as
September 1919, during the Sivas Congress, he decided to send
a delegation to Moscow to ask for military aid. Ali Fuat Cebesoy,
Kemal's comrade from military college, was appointed as the
Republic's first ambassador to the Soviet Union, a key position
at this critical juncture. In April 1920, three days after the formation
of the National Assembly in Ankara, Kemal sent Lenin a telegram
signalling a radical reorientation in Turkish foreign policy: 'In
order to liberate the people who are being oppressed by the
imperialist powers, I am willing to collaborate with the Soviet
Union. If the Bolsheviks wish to fight against the Mensheviks in
Georgia, Turkey will undertake to fight against the imperialist
Armenian government and to allow Azerbaijan to join the Bolshevik

community' (Tunçay, 71). The Treaty of Sèvres, signed by the Ottoman government in May 1920, assigned swathes of territory in southern and western Anatolia to Italy and Greece, while recognizing an Armenian Republic in the east. In June the Greek army advanced into Anatolia, capturing Bursa while the Turkish forces retreated in disarray. The Grand National Assembly, meeting in Ankara, found itself internationally isolated, and in the war against Greece the only possible ally was the Soviet Union.

These events made a powerful impression on the intellectuals assembled in the Swan Café, since the Turkish-Soviet rapprochement focused attention on the transformations taking place in Russia. The new Turkish government was formally recognized by the Soviet Union at a time when, in Western eyes, Kemal was still a dangerous rebel and traitor to the Ottoman Sultanate. Moreover, the Soviet consulate opened in Ankara rapidly became a meeting place for the Spartacists and other radical groups. After his arrival on 20 February 1921 the Soviet consul, Prince Budu Mdivani, later President of Georgia, became a catalyst for social life in Ankara. The treaty of Moscow, signed on 16 March, and the opening-up of relations with the Soviet Union became the key topics of discussion. These developments gave an important impetus to the Turkish communist movement, which Kemal initially felt obliged to tolerate as part of the pro-Soviet strategy. However, even the officially recognized Turkish Communist Group, which was controlled by Kemal's own associates, did not survive long. His authoritarian style allowed little scope for opposition, least of all from the far left.

It was not only internal politics that caused tensions within the Kemalist camp. A more serious crisis was developing in western Anatolia during the spring of 1921, when the Greek army made dramatic advances. The invaders were checked on 31 March at the second battle of Inönü by Turkish troops commanded by Ismet Pasha (later known as Ismet Inönü). A new Greek advance began in July, leading to the capture of the important railway junction of Eskishehir, after which the Turkish forces retreated to within 80 kilometers of Ankara. At this moment of crisis the National Assembly appointed Mustafa Kemal commander-in-chief with unlimited powers, and he began to mobilize the population of central Anatolia for what he described as a new form of war: not 'two armies fighting against each other, but two nations who are both risking their existence' (Kinross, 272). Even Turkish women were summoned from their hearths to transport artillery shells to the battlefront on ox-carts laden with hay. The Greek advance was finally checked at the battle of the Sakarya River, which began on 13 August and lasted twenty-two days. From the autumn of 1921 onwards, the Kemalist government rapidly gained both in military strength and in international prestige, although the war with Greece continued for a further twelve months.

There were weeks of tension and uncertainty, as the poets waited to hear whether they would be sent to the front. Fortunately, Nazım's friend Nüzhet was also in Ankara, staying with her brother-in-law Muhiddin Birgen, the Kemalist government's press officer. Birgen was an enthusiastic supporter of the Russian revolution, and his house was a meeting place for journalists and diplomats, including Budu Mdivani. Nazım and Va-Nu also made contact with members of the government – Ali Fuat Cebesoy was his mother's cousin. Although Cebesoy had already left for Moscow, they were taken in hand by his father, Ismail Fazıl Pasha, who introduced them to Mustafa Kemal. When they were presented to the great man as 'two young poets', Kemal immediately turned the subject to poetry. Some young poets (he said) were writing simply for the sake of being modern; 'I recommend you to write poetry with a purpose' (Va-Nu, 95). Nazım and Va-Nu soon found an opportunity to put their poetic talents in the service of the patriotic cause. As director of the Press Office, Muhiddin Birgen suggested that the two poets should compose an appeal urging other young people to join the liberation movement. Within a matter of days, as Va-Nu recalls, a three-page poem was published, addressed to the youth of Istanbul:

> Come, you long-awaited loyal youth!
> Come, join the cause of Anatolia,
> for people's hopes depend upon your faith
> and fortitude, unbending, strong as steel. [...]
> Have you too joined those men who have sold out,
> the sold-out Sultan and sold-out Vizier?

This daring formulation did the poets more harm than good. After several thousand copies had been issued by the Press Office in March 1921, the poem provoked a debate in the National Assembly. Muhiddin Birgen faced a barrage of criticism, as Nazım and Va-Nu listened from the balcony. Deputies loyal to the Sultan were outraged by the suggestion that he was guilty of a 'sell-out'. The future of Turkey was still in the balance, and it was far from certain that the Ottoman dynasty would be deposed. Others were concerned about the positive effects of the poem, fearing that Ankara would be flooded by enthusiastic but untrained volunteers (Va-Nu, 86-7). Shortly afterwards Birgen resigned, moving with his family to Tiflis in Georgia as the representative of a commercial firm. The file on the two poets was transferred to the Ministry of Education.

The two young men were surprised not to be enlisted in the armed forces, as they had expected. But for Mustafa Kemal military victory was not the only aim; equally important was what he described as 'the battle for education' (Kinross, 342). Only through a programme of re-education would it be possible to transform a quasi-feudal Islamic society into a modern secular state. In June 1921 he made a speech at an educational convention in Ankara setting out his aims:

Even in these war years we must develop carefully devised programmes of national education and prepare the grounds upon which our entire educational system shall operate efficiently. [...] I firmly believe that our traditional educational methods have been the most important factor in the history of our national decline. When I speak of national education I mean an education that will be free from all traditional superstitions as well as from all foreign influences, Eastern and Western, that are incompatible with our national character (Berkes, 476-7).

The appointment of Nazım and Va-Nu as schoolteachers formed part of this strategy. In April 1921 they were posted to Bolu, a small town mid-way between Ankara and Istanbul; only a few months earlier there had been an anti-Nationalist revolt in the Bolu region, led by Ottoman loyalists who supported Sultan Vahdettin. Troops had been sent from Ankara to occupy the town, and the ringleaders were executed. Thus in Bolu the two friends faced a formidable task. Although neither had any training, the Ministry issued them with impressive teacher's certificates in elegant Arabic calligraphy (Coşkun K 1990, 28).

Teaching in Bolu

The distance from Ankara to Bolu is over 200 kilometers, but once again the two friends had to travel on foot, hiring a man with a mule to transport their bags. On leaving Ankara they climbed the mountain road towards the resort of Kızılcahamam. With its luxuriant woods and meadows, this region offered a magnificent spectacle as the snows were beginning to melt, revealing the first shoots of spring. To reach the town of Gerede, they had to face an exhausting climb over a 1,500-metre mountain pass. 'We recited poems as we walked along,' Va-Nu recalls. 'A day before we got there Nazım had a splitting headache. When I touched his head it was hot like fire. He had a black-out. I tried to get him on to the mule, but the owner refused to unload the luggage, so I carried him on my back for several miles' (Va-Nu, 105). Va-Nu fed him with chicken soup, and the following morning he was sufficiently recovered to continue the walk to Gerede, where they paused for a day's rest. Walking round the market, they were astonished to find a shop full of animal skins. On impulse, they invested in 5 Lira worth of rabbit skins, together with the skin of a wildcat, hoping they would be able to sell them later at a profit.

Four days later they arrived in Bolu, a cluster of houses, orchards and minarets in the foothills of the range of mountains associated with legends about Köroğlu, the Turkish Robin Hood. Arriving at midnight, Nazım and Va-Nu spent the night at an inn and were woken at dawn by the sound of animals in the courtyard. On the advice of the landlord, they made their way to Beyler Kahvesi, the 'Gentlemen's Café' frequented by teachers and officials. They were soon introduced to the ideological debates which dominated the life of this provincial community. 'Before we got there we found out about the politics of the place', Va-Nu recalls. 'There were two groups of teachers. One group was young and progressive, so we thought we should make common cause with them against the old conservatives. The bearded head teacher, Hilmi Bey, was the worst of all' (Va-Nu, 109). However, Hilmi Bey did find them a place to live – a house with newly painted ceilings and beautifully whitewashed walls. The divans had comfortable mattresses, covered with embroidered materials, while there were cushions propped against the walls and shelves with tulip designs. They soon transformed this house into their home, decorating the walls with the rabbit skins they had brought from Gerede. Nazım even drew a map on the wall to help plan their future.

It was not only geographically that Bolu was the mid-point between Istanbul and Ankara: it also mirrored the divisions between traditionalists and progressives which threatened to tear Turkey apart. The supporters of Vahdettin, the Ottoman Sultan who was still head of state and Caliph of Islam, were fundamentalists who insisted on maintaining traditional religious customs. This faction, though intensely patriotic, was intolerant of social reform and hostile to the Kemalist revolution. There were even rumours that two of Kemal's supporters had been imprisoned and killed in the school-house, and Nazım and Va-Nu wondered whether, beneath the whitewashed walls, they could discern traces of blood. The Kemalists in Bolu, too, were Turkish nationalists, but they no longer believed in the restoration of the Empire. There was a third faction which still believed in the Pan-Turanist ideals of the Committee of Union and Progress, dreaming that Enver Pasha would one day return to power. Meanwhile the silent majority, bewildered and illiterate, hesitated to throw in their lot with any of the rival groups. In this confused situation, the newly-fledged schoolteachers found themselves engaged in a struggle for hearts and minds. Nazım was formally a teacher of Turkish, while Va-Nu was to teach French. But their main task was to challenge religious superstitions, which were so strong that Nazım felt they had re-entered the Dark Ages. His position is forcefully expressed in a satirical poem written towards the end of 1921, 'The Book with the Leather Cover', which makes light of the contents of the scriptures, identifying narratives like Noah's Ark and the virgin birth of Jesus as fairy tales. The Book deserves to be thrown down a well, since it serves to justify the exploitation of im-poverished labourers and the pernicious influence of 'masters, gentry, lords, saints, priests and rabbis' ('Meşin Kaplı Kitap', A 1, 176).

It was no easy task to propagate secular ideas in an overwhelm-ingly Islamic community, where everyone was expected to pray five times a day. The rituals of Islam reach their climax during Ramadan, which in 1921 fell in May, and there was intense pressure to fast between dawn and dusk. All restaurants were closed, and it was not permissible to eat food in public, so the young teachers were unable to take their usual midday meal. One day around lunch time they were surreptitiously eating at home, enjoying Nazım's favourite snack of bread and rose-petal jam, when they had surprise visitors: the head teacher, Hilmi Bey, accompanied by the teacher of religious education. To their relief it transpired that these teachers themselves wished to break their fast. On another occasion Nazım and Va-Nu were invited to a gathering of the Bektashi religious sect, where they witnessed displays of religious ecstasy which culminated in some devotees thrusting metal spikes through their cheeks. Reacting against this climate of obscurantism, Nazım felt he had to make a provocative public gesture. He refused to shave his side-boards, as the traditionalists demanded, and on hearing the evening call to prayer from the minaret, he would ostentatiously walk in the opposite direction, wearing his kalpak at a jaunty angle. Despite the oppressive atmosphere, Nazım made a study of the local dialect, which helped him to move beyond traditional diction and to incorporate popular usage in his poetry. The two poets also collaborated on a folk play about a hard-hearted landlord, 'Osman with a Heart of Stone'. When the long-suffering peasants attempt to remove the stone, they discover that Osman hasn't got a heart at all ('Taşyürek Osman', A 8, 60).

At the end of Ramadan, Nazım and Va-Nu resumed their convivial meetings in the café, discussing politics and gathering small-town gossip. It gradually dawned on the two friends that they were making little progress with a community still in the grip of religious fanaticism and that their own safety could by no means be guaranteed. Moreover, they themselves were becoming restless, longing for contact with a wider world, and they began to consider the possibility of travelling abroad, perhaps to Germany. However, two factors led them to turn their eyes East. The first was their friendship with a young man called Ziya Hilmi, a committed socialist who held an appointment at the law court in Bolu. The three became such close friends that they decided to move together into a house in a nearby village, sharing running costs and household chores. Ziya particularly impressed them with his knowledge of French literature and politics. Sitting in the café, he would recite Baudelaire by heart and tell stories about the Paris Commune of 1871 and the disputes between Lenin and Kautsky. One day Ziya suggested that they should all three travel together to the Soviet Union. This idea became irresistible when Nazım received a card from Nüzhet saying that she was planning to travel to Tiflis (Tiblisi in Georgia) with her sister and her brother-in-law, Muhiddin Birgen (Va-Nu, 132 & 138). Travelling to the Soviet Union would enable Nazım to combine personal romance with political education.

An invitation to attend an educational conference held in Ankara provided the opportunity to obtain the necessary funds. Since Va-Nu was far more diplomatic than Nazım, it was agreed that he should represent them. Borrowing a horse, he set off one blazing August day in the company of Kerim Bey, the police chief, and a number of gendarmes. They chose to take the longer but safer route to Ankara, avoiding the bandits who roamed the countryside. Their road passed through Mudurnu to the southwest of Bolu, which lay so near to the battlefront that they could hear the sound of gunfire. There were rumours that the Kemalist army was losing the war and that they might be attacked by deserters. During this journey Va-Nu witnessed the enforced migration of Armenians from Nallıhan, noticing that members of the Muslim population were already moving into the vacated houses. The police chief tried to reassure the Armenians that this was a merely precautionary measure and that they would come to no harm. When Va-Nu and his companions reached the town of Beypazarı, they found it full of Turkish refugees fleeing before the threat of enemy occupation. It was also reported that the forces of Enver Pasha in eastern Turkey were poised to seize power after Kemal's defeat (Va-Nu, 151). However, Va-Nu reached Ankara safely, and the faith which Nazım had placed in his negotiating skills proved well founded: the Ministry of Education paid their salaries in full. Returning to Bolu, he was also able to advise his friends that the best way to travel to Tiflis was to take the sea route via Batum, the Soviet port on the Black Sea.

Treachery in Trebizond

Early in September they set out along the precipitous road from Bolu to the port of Akçakoca, a distance of 80 kilometers. The three friends were able to hire a horse-drawn carriage, and wherever they stopped they treated themselves to lavish meals, since Ziya had assured them that money would be obsolete in the Soviet Union. From Akçakoca they took the boat to Zonguldak, and it was only there that they learned that this report was untrue. However, they still had sufficient funds to book their passage on a Russian ship from Zonguldak to Trebizond (Trabzon), where they arrived on 21 September (Va–Nu, 177 & 182). To obtain a permit to cross the frontier into the Soviet Union, they applied to be posted as teachers to the Turkish frontier town of Kars. Since the overland route from Trebizond to Kars was all but impassable, they persuaded the authorities to allow them to travel by boat to Batum, so that they could then take the road to Kars through Soviet Armenia. Ziya, who had been offered a job as a lawyer in Trebizond, decided to remain behind.

While they were waiting for their papers, they learnt of the fate of Mustafa Suphi and the founder-members of the Turkish Communist Party, murdered eight months earlier while crossing the Black Sea. This extraordinary episode illustrates the complexity of Turkish-Russian relations during a period when all the frontiers were being redrawn. Suphi, who was born near Trebizond in 1883, had attended Istanbul Law School before going to Paris to study political science. He returned to Istanbul to work as a journalist, but in 1913 he was exiled by Enver Pasha to Sinop on the Black Sea coast. The following year he escaped to Russia, but on the outbreak of war in August 1914 he was interned and sent to a labour camp in the Urals. After the October revolution he joined the Bolshevik Party and moved to Moscow. He was appointed head of the Turkish section in the Central Committee for the Eastern Nations and sent to organize a Red Army detachment in Tashkent. On 27 May 1920, after Soviet authority had been extended to Azerbaijan, Suphi moved to Baku on the Caspian Sea, where he organized Turkish prisoners-of-war into military units (Tunçay, 101-7). The Turkish-Soviet agreement provided him with the opportunity to play a more public role.

In a letter of 15 June 1920 Suphi informed Kemal that the Bolsheviks were willing to support the Turkish liberation struggle through his committee in Baku, which had at its disposal fifty cannons, seventy machine-guns, 17,000 rifles and ammunition, ready to be sent to Anatolia. Kemal's answer, dated 13 September 1920, insisted that all military operations should be controlled by the National Assembly. Suphi's forces would have to operate under a unified Turkish military command, and his group should send a delegation to National Assembly in Ankara. Negotiations continued during September 1920 at the Congress of Peoples of the East, convened in Baku by the leaders of the Third International,

Gregory Zinoviev and Karl Radek, with the aim of mobilizing anti-colonial movements in the Islamic world. Suphi was a member of the organizing committee for the congress, which was attended by over two thousand delegates of forty different nationalities (Riddell, 20-2). They included a large delegation from Ankara, as well as Enver Pasha and his followers. Immediately after the Baku Congress, Suphi reorganized the Turkish Communist Party, eliminating most of Enver's supporters (Ileri, 143-50). His aim was to unify the three strands of the communist movement: his own group, recruited largely from Turkish prisoners-of-war in Russia, which operated from Soviet territory; the 'Spartacus' group from Ankara, where a clandestine communist party had been founded in June 1920; and the indigenous groups in Asia Minor which, though not strictly Marxist in doctrine, professed a 'vague sympathy for communism' (Carr, 3, 298-9).

Collaboration between Turkey and the Soviet Union involved adjustments of their common frontier which benefited both sides. Repudiating the dreams of Pan-Turanism, Kemal recognized Soviet claims to Azerbaijan, where the Bolsheviks took power in April 1920 after suppressing the national government in Baku. In exchange, Kemal gained a free hand to occupy certain areas of Armenia. Both countries were determined to frustrate the plans of the Western powers to establish an independent Armenian republic, and during the summer of 1920 General Kazım Karabekir, commander of the Turkish forces in Erzurum, began to organize covert anti-Armenian operations. In September the Turkish army went on the offensive, occupying the Armenian-populated regions of Kars, Ardahan and Artvin. The Soviet Union had no option but to accept this situation, and the Treaty of Gümrü, signed in December 1920, realigned the Turko-Soviet border so as to acknowledge Turkish sovereignty over the occupied territories. The Red Army then occupied Erivan and Batum and proclaimed a socialist republic of Armenia under Soviet control.

Kemal's success in dealing with the Armenian question demonstrated that he could assert his authority in eastern Anatolia without Suphi's support. A letter he had written in August 1920 to Cebesoy, his representative in Moscow, shows that he was firmly opposed to Suphi's attempts to establish a communist movement in Turkey (Ileri, 151). Kemal had good reason to be suspicious of organizations not directly under his command. It was in this same period that he eliminated the irregular forces – the so-called Green Army – commanded by Çerkes Ethem on the western front, which was also suspected of communist tendencies. Suphi now decided to take up Kemal's invitation to lead a delegation to the National Assembly in Ankara. After setting out from Baku with his wife and other members of the central committee, Suphi arrived in Kars on 28 November, accompanied by the newly-appointed Soviet consul, Prince Mdivani, who was also travelling to Ankara. However, a telegram dated 2 January 1921 from Karabekir to the mayor of Erzurum indicates that orders had been received from the National Assembly to obstruct the progress of Suphi's delegation. They remained in Kars for three weeks, after being warned that if they travelled south by land they were likely to be attacked. On 22 January they finally took the train to Erzurum, where they were met by hostile demonstrations. The aim was to make it clear to the Russians that Suphi's communist followers had no support in Turkey. The group decided to continue their journey by the circuitous coastal route, heading first for Trebizond. But here the authorities again organized a hostile reception, which made them all the more anxious to travel on by boat to Inebolu, before taking the overland route to Ankara. Through the intervention of Mdivani, they obtained assurances that they would be allowed to continue their journey unmolested, and on the evening of 28 January boarded a boat hired from Yahya Kahya, harbour master of Trebizond.

Although Nazım always speaks of 'fifteen' comrades, the number of communists who actually embarked with Suphi is in dispute, and only eight of those who died have been identified by name. The sequence of events has never been definitively explained, but it seems clear that Yahya Kahya arranged for the communists to be followed in a motorboat by a group of armed confederates who killed them. Suphi's wife Semra, a Turkish-speaking woman born in the Crimea, was one of those who remained behind, and she was placed under house arrest. After trying to smuggle out a note appealing for help from the Russian authorities, she too disappeared. Since Suphi's group was nominally under Soviet protection, the Ankara government had some explaining to do. The most implausible justification for the murders was Karabekir's claim that Suphi was an agent of the British government and perhaps in league with the Greeks. There were exchanges of telegrams between Kemal, Karabekir and the mayor of Erzurum, indicating some involvement among the higher echelons of the Turkish administration. The picture is complicated by the fact that Yahya Kahya was one of the principal supporters of Enver Pasha, whose uncle, Halil Pasha, was living clandestinely in Trebizond. Indeed, the whole town swarmed with Enver's supporters. To repair the damage to relations with Moscow, the Turkish government announced that it would 'hand over to justice those guilty of the murder of the Turkish communist Mustafa Suphi' (Carr, 3, 303-4). But it was not till December 1921, after the Ankara gorvernment had sent a new military commander to Trebizond, that Yahya was arrested. The incriminating evidence included a letter from Enver Pasha asking Yahya to infiltrate his supporters into Turkey. Although the charges also included embezzling a hoard of gold and jewellery, Yahya was acquitted. However, on 3 July 1922, seven months after the trial, he was killed by unidentified assailants outside the military headquarters in Trebizond (Ileri, 203-29).

These events made a profound impression on Nazım, hastening his disillusionment with the Kemalist regime, and Mustafa Suphi became one of his heroes. In a poem entitled 'For the Fifteen', written in Batum in 1922, he and Va-Nu paid tribute to the victims ('Onbeşler İçin', A 8, 120). The date of their death, 28 January 1921, imprinted itself so deeply on his mind that the following year he wrote a verse play entitled '28 January' with a jacket design incorporating Suphi's dignified features. As they prepared for their own crossing of the Black Sea in the autumn of 1921, he and Va-Nu must have been aware that they were embarking on a life-and-death adventure. It was a calm autumn day when they boarded a ship from Trebizond, leaving war-torn Turkey behind them, but before long a storm blew up and the passengers had to take refuge in the hold. The following morning the skies cleared and they were able to mix with other passengers, who included White Russian soldiers from Wrangel's defeated army, returning home from Poland via Turkey. The Soviet Union proved not to be the utopia of which they dreamed but a country convulsed by the consequences of war and revolution.

3

Communism under the Spotlight
1921-1928

After a stormy night at sea, the clouds lifted and the silhouette of Batum appeared on the horizon. The scene on board as they approached the Soviet Union was full of surprises. 'When we went on deck,' Va-Nu recalls, 'we couldn't believe our eyes: a group of fifteen or twenty Russian people [...] were sunbathing in their bathing costumes, men and women cuddling each other.' These were remnants of Wrangel's army, which had been evacuated from the Crimea in November 1920 after being defeated by the Red Army. After an unsuccessful attempt to settle in Istanbul, they were returning home. Towards lunch-time the ship was within hailing distance of the harbour. The Russian soldiers grouped together as if they were posing for the camera, rehearsing for the photographers who were awaiting their arrival. The soldiers even produced a red flag and sang the International to give the impression that they supported the Revolution (Va-Nu, 191-2).

Batum had become part of the Soviet Union as a result of the Soviet-Turkish Treaty of 16 March 1921, which finally resolved the frontier question. The port had been occupied by Turkish troops only a few months earlier; Turkish nationals were still regarded there with suspicion, and Nazım and Va-Nu had to undergo strict immigration controls. When they began to explore, they were amazed to find the churches still open, even though religion was supposed to be the opium of the people. Having been told that bourgeois institutions like money and the family had been abolished, they were also disconcerted to see parents holding their children by the hand and to discover that money was indispensable. Mingling with the crowds, they strolled through a park full of palm trees and tropical plants, where peasant women sold cheap black grapes scented like strawberries. Soon an even more astonishing sight met their eyes: men and women relaxing together on the beach and sunbathing completely naked. Such a scene was inconceivable in Istanbul, where women were obliged to wear head-scarves and veils.

In Batum they began to learn the Russian alphabet by studying propaganda posters on the walls. Nazım was particularly struck by a poster depicting the capitalist social pyramid: the base consisted of the oppressed ranks of workers and peasants, bearing on their shoulders the successive tiers of the petty bourgeoisie, the middle classes, the priesthood, the aristocracy and the capitalists, crowned finally by the Tsar and God (Babayev, 69-70). Such broadsheets were widely circulated in the Soviet Union to discredit the traditional social hierarchy. Soon they were soaking up the ethos of the new society, joining demonstrations and singing revolutionary songs. Seeing units of the Red Army riding by on horseback, they exulted in the cheering of the crowds. In a late essay Nazım recalls the political and literary stimuli of those Batum days: 'I took my meals in the Hôtel de France, living on two bowls of corn-soup and a quarter loaf of bread a day. Yet I also attended demonstrations wearing my wooden clogs, worked on the 'Red Trade Union' magazine, which was published by the Turkish Communist Party foreign section, and read hundreds of French plays published before 1914 in the 'Little Illustrations' series, which I found in the room I was occupying. In those six months I immersed myself in the repertoire of the French boulevard theatre' (A 21, 265-6). This was the moment when the poet began to imagine writing a play about Karl Marx.

It was in Batum that Nazım and Va-Nu took the decision to join the Turkish Communist Party (Babayev, 70 & 370). The minutes of a branch meeting of September 1921 record that they were delegated to work for the literary section of the journal *Kızıl Sendika* (Red Trade Union). Towards the end of his life Nazım reflected on these events in his autobiographical novel, 'The Romantics'. There, in a scene set in the comfort of the Hôtel de France, he recalls the soul-searching that led to his decision to join the Party: 'You must decide, my son, I say to myself, you must decide. [...] What can you give to Anatolia, what can you give? Everything [...] Your freedom? Yes! How many years will you be able stay in prison for this cause? All my life, if necessary! But you love women, you enjoy the good life. [...] If you become a communist, you might end up being drowned like Suphi' (A 17, 30). Despite the hazards associated with communism, he now made the fateful decision that was to shape his whole career.

The Social Family

Life in Batum offered limited possibilities, since they had no way of earning a living. Their most promising contact, Muhiddin Birgen, was based in Tiflis, the capital of Georgia. An alliance had been formed between Georgia and Turkey in the summer of 1918 when the Treaty of Brest-Litovsk established Georgia as an independent state under German and Turkish protection. Between 1919 and 1921, the period when Georgia achieved real independence under an elected Menshevik government, the links between Ankara and Tiflis were consolidated. After the Bolsheviks, led by Orjenikitze, had crushed Georgian independence in the summer of 1921, Tiflis gained an additional interest for Turkish radicals. Moreover Nazım hoped to resume contact with Nüzhet, who was staying in the Georgian capital with the Birgen family. In the spring of 1922 he and Va-Nu took the overnight train from Batum to Tiflis, a distance of 330 kilometres. They had been told that the Birgen family were staying at the Orient Hotel, but when they arrived they found that only Muhiddin's wife, Melahat Hanım, was actually there. Her husband and her sister Nüzhet were both away in Moscow.

They were made welcome by Melahat Hanım, who invited them to stay at the hotel. But soon after midnight they were told by the management that they had to leave, since the regulations did not permit visitors after midnight. They were reduced to walking the streets looking for another hotel at a price they could afford. However, on the next day their luck turned. When they went to visit Melahat Hanım, they received an invitation from Budu Mdivani, the former Soviet Consul in Ankara, who had recently been appointed President of Georgia. After visiting the President, they were conveyed in his official car back to the Orient Hotel, where Mdivani instructed the hotel manager to take particular care of his guests while he himself was away in Moscow. The poets thus found themselves in a **contradictory** position, as party members enjoying the privileges reserved for the élite (Va-Nu, 207). They settled into a room on the same floor as Nüzhet's family and were given food coupons for the restaurant, where they dined with silver cutlery beneath glinting chandeliers.

In this hotel they met some members of the Committee of Union and Progress, followers of Enver Pasha, who was in self-imposed exile in the Soviet Union. They included Ahmet Cevat, who had been involved with the Young Turk movement before the First World War and was now negotiating complicated deals in Tiflis, involving the sale of Turkish books to the Azeri Ministry of Education and the purchase of carpets to be imported into Turkey. He was also planning to relaunch in Batum the newspaper *Yeni Dünya* (New World), originally founded by Suphi in 1919. Taking a liking to the two young writers, he offered them jobs as journalists if they would return with him to Batum. They found this offer tempting, but they first had to raise enough cash to cover their expenses. Since Western clothing was very expensive in Tiflis, they decided to sell some of their clothes at the local flea market. The cash they raised from selling a two-piece suit and patent leather shoes, supplemented by a small advance from Ahmet Cevat, enabled them to book their tickets for the train journey back to the Black Sea (Va-Nu, 213-14). On reaching Batum they established themselves in two rooms at the Hôtel de France, one of which served as an office for *Yeni Dünya* while the other was used as a bedroom. Shortly after they had settled in, Nüzhet also arrived in Batum. Living in the Soviet Union with her sister's family had proved frustrating, and she was planning to return to Turkey and attend a German college (Sülker 1, 180). During these weeks in Batum, Nazım and Nüzhet grew very fond of each other, and he did his best to persuade her to stay in Soviet Union. In the event she was unable to obtain the necessary travel permits and reluctantly returned to Tiflis.

The political situation on the Black Sea coast was extremely confused. Batum was not simply the gateway to the Soviet Union, but also the testing ground for competing ideologies. Among those who had set up camp in Batum were members of the Pan-Turanist branch of the Committee of Union and Progress. The collapse of the Tsarist Empire had given new momentum to those who dreamed of creating an alliance of the Turkic-speaking peoples of the Central Asia, and the frontiers in the Caucusus remained fluid. Enver Pasha had not yet abandoned his dream of creating a 'union of all Turkic peoples from Edirne (Adrianople) to the Chinese oases along the road of the silk-trade' with its capital in Samarkand (Landau, 51-2). The Bolsheviks, who were keeping their options open, had given Enver's faction certain privileges, since it was still possible that he might help them to extend and consolidate their power. One of his aims was to build up support for his movement among wealthy landowners in eastern Turkey. After Kemal's victories had frustrated his hopes of seizing power in Ankara, Enver returned to the Caucasus, proclaimed himself Emir of Bokhara and organised armed resistance among Islamic peoples hostile to the extension of Soviet power. In August 1922 this short-lived revolt was crushed and Enver himself was killed in a burst of machine-gun fire (Kinross, 297).

Nazım and Va-Nu made contact with the Pan-Turanists through Enver's uncle, Halil Pasha, who was based in Batum. Living in a mansion with his own staff officers and servants, Halil Pasha would give lavish dinner parties, and Va-Nu and Nazım became regular visitors. But their willingness to mix with the Turanists attracted the suspicion of the communist authorities, which led to their rooms at the Hôtel de France being searched. Feeling that the hotel was no longer safe, they began to search for alternative accommodation. Once again Ahmet Cevat's contacts proved invaluable. Hearing of their difficulties, his printer Ali Riza invited them to move into his villa, and they now developed a set of domestic arrangements known as the 'social family' (Va-Nu, 235). Ahmet Cevat took responsibility for cooking, while Nazım would compose articles and poems. Their finances also improved, since Va-Nu supplemented their income by giving Turkish lessons to Azeri children. At Ali Riza's house they were joined by Şevket Süreyya, an idealistic young schoolteacher with Pan-Turanist sympathies. After serving in the Ottoman army during the First World War, Süreyya had taken a teaching post in a village in Azerbaijan, then still within the Turkish sphere of influence. The occupation of Azerbaijan by the Red Army made such an impression on him that he became a communist (Süreyya, 169). Soon after moving to a school in Batum, he was accepted as a member of the social family, and the four men became close friends; indeed, so strong were the affinities between them that their paths did not radically diverge till the late 1920s, when Va-Nu became a professional journalist and both Cevat and Süreyya decided to join the Kemalist administration. During these early days in Batum they spent their evenings engaged in passionate debates about politics and personal relationships. When Nazım visited friends, he would carry a notebook to jot down ideas for poems or make sketches of the people he met. One evening at a dinner party he made a drawing of a young woman called Leyla, the sister of a teacher at Süreyya's school. This sketch was so entrancing that Süreyya fell head over heels in love. Shortly afterwards he and Leyla married, and the social family acquired its first female member.

It was through the social family that Nazım and Va-Nu finally obtained the opening they had dreamed of – the opportunity to visit Moscow. The Oriental Institute at Moscow University decided to appoint a professor of Turkish and asked for a recommendation from Orjenikitze, head of the Georgian communist government. Orjenikitze, a close associate of Stalin, recommended Ahmet Cevat, knowing that he had written textbooks for the Turkish Ministry of Education. On accepting the post, Cevat persuaded the authorities to allow his three friends to accompany him; they would enrol at a newly-established university in Moscow, the Communist University for the Workers of the East. The social family wasted little time in preparing for the journey to Moscow. They stopped at Tiflis to spend a few days with Nüzhet, and this time succeeded in persuading her to follow them to Moscow. They then embarked on an epic journey full of scenes reminiscent of Maxim Gorki. The trains were so crowded that some passengers stowed away under the floor. Va-Nu recalls that he and Nazım themselves ended up sleeping on the roof, giving up their seats to pregnant women and children (Va-Nu, 253-8). To cross the Caucasus, the train first wound its way south-east to Baku on the Caspian Sea, before turning north to Rostov. Altogether, it took them eleven days to cover the 1,000 miles to Moscow.

The Soviet Union was still gripped by the effects of revolution and civil war, the campaign against peasant landowners and a devastating drought which resulted in several million deaths from famine. During this train journey the travellers from Turkey witnessed appalling sights – the countryside barren with drought and the peasants tortured by hunger – and these confronted Nazım with a challenge both as a communist and as a poet. He had to abandon his idealistic conceptions of the Soviet Union as a liberated

and egalitarian society. At the same time he had to develop a
new poetic style to express the convulsions of this modern politics:
'When we were travelling from Baku to Moscow [...] we passed
through the famine areas. What we witnessed there affected me
deeply. But I wanted to shout that even a famine like this cannot
reverse the revolution. I tried, in vain, to write about the famine
in various combinations of regular metrical patterns. Then I remembered the form of a poem I had seen in Batum. I realised that
it wasn't the form of French vers libre that I already knew very
well, but it was something completely new: the poet was thinking
in waves' (A 26, 175). It may have been a poem by Mayakovsky
which gave the first hint of an appropriate new style. During his
time in Batum his knowledge of Russian was still very inadequate,
but although he did not understand the theme of the poem, he
was fascinated by its experimental form. As the train wound its
way through the devastated countryside, the crooked lines of
starving people became associated in his mind with the fracturing
of metrical form, and on arriving in Moscow he began to experiment
with poetry in the Mayakovskian mode.

Moscow, commune and Communist University

When the social family arrived in Moscow, they settled into the
Lux Hotel on Tverskaya Boulevard, an elegant street full of disused
banks and businesses now being converted into co-operatives or
campaign centres. The hotel housed official visitors, foreign communists and political refugees. Thanks to the position of Ahmet
Cevat at the Oriental Institute, the Turkish guests were assigned
three separate rooms. At the hotel they met revolutionaries from
all over the world. They were also introduced to two young
women, Shura and Lyolya, who were to act as their interpreters
and guides; the two women had defied their aristocratic families
and joined the revolution, and were now art students. The four
of them soon became close friends. It was in this bohemian circle
that Nazım first heard the names of Yasenin and Alexander Blok
and began to assimilate the ideas of the avant-garde, even meeting
Mayakovsky himself.

By the time they had found their bearings in Moscow, the
holidays had begun, so Nazım and Va-Nu were able to move
into vacant rooms in a student hostel – a fine two-storeyed building

in Pushkin Square. Previously the headquarters of the Bank of Holland, it had only recently been converted into a hostel, and although the building was lavishly decorated, their room had no furniture. In Moscow everything was rationed, with only the most basic food and clothing available. Some students, as was later recalled by the poet Nikolay Zabolotsky, hit on the ruse of registering in two faculties at once, in the hope of obtaining two ration cards (Zabolotsky, 24-5). Nazım and Va-Nu had very little money, but they were still able to use Cevat's facilities at the Lux Hotel, which provided a communal kitchen for the social family. Their daily ration, if they were lucky, was a quarter loaf of black bread, half a cabbage and a couple of carrots. Va-Nu discovered a way of enhancing the flavour of their food by pur-loining ingredients from some of the other cosmopolitan users of the kitchen – tasty Indian spices and succulent vegetables. But when he confessed his misdeeds to the others, he had to endure a lecture from Şevket Süreyya, the social family's mentor. As students they were assigned various community duties, including one month spent guarding the city's stores of fish. When it came to Va-Nu's turn, he was again severely censured – this time for purloining some of the fish for himself and his friends. Confession and self-criticism helped to keep bourgeois tendencies under control (Va-Nu, 279-86).

The flood of new impressions during their first weeks in Moscow stimulated Nazım to a renewed burst of creativity. He was still trying to digest the painful impressions of their journey through the famine areas. In the early summer of 1922 they studied documentary films shown in the public squares by mobile cinemas, as well as photographs of the famine areas displayed in Moscow shop windows. Süreyya has left an account of one particularly memorable episode: 'One evening we were walking along the crowded streets. Two lorries stopped in the middle of the square, one with a screen, the other with a film projector. The name of the film was *Hunger*. [...] It showed people leaving river areas like Kuban, Volga and Don, as if starvation was burning their bodies. The earth was cracked because of the drought in such a way that it would have made a grave for the staggering children holding on to their mother's skirts. Starving people were walking and running away in crooked lines in the midst of an unending wasteland towards an unknown horizon' (*Kadro*, April 1932).

The same night Nazım read out a poem he had just composed, 'Eyes of the Starving People'. This poem exemplifies his new Mayakovskian style of poetry written 'in waves':

> Hungry people, lines of hungry people!
> Not men, not women, not boys or girls
> skin and bones
> > bent twisted branches
> > > of bent twisted trees! [...]
> But
> we shall not lose our faith!
> Our hearts are strong as steel
> for the pains we feel
> > are 30,000,000
> > > fervent piercing eyes!
> > > ('Açların Gözbebekleri', A 1, 24-7)

The poet's faith was strengthened by his enthusiastic study of Marxism, recalled in the poem 'My Nineteenth Year', which suggests with characteristic hyperbole that he was so absorbed by the study of Marxism that there was little time for making love:

> In 24 hours 24 hours of Lenin
> > 24 hours of Marx
> > > 24 hours of Engels
> a hundred grammes of black bread
> > 20 tons of books
> and 20 minutes of the other thing!
> > ('19 Yaşım', A 1, 212)

During the summer they enjoyed a more relaxed interlude in the countryside, joining a commune organised by the University. The four members of the social family set out together by train. They then walked through the woods past a number of holiday villages with log cabins rented by families during the summer. Skirting a cluster of small lakes, they finally reached Udelnaya, a holiday village constructed for wealthy families before the revolution; forty or fifty of the buildings were now assigned to the University. The village had a communal kitchen and social facilities, which were used not only for meals but also for study and discussion. Everybody had to contribute to the rota of duties such as cooking, cleaning, chopping wood, and even looking after orphaned children. They started systematically learning Russian, but life in the commune did not only consist of classes and discussions. Nazım continued to write poetry, discovering a new and appreciative audience. One of the privately owned villas was occupied by a family who were prospering under Lenin's New Economic Policy. The husband, a chemical engineer, was often away, reportedly visiting his mistress. His wife Sophia Isk would entertain writers and artists at the villa, in the company of like-minded friends and relatives. Nazım and Va-Nu were soon enjoying her parties and picnics, with an abundance of food and delicious tea simmering on the samovar (Va-Nu, 286 & 321). He would recite poetry, and Sophia would respond by singing Russian songs. Nazım's friendship with Sophia continued until he received the news that Nüzhet had arrived in Moscow.

In the evenings the members of the commune would sit around the fire analysing each other's characters. Nazım would impetuously denounce Süreyya as a 'peasant' whose cautious approach to communism was an obstacle to the revolution (Süreyya, 240). The poet in his turn was criticised as self-indulgent. Indeed, all the members of his group were censured for giving priority to relationships within their social family instead of becoming fully committed to the commune. Their weakness for women, especially their contacts with bourgeois girls outside the university group, was also criticised. These discussions were led by a comrade named Abit Alimov, the son of an Islamic mullah from Kazakhistan who spoke Turkish fluently – he was to be the first translator of Nazım's work into Russian. Since he was a gifted political theorist, Alimov became one of Nazım's models (Va-Nu, 291, 304-15 & 336). Excerpts from the poems Nazım wrote at Udelnaya, such as 'We Believed', show how fervent his faith had become – not only in the revolution but also in the accompanying technocratic ethos:

> We believed!
> We believed with our brains!
> We believed in the flight of aeroplanes
> every line of which was created
> by the science of numbers [...]
> ('İnandık', A 8, 151)

Echoes of the Russian Futurists can be detected in these celebrations of technology with their emphasis on the superhuman energy required by the revolutionary struggle. In a poem dated 10 August 1922 he wrote with characteristic exuberance: 'I am like the

Colossus of Rhodes / wearing American shoes size 45!' ('Rodos Heykeli', A 1, 39)

An even more striking example, which combines technological optimism with images of erotic desire, is 'The Means of Production in our Hands or the Conquest of Mars'. Here the poet expresses the hope that modern machines, which he calls 'our children', will not be used for the wrong purpose by the wrong people, as was the case in the past. Control of nature should now be in the hands of the workers:

> Nature [...]
> is ours!
> Like a healthy peasant bride
> wriggling with her firm breasts
> under her husband's broad hairy chest!
> ('Istihsal Aletleri ve biz yahut Merihe uçacak zafer', A 8, 152)

Man's power over nature is associated with holding a woman, naked like a peeled apple in his hands, as she yields to his oriental possessiveness. This poem, from the summer of 1922, was not included in the first edition of Nazım's work. Like other juvenilia, it only survives because it was transcribed by Nüzhet into her notebook. One wonders how she responded.

On their return to Moscow in autumn 1922, they began their studies at the Communist University for the Workers of the East, founded to train revolutionary cadres from newly-formed Soviet republics like Turkmenistan and Uzbekistan. Its second main task, as defined by Stalin in an address to students delivered in May 1925, was to educate workers, peasants and revolutionary intelligentsia from colonial countries like India and Egypt as 'real revolutionaries, armed with the theory of Leninism' (Stalin 7, 153). The curriculum was flexible, with instruction in many languages. In addition to courses on Marxism-Leninism, Nazım and Va-Nu studied French and Russian, and they soon began to take on some of the teaching duties themselves. The University was run as a commune with its own restaurant, where the poorest students were able to obtain free meals. Most students were accommodated in dormitories, but there were also smaller rooms for close friends or married couples. Initially the two poets shared a room, but the situation changed after the arrival of Nüzhet, who was photographed with Nazım in a striking picture taken in 1921 (Fig. 5). Unable to return to Turkey, she had persuaded

5. Nazım and Nüzhet in Moscow.

her brother-in-law to allow her to join the Turkish group in Moscow, and later that year she and Nazım announced that they were married. In this period of revolutionary reconstruction no formal ceremony was necessary. They simply went together to a registry office and made a declaration that they had become partners, which entitled them to a room of their own (Va-Nu, 297 & 405). In addition to his studies, Nazım became increasingly involved with the student theatre. Nüzhet, who also attended courses at the university, has left a glowing account of his charismatic role: 'In this circle, which included many male and female friends, Nazım was the most popular person; he was in a position of leadership with his good looks, striking behaviour and animated gestures, and through his poems and plays, which conveyed the strength of his convictions and ideals' (Sülker 1, 181).

At the university Nazım met revolutionaries from all parts of Asia, including a Chinese student called Emi Siao (transliterated by Nazım as Si-Ya-U). Siao, who had studied in Paris in 1920 and spoke fluent French, was later to become a leading figure in the Chinese revolution and a well-known poet. His dandified appearance so caught Nazım's imagination that he reappears in the 'The Romantics' complete with satin trousers, patent-leather shoes, a tie and a trilby hat. Fellow students also included two Indians named Zafer Hasan and Banerjee. Zafer was a practising Muslim who had studied in England before becoming involved in the anti-colonial movement in India. Threatened with imprisonment and even a death sentence because of his agitation against the British Raj, he escaped to the Soviet Union. Later he married a Turkish woman and settled in Turkey, where he worked as a teacher and researcher. Banerjee was a revolutionary of a very different type, striking Nazım as a real gentleman. Apart from English and Russian, he was studying Sanskrit and Indian mysticism. The deep impression made by these idealistic communists later led Nazım to make them key figures in two of his narrative poems, *Jokond ile Si-Ya-U* ('Mona Lisa and Si-Ya-U', 1929) and *Benerci Kendini Niçin Öldürdü?* ('Why Did Banerjee Kill Himself', 1932).

Nazım's circle also included Siao's girlfriend, a tall Russian woman with red hair and green eyes. According to one account, this woman actually fell in love with Nazım, although their friendship never developed into an affair, since he did not want to hurt the feelings of his sensitive Chinese friend (Va-Nu, 299). She must have made quite an impression on him, since many years later she resurfaces as a character named Anushka in his autobiographical novel 'The Romantics'. The hero of Nazım's narrative listens entranced as Anushka recounts how she has survived terrible ordeals, including the death of both her parents, before joining the partisans in Siberia and becoming a communist. After Siao returns to China, she and the hero fall passionately in love, but the relationship has to end when he is instructed by the communist party to return to Turkey. In a poignant episode set in a dacha during the summer of 1924, the hero, lying in bed beside the naked Anushka, wrestles with his conscience before finally deciding to leave (A 17, 140-3). How much these sections of the novel owe to actual experience, how much to subjective fantasy, has always perplexed Nazım's biographers.

The students of the Communist University were exposed to a variety of competing arguments. This was a period of exhilarating ideological debate, when Leninist theory had not yet hardened into Stalinist dogma. But even at this early stage there was an awareness of the conflict between the internationalism of Trotsky and Stalin's more pragmatic concept of socialism in one country. Trotsky's lectures to students at the Communist University insisted on the need for international solidarity. Nazım was so impressed that in the original version of his poem 'Farewell' ('Veda') he paid tribute to Trotsky's voice 'resounding like a great bell' (Va-Nu, 308). He too dreamed of a revolution that would liberate oppressed peoples throughout the world. In autumn 1922 he witnessed the spectacular parades to mark the fifth anniversary of the Revolution. This inspired him to write the first of his poems that was actually translated and published in the Soviet Union, 'On the Fifth Anniversary of the Revolution'. This poem ends with a celebration of Lenin's programme of modernisation and electrification, but it is also remarkable in that it acknowledges suffering and refuses to idealise the revolution ('Inkilabın Beşinci Senesine', B 1, 58).

Events in Germany seemed for a time to confirm the Trotskyist strategy of international revolution, especially when the communists briefly seized power in Thüringen in October 1923. This inspired Nazım's poem 'Waiting for the German Revolution': 'The streets of Berlin are listening again / to the footsteps of Spartacus!' ('Almanya Inkilabını Beklerken', B 1, 83). However, from 1924 onwards the economic and political situation in Germany became more stable, and Nazım realised that his hopes were unlikely to be fulfilled. He also became aware that Trotsky's internationalism might involve the Soviet people in international class wars, and the admiration he had felt for him soon cooled (Va-Nu, 313). Meanwhile developments in the Soviet Union gave grounds for renewed optimism. In the spring of 1921, at the 10th Congress, Lenin had announced his New Economic Policy (NEP), designed to alleviate the crippling shortages of food and consumer goods by allowing small private enterprises and more scope for peasants to market their agricultural products. The success of this policy created a mood of confidence, and Nazım became a staunch supporter. There was also a drive to increase agricultural productivity through collectivisation. Nazım, blissfully unaware that these policies might have destructive consequences, celebrated them in romantic terms in poems like 'Love of the Earth' ('Toprak Sevgisi', A 8, 156).

Social reconstruction assigned new roles to women, and International Women's Day was celebrated on 8 March 1923 with a poetry reading at the Polytechnic Museum, led by Mayakovsky

(Fevralski, 11). Nazım too read a number of his poems, including one provocatively entitled 'Trousers and Skirts in our Time' ('Bizde Pantalonla Eteklik'). The erotic undertones in this poem, so characteristic of his vision of a liberated society, can hardly be described as politically correct, either by the Leninist principles of the time or by those of a more recent puritanism. His ostensible theme is that female revolutionaries are just as important as males, Clara Zetkin as significant as Karl Radek. The only difference is 'the little thing between the legs' (Sülker 1980, 113). The celebration concluded with a student performance of Nazım's short play about the murder of fifteen members of the Turkish Communist Party on 28 January 1921 ('28 Kanuni Sani', B 1, 78-80). The play ridiculed the attempted cover-up by the Turkish police, who in a series of farcical episodes threaten to imprison anyone mentioning the fatal number '28' (Fevralski, 14). A year later, on 12 February 1924, the play was staged in a workers' club in the Krasno-Presnenski district of Moscow by the student theatre group under the direction of Nicolai Ekk, a member of Meyerhold's theatre workshop. This time, as Nazım proudly recalled, the production was even reviewed in *Pravda* (A 21, 268). With Ekk's assistance, he now began to develop a new style of political drama, inspired not only by the experimental poetry of Mayakovsky but also by the avant-garde theatre of Meyerhold.

Mayakovsky, Meyerhold and the 'mechanised theatre'

Nazım first met Mayakovsky in Shura and Lyolya's room at the Lux Hotel, shortly after first arriving in Moscow (Babayev, 76). Since he went on to share the stage with Mayakovsky in March 1923, it is often assumed that the Russian poet strongly influenced his work. Looking back on these contacts many years later, Nazım was to give rather contradictory accounts. In an interview published in *Her Ay* in April 1937 he claimed: 'Once I learned Russian and was able to get to know Mayakovsky's work and personality, I learned a lot from him. [...] But this Futurist phase passed very quickly' (A 26, 33). This seems to imply a genuine familiarity with Mayakovsky's work. In 1941, however, Nazım explains in a letter to Kemal Tahir, that he is reading the collected works of Mayakovsky in one volume:

I am going to confess something, but it has to remain a secret between us: Mayakovsky's work is a new discovery for me. What I mean is that apart from a couple of poems which I heard from his own lips, this is the first time I am reading his works in print. [...] Don't take any notice of the fact that on numerous occasions, out of a sense of embarrassment, I claimed that I am familiar with Mayakovsky, even though I actually had no knowledge of his work (AM 3, 69–70).

In a conversation with Fevralski in June 1955, Nâzım attempts to strike a balance between these two positions, acknowledging Mayakovsky as his teacher while at the same time asserting his own independence:

What my poetry and Mayakovsky's have in common is breaking down, first, the division between poetry and prose, secondly between different styles (lyrical, satirical etc), and thirdly bringing the language of politics into poetry. However, we used different forms. Mayakovsky is my teacher, but I do not write like him. When I was a student in Moscow, I was a poet of the public platform like Mayakovsky. When I read to the audience, my poetry produced the sounds of an orchestra of wind instruments. But on my return to Turkey, I was only once able to read my poetry in public. After that I had to use softer words because I had to whisper my poems into the ears of the audience (A 26, 168).

Nâzım was privileged to be in Moscow during the magical early years of Soviet modernism. The city was perceived not as the centre of Russian imperialism but as the heart of a revolution that would transform the world (Fig. 6). And art was assigned a formative role in the building of the new society. The Commissar for Education, Anatoly Lunacharsky, himself an essayist and playwright, had decided to back the avant-garde both ideologically and financially. The Soviet theatre of the 1920s combined daring formal experiment with directness of political impact, using innovative techniques to convey the dynamics of a new technological civilisation. The innovations of Meyerhold had not yet been subordinated to the more philistine priorities of the Proletcult and Socialist Realism, and Nâzım was captivated by the innovative spirit of the avant-garde.

In Nâzım's development during this period, Marxist theory and avant-garde aesthetics converged: 'I read the courses on Marxism, which I was studying at the Communist University for the Workers of the East, under the spotlights of the contemporary Soviet theatre' (A 21, 268). He envisaged a synthesis of communism

6. 'RED MOSCOW the heart of the World Revolution',
Soviet poster, 1920.

and constructivism, as indicated by a programmatic passage from
'The Poet', written in Moscow in 1922:

> I am a poet
> I have written as much poetry as it rains in a year.
> But in order to start writing my masterpiece
> my 'Constructivist-Marxist' novel
> I shall have to wait till I've learned
> 'Das Kapital' by heart !
> ('Şair', B 1, 64; A 1, 97)

The impact of Nazım's early writings derives not from theoretical
sophistication, but from the immediacy of their imaginative appeal.
Like the Futurists, he was committed to publicising political issues
by means of arresting poetic images rather than simplistic political
slogans. Since many of these poems were written for the public
platform, he devised ingenious sound effects to express the energies

of the social and technological revolutions. The poem 'Mechanisation' (1923), which also makes use of experimental typography, is a characteristic example:

trrrrum,

trrrrum,

trrrrum

trak tiki tak!

I want to be

Mechanized

I will find a solution to this
and I shall only be happy
on the day I fix a turbine to my belly
and a couple of propellers to my tail!
('Makinalaşmak', A 1, 22)

The use of onomatopoeia proved remarkably effective. At an International Art Festival presented at the Meyerhold Theatre on 14 January 1923, Nazım read another programmatic poem, 'New Art', in which the melancholy sound of nightingales is disrupted by the full blast of the modern poetic orchestra. After this reading Fevralski noted: 'Despite the fact that the audience did not understand Turkish, they could feel the revolutionary spirit and the enthusiasm he expressed in his poetry. The language didn't seem a barrier because of the rhythm and phonetic expressions and the way he read his poetry' (Fevralski, 10).

Nazım's position as director of a student drama group at the Communist University enabled him to make personal contact with Meyerhold himself. The Soviet director, who had a particular interest in oriental theatre, encouraged the students to use folkloristic elements in their productions, deriving from national traditions that would be familiar to an audience of workers. When Nazım showed him the typescript of a play he had written entitled 'The Pyramid', Meyerhold found time to read it and suggested that it might be adapted as a ballet or pantomime. Everything depended on 'music and movement' (SF, 918-19). Nazım did not take up this suggestion, perhaps because his attitude to the Russian ballet was rather critical. In an essay in praise of the Meyerhold Theatre

he even had the effrontery to suggest that the Bolshoi Theatre
'would be more useful if converted into a grain silo' (A 8, 164).
But towards the end of his life he modified his views: 'From the
operas I saw at the Bolshoi Theatre I learned the necessity of
being brief, plain, unadorned and unpolished in the arts as in
life.' He vividly recalled Vassilenko's ballet 'Handsome Joseph':
with its fluidity of theme, it suggested that similar effects might
be achieved in poetry.

His real passion, however, was for the theatre: 'I saw plays
produced by Stanislavsky, Meyerhold, Vakhtangov, Tairov, freshly
baked and fragrant, smelling of life, revolution, beauty, heroism,
goodness, rationality and intelligence' (A 21, 267). The plays which
he saw during this first visit to Moscow included Maxim Gorki's
The Lower Depths at the Moscow Arts Theatre. But he also records
the stimulus he received from more experimental productions,
like Sukhovo-Kobylin's *Tarelkin's Death*, staged by Meyerhold in
the autumn of 1922 with stage effects borrowed from the circus
and with constructivist stage designs by Varvara Stepanova. Nazım
also saw Racine's *Phèdre*, directed by Tairov at the Kamerny
Theatre in 1923 with Alisa Koonen in the title role; austerely
geometrical sets were designed by Alexander Vesnin. Even more
memorable was Vakhtangov's staging of Carlo Gozzi's fairy tale
Princess Turandot, which combined the verve of Commedia dell'Arte
with pre-Brechtian techniques of estrangement (Rudnisky, 54-5
& 105-6). In 1924 Nazım also saw the celebrated production of
Ostrovski's *The Storm* at the Kamerny Theatre, directed by
Alexander Tairov with Alisa Koonen as the indomitable heroine.
The performance blended realistic peasant drama with constructivist
stage design. His enthusiasm for the theatre was shared by his
friends Siao and Anushka, who accompanied him to Ostrovski's
The Forest at the Meyerhold Theatre (A 17, 107).

For his most memorable theatrical experience, however, he
had to wait till his second stay in Moscow. This was Meyerhold's
adaptation of Gogol's *The Government Inspector* (1926) with its
grotesque social satire, haunting musicality and pantomimic use
of costume and gesture. Summing up these experiences many
years later, Nazım observed: 'Isn't your rigid, static conception
of art transformed when you see such things? Do not new horizons
open up, becoming wider and wider? Don't you burn with desire
to write works full of hope and light for your people, for the

nations, for mankind, works appealing for progress, justice, truth, beauty, freedom and brotherhood?' Nazım goes on to explain that his own writing received a decisive stimulus from these direc- tors, especially Meyerhold, Stanislavsky and Vakhtangov: 'The influence of the Soviet theatre on my lyric poetry is greater than the influence of Soviet poetry' (A 21, 267-8). In short, the stimulus towards a new poetic style derived less from Mayakovsky than from Meyerhold. On 2 April 1923, at a celebration to mark the twenty-fifth anniversary of Meyerhold's debut in the theatre, Nazım represented his university, reading in Turkish his poem on 'The Meyerhold Theatre'; it was followed by a Russian translation read by the Sergei Tretyakov (Babayev, 86). This enthusiastic celebration of Meyerhold's innovations culminated in the line: 'Long live the mechanised theatre!' (A 8, 164).

The summer of 1923 was again spent in the Russian countryside. As soon as the university term was over, the social family left Moscow and stayed for several weeks in a student commune at Vaskin, set up in a mansion among picturesque woods and gardens and lakes teeming with fish. Şevket Süreyya was again the leader of the social family. However, despite the idyllic surroundings the summer break proved less auspicious than the previous year. Va-Nu fell ill and had to be sent south to a sanatorium in Caucasia, and there were anxious weeks of waiting before at last he returned safely (Va-Nu, 323). Nüzhet too developed some health problems and had to return to Baku, where her brother-in-law Birgen had been appointed as professor. Nazım accompanied her on this ar- duous journey, which was to mark the end of their short-lived 'marriage'. Towards the end of the year she returned to Turkey with Birgen's family, having convinced Nazım that she had to return to Istanbul for the sake of her health, although the separation was only supposed to be temporary. Family pressures may have played their part in the break-up of this partnership: Nüzhet was under the influence of her brother-in-law, a member of the Union and Progress Party, who was sceptical about Nazım for both political and personal reasons. Birgen had never approved of their relation- ship, and one of his letters openly expressed his hostility: 'How could a delicate quiet girl like you want to marry someone who is rebelling against everything so strongly, with words and with all his personality, that even his hair rebels against the barber's comb' (Va-Nu, 405).

After Nüzhet reached Istanbul, Nazım experienced several months of anxiety, when he received no letters. It was Nüzhet who finally decided that she and Nazım were incompatible; during her stay at a sanatorium in Europe, she had realized that she could never keep up with a giant like Nazım: 'I never considered myself to be worthy of him. Me a timid, quiet, delicate and physically sensitive girl. Him a blue-eyed giant' (Sülker, 1980, 24-26). This alludes to a poem written in the early 1930s, in which Nazım arrogantly suggests that no 'little woman' is likely to measure up to a 'blue-eyed giant' like himself ('Mavi Gözlü Dev, Minnacık Kadın ve Hanımelleri', A 2, 104). One might expect the tensions created by Nüzhet's departure to figure prominently in his poetry of the mid-1920s; after all, she had not only shared his life in Moscow but encouraged his creativity, faithfully transcribing his poems of the years 1922-4 into her own albums. But Nazım was too strongly committed to politics to write poetry about unrequited love. Only in one poem of this period, 'A Worm in My Body', did his ambivalent feelings for Nüzhet find expression:

> Like a worm,
> soft,
> white,
> you penetrated
> my body,
> strong as a minaret or a pine-tree,
> [...]
> Soft,
>   white,
>   you wriggle
>   and nibble your way
>   into my brain!
>   ('Gövdemdeki Kurt'; A 1, 28)

In this poem the seductive effects of femininity are seen not only as emotionally debilitating, but also as politically suspect, comparable to the intrigues of Western politicians like the British Labour Party leader Ramsay MacDonald or the French premier Poincaré. According to Nüzhet's reminiscences, this poem was written in 1922 while they were a temporarily estranged and Nazım was undergoing pangs of jealousy (Sülker 1980, 39).

In both political and personal terms, the end of 1923 marked a turning point. Nüzhet's departure reinforced Nazım's growing impatience to return to Turkey and put his newly-acquired knowledge into practice, and the death of Lenin on 21 January 1924 reinforced his sense of mission. The scenes of public mourning made a profound impression: 'I had once, when my grandfather was buried, experienced ten or perhaps twenty people grieving together,' he wrote many years later in his autobiographical novel. 'It is even possible to imagine a hundred people sobbing in chorus, but the sound I heard was a whole city sobbing from a single mouth.' He goes on to describe the experience of keeping vigil in the great hall where Lenin's body lay in state: 'I see Lenin's head from behind, or rather his huge forehead. I hear the funeral march. I have no connection any longer with the endless flow of people coming from four sides. I gaze at Lenin and I want to cry' (A 17, 84-6). This communal mourning set the seal on his commitment. His poem 'Echo of the Death of our Master' expresses the theme of collective bereavement through echoing voices. When the mourners, unable to believe that their hero is dead, call out in chorus 'It's a lie', they hear the answering echo 'He must die'. But the poem culminates in the uplifting lines: 'Tomorrow, in a classless society, all new-born children / will find the sprit of Lenin within themselves' ('Ustamızın Ölümü'; B 1, 95-7).

Turkish interlude: spreading the light

The Turkish Communist Party was planning to hold a congress in January 1925, and members who had been at the Communist University for more than a year were asked to return. This was the moment when the social family, which had sustained them through so many adventures, began to disintegrate. Va-Nu, who had recently married a Russian woman, decided to remain for a few more months in Moscow. Ahmet Cevat had already been obliged to leave because of doubts over his political commitment and questions raised by his involvement with the carpet trade (Topcuoğlu 2, 89-93). Then Şevket Süreyya left Moscow, followed in December 1924 by Nazım himself. Anxiety about his relationship with Nüzhet made him all the more eager to return to Istanbul, but as soon as he arrived he was confronted with her decision to leave him. His first reaction was to suggest that they should rebuild their relationship and even formally get married, but after being pointedly cut by her one evening at the theatre, he was compelled to acknowledge that the relationship was at an end (Sülker 1980, 25-6). Since they were not married according to Turkish law, no divorce proceedings were necessary, and Nüzhet was free to choose another partner. In 1926 she married a teacher of philosophy named Mehmet Servet Berkin, by whom she had two children (Karaca 1995, 36).

Grief did not deter Nazım from pursuing his political commitments. The Turkey to which he returned late in 1924 was a very different country from the one he had left three years earlier. In November 1922, three months after Kemal's forces had driven the Greeks into the sea, the last Ottoman Sultan had fled from Istanbul abroad a British warship. After protracted negotiations the Treaty of Lausanne was signed in July 1923, setting the seal of international recognition on Kemal's victory. Exploiting differences between the Allied powers, the chief negotiator Ismet Pasha had succeeded in securing for Turkey extremely favourable terms. Britain withdrew its forces from Istanbul and the Dardanelles, and Kemal was also able to reoccupy Eastern Thrace and consolidate his power throughout Anatolia. On 29 October 1923 he proclaimed Turkey a republic, with himself as its first President. On the 3 March 1924 he took the even bolder step of abolishing the Caliphate with the aim of converting Turkey into a secular state, and the following day the last Caliph, Abdul Mecit, was deported on the Orient Express.

The abolition of the caliphate was followed by a radical reform of the education system, involving the replacement of religious seminaries by secular schools. Some of Kemal's staunchest supporters found these measures too radical, arguing that Turkey needed a period of consolidation, not social revolution. They resigned from the Kemalist Republican People's Party and began to organize an opposition group. On 17 November 1924 the Progressive Republican Party was founded under the leadership of Rauf Orbay, Kazım Karabekir, Ali Fuat Cebesoy and Adnan Adıvar; this was the party that would represent 'the religious sensibilities of the people' (Heper, 79). At this stage the young Republic was still searching for its identity, and Kemal had not yet gained absolute authority over the National Assembly, although he regarded the so-called Progressive Party with deep suspicion. The press enjoyed considerable freedom, and there were opportunities to debate the merits of different political systems and explore new ideas in literature and politics. One of Kemal's first steps after the proclamation of the Republic was to establish Ankara as his capital. But Istanbul remained dominant in commerce and industry, as well as publishing and the press, and it was here that the Communist Party centred its activities.

When Nazım arrived in Istanbul in December 1924, he moved in with his father, Hikmet Bey, who was living in the Kadıköy district with his new wife Cavide and with Nazım's sister Samiye (Aydemir 1970, 136). Hikmet Bey was working in Süreyya Cinema and publishing *Cinema Post*, a magazine devoted to film reviews and other news about the cinema. The family tried to encourage Nazım to apply for a job in Kemal's government, but he had no intention of joining the establishment. However, his relationship with his father remained cordial, and he helped him with the production of *Cinema Post*. Şevket Süreyya and Ahmet Cevat had already returned to Turkey and started working for *Aydınlık* (The Light), the monthly magazine of the Party edited by Şefik Hüsnü, which had been founded in July 1921. In its early phase *Aydınlık* adopted an anti-imperialist stance, campaigning against the capitulations (the economic privileges enjoyed by the Western powers), rather than undertaking a Marxist critique of domestic economic policies. Not surprisingly, at the Fifth Congress of the Comintern held in Moscow between 17 June and 8 July 1924, *Aydınlık* was criticised for supporting Turkish national capitalism against foreign imperialism (Tunçay, 177). This led the Comintern to recommend that trained members should return to Turkey to attend the Congress of the Turkish Communist Party and reactivate its propaganda.

The Congress took place in Istanbul in January 1925, within a few days of Nazım's arrival, and it was agreed that *Aydınlık* should adopt a more explicitly Marxist stance (TKP, 57). It is significant that the first number to be published in 1925 (no. 29) contains a critique of Trotsky, whose position had been defended in another article only two months earlier (Tunçay, 181). This was followed by the publication of Nazım's poem on the first anniversary of Lenin's death (no. 30). Physically Lenin might be dead, but the poem proclaims that all proletarians will feel his spirit alive within themselves (A 2, 98). Despite these changes of emphasis, *Aydınlık* remained essentially a magazine for intellectuals. In an attempt to appeal to a wider audience, the Party launched on 25 January 1925 a new weekly political magazine for workers and peasants: *Orak-Çekiç* (Hammer and Sickle). This short-lived publication, also edited by Şefik Hüsnü, concentrated on more basic political issues. The contributors formed a collective, going out on to the streets to sell copies of the magazine with its provocative 'Hammer and Sickle' design (Fig. 7). In his autobiographical novel Nazım recalls his mixed feelings selling the first issue on Galata Bridge – a pasha's son shouting socialist slogans (A 17, 86).

Nazım's contributions to *Aydınlık* marked a new phase in his development – the first attempt to make the complexities of Marxist theory accessible to Turkish readers. His earliest contribution, published under the pseudonym Ahmet, had appeared in September 1924 while he was still in the Soviet Union. A spate of further articles and poems appeared in the following months, until this brief experiment in political freedom was brought to an abrupt end with the closure of *Aydınlık* in February 1925. For a short time he threw his full energy into this ambitious project. His most significant themes were the critique of capitalism, the exposition of dialectical materialism, and the satirising of romanticism and cultural imperialism. In these writings the 'fiery light' of Marxism becomes a dominant motif, as in a poem of September 1924 which actually bears the title 'Aydınlık' (A 8, 177). A further poem, 'Spreaders of Light', summarizes the aims of the group, 'writing with the head of Marx / and the eyes of Lenin' ('Aydınlıkçlar', A 8, 179). Nazım claims that the group includes ordinary working people like engine drivers, sailors and seamstresses, as well as the poet himself, all rallying to the sign of the hammer and sickle (B 1, 105-6).

The October issue included a philosophical article by Nazım entitled 'A Brief Introduction to Dialectical Materialism' ('Diyalektik Materyalizme Küçük Bir Methal'), as well as two poems about dialectical materialism and science (A 22, 13). In this article Nazım argues that 'scientific and dialectical materialist thinking has demolished that absolutism and abstract ideology which forms the foundation of metaphysical thinking'. He is visibly struggling to develop a conceptual language to convey Marxist theory in Turkish, relying so heavily on abstractions of Arabic origin that the modern editor feels obliged to add a glossary almost half as long as the article itself. Compared with this inflated terminology, the language

« اوراق چكيج. غزئته سى بوتون توركيا عمله سنك ماليدر.

7. Hammer and Sickle design from the magazine *Orak Çekiç*.

of his verse is crisp and clear, as in the short poem 'Again on the Same Subject: Science':

> Life means movement!..
> movement means contradiction!..
> Society is at the throat of nature
> and the different classes are ready to knife each other!..
> Watch out!
> That which is called 'science' is beyond our control
> yet we take part in it
> like a film reflected in our brains!..
> 'Science' is born out of struggle
> and struggle creates 'science'.
> ('Yine Bu Bahse Dair: Ilim', A 8, 178)

The most powerful poem of the period, 'The Orient and the West' (Şark-Garp), appeared first in *Aydınlık* No 27 in November 1924. Focusing on the figure of Pierre Loti, it is a devastating satire on cultural imperialism and the sentimental cult of the Orient. The poet and novelist Pierre Loti (1850-1923) was an officer in the French navy who first visited Turkey in 1876. His experiences

in Salonika and Istanbul inspired his first novel *Aziyade* (1879),
a romance about a young naval officer's passion for a Circassian
slave-girl. The beauty of Aziyade, whose green eyes are first
glimpsed through a lattice window in Salonika, becomes identified
with the romance of the orient and the seductive city of Istanbul.
Aziyade celebrates the attraction of mosques and minarets, picnics
on the Golden Horn and romantic excursions along the Bosphorus,
culminating in a melancholy evocation of the hero's final parting
from Aziyade among the cypress trees of the Eyub cemetery. Loti
returned to these themes in many of his later writings, which
contrast the timeless wisdom of the East with the shallow civilisation
of the West. But although his cult of the orient had such a
powerful appeal for earlier generations of readers, it can now be
seen as a blend of sexual fantasy and political nostalgia.

Nazım's Marxist schooling enabled him to expose this form
of mystification in a poem which juxtaposes the lure of the orient
against the harsh realities of suffering. In an exemplary attack,
Loti is identified as the perpetrator of poetic myths grotesquely
at odds with the true condition of the Turkish people:

> 'Opium!
> Submission!
> Kısmet!
> Lattice work, caravanserai
>   fountains
> a sultan dancing on a tray!
> Maharajah, rajah
> a thousand-year-old shah!
> Waving from minarets
> clogs made of mother-of-pearl;
> women with henna-stained noses
> working their looms with their feet.
> In the wind, green-turbaned imams
>   calling the people to prayer.'
> This is the Orient the French poet sees.
> [...]
> Orient!
> The soil on which naked slaves die of hunger.
> The common property of everyone
> except those born on it.
> The land where hunger itself
>   perishes with famine!

> But the silos are full to the brim,
> full of grain –
> > only for Europe
> (A 1, 18-21; SP 19)

The quotation marks enclose a collage of motifs from Loti's writings, from the alluring lattice-window which sets the scene for *Aziyade* to the splendours of the Ottoman Sultanate which are celebrated in his reminiscences. Loti may have 'planted the tombstone of Aziyade in our hearts' – a reference to the sequel, *Fantôme d'Orient* (1892), in which the protagonist returns to search for the grave of his beloved. But for Nazım he is 'a charlatan / who sells in the East / rotten French fabrics / at a profit of five hundred per cent'. By deconstructing the sentimental tourist's image of a world untouched by Western civilisation, Nazım exposes one of the persistent myths of the modern age.

Nazım was concerned too about other aspects of cultural imperialism, notably the indoctrination of young Turkish readers with a flood of popular magazines featuring Western cultural heroes and cartoon characters like Nat Pinkerton and Sherlock Holmes. He argues that Turkish literature should celebrate its own folk heroes – the rebels against Ottoman rule who fought for equality and justice. A further target for satire was provided by romantic poets like Faruk Nafiz, Ruşen Eşref and Falih Rıfkı. The poem 'Gentlemen! Stand Up' (Ayağa Kalkın Efendiler, A 1, 141) ridicules such writers, who were still concocting beautiful love lyrics and then 'selling their poems as if they were pears' (*Aydınlık*, No 28, December 1924). It is time, he declares, for such poets to pack up their bags and go. Nazım even has the temerity to cite some lines by the leading Ottoman poet Yahya Kemal from his celebrated love poem 'Gaze'. The Turkish romantics are ridiculed for still writing in Yahya Kemal's style, 'wearing your powdered mustachios, your eyes still gazing at Leila bathing in the bay'. To press home this attack, Nazım published a further article in January 1925, praising the work of the theatre director Muhsin Ertuğrul as authentic modern art for revolutionary Turkey (A 21, 7).

Nazım was the first writer to introduce into Turkish poetry the language of modern politics. The impact of these revolutionary new themes is reinforced by a new poetic style shot through with irony and dissonance, disrupting the melodious rhythms of Ottoman diction with the rugged irregularity of its lines. At the same time his articles focus on the role of the artist in a rapidly changing society. The originality of Nazım's writings soon gained him many admirers both inside and outside the communist movement. His contributions to *Aydınlık* marked a decisive stage in the redefinition both of the role of art and of the Party's ideological basis. But these developments were brought to an abrupt halt in February 1925 by a crisis which arose in the remote eastern provinces of Turkey. The authority of the Republic was rudely challenged by a Kurdish rebellion, which provided Kemal's government with a pretext for reppressing all forms of political dissent.

The Kurdish rebellion was led by Sheikh Said, a tribal chieftain whose authority was based on both wealth and religious prestige. Traditional feudal power and Islamic piety were clearly under threat from the infidels in Ankara with their programme of secularisation. Denouncing the godless policy of the Kemalist regime, the Sheikh raised the green banner of Islam against the red and white flag of the Republic. The news of this revolt provoked acrimonious debates in the National Assembly, some of whose members were sympathetic to the call to uphold Islamic traditions. Kemal brushed this opposition aside and appointed a hawkish new prime minister – Ismet Pasha, hero of the battle of Inönü and leader of the delegation at Lausanne. Martial Law was declared on 21 February, and on 4 March a draconian Public Order Act was pushed through the Assembly, giving the government dictatorial powers. A strong military force, supported by aircraft, was dispatched to the east to crush the Kurdish revolt, and within two months the irregulars were encircled and forced to surrender. The Sheikh himself was put on trial for treason, sentenced to death and hanged.

Kemal's policy was to act decisively against any threat to his power. 'If we can manage to keep the right wing under control', he is quoted as saying, 'we do not need to fear the left' (Kinross, 398). Since he regarded the leaders of the Progressive Republican Party, who had dared to challenge his authority in the National Assembly, as 'traitors' and 'reactionaries', he had little hesitation in closing the party down (Heper, 77-8). Using the Kurdish threat as a pretext, the government also turned its attention to the liberal press, which had expressed certain reservations about the military action, and on 12 March it used its new powers to close down five Istanbul newspapers. Ahmet Emin Yalman, proprietor of the independent daily *Vatan*, has left a circumstantial account of the indignities suffered by newspaper editors, as they were taken under arrest to the Kurdish regions of eastern Anatolia to be confronted with the consequences of their folly in questioning official policy. They were then put on trial by newly established Independence Tribunals ('Istiklal Mahkemeleri'), accused of 'undermining the authority of the government and indirectly causing the revolt'. Yalman admits that he had failed to recognize the seriousness of the Kurdish problem: 'The more we saw of the interior, the more we recognized our share of responsibility for the existing crisis.' Intimidated by the threat of imprisonment, he joined a number of other editors in issuing a public apology and abandoning his career as a journalist. It was not till fifteen years later, in the summer of 1940, that Yalman resumed it and refounded *Vatan* (Yalman 1956, 151-7 and 187).

The Independence Tribunals had extensive powers and imposed a number of death sentences during their two-year reign of terror. An abortive conspiracy against Kemal's life, which came to light in June 1926, provided a pretext for a further spate of arrests, which included former leaders of the Progressive Party like Karabekir and Cebesoy, who had nothing to do with the plot. Those condemned and executed by the Tribunals included Javid, a prominent figure from the Union and Progress movement who had been financial adviser to Enver Pasha's goverment, and Colonel Arif, one of Kemal's comrades-in-arms during the War of Liberation. Karabekir and Cebesoy were acquitted and released, probably through the intervention of the Prime Minister, but they had been taught their lesson. Executions were carried out in public, and the bodies of those hanged were displayed in Ankara's main square with placards pinned to their chests denouncing their crimes (Kinross, 403 & 425-43). It was by such ruthless measures that Kemal succeeded in keeping the conservatives under control. In a country with no organized working-class movement, he had little to fear from the left.

Communist journals were nevertheless among the first casualties of the crack-down in 1925. On 5 March *Orak-Çekiç* printed an article which deplored the Kurdish rebellion and denounced Sheikh Said as the puppet of British imperialism. It went on to advocate land reform: 'The thing to do is not just to suppress the rebellion and to punish its leaders, but also to abolish the feudal order in the east. The problems of ownership of land should be solved and the land should be redistributed for the benefit of the peasants.' This was the final number of the magazine to appear before it too was suppressed (Tunçay, 186-7). This equivocating approach was characteristic of the Party's attitude to the Kurdish question. In theory, it condemned the chauvinism of Kemalist policy, but in practice had to acknowledge that the suppression of the Kurdish revolt was 'favourably received by the masses of the Turkish workers' (IISH Archive, 'La situation du Parti', 5 July 1926). During the following decades the Kurdish question was to prove just as intractable for Commmunist Party theorists as for the representatives of the Turkish government.

The suppression of opposition newspapers under the Public Order Act was followed on 30 March 1925 by the arrest of editors and staff of *Aydınlık*, together with nine members of the Communist Party (Coşkun, 21). Further arrests followed after the May Day celebrations, held in defiance of the government. This resulted in the arrest of thirty-eight left- wingers, including members of the Workers Advancement Society (Harris, 134). Their houses were raided by the police, who confiscated books and other material regarded as subversive. The thirty-eight left-wingers, who were sent to Ankara to face the Tribunals, included Şevket Süreyya, leader of Nazım's social family. Nazım himself fled to Izmir to avoid arrest, but he was tried in his absence and given a fifteen-year prison sentence (Tunçay, 190). While he was away, Nazım's father and his family were harrassed by the police, the house was searched and Nazım's letters to the family were confiscated.

According to one account, Nazım was sent to Izmir by the Party with the mission of starting an underground newspaper (Coşkun, 27-8). The city was still recovering from the conflagration caused by the war against the Greeks, and the authorities were preoccupied with programmes of reconstruction and resettlement, after the enforced exodus of thousands of Greek inhabitants. The ordeal of these months on the run in Izmir is recalled in a personal reminiscence published many years later: 'I had to live in an underground stone cave. It was a small house with a heavy wooden door with no window and no light. I could only go out at night to attend meetings. I didn't even have money to buy an oil lamp. For two months I lived in darkness' (Babayev, 114). Eventually Nazım succeeded in obtaining false identity papers, and by the middle of June he was back at his mother's house in Istanbul (Aydemir 1970, 144-5). Soon after his return, the hide-out in Izmir was raided and several comrades were arrested. It was not safe to remain in Turkey, so he asked his mother to use her artistic skills to disguise him as a sailor. Shortly afterwards Nazım left Istanbul by boat, embarking from Mühürdar near his mother's house in Kadıköy, and by September 1925 he was back in the Soviet Union.

A new broom in the theatre

When Nazım returned to the Soviet Union in the autumn of 1925, he found the mood significantly altered. During the early years of the New Economic Plan there was still scope for a diversity of artistic methods and ideological positions. But by the summer of 1925 the debate about the function of art was entering a new phase. The heady experiments associated with Mayakovsky and Meyerhold were being challenged. Influential critics began to argue for a more systematic integration of cultural policy with the Five Year Plan to modernise the Soviet economy. Towards the end of the 1920s, newly established groups like RAPP (Revolutionary Association of Proletarian Writers) began to have a dominating influence on literary organisations and editorial boards, joining forces with dogmatic thinkers in the Communist Party. Their manifestos spoke a new language, subordinating the playfulness of Futurist aesthetics to the militant rhetoric of class warfare. The aim of these zealots was to subject all creative activity to the discipline of political and economic reconstruction. The most influential figure in this new wave of the Soviet theatre was Sergei Tretyakov, the playwright who in 1926 became famous overnight through the revolutionary impact of *Roar China*. The new heroes of the Soviet stage were to be exemplary figures, so committed to communism that they appeared to be completely free from human psychological failings or spiritual needs. The shift towards more a more dogmatic conception of culture became irreversible after Stalin took control of the Party in December 1927, a development followed by the exile of Trotsky to Alma Ata in January 1928 and finally his deportation to Turkey on 12 February 1929.

During this period Nazım re-established himself in Moscow

with the aim of developing a new style of political theatre. He settled once again in a room in Tverskaya Boulevard, in a block of flats opposite the TASS news agency. One of his first moves was to visit his old friend Va-Nu in Udelnaya. This reunion was not without its hazards. On the day before their visitor arrived, Va-Nu and his wife Anna had gone mushroom-picking in the forest, and in Nazım's honour they then cooked the freshly picked mushrooms with onions and kidneys. Unfortunately the wild mushrooms turned out to be totally indigestible. While Va-Nu wanted to hear all about the changing political climate in Turkey, Nazım couldn't wait to recite his latest poems to his friend, striding up and down, his face flushed and his eyes flashing. But he also had to face up to new political responsibilities associated with the forthcoming conference of the Turkish Communist Party.

The Party was in a state of turmoil as a result of the government crack-down of 1925, and the majority of the leadership were now in prison or exile. Şefik Hüsnü, who had escaped to Austria, made an attempt to reorganize the Party from outside, and in 1926 he convened a party conference in Vienna. Nazım was one of those who attended as a delegate from the Moscow-based Foreign Section of the Party, while other members, including Vedat Nedim and Hamdi Şamilof, arrived from Turkey. But far from solving the conflict, the discussions merely accentuated the divisions within the Party. One issue debated at the conference was the cautious line adopted by the magazine *Aydınlık*, which had been criticised by the Comintern for supporting 'legal Marxism' (Bursalı, 120). The group with which Nazım was associated, though strictly Leninist, was in favour of working to gain popular support within the limits of the constitution, while the rival group, led by Şefik Hüsnü, wanted an increase in underground activity (Coşkun, 30). Among the decisions taken in Vienna was the appointment of Vedat Nedim as general secretary. Although Vedat wanted the Turkish Party to be less dependent on the Comintern, it was decided that they had no alternative but to accept directions from Moscow and that the Foreign Section would return there to represent the Party. The atmosphere during these debates was highly charged, marking the beginning of the splits which were to continue for decades.

Back in Moscow, Nazım continued to develop new projects in the theatre. Within a few months he was joined by another kindred spirit, the young Turkish theatre director Muhsin Ertuğrul. In the January 1925 issue of *Aydınlık* Nazım had already written appreciatively about Muhsin's work, praising him for his progressive ideas. He now introduced Muhsin to Lunacharsky and obtained permission for him to visit theatres and attend rehearsals. Muhsin was also introduced to leading directors like Stanislavsky, Meyerhold and Treytakov. At the suggestion of Vladimir Gardin of the Goskino Theatre Company, he was given a room next to Eisenstein, and he was present at the rehearsal for *Roar China*, first performed on 23 January 1926. In March 1926, with the support of Tretyakov, Muhsin became the director of the Vufku film company in Odessa. After directing a number of films, including *Tamilla* and *Spartacus*, he returned to Turkey in January 1927, later becoming director of Istanbul City Theatre (Ertuğrul, 496-8).

Another contributor to Nazım's theatrical projects was Nicolai Ekk, the friend who had ealier helped organize student drama groups. Early in 1926, when Nazım was just recovering from an attack of flu, they met again and had a stimulating discussion. 'It is time for us to have our own theatre to rival the Kamerny', Nazım declared (Fish, 132). It was this meeting that inspired their new theatre, which opened in the autumn of 1926 at the Central Cinema, formerly known as the Black Cat ('*Chat Noir*'). They decided to call their theatre company METLA, an acronym for Moscow's Only Leninist Theatre Studio, which in Russian also forms the word 'broom'. In the introduction to his collected plays Nazım recalls that this new broom was to sweep traditional psychological and melodramatic elements off the stage and develop new forms of agitational art (A 21, 269). A model for this venture was provided by the mobile theatre units used for propaganda immediately after the revolution (Babayev, 300). Nazım was the resident poet and playwright, since by this date his command of Russian enabled him to organize a Russian-language theatre. He and Ekk developed a double strategy for recruiting actors, most of whom came either from the Meyerhold Theatre or the Communist University. Ekk would test their acting talents, while Nazım assessed their political orientation. During rehearsals the actors were encouraged to depart from their script, so that in a sense they became co-authors. They would appear in their working clothes, 'demonstrating' their roles (in a style analogous to Brecht's epic theatre), rather than becoming fully absorbed in the dramatic

characters. The decor was sparse and relied on geometrical con-
structions, and they favoured short plays with a direct political
impact. In search of the most effective techniques for representing
contemporary history, they introduced elements of cabaret and
pantomime, as Meyerhold and Eisenstein had done before them,
and even motifs from the Turkish puppet theatre.

The theatre officially opened on 19 September 1926 with a
series of one-act revues about the First World War and the achievements of the October Revolution (Fevralski, 16). The leitmotif
was provided by a popular Russian song, 'Kirpichiki' ('Little
Bricks'), in praise of a woman worker who helps to rebuild a
factory after the war. They used cinematographic techniques to
correlate political events with the domestic interiors represented
on stage. For example, the audience would first be shown shots
of a political demonstration, and then someone coming home
from the demonstration would enter the scene, the actor apparently
stepping out of the cinema screen on to the stage (A 21, 269).
Documentary film footage was used to convey contemporary political events, in the style popularized by the revolutionary German
theatre of Piscator. The spirit of improvisation which inspired
their productions has been described by Isidor Stok, an actor in
the METLA company who also made his name as a playwright:

We used to run around carrying props, sometimes acting the role of soldiers
shooting at the people, the next moment representing the people taking
the guns out of the hands of the soldiers, sometimes bourgeois, sometimes
workers. [...] A loud accordion would play the song of the bricklayers in
the background, while clips from films were shown (Fish, 135).

Nazım's own account of his aims is more formal: 'Our theatre
was to build an organic relation between politics and the stage.'
At the end of the peformance, audience and actors would join
in the singing of revolutionary songs. The political message conveyed by METLA is exemplified by the play *Kabahat kimde?* (Who
Is To Blame?) about the corrupting influence of capitalism (A
21, 269). A more complex study of the insidious effects of social
institutions is offered by *Herşey Mal* (Wealth is Everything), originally subtitled 'A Theatrical Lesson in Marxism' (Babayev, 307). In
this play Nazım explored the relationship between scientific research
and capitalist exploitation. The plot centres on a medical scientist
desperately seeking a cure for tuberculosis, since his daughter is
dying of the disease. His work is sabotaged by the owners of

sanatoriums who fear that the discovery of a miracle drug will deprive them of a profitable market.

Although the METLA company enjoyed some success, attendance gradually fell and in March 1927 the theatre had to close (Fish, 132-8). Looking back on this project years later, Nazım modestly attributes its failure to their own shortcomings: 'We needed to fight against our old patterns with deeper and more progressive and mature weapons' (A 21, 270). This face-saving formula perhaps conceals the significance of external political factors. It can hardly be a coincidence that the closure of METLA followed so soon after the 15th Congress of the Soviet Communist Party in January 1927, which resulted in the defeat of Trotsky and the imposition of tighter political controls. Nazım's project foundered at a time when the Kremlin was becoming increasingly hostile to experimental artistic activities. After METLA closed, Nazım, Ekk, Stok and some of their colleagues joined another theatre group which enjoyed greater official approval, the Young Playwrights Productive Unit (PROMD); it encouraged people to write collective plays and criticise each other's work in the approved communist manner. The METLA experiment may have been short-lived, but for Nazım it had a long-term value, stimulating him to develop new skills. Several dramatic sketches from this period were later incorporated in more ambitious works, and his involvement with the theatre encouraged him to make increasing use of dialogue in his poetry.

Philosophical poetry: flowing waters and fallen comrades

Although best known as a lyric poet, Nazım was never afraid of tackling more philosophical themes. He recalls that he was so immersed in Marxism-Leninism that he decided 'to elucidate Lenin's *Materialism and Empiriocriticism* by means of two poems' (A 26, 179). The finest of these, 'Berkeley' (1926), uses implicit dialogue to challenge the claim that material objects have no reality beyond subjective consciousness:

> Well if you say so
> > if you argue
> that the sea is your idea
> the boat is your own idea,
> Time doesn't exist

Space does not exist
and nobody exists outside your own self
[...]
Oh, but you the drunk bishop of dark taverns:
wasn't the publican's young daughter
who kept wriggling in your hairy arms
outside your own filthy body?
Or, should we assume that you slept
with Bishop Berkeley?
(A 1, 49-56; SP 26)

Another poem of this period, 'Thinking of Heraclitus in Moscow'
(1925), expresses Nazım's affinity with the natural philosophy of
Heraclitus:

I could not have survived
here for long
if I did not understand the meaning of flowing waters
Perhaps, one evening
Heraclitus leaned over the water
running though the green olive groves
and said:
'everything is changing and flowing
that makes me adoring'
('Moskova'da Heraklit'i Düşünüş', A 8, 166)

Images of the material world reflected in water often recur in
Nazım's poetry. In 'Longing', another poem of the late 1920s,
the impulse is 'to burn out / like a light falling into the sea'.
Man is inescapably part of the material world and must return
to nature, but this tells only half the story. At another level we
may detect the voice of the exile longing to return to Istanbul
('Hasret', A 1, 197).

In some of the finest poems of this period, philosophical themes
are blended with a gentler lyricism, very different from the strident
verses written during his first visit to Soviet Union. The political
lyrics of the late 1920s involve the use of softer words, as in the
poems 'Caspian Sea' ('Hazer Denizi', 1928) and 'Weeping Willow'
('Salkım Söğüt', also 1928). In 'Caspian Sea' the breaking waves
allude to conflicts within the Turkish Communist Party which
have to be accepted by the resilient helmsman. In 'Weeping Willow'
musical rhythms interspersed with sonorous rhymes are used to
validate events from the Russian Revolution:

Flowing
was the water, showing
in its mirror the willow trees.
The weeping willows in the water washed their hair.
Striking the willows with swords burning, bare,
ran the red horsemen to where
        the sun sets.

Once again the motif of reflection represents the mystery of the
material world, while the horsemen recall the heroism of the
Red Army cavalry – one of Nazım's most vivid memories from
his first visit to Batum:

Suddenly
like a bird
        struck in the wing,
a wounded horseman rolled from his horse.
        (A 1, 14; T 197)

Despite the acknowledgement of pain and sacrifice, the poem
ends with images of consolation, suggesting that nature and revolution may be reconciled.

This poem of restrained lament over the loss of a comrade
may have specific contemporary application, since the image of
the fallen comrade also alludes to defections from the Turkish
Communist Party. A crisis had arisen in October 1927 when the
general secretary Vedat Nedim, disillusioned by splits within the
party and the oppressiveness of the Moscow line, revealed names
and details to the police. Ninety-eight people were arrested and
the communist movement was decisively weakened. For Nazım's
old friend Şevket Süreyya this debacle marked the decisive turning-point. After being convicted under the Public Order Act of
March 1925, he had spent eighteen months in Afyon prison before
being released under an amnesty on 29 October 1926. By the
end of 1927 Süreyya felt so disillusioned that he decided to leave
the Party. This marked the demise of the social family which
had sustained Nazım for so long.

A further effect of the amnesty of October 1926 was to lift
the fifteen-year prison sentence on Nazım himself. But the decision
whether or not to return to Turkey was not entirely in his hands.
As a party member he was subject to decisions taken by the
Central Committee, which met in Istanbul and reported back to
the Comintern in Moscow. The minutes and reports of the Central

Committee, copies of which are now in the Archive for the History of Socialism in Amsterdam, help us to understand the difficulties which Nazım and his comrades had to face: the 'white terror' of the Kemalist regime (according to a detailed report on 'The Situation of the Party' in July 1926) had crippled the organization in Turkey, severing the links between the Central Committee and the cells in other urban centres. The persecution' of the left had deterred many potential supporters, and the Party had fewer than 350 members in the whole of Turkey, 120 of them in Istanbul; and now that communist newspapers were banned, some left-wing writers associated with *Aydınlık* had committed the error of collaborating with journals opposed to the party line. To remedy these failings, a fundamental reassessment of strategy had been undertaken at the Vienna Conference (IISH Archive, 'La Situation du Parti', 5 July 1926).

The difficulties involved in rebuilding the Party are reflected in the records of the Central Committee, which repeatedly stress the need for more regular financial support from Moscow. A particular priority, according to the Minutes of 10 February 1927, would be a printing press to produce party literature, and here Nazım was evidently expected to play a leading role. The Minutes of 25 February resolve that he should be recalled to Turkey, not least because he is protected by his growing reputation as a poet:

As far as Nazım is concerned, his poem about 'The Holy Book' ['Meşin Kaplı Kitap'], recently published in a literary review in Istanbul, was read by Mustafa Kemal, who was very enthusiastic about it. When members of his entourage intimated that the author was a communist, Kemal apparently replied: 'Who cares what he is! One thing is certain – no one has ever written anything as powerful as this in the Turkish language.' This information, passed on by a member of his entourage, leads one to believe that the authorities will not be too severe towards Nazım (IISH Archive, 'Séance du 25 février 1927').

This view of the Turkish authorities was to prove over-optimistic. However, it is hardly surprising that Nazım's satire on religious supersition should have appealed to Kemal, whose programme of secularization was to lead in April 1928 in the removal of all reference to Islam from the constitution.

In the event Nazım did not return to Turkey till July 1928. Several factors prolonged his stay in Soviet Union, particularly the difficulty he had in obtaining a Turkish passport. He also seems to have become embroiled in an internal party dispute about his links with the faction of Abit Alimov. A confidential memo addressed to the Comintern in February 1927 identifies Alimov as ring-leader in a 'plot' designed to undermine the authority of the Central Committee in Istanbul (IISH Archive, 'A l'Executif de l'I. C.', 7 February 1927). Alimov was one of Nazım's mentors, and he too seems to have become involved in the alleged conspiracy. Later that same year, an unsigned letter and accompanying memo written in German specifically suggest that Nazım and one of his comrades should be removed from Moscow for a month to give them a chance to change their attitudes. They should then return to Turkey, because of the urgent need for more activists (IISH Archive, 'Uebersetzung des Briefes des Genossen F. vom 9. Oktober 1927' & 'An Genossen Smeral und Petroff', 24 October 1927).

Nazım's position was complicated by personal factors. He had fallen in love again, this time with a young woman called Lena Yurchenko, whom he had met while working at the METLA theatre. He refers to this 'Dr Lena' as his wife, but there is little firm information about their relationship. According to Şükrü Mertel, a Turkish worker studying in Moscow at this time, her real name was Ludmilla Yurchenko and she was a dentist. She and Nazım lived together in a second-floor flat in Tverskaya Boulevard, and Şükrü used to keep them supplied with agricultural produce, saving them from disaster one evening when they had invited Mayakovsky to dinner and had nothing in the larder (*Vatan*, 10 July 1976). A further clue is provided by a photograph of them together, published in the magazine *Resimli Ay* in May 1929 after Nazım's return to Turkey, with the caption 'Nazım with his wife Lena'. Beyond this we know little about her apart from her shoe size, mentioned by Nazım in a letter to his sister Samiye asking her to buy a pair of shoes for Lena. This letter is undated, but certain details suggest that it was written before August 1926. Thus the relationship with Lena must have lasted at least two years.

Once Nazım had decided to return to Turkey, his father tried to obtain a visa for Lena so that she might accompany him (Aydemir 1970, 147-9). Nazım's sister Samiye recalled (Interview 1988) that Lena travelled as far as Odessa in the hope of finally joining him in Istanbul, but one year after they parted a final postcard was received from Lena in Odessa, postmarked 23 May 1929.

Her Cyrillic script is hard to decipher, but it is clear that she identified with Nazım's family, as well as with the poet himself:

My dear Nazım,
I am happy to have had your letter. [...] Please write more frequently, this long silence has cost me dear. [...] How do they explain the refusal to grant a visa? My regards to your father, uncle, Samiye. [...] If you have no time, ask somebody else to write. Please send me a Turkish textbook and a kilo of coffee. Your book and magazines arrived by post, but I did not receive them. I was told that they were kept somewhere and they do not want to give them to me. I miss you very much my love. It is summer now. It will soon be a year since we parted. I miss you so much that sometimes it seems that the door will open and I will see you. I've lost all hope that this will happen. [...] Lots of kisses, Lena
(Coşkun K, 1990, 33).

The rest of the story is shrouded in mystery. It is reported that in Odessa she contracted a disease, possibly cholera, from which she died (Tulyakova, 196). In some studies Lena has been confused with another young Russian woman named Lyolya, who, with her sister Shura, had acted as interpreter for Nazım and Va-Nu in 1922 (Fish, 146). In Nazım's autobiographical novel, written thirty years later, there is an enigmatic reference to a young woman from the Ukraine named Lena Yurchenko, a brunette with dimples on both cheeks who 'looks like the girls from Istanbul' (A 17, 37). Although the full significance of this relationship cannot be reconstructed, it forms part of a pattern of love-and-separation which would haunt Nazım throughout his life.

4

Literature and Marxism: A Borrowed Shirt?

1928-1938

Just before Nazım left the Soviet Union, a first collection of his poems appeared in book form, published in 1928 in Baku under the title *Güneşi İçenlerin Türküsü* (Ballad of Those Who Drink the Sun) with a striking cover design that linked the Arabic lettering with the brilliant disk of the sun. Writing to his father around this date, Nazım proudly explains that he is now well known in Azerbaijan, and that his work has been praised and his photograph published in several magazines (Aydemir 1970, 152). Baku was important for Nazım not simply as an outpost of Turkish culture in the Soviet Union, but also as a dynamic centre of industrial development. During the four-day train journey there from Moscow, he wrote a diary in verse entitled 'Nefte Doğru' (Towards Petrol), subsequently revised under the title 'Seyahat Notları' (Travel Notes, A 1, 151). These poems, written with a Mayakovskian exuberance, celebrate the triumphs of industrialisation, describing the Don valley as a land of factories, coal, oil and telegraph poles. Recording his impressions as the train approaches an industrial town, he writes: 'Black clothes are not the signs of mourning / but of coal on our right and on our left.' The arrival in Baku inspired a panegyric: 'I want to kiss the black-eyed workers with their greasy overalls. / I want to prostrate myself on the holy earth of Baku / taking a handful of oil and drinking it like black wine.' Oil even becomes associated with the girls from Azerbaijan 'with their glittering black hair' (B 1, 148).

Homecoming in handcuffs

After failing to obtain a permit to re-enter Turkey legally, Nazım decided in July 1928 to cross the frontier without a visa, accompanied by a comrade named Ismail Bilen (Laz Ismail). Born in Rize in 1902, Bilen studied at University for the Workers of the East from 1923-5. He was a party activist whom the Turkish authorities imprisoned several times before he returned to Moscow in 1934 to become a dominant figure in the foreign section of the Turkish Communist Party for the next fifty years. As they arrived in the Turkish border town of Hopa on the Black Sea coast, the two comrades were arrested for entering the country under an assumed identity. This was Nazım's first experience of prison – with cramped and crowded cells and no sanitary facilities. Most of the inmates in Hopa prison were poor country people, who at first were suspicious of this aristocratic-looking newcomer. But when they heard that Nazım had been arrested for campaigning against the landowners, they began to treat him as their friend, sharing both their food and their life stories with him.

These experiences inspired him to write the poems collected under the title of 'Notes from Hopa Prison' ('Hopa Mahpusanesi Notlarından'). Imprisonment curbed his tendency towards Mayakovskian rhetoric, and we now find him using more condensed images to create vivid characters and poignant scenes:

> An oil lamp...
> nailed to the wall...
> a crooked nail
>   through the heart of a page
>   torn from a writing-pad.
> The clear white paper
>   has faded...
> The nail has drunk the blood of the paper.
> The lamp is burning like sunshine on a rainy morning
> and the paper is dangling
>   like a hanged man's
>   white shirt...
> On the chest of the white shirt it says:
> 'Weekly rota:
>   carrying water
>   emptying slops
>   scrubbing floors [...]'
> ('Kızkapan Oğlu Vehbi ve Çocuk Muhittine Dair'; A 1, 225)

Identifying closely with his fellow inmates, the poet acknowledges that the prisoners themselves have no voice. In the poem 'Sükut'

(Silence) he speaks for them, suggesting that their inability to argue their case is not a passive silence but 'like a bullet in the breech of a gun'. Their suppressed anger is echoed by the sounds of the sea beyond the prison walls:

> Outside,
> in the darkness
> the sea is breaking like a forest stabbed in the chest.
> Inside we are silent,
> the dungeon is silent
> like a wounded animal
> bleeding inside ...
> (A 1, 175)

The images of suffering and injustice culminate in a poem describing an impending execution, named after the condemned man, 'Bayram Oğlu'. This sombre poem creates a mood of foreboding as the prisoner's hands are tied and at two o'clock in the morning the carriage arrives, drawn by skeletal horses: 'The carriage lanterns are filled with the terror / of your deep blind eyes / as if gouged with a knife' (A 1, 199-201).

After an initial hearing in Hopa, Nazım and Laz Ismail were transferred to Rize to be tried in the central criminal court. According to Va-Nu they were even accused, under Section 146 of the Turkish Criminal Code, of planning an uprising among the minorities, an offence which carried the death penalty. Nazım had brought with him a copy of *Güneşi İçenlerin Türküsü* together with other notes and manuscripts, including the philosophical poem 'Thinking of Heraclitus in Moscow'. The authorities in Hopa read this as '*Her ekalliyet*', which in Turkish means 'all the minorities'. This was taken to refer to the position of the Greeks, Armenians and Kurds, explosive issues in the newly founded Turkish Republic. 'So you're thinking of all the minorities, that means you are a provocateur inciting them to revolt,' one of their interrogators insisted. 'But Heraclitus is a Greek philosopher', Nazım replied. 'Aha, so you admit that he's a Greek! That makes it far worse!' (Va-Nu, 349). They had to wait two months for their trial and then received a three-day sentence for using false papers.

This was not the end of their adventures, since they also had to answer more serious charges arising from the court cases initiated in their absence in 1925 and 1927. From Rize, near the Russian border, the two prisoners had to travel by boat the whole length of the Black Sea to Istanbul. When they arrived on 4 October, they were forced to walk through the streets handcuffed with three armed guards. After twenty-four hours in the detention centre, where the charges were read to them by the public prosecutor, they were transferred to the notorious Sultanahmet prison to await trial. Here they had the consolation of being able to compare notes with other members of the Turkish Communist Party, who were serving long sentences imposed during the 1927 trials. The poet's spirits remained undaunted. Va-Nu, visiting Nazım, found him 'sitting on a wooden bench in the basement of a building which was dirty, had no ventilation, and was stinking very badly. He looked unshaven, had no buttons on his coat, his clothes were stained and his shoes were muddy. He could not even hug me because he was handcuffed. [...] But he immediately wanted to read me his most recent poems' (Va-Nu, 349).

The courtroom was packed with reporters, since news of their arrest had provoked protests against their imprisonment. Istanbul was the centre of a thriving press, and the founding of *Cumhuriyet* ('Republic') by Yunus Nadi in 1924 had provided Turkey with a modern daily newspaper modelled on Western lines. A photograph in *Cumhuriyet* (5 October 1928) shows Nazım and Laz Ismail being escorted through the streets under armed guard (Fig. 8). The court decided that all the charges should be heard together, which meant that the prisoners had to be transferred to Ankara. They arrived there on 14 October, and the trials lasted from 4 November till 23 December 1928. Nazım's six-month ordeal finally ended when he was acquitted of the charges dating from 1925, but sentenced to three months' imprisonment under the anti-communist measures of 1927. Since he had already served almost twice as long, he was immediately released.

During his early days of freedom in Ankara at the end of 1928, Nazım was faced with a new challenge. By this date the Kemalist regime had consolidated its power, having suppressed both Kurdish rebels and religious opponents. Kemal acquired almost dictatorial powers, and after the suppression of the Progressive Party there was no faction in the National Assembly that could challenge him. But if the system he created had elements of dictatorship, it was a still one inspired by progressive aims and regulated by constitutional principles. Moreover Kemal's westernising policies had enhanced his prestige abroad, so that there was even a prospect

8. Nazım and Ismail Bilen under escort in Istanbul.

of the country being admitted to the League of Nations. In September 1927 he delivered his famous six-day speech to the National Assembly setting out the achievements of the War of Independence and the Turkish revolution. It was now clear even to his most principled opponents that Kemalism was there to stay.

For writers of progressive outlook, the Kemalist reforms held an additional attraction. One of the keys to the programme of modernisation was the replacement by the Latin alphabet of the Arabic characters in which Turkish was traditionally written. This reform, announced by Kemal in August 1928, was implemented by the National Assembly on 3 November, shortly before Nazım's release. From this date all books, newspapers and magazines were printed in Latin characters. This was followed by a further series of language reforms designed to reduce the number of obscure loan-words of Persian or Arabic origin. These breaks with Ottoman tradition helped to win over many left-wing Turkish intellectuals, including Şevket Süreyya, founding father of the 'social family'. The way forward, they concluded, lay with Kemalist reform rather than Leninist revolution. After Süreyya had served eighteen months in Afyon prison, as a result of the anti-communist trials of 1927, his case came up for review. 'I was acquitted and freed,' he recalls. 'Quietly, I said farewell to my old friends. From then onwards our paths diverged' (Süreyya, 408). He became a government adviser on economic policy, setting up a new group in Ankara associated with the journal *Kadro* ('Cadre'), which aimed at finding a middle way between socialism and capitalism based on state planning. Süreya suggested that Nazım should follow his example, but the prospect of settling in Ankara and becoming a bureaucrat neither appealed to the poet's romantic temperament nor agreed with his political conscience. Shortly after his release, he returned to Istanbul to try his luck in Babıali, the journalistic quarter where literary reputations were made. During the crisis years 1925-6, the Public Order Act had imposed severe constraints on the press, but the lifting of these restrictions created new opportunities for radical journalism and political agitation.

Constructivist poems and communist cells

When Nazım resettled in Istanbul towards the end of 1928, he found the Turkish Communist Party weakened by splits, arrests and defections. The general secretary, Vedat Nedim Tör, had not only left the party but also informed on his comrades, which resulted in yet more members being imprisoned and tortured. For a time Şefik Hüsnü attempted to lead the party from prison in Istanbul, but in April 1929, after his release, he decided to escape to Europe and remained in exile for ten years. Meanwhile, the remnants of the party were being reorganised by Hüsamettin Özdoğdu, who had been released in January 1928. He tried to strengthen communist groups in various industrial and commercial centres, but these activities were leaked to the police, resulting in the arrest of thirty-five party members on 4 May 1929 (Topcuoğlu, 126-7). Nazım himself escaped arrest, since he was not implicated in underground activities. A report in *Cumhuriyet* claimed that those arrested included people employed by a Soviet firm named Arkos, suspected of providing links with Moscow. The trials began on 25 June, resulting in prison sentences of between two and five years. Among those imprisoned was Dr Hikmet Kıvılcımlı, a life-long communist born in 1902 who wrote several books of political theory. Since he espoused a dogmatic form of Marxism, he and Nazım found themselves in opposite camps.

These arrests created a vacuum in the party leadership. Nazım became associated with an oppositional faction – the 'muhalefet' group – which organised a meeting of the party in 1929 at his friend Hamdi Şamilov's house on Pavli Island near Istanbul. This led to the setting-up of a committee headed by Şamilov and Mustafa Börlükce, with Nazım as a secretary. The rival faction was led by Hasan Ali Ediz, who had returned to Turkey from Moscow to co-ordinate communist policy, and claimed that he represented the official party – the 'muvafakat' group (Tevetoğlu, 146-7). During 1930-1 the Ediz group extended it campaign to include not only the workers but also cadets at the military schools in Istanbul (Sayılgan, 198-9). However, this tactic backfired, since the Turkish authorities were particularly sensitive to any attempt to subvert the armed forces, and in August 1930 Ediz and other members of his group were arrested. In February 1931 Ediz received a two-year prison sentence, so he too lost control of the party. The campaign against Nazım's group culminated in a confrontation at the party congress of February 1932, held at Zeki Baştımar's house in the Defterdar suburb of Istanbul, and attended by a representative of the Comintern from Moscow. After a heated debate, it was decided that Nazım should formally be expelled. According to report sent to the Comintern in August 1932, Nazım's group had campaigned for greater 'internal democracy' and for the freedom to criticise decisions of the Comintern (IISH Archive, 19 August 1932, 'Muhalefet Hakkında'). A further report sent to Stalin in March 1935 by Şefik Hüsnü, who was still trying to exert his authority from exile, claims that Nazım was expelled for anti-Stalinist activities (Tevetoğlu, 163). This unwitting tribute to the poet's integrity was circulated through the bulletin of the Comintern and also distributed in Turkey (Coşkun, 88 & 105).

Nazım's work as a political activist pales by comparison with his achievements as a poet, since for him 1928-38 was a decade of exceptional productivity. The campaign for communism was being conducted on two levels, publicly through legal publications and secretly by underground cells. Nazım spearheaded the legal campaign, disseminating radical ideas through the weekly magazine *Resimli Perşembe* (Thursday Illustrated) and the monthly *Resimli Ay*. The underground campaign was conducted by means of the clandestine news-sheets *Kızıl Yıldız* (Red Star) and *Komunist*. Even though no longer formally a member of the party, Nazım continued to express solidarity with the working class. His confidence in the ability of rank-and-file members to finish the task is expressed in the poem 'Ordinary Man' ('Sıradaki', A 1, 206). However, Nazım's independence did not endear him to his former comrades. The criticism he had to endure is exemplified by a passage from Hikmet Kıvılcımlı's book, *Markisizmin Kalpazanları* (Impostors of Marxism, 1936): 'The poet Nazım Hikmet pretends to include Marxism in his poetry, like a borrowed shirt. If you take this shirt off his poetry, you will see any ordinary bourgeois poet in Babıali Street' (Korcan 1989, 88). For dogmatic Marxists, Nazım's individualistic approach remained suspect, despite his literary success. On 1 June 1936 *Orak Çekiç* published his name in their 'black list', declaring that he had been expelled from the Party as a bourgeois deviationist (Tunçay 2, 421).

It is against this background that we must interpret the most explicitly pro-Soviet of Nazım's publications, a 32-page pamphlet on 'Soviet Democracy', published in 1936 with a portrait of Stalin on the cover (*Sovyet Demokrasisi: Sovyetlerin Yeni Ana Kanun Projesi Dolayısıyla*). A new Soviet Constitution had been promulgated that year, which supposedly guaranteed freedom of speech and assembly, protection from arbitrary arrest, and the right to demonstrate. This document was welcomed by a whole generation of fellow-travellers as conclusive proof of Stalin's genius. Nazım's tone, by contrast, was somewhat cautious, avoiding any idealisation of Stalin. In making out a rational case for communism in this pamphlet, he both reaffirmed his own left-wing credentials and at the same time distances himself from his more dogmatic comrades. He argued that Lenin's conception of 'proletarian democracy' was far superior to bourgeois democracy, since workers, peasants and soldiers were to be represented in the legislature by members of their own class. Moreover, workers' rights in the Soviet Union included equal opportunities for women and guaranteed employment, sick pay and invalidity benefits. These arguments suggest that Nazım was unaware of the terrible consequences of Stalin's programme for the collectivisation of agriculture. The idealistic conception of communism formed in Moscow during the 1920s continued to shape the poet's vision.

Far from being a borrowed shirt, Nazım's Marxism proved a lifelong commitment, but his overriding aim was to transpose party dogmas into poetic forms. He had already set out his position six years earlier, in the interview published in *Cumhuriyet* on 5 October 1928 at the time of the Istanbul trial. Here Nazım is reported as saying: 'I am a believer in communism. I do not belong to any organization. I am only interested in the expression of the Marxist and Communist ideologies in literature' (Coşkun, 48). Three weeks later, in an article of 28 October, *Cumhuriyet* reported that his main intention in returning to Turkey was to found a literary magazine under the title *Sol Cenah* ('Left Wing'), reflecting the literature of the workers and peasants: 'There is a literary school in Russia called LEF. They are thought to be Futurists. But they are actually Constructivists. I belong to that school and I want to promote these developments' (A 26, 7). This literary conception of Marxism is reflected in a spate of publications. In April 1929, within a few months of his return to Istanbul, Nazım's first collection of poems in Latin type was published, with a bold jacket design, under the cryptic title, *835 Satır* ('835 Lines'). The book included experimental poems written in the Soviet Union under the influence of constructivism, including 'Mechanisation', 'Hungry Eyes', 'East and West (Pierre Loti)' and 'Berkeley'. The impact of the collection was enhanced by the opening poem, 'The Ballad of Those Who Drink the Sun' ('Güneşi İçenlerin Türküsü'), an appeal for political commitment peppered with exclamation marks:

> In that fire
> which has fallen
> from the sun
> millions of red hearts are burning!
>
> (A 1, 10)

Drawing on elemental imagery, the poem presents the power of the sun as an implicit endorsement of communism. For Nazım constructivism meant the combination of revolutionary themes with daring experiments in poetic form, especially the use of short lines and broken rhythms. *835 Satır* took the Turkish public by storm, selling 3,000 copies, and in 1932 Nazım's publisher, Ahmet Halit, issued a second edition. Established reviewers like Nurullah Ataç praised the book for bringing a breath of fresh air into Turkish literature, and Nazım's fame even reached New York, where a perceptive appreciation of his poetry appeared in *The Bookman* with the title 'A Poet of the New Turkey', accompanied by eye-catching illustrations.

The author of this article was Nermine Mouvafac (Nermin Menemencioğlu), a young Turkish woman studying at Brown University in Providence, Rhode Island. On 10 July 1930, after interviewing Nazım at the office of his publisher Ahmet Halit in Babıali, she noted in her diary: 'I have met a MAN!' Nazım Hikmet, she later recalled, was the 'epitome of a poet – handsome, courageous, generous, modest though sure of himself, dedicated to a cause. As Byron, with his dark beauty and romantic pessimism, was the symbol of the nineteenth century poet, so is Nazım Hikmet, with his flashing blue eyes and his positive outlook on the world and the people living on it, that of the twentieth century' (Menemencioğlu, 1). So eloquent was Nermine's account of the poet's achievements that even the editors of *The Bookman* were carried away. 'We should hardly have thought in advance', they wrote, 'that a paper on an obscure Communist poet in Turkey could find space in the crowded pages of the 'Bookman'. But the charm of Miss Mouvafac's account immediately won us over, and when we had finished we realised that however "marginal" from a local and literary view the story of Nazım Hikmet might be, it had great general interest in illustrating the sweep of the Communist fever in every country.'

Nermin Mouvafac's article offers an atmospheric account of the journalistic quarter of Babaılı, the street that winds up from the Sirkeci railway terminus towards the Blue Mosque: 'Here in their little musty shops the publishers sit drinking tea out of Persian glasses. [...] It seems a quiet enough world, and yet ideas – a strange intermingling of the classic arrogance of years ago, the romantic pessimism of yesterday and the chaotic vitality of today – are being constantly passed from one to another.' Describing the excitement created by the transition from Arabic to Latin characters, she caught the mood of Nazım's poetry in his constructivist phase: 'His verse is always bold, striking, the metaphors chosen from the world of machines, factories, railways and bridges. He believes the most beautiful language to be the industrial language – more exact and more to the point than the language of literature. He likes bright, naked colours, red in all its shades predominating, copper and brass, and sunlight. He likes swift images – "The news travelled in the air like fiery greyhounds". When he is angry, and even when he isn't, he abounds in oaths' (*Bookman*, Jan–Feb 1932, 508-15).

Another of Nazım's admirers was Peyami Safa, a young author with mystical tendencies who was secretary of the Fine Arts Society. In 1928, while Nazım was still under arrest, Safa had published his poem 'Yanardağ' (Volcano) in the literary supplement of *Cumhuriyet*. In this poem, originally written in 1925, the eruption of a volcano represents the revolutionary potential of the people, with the molten lava acting as an image of political energy (A 1, 35). This action cost Safa his job on the cautiously liberal newspaper. Nazım was keen to meet the man who had the courage to publish such a poem, and the two soon became friends. Peyami then invited Nazım to give a public reading at the Fine Arts Society, introducing the relatively unknown twenty-seven-year-old as a 'great poet'. Following a tradition which dated back to the Ottoman period, the Society held its meetings at Alay Köşkü, a handsome building near Topkapı Palace where even the Sultans had attended performances. Nazım had such a gift for recitation that he stole the show from established authors like Ahmet Haşim and Hamdullah Suphi.

These successes provoked hostile reactions from representatives of the old school. The poet Yaşar Nabi opened the attack, condemning *835 Satır* as ideologically slanted. The novelist Yakup Kadri Karaosmanoğlu, writing in *Milliyet* on 14 May 1929, repudiated the whole concept of socialist poetry: 'Socialist poets are like the rest of humanity, loud, vulgar, irrational and thoughtless.' Yakup Kadri's most outspoken attack followed in the *Milliyet* of 30 May, where he condemned all the writers of the younger generation, calling them spineless and uneducated. 'They have emerged', he wrote, 'out of the chaos of the war years, in which we adults did not manage to provide them with the opportunity to read, to learn, even to eat. [...] This generation was brought up eating bran, not bread.' This final phrase caused a furore, since bran is normally fed to animals. Kadri was forced to modify his position, explaining in *Milliyet* on 16 June that he was not referring to the patriotic Turkish students of today, but 'to those youngish writers who are 25-35 years old and somehow claim to represent the intellectual and literary élite. Some of them believe in defeating the giants, some claim that they carry the blood of thousands of people in their fingernails, some are convinced that they can turn idols to dust at a single blow' (Sülker 2, 38-40, 74-5, 90 & 111). Kadri was so compromised by this affair that on 28 June he resigned from the Fine Arts Society with a group of his supporters. Meanwhile Nazım launched a sustained campaign against the literary establishment.

Demolishing the idols

Nazım now formed a new alliance with Zekeriya and Sabiha Sertel, who had been leading figures in the anti-imperialist agitation ten years earlier. Between 1920 and 1923 they had studied at Columbia University in New York before returning to Istanbul to make their careers in journalism. In their magazine *Resimli Ay* (Illustrated Monthly), founded in 1924, they introduced a modern American lay-out with eye-catching illustrations. Initially the magazine pursued a liberal line, dealing critically with social problems without challenging middle-class interests. Nazım's recruitment to the staff in April 1929 resulted in a decisive radicalisation. Zekeriya Sertel has left a vivid account of their first meeting: 'Va-Nu arrived with an extremely lovable man, tall with blue eyes and curly blond hair, who looked reserved and restless. [...]

I asked him to read one of his poems to break the silence. He closed his eyes as if he were in a different world. He recited with a loud voice emphasising each rhythmical unit separately. [...] My god, what a richness of harmony and symbolism, what originality!' (Sertel 1991, 166). Nazım was initially employed as a proof reader, a task he took very seriously, but he also became involved as a designer, helping to illustrate the stories and strengthen the visual impact.

The magazine soon became a forum for younger poets and intellectuals. Nazım's arrival, as Sabiha Sertel recalls, had a dramatic effect: 'Once Nazım started writing for *Resimli Ay*, many poets who followed his technique gathered around him. [...] Only stories by left-wing writers like Sadri Ertem, Suat Derviş and Sabahattin Ali were to be published. This new group of writers was concerned with social questions, writing about the problems of the working class, peasants and people oppressed by the ruling class. Nazım was not only laying the foundation for a new kind of literature, but also trying to win people over to the cause of socialism' (Sertel S, 130). Taking Sabiha's lead, the journal also supported the cause of women's emancipation, giving prominence to a critique of repressive religious and social institutions by Suat Derviş (*Resimli Ay*, August 1929). Nazım also proved an asset in other ways: 'Most writers in our group were bohemians in the Parisian tradition, while Nazım did not smoke or drink, but worked regularly and disliked the bohemian lifestyle. He would arrive early in the morning and work non-stop. [...] He loved being in the print room, binding the pages with the workers' (Sertel 1991, 167).

Nazım worked for *Resimli Ay* from April 1929 till October 1930, during the short-lived golden age of the Turkish avant-garde, and can take the credit both for typographical innovations and for the striking use of photography and photomontage, reminiscent of Russian Constructivism. In July 1929 the journal featured one of his most provocative political poems, written in support of a taxi drivers' strike in Istanbul, 'Sesini Kaybeden Şehir' (The City Which Lost its Voice). Knowing the dangers that Nazım was facing, Va-Nu tried to persuade him to avoid direct political engagement: 'One can survive as a rebellious dissident writer, but you are different, you will be considered the leader of revolution. [...] You must avoid challenging the system.' He warned Nazım that there were informers in his own camp: 'But when I suggested that he should adapt his politics to what was possible, his so-called comrades in the organisation told him that I was trying to corrupt his idealism by offering him an easy life' (Va-Nu, 358-61). Va-Nu also recalled the fate of Kerem, a folk hero burnt to death by the flames of his own passion. This stimulated Nazım to write one of his most powerful poems, 'Like Kerem', a call to political commitment published in *Resimli Ay* in June 1930. In the romantic legend Kerem, unbuttoning the dress of his beloved Şirin on their wedding night, fails to undo all the buttons within the allotted time and is consumed by fire. In Nazım's poem this becomes an image of political passion:

If I don't burn	*Ben yanmasam*
If you don't burn	*Sen yanmasan*
If we don't burn	*Biz yanmasak,*
how will	*nasıl*
the darkness	*çıkar*
change	*karan-*
into	*-lıklar*
light?	*aydınlığa?*

('Kerem Gibi', A 1, 188)

The resonance of this poem is difficult to convey in translation, since Turkish is an inflected language whose extended verbal forms acquire a cumulative power, with vocalic modulations for which there is no equivalent in English. Turkish is also governed by patterns of vowel harmony which endow spoken verse with elements of incantation (a significant number of Nazım's poems have been popularised by musical settings). The power of the poem derives from the tension between sonorous repetitions and staccato line-breaks, accentuated by experimental typography. Even in translation the suggestive power of this image of burning is clear, conveying a passionate commitment which may involve anguished suffering – as the price to be paid for fundamental change.

The campaign against the old guard was intensified in the pages of *Hareket* (Movement), a twice-weekly magazine founded by Peyami Safa. The first issue appeared on 11 May 1929 and featured the poem 'Çıplak Ayak' (Barefoot), which Nazım wrote in 1922 during the long march through Anatolia. The poem describes the conditions endured by Turkish peasants, interpreting their poverty in Marxist terms and suggesting that their salvation lies in mechanisa-

tion. *Hareket* and *Resimli Ay* formed an alliance against the conservatives who, as Safa scathingly put it in *Hareket* on 22 May,
claimed the title of 'master' as if it were an honour bestowed by
the government in exchange for services to the state (Sülker 2,
80). A further attack appeared in *Hareket* on 1 June, when Safa
recalled that Kadri had spent the war years in a Swiss sanatorium.
What right had he to condemn those who had endured deprivation
in Turkey while he was enjoying the comforts of Switzerland?
This was followed on 4 June 1929 by Nazım's poem 'Yarıda
Kalan Bir Bahar Yazısı' (An Unfinished Writing in the Spring),
published in *Resimli Ay* over the by-line 'Man Without Signature'.
The poem ridicules the bourgeois hacks of Babıali who write
pretty verses to please their masters: 'It is spring, spring, spring,
and I, the poetry editor, have to read 2,000 badly written lines
every day' (A 1, 123).

The controversy intensified after Nazım circulated a questionnaire to a number of leading writers asking 'How do you compose
your work?'. Sabiha Sertel recalls his reaction to their replies.
After reading the answers received from well-known poets like
Abdülhak Hamit and Halit Ziya, Nazım threw down his pen in
disgust and said: 'Which of these are our national poets? Some
are only concerned about the other world, others portray the
degenerate personalities of their own cliques. Aren't there any
workers or peasants in this country? These men are not interested
in them. They do not want to see the realities. We have to
demolish these idols' (Sertel S, 125). With the approval of Zekeriya
Sertel, the slogan 'Demolishing the Idols' ('Putları Yıkıyoruz') was
then used as the general title for a series of polemical articles.
Nazım insisted that contemporary writers should face the challenge
of social change and place themselves at the service of people.
The principal aim of the polemic, as announced in *Resimli Ay*
in June 1929, was 'to strip off the halo from figures who have
been made into idols and worshipped undeservedly'. In the first
of these attacks, Abdülhak Hamit was mocked for his aspiration
to be 'a great international genius'. The article was embellished
with a photograph of this eminent man of letters sitting at his
desk, an icon of literary respectability defaced by a bold red cross.

The 'Demolishing the Idols' controversy divided the literary
world into two camps: the progressives of *Resimli Ay*, *Hareket*
and *Akşam* versus the traditionalists, who enjoyed the support of

conservative newspapers like *Milliyet* and *Ikdam* and of a patriotic association called 'the Turkish Hearths' (Halk Ocakları). The second instalment of 'Demolishing the Idols' appeared on 1 July. In this article Nazım disputed the credentials of the supposed 'national poet', Mehmet Emin. On 10 June, Emin's sixtieth birthday had been marked by an official celebration organised by the Ministry of Justice. The fact that a minister was willing to intervene, defending patriotic cultural traditions in a speech addressed to young Turkish nationalists, shows that the campaign to counteract Nazım's growing popularity enjoyed official support. Nazım's response was scathing: 'How could anyone be called the national poet if he never marked any turning-point in the language of the people, if he never voiced the great struggles of its people?' Emin is denounced as a conformist who never raised any objection to Ottoman despotism, and *Resimli Ay* printed a photograph of its distinguished victim, his head overprinted with the word 'IPTAL' (Cancelled).

In this same issue Nazım also published a poem attacking his most formidable opponent, Yakup Kadri, who had declared that the writers of *Resimli Ay* were unpatriotic communists blinded by dogma. Kadri's response was to denounce his critics as 'rabid, hungry dogs, attacking a man innocently walking down the street'. Using the form of an interview in *Ikdam* on 27 June, Kadri continues: 'Some of these writers are hardened criminals who have only just escaped being hanged or impaled. [...] Some kissed the blood-stained hands of the communist secret police. [...] During the Anatolian War two of them, who were scared of fighting the enemy, escaped to the Bolsheviks across the waters of the Black Sea with money stolen from the Ministry of Education' (*Ikdam*, 27 June 1929). The reference to Nazım and Va-Nu, and the implication that both were criminals and traitors, was unmistakable. The allegation of embezzlement was manifestly false, since one of their opponents, Hamdullah Suphi, who was Minister of Education at the time, had signed the document entitling Nazım and Va-Nu to their pay as teachers (Sülker 2, 108). However, it is true that in the autumn of 1921 they were technically supposed to be taking up teaching posts in Kars and not travelling to Moscow.

In the poem 'Answer No. 1', replying to Kadri in *Resimli Ay* of July 1929, Nazım sets out the opposing positions with exemplary clarity: 'It is I who wore the handcuffs / like a golden bracelet,

/ it is I who looked at the greasy rope, / scratching my thick hairy neck, / do you think you can scare / the pants off me?' He also ridicules Kadri's surname Karaosmanoğlu, which literally means 'Son of Black Osman': 'You with the head of a black beast, [...] you turned your head into the room of a whore, / stealing money out of the pockets of dead men's uniforms / buying yourself the mountain air of Switzerland' ('Cevap 1', A 2, 159). Here the implication was that Kadri used public funds to pay for his treatment at a Swiss sanatorium, while in Turkey people were dying for lack of medical care. This was too much for the conservatives, who orchestrated a chorus of counterattacks. Reviewing *835 Lines* in *Ikdam* on 6 July, the critic Yusuf Ziya, who had been one of Nazım's companions on the journey from Istanbul to Inebolu in January 1921, observed: 'This is not the work of an artist or even an art lover, it is the work of a vandal' (Sülker 2, 94). Hamdullah Suphi joined the attack in an even more extreme form. Having served both as an Ottoman official and as chairman of the patriotic 'Turkish Hearths', he had a political axe to grind. 'How are the idols to be demolished?' he asked in a long article in *Ikdam*. Without mincing his words he went on: 'We need to know which religious idols they are replacing the old ones with – [they are] the idols of the Bolshevik religion! [...] Behind the curtain of Turco-Russian friendship a tragic game is being staged. Wherever there is Soviet foreign trade, there is money, propaganda and the secret service. The effects of this ominous development can be seen in all corners of Turkey. [...] Who do we have facing us? Lackeys at the door of the Bolsheviks!' ('Putlar Nasıl Kırılır?' *Ikdam*, 7 July 1929).

The publication of his article marked the point at which the war of words degenerated into a threat of physical assault. On the day that this polemic was published, about thirty young nationalists appeared outside the offices of *Resimli Ay*. The police did nothing to prevent the demonstration, having apparently been instructed not to intervene. Nazım, who was at the office with the editors Zekeriya and Sabiha Sertel, had to listen to agitated young men chanting 'You are killing our heroes, destroying our heritage'. Sertel succeeded in gaining a hearing by saying: 'As you are students, you should listen to both sides of the argument and make up your own minds.' Once they had calmed down, Nazım was able to explain to them that every social change requires changes in the character of literature, which should not be confused with communist propaganda (Sertel 1991, 191). The following day a protest meeting was organized at the Turkish Hearth with no less than twenty speakers, including Hamdullah Suphi, in an attempt to mobilise the authorities. Communist propaganda should not be allowed to infiltrate the country 'under the mask of demolishing the idols' (*Ikdam*, 9 July 1929).

Responding to this attack in August 1929, *Resimli Ay* published a cartoon showing Hamdullah Suphi climbing into the boxing ring to face the indomitable Nazım, while an exhausted Yakub Kadri cowers in his corner and Nazım's second, Payami Safa, gives him an encouraging pat on the back (Fig. 9). After reporting the attack on their editorial office, Zekeriya Sertel answered the militant students in an editorial which insisted on the distinction between open-minded literary debate and dogmatic political argument: 'It is not a question of communism, it is choice between old and new.' Articles designed to discredit their two principal opponents, Hamdullah Suphi and Yakup Kadri, were accompanied by photos of the two traditionalists, printed upside down and split down the middle. This time the commentary was written by Sadri Etem, while Nazım added an article of his own explaining 'Why are we demolishing the idols' ('Putlar Niçin Kırıyoruz?').

The controversies of the summer of 1929 caused by *835 lines* and 'Demolishing the Idols' intensified after the publication of the narrative poem *Jokond ile Si-Ya-U* (Gioconda and Si-Ya-U) at the end of the year. Conservative critics were shocked by Nazım's temerity in appropriating one of the most hallowed icons of bourgeois culture to the communist cause, especially as Leonardo da Vinci's benignly smiling Gioconda (the Mona Lisa) is transformed into a fervent revolutionary. Nazım had started work on this poem while still in Moscow, inspired by his friendship with Emi Siao, the Chinese revolutionary who had studied first in Paris and later at the Communist University. After Siao returned to China in 1924 to join the armed struggle, it was reported that he had been killed in the crackdown against communists in Shanghai (it was more than twenty years later that Nazım discovered his friend had actually survived). The news of his supposed death led Nazım to commemorate his friend in a thirty-page narrative poem, which characteristically combines the personal with the political, beginning with the figure of Siao – Si-Ya-U – falling in love with

9. Nazım as boxing champion: cartoon from *Resimli Ay*, August 1929.

Leonardo's painting in the Louvre and culminating in his death in Shanghai.

Jokond ile Si-Ya-U subverts traditional gender roles by emphasizing the involvement of women in the revolutionary struggle. The narrative, beginning '15 March 1924: Paris, Louvre Museum', develops into a miniature drama of many voices, with the poet himself playfully intervening in the action. Nazım sets up a counterpoint between poetry and politics, combining surrealist fantasy with revolutionary fervour. The poem also becomes self-reflexive, questioning the role of art in a period of social transformation as well as the implications of political commitment. Gioconda breaks free from the passivity assigned her by the culture of the museum and becomes an active subject whose ideas challenge both bourgeois aestheticism and the patriarchal cult of femininity. Overcome by boredom on the wall of the Louvre, she falls in love with the Chinese student Si-Ya-U and is grief-stricken when he is deported for taking part in a political demonstration. Her enigmatic smile modulates into an expression of passionate commitment, powerfully conveyed by the cover design of the book (Fig. 10a). Stepping boldly out of her frame, the 'lion-hearted woman' follows Si-Ya-U by plane and ship to China, where the struggle against Chiang Kai-shek's forces has begun. But shortly after her arrival in Shanghai,

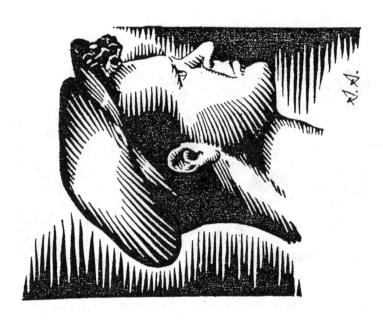

she witnesses the execution of her lover. Gioconda herself is arrested, put on trial by a French military court and condemned to death by burning. The poem ends with the paradox that she finally has a genuine smile on her face, happy to be dying in the struggle for liberation.

The structure of *Jokond ile Si-Ya-U* bears traces of Nazım's indebtedness to Meyerhold, especially through the orchestration of a medley of voices and the disconcerting use of transitions. The setting is vividly scenic, and the narrative is enlivened by witty and poignant dialogue. Although the poem was denounced by conservative critics, more discerning reviewers praised the flexibility of its approach to the theme of revolution. Writing in *Resimli Ay* in December 1929, Peyami Safa shrewdly observed: 'The Gioconda and Si-Ya-U are symbols. Their love is the love of the poet, their ideals are the poet's ideals. [...] What I like most is when Nazım moves away from his claims, when he is sceptical about every idea, even about his own ideology. [...] I like his love of unattainable ideals. I love him because underneath the materialist, pessimist, vulgar humorist there is a passionate, lyrical, melancholic, painful and pessimistic love for the unknown and impossible, always rebelling, always asking for more'. Nazım was not entirely happy with this review, sensing that Safa was unwilling to abandon his mystical philosophy.

Nazım's position was strengthened by an extraordinary burst of creativity. During the spring of 1930, while the debate was still raging about Nazım's 'Mona Lisa', Ahmet Halit published two further collections of his poetry, *Varan 3* and *1 + 1 = 1*, followed in 1931 by in *Sesini Kaybeden Şehir* ('The City Which Lost its Voice'), with a frontispiece by Sedat Simavi showing the poet wearing a cloth cap (Fig. 10b). Nazım had a gift for attracting the support of younger collaborators, and the text of 'The City' was enhanced by illustrations by Abidin Dino. Abidin, from a wealthy Istanbul family, was brought up in France and Switzerland before studying at Robert College in Istanbul. In 1930, at the age of seventeen, he joined a left-wing group for which he began to produce political cartoons, and his bold designs caught Nazım's eye. In 1934 Abidin's artistic talents won him a scholarship to the Soviet Union, and he was later to become the best known of Nazım's illustrators and a lifelong friend. A further collaborator was a young communist known as Nail V., co-author of *1 + 1*

= *1*. The initial 'V.' derived from a misreading of the first letter of Nail's surname, Çakırhan, by a publisher accustomed to Arabic script (Çakırhan, Interview 1995). This is the only occasion when Nazım wrote a book with another poet, a mark of the strong bond between them. Nail, who had come to Istanbul from Konya to study medicine, had made a name for himself at the age of eighteen by writing a subversive poem entitled 'Alev Yağmuru' (The Rain of Fire). Nazım took such a strong liking to the young man that he persuaded him to give up medicine and join the communist party, arranging for him him to stay at his father's house for more than a year.

Nazım's solidarity with the working class was expressed not only in his writings but also through a casual style of dress. He was fond of wearing a cloth-cap, his jacket casually slung over his shoulder, his shirt unbuttoned, his trousers ostentatiously crumpled. A photo printed in *Resimli Ay* in May 1929, showing Nazım in an open-necked shirt, his Russian wife Lena Yurcenko leaning affectionately on his shoulder, served to accentuate the campaign against the stuffed shirts of the literary establishment. This photo may be contrasted with the picture of another celebrated poet, Tevfik Fikret, published in *Resimli Ay* in September 1930, showing him amid the clutter of an antiquated book-lined interior. Writing under the pseudonym Süleyman, Nazım presented Fikret as a petit-bourgeois intellectual with outdated conceptions of the writer's mission. In a further diatribe, 'Cevap No. 2' ('Answer No. 2'), also published in the September number of *Resimli Ay*, Nazım ridicules the symbolist poet Ahmet Haşim. The discrepancy between Haşim's sentimental poetry and his materialistic public position is condensed into the image of 'two dimwits'. Taking up one of Ahmet Haşim's favourite motifs, the image of reflections on water, Nazım contrasts the poet who 'counts the stars in the water at night' with the 'member of the French imperialists' management committee' (A 2, 162). Haşim was on the board of a French-owned company which operated the railway between Adana and Mersin (Sertel 1991, 187).

In this period Nazım's reputation was spreading far beyond the confines of the literary élite, not least because a gramophone recording had been made by the leading American company Columbia of him reading two of his own poems. In the summer of 1930 *Resimli Ay* carried an eye-catching article announcing

that 'for the first time in Turkey we can listen to POEMS on
the gramophone': headed by a photomontage of Nazım's face
with a typewriter and a gramophone, it praised him as the poet
of dialectical materialism. However, for most listeners it was not
the politics but the musicality of the recording that made the
greatest impact, especially since one of the poems was 'Weeping
Willow' ('Salkımsöğüt'), with its haunting use of vowel harmony
and its play on the assonance between '*atlılar*' (horsemen) and
'*kanatlı*' (with wings):

> Life has gone past like horsemen on the wings of the wind!
> *Rüzgar kanatlı atlılar gibi geçti hayat!*
> (A 1, 15).

This recording won Nazım many new admirers, even bringing
his voice to the attention of Mustafa Kemal. During the 1930s
the Turkish President increasingly centred his social life in Istanbul
rather than Ankara, taking up residence in Dolmabahce Palace.
There are many accounts of his late-night drinking parties with
political cronies and passionate debates with members of the diplomatic
corps. Some evenings were devoted to poetry, and in the small
hours he would call in cabaret artistes to entertain his guests, one
of the most celebrated being the singer Deniz Kızı Eftalya ('Eftalya
the Mermaid'). He also enjoyed listening to the gramophone:

One evening when Mustafa Kemal was in Istanbul dining at Dolmabahce
Palace, Nazım's name was mentioned. People present talked about Nazım
with great admiration. They told him that Nazım was the greatest Turkish
poet of the day. He became curious and wanted to hear one of his poems.
Records of Nazım's poetry were brought in, and Mustafa Kemal listened
attentively and with amazement. Then he said: 'This poet is different from
the rest of you.' He requested that Nazım should be brought in, so that he
could hear him speaking in his own voice. However, it was past midnight.
They phoned Kadıköy police station and instructed them to fetch Nazım.
Late at night a policeman knocked at Nazım's door. Nazım woke, got up
and opened the door. He was surprised to see the policeman and for a
moment went into a cold sweat. The policeman courteously informed him
that Mustafa Kemal was waiting for him at Dolmabahce Palace. Then
Nazım pulled himself together. 'My son', he said, 'give my greetings to
Kemal Pasha and tell him that I am not Eftalya the Mermaid.'

When this was reported at Dolmabahce Palace, Kemal (according
to this version of the story) reacted with the words: 'Well done,
my boy... That is how a poet should be!' (Sertel 1977, 166).

Looking back on this episode, Nazım reportedly observed: 'I did not accept the invitation I received from Mustafa Kemal. But I cannot refuse a poet.' The reference is to an invitation he received during this same period from Abdülhak Hamit, the poet of the older generation who was criticized in *Resimli Ay*. A year or so after that attack, Hamit and his wife invited Nazım to tea so that they could resolve their differences in a civilised manner. Hamit showed some sympathy for the programme of 'demolishing the idols', explaining that his generation had taken a similar line thirty years earlier. He and Namık Kemal had initiated new trends in Ottoman literature by introducing modern Turkish words and Western metrical systems in place of the traditional modes of Divan poetry. 'We demolished them, now it is your task to demolish us,' he concluded (Sertel S, 131). Nazım was delighted to meet a poet who remained active even in his eighties, and writing in *Akşam* under the pseudonym Orhan Selim, paid tribute to this 'Young Man of 83'. When reminded of his earlier attacks, he explained that he had criticized the 'personality cult' surrounding the older poets, not their art (A 21, 64 & 66).

Resimli Ay was closed in January 1931, after political pressures led to a dispute with the proprietors, who were unhappy about the radical line which the majority of the contributors were taking. One article criticising authoritarian leadership, translated by Sabiha Sertel, was construed as a disguised attack on Atatürk and resulted in costly legal proceedings. There followed a dispute over copyright to the title *Resimli Ay*, which brought about a complete break between Zekeriya Sertel and the magazine's owners. Sertel then founded a new daily newspaper, *Son Posta*, which continued to campaign for radical causes, including an exposure of profiteering in the wholesale sugar market by government officials, which resulted in his being arrested and sentenced to three years' imprisonment. Although Sertel was released after serving only eighteen months, this episode reflects the growing intolerance of the Turkish authorities towards crusading journalism. Meanwhile Nazım started writing a humorous column in the daily paper *Yeni Gün* under the pseudonym 'Ben', the Turkish word for 'me'. And he supplemented his income by translating short stories for publication in the same paper, including a whole series by Mihael Zoshchenko (A 18 and A 19).

Nazım's determination to confront his bourgeois opponents

continued in book form. In 'Answer No. 3', published in 1931 in *Sesini Kaybeden Şehir*, he again denounce that 'absurd man', Hamdullah Suphi, with his wealth of 'houses, hotels, public baths, apartments and villas' (A 1, 236). 'Answer No. 4' appeared the following year in a further volume of poems entitled *Gece Gelen Telegraf* ('Telegram Received at Night'). The focus of this fourth 'Answer' points beyond the literary feuding of 1929-31 to a far more threatening development: the tendency of bourgeois intellectuals to succumb to the lure of fascism (A 2, 112). The title of this collection alludes to a telegram bringing news of the death of a political activist, apparently Ismail Bilen (C 2, 299). The news turned out to be premature, for although Bilen was repeatedly arrested, he survived into ripe old age. But Nazım was stimulated to write several poems about his comrade's disappearance, including the subtly understated 'A Portable Bed', which uses the imagery of the abandoned bed in an empty room to evoke the transient existence of the revolutionary ('Portatif Karyola', A 2, 99).

Nazım's admiration for activists like Bilen possibly made him unduly harsh on former comrades who made their peace with the establishment. The break with Va-Nu, whom he had known since their schooldays, was particularly painful. Since it was difficult for a writer with communist connections to obtain a regular job, Va-Nu had distanced himself from the party and accepted a position with *Akşam*, a daily newspaper which supported the government. Nazım was himself writing for the bourgeois press under various pseudonyms, so he was not really in a position to throw stones. But he evidently felt that Va-Nu was betraying the cause in accepting a permanent appointment with a handsome salary of 300 Lira (Va-Nu, 361). There may be a hint of envy in Nazım's reaction, since his own earnings were so meagre. The motif of the 'three hundred bucks' features in a poem of 1932 entitled simply 'You', which laments the defection of three unidentified comrades. Without mentioning Va-Nu by name, Nazım denounces his friend for betraying 'our most beautiful days'. Unlike Caesar and Brutus, 'you and I from henceforth / cannot even be enemies' ('Sen', A 2, 136-7). It was to be fifteen years before their friendship recovered from this rupture.

During this time Nazım was also preoccupied with tensions within the Communist Party. Aspects of the internal struggle are reflected in *Benerci Kendini Niçin Öldürdü?* ('Why Did Banerjee

Kill Himself?', 1932). This eighty-page narrative poem ostensibly deals with the struggle against British imperialism in India. Set in Calcutta, it explores the dilemmas faced by revolutionaries in extreme conditions. Nazım had been planning this work since 1926, and it was partly inspired by two Indians whom he had met in Moscow. The early sections foreground the figure of Somedeva, a revolutionary writer imprisoned and tortured by the British police after organizing a strike. He escapes from prison and goes into hiding. Although he is suffering from tuberculosis, he resolves to devote all his remaining energies to the revolution, selflessly sending money and food to his comrades in prison so that they can survive and continue the struggle. Meanwhile his friend Banerjee, who has fallen in love with an Englishwoman, is suspected of being an informer after several comrades are arrested. When Banerjee himself is allowed to go free by the police, he is denounced as a traitor by Somedeva and the other party members, but it turns out that it was his girlfriend who was the informer. Another problematic figure is a comrade named Roy Dranat, an individualist who leaves the party and becomes a supporter of the national bourgeoisie. Banerjee, in his isolation and despair, considers suicide but resists the temptation, remembering Lenin's precept that 'you must devote your whole life to the revolution' (A 2, 44). After rejoining the movement, he too is imprisoned by the British for political activities. When he is released fifteen years later his admirers hail him as their leader, but he has become ill and incapable of providing the dynamic leadership which the party requires, so he decides to make room for the new generation by ending his own life. The question is whether there are any circumstances which can justify a revolutionary committing suicide.

Formally this poem is characteristic of Nazım's work in this period – a flexible style of free-verse, enlivened by humorous episodes, ironic interventions and interludes of prose commentary and dramatic dialogue. Elements of self-parody subvert the conventions of orientalism, familiar to the poet from his childhood reading of *Around the World in Eighty Days*. Unlike Phileas Fogg, Nazım's hero does not rescue his beloved from a Buddhist temple – he meets her on a bus. Traditional poetic motifs are subverted by an ironic modernism: the moon rising over Calcutta provides a good light for burglars. Among the medley of voices one scene stands out, in which three policemen are overheard comparing notes about techniques of torture: pouring molten lead into the prisoner's ears is surely more effective than simply extracting his fingernails! (A 2, 36). Although the setting is ostensibly Calcutta, the implicit critique of Turkish police methods is effective. Even more striking is a surrealistic use of montage, which reflects Nazım's involvement with the cinema. 'As a baby I was wrapped up in a cinema ticket,' Somedeva observes in a phrase which encapsulates the formative influence of the movies on this whole generation. The book which he is writing includes an episode set in a cinema, a device which enables Nazım to explore the global effects of capitalism through a filmic fantasy entitled 'Famous Dramatic Exploits of the 20th Century'. After clips showing factory chimneys producing so much pollution that even the angels have to be provided with plastic raincoats (made in the USA), a Chicago millionaire is seen kissing his girlfriend in Tokyo by long-distance telephone, while a sausage-making machine goes into reverse and churns out cows.

The interest of this work lies not only in its imaginative qualities, but also in its coded references to identifiable members of the Turkish left. Roy Dranat, the renegade, can be seen as a thinly disguised portrait of Şevket Süreyya, who at one point is specifically censured in a footnote by name for abandoning the struggle against imperialism and sympathizing with 'neo-Hitlerist social fascism' (A 2, 75). The allusion to an informer named 'Nedim Vedat Bey' is even more obviously directed at Vedat Nedim, the secretary of the Turkish Communist Party who in 1927 had shopped his comrades to the police. In the figure of Somedeva, some commentators have seen allusions to Hasan Ali Ediz, the leader whose inflexibility had exacerbated the split in the Turkish Communist Party in 1929, leading ultimately to Nazım's expulsion (Karaca 1992, 80-5). But there are traces of Nazım's own position in the characterization of both Somedeva and Banerjee. Somedeva is the writer concerned to convey a global critique of capitalism, Banerjee the individualist rejected by his own party.

It is likely that the 'death of a revolutionary' theme also alludes to the suicide of Mayakovsky in April 1930. Since the two poets had been close during the 1920s, Nazım must have found the news of his death particularly distressing. In July 1930 he published an article in *Resimli Ay* about the possible motives for Mayakovsky's action, criticising his suicide as an individualistic solution to personal problems. Committed communists (he argues) have an overriding duty to the revolution, and they should be able to overcome personal unhappiness. The article contrasts the Futurist poet, isolated from the Russian people, with the later revolutionary writer who overcame his individualism to become the poet of the working class. Drawing on an analysis by Demyan Bedny, a member of the Proletarian Writers Group RAPP, Nazım offers the following summary: 'Personal unhappiness, at a time of serious illness intensified by loneliness, led to a revival of the old individualistic attitudes. It was the old Mayakovsky who killed the new Mayakovsky.'

Nazım was probably unaware of the Russian poet's difficulties with the Soviet authorities. He makes no reference to the conflicts between the experimental poets of LEF and the party-liners of RAPP, which exacerbated Mayakovsky's sense of isolation. Nor is there any allusion to the tormented love affairs which intensified his despair, although the article is accompanied by a photograph with the caption 'Mayakovsky with his wife' (actually, his mistress Lili Brik). Nevertheless, Nazım does succeed in identifying the tension between social responsibility and artistic individualism which runs through the Russian poet's career. Mayakovsky, as his friend the aesthetician Viktor Shklovsky saw it, 'was a double personality, an unstable mixture of a tough exterior and a soft interior, and the circumstances of his life had defeated him' (Charters, 362). Although Nazım himself was familiar with this tension, he was more successful in reconciling art and politics. Moreover, where Mayakovsky was driven to distraction by passionate love affairs, Nazım was sustained by relationships which enhanced his creativity.

The red-haired woman and the scent of the sun

The years 1929-33 mark the longest period of freedom the poet ever experienced in Turkey. His social life was active: on Mondays he and his friends used to meet for poetry readings at the house of Suat Derviş, an old flame from the autumn of 1920 when they both wrote poems for *Alemdar*. By this date Suat had developed into one of the most successful women novelists of her generation. Sometimes Nazım would meet his friends at the Sertels' house in the fashionable suburb of Moda, where he would read his poems, listen to music and join in the singing (Sertel 1991, 210).

He rarely touched alcohol, but his eloquence was intoxicating, especially when he declaimed verses like 'The Ballad of Those Who Drink the Sun'. The atmosphere of those convivial evenings is recaptured in a variant on this theme written in 1930, 'The Song That Was Sung While Dining with the Sun' ('Güneşin Sofrasında Söylenen Türkü'): 'Before us are copper mugs filled with sun. [...] Let us drink a toast, my friends. [...] Let us all go, barefoot, running, following in the footsteps of the giants' (A 2, 106).

At first, in December 1928, Nazım had settled in his father's house in Kadıköy, a pleasant district on the Anatolian shore. His father Hikmet Bey had remarried in 1924 and now lived with his second wife, Cavide Hanım, and their twin children, Fatma and Metin. Nazım's sister Samiye also formed part of the household. Nazım was an intensely sociable person, and as hopes of Lena being permitted to travel to Turkey faded, he formed a new relationship with a friend of his sister Samiye. This was Piraye, a married woman with striking red hair who had separated from her husband and lived with her mother in Kadıköy. From 1929 onwards Piraye was a frequent guest at Hikmet Bey's house. She is described as rather reserved and formal with a strong personality and a progressive outlook. Born on 23 December 1906, she came from a wealthy family called Altunizade, who were so well known that a district of Istanbul is named after their villa. Piraye did not have a university education, but since her father was editor of the newspaper *Tercuman-i Ahval*, she had grown up in a cultivated environment. Nazım soon came to respect her judgement and would always ask her opinion about his poetry or other books which they read together. Through the love poems which Nazım later sent her from prison, Piraye has become one of the icons of Turkish literature. But her identity as a private person remains an enigma. Although she lived to a great age (she died in 1995), she steadfastly declined to be interviewed or to publish her memoirs. Since few of her letters are available, it is difficult to form an impression of her personality, as distinct from her mirror image in Nazım's writings.

Piraye's first marriage from which there were two children, Suzan and Memet Fuat, was evidently unhappy, and her husband Vedat Örfi Bengü, an actor, pianist, novelist and film director, deserted the family and moved to Paris just before their second child was born in 1926 (AM 1, 15). Vedat's father, Mehmet Ali

Pasha, remained attached to his daughter-in-law and her children, especially Suzan. He looked after the family for a time at his mansion in Erenköy, while they waited for Vedat's return, and continued to support them intermittently up till his death in 1950 (Memet Fuat, Interview, March 1996). By 1930 it had become clear that Vedat would never return (their divorce was finalized on 13 September 1932), and Piraye decided to leave her father-in-law's house and move in with her mother at Kadıköy – thus Piraye and Nazım became neighbours (AM 1, 15). Their relationship took a new turn after Hikmet Bey's unexpected death on 17 March 1932, when Nazım found himself obliged to take over responsibility for the family under difficult circumstances. These were the years following the American stock market crash, and the resulting impact on the Turkish economy was only partially alleviated by étatist policies of state intervention (Lewis, 469). To cope with the economic hardships, Nazım decided to pool resources with other members of his family, inviting his sister and his brother-in law to share a house with him (Aydemir 1986a, 197). Piraye's family household now included her son Memet Fuat, her mother Nurhayat, her sister Fahamet with her husband Vedat Başar, and another sister, Selma, and plucking up his courage Nazım suggested that they too should join his extended family. The resulting commune was based on practical convenience rather than ideological solidarity. Neither Nurhayat, a woman of aristocratic temperament, nor Vedat Başar, who was a Freemason, had any left-wing sympathies.

They found the ideal place, a large ramshackle house called Mithat Pasha Villa, also on the Anatolian side of the Bosphorus opposite Mehmet Ali Pasha's mansion in Erenköy (AM 1, 15). The villa was set amid fertile fields and pine woods with scope for growing vegetables and rearing animals. For two years they lived there as an extended family, while Piraye's daughter Suzan stayed with her grandparents nearby, and shared the costs of running a seven-bedroomed house, with chickens running wild in the rambling garden. Nurhayat organized the cooking with the help of a housekeeper. Although their home was rather remote from the centre of Istanbul, they occasionally entertained writers and poets, who would join them for meals and discussions under the pine trees in the warm evenings after Nazım arrived home from work. They included Nazım's journalist friend Naci Sadullah and the celebrated woman singer Safiye Ayla. This idyllic interlude forms a striking contrast to the ordeals that followed, and Piraye was happy to live in a familiar environment with friendly neighbours and relatives living nearby (Memet Fuat, Interview, November 1988). But on 18 March 1933 the Anatolian idyll was rudely disrupted when Nazım was again arrested.

This time he faced charges not only for political activities but also for defamation. The circumstances of the case were extremely poignant. The poet had been deeply affected by his father's death, which had resulted from an accidental injury followed by botched medical treatment. One day in March 1932 Hikmet Bey was bitten by a dog and given an anti-rabies injection. However, a few days earlier he had suffered another injury and been treated with a tetanus vaccine. The two vaccines proved incompatible, and Hikmet Bey developed a high temperature, fell into a delirium and died (Sertel 1991, 197). The cinema where Nazım's father had been employed was owned by Süreyya Pasha, a prominent member of Istanbul society who had served as a commander during Abdulhamid's reign. While Hikmet Bey was on his deathbed, Süreyya Pasha (Ilmen) arrived at his home to question him about some discrepancy in the accounts. Nazım and the family were extremely distressed by this insensitivity, which seemed to exemplify the rapacious capitalism of the ruling class. This visit occurred just three days before his father died.

The poet felt so incensed that he sat down and wrote a satirical poem about the greed of the owning class, entitled 'Hiciv Vadisinde bir Tecrübei Kalemiye' (An Experiment with Satire). It appeared at the end of 1932 in the collection *Gece Gelen Telegraf.* The poet presents his own father as a humble man, while Süreyya Pasha's father is a war profiteer who has enriched himself while the soldiers suffered and died in the deserts of Yemen during the First World War:

> The father of this honourable man
> constructed hotels and public baths
>   by stealing bread and water
> from the men who starved in the Yemen desert,
>   by taking 100% commission
> from the blood flowing on the sand...
> ...
> Calling my father to account for five Lira before he died,

you counted his heartbeats.
...
My father's eyes were not able
        to see the pitch black books any more...
But you were right:
it was the final Day of Reckoning.
With your own hands you condescendingly put
the spectacles on the nose of a dead man,
demanding an explanation for the missing five Lira.

(A 2, 128)

Generalised denunciations of the bourgeoisie were the stock-in-trade of a whole generation of left-wing intellectuals. Nazım's satire is exceptional for its chilling precision, targeting a member of the ruling élite. This proved to be too much for the political establishment, and four months after its publication the book was banned and Nazım was arrested.

While awaiting trial, Nazım was transferred to Bursa prison, 250 kilometres from Istanbul. The enforced separation, far from alienating the lovers, served to strengthen their attachment, and it was during this period that Nazım and Piraye decided to get married. His letters from prison are filled with longing for his 'red-haired woman', which became a recurrent motif in his poetry. In a letter to her dated 5 July 1933, he explains that he has told the prison governor they are engaged (AM 1, 22). Nazım was finally freed in August 1934 after an amnesty, and he and Piraye resumed their life together at the house in Erenköy. On 31 January 1935, five months after his release, they were quietly married at the local registry office in Kadıköy with only two of his relatives present as witnesses (AM 1, 60). A photograph taken shortly afterwards shows the young couple together in the garden at Erenköy (Fig. 11). It was at the time of their marriage that they were required to choose a surname, under legislation introduced the previous year as part of Atatürk's modernization programme (Hikmet, the forename borrowed from Nazım's father, was only a *nom de plume*). Nazım had been reluctant to adopt a surname, not least because so many of his contemporaries were choosing sonorous and pretentious names like 'Başaran' ('Successful') or 'Kurtaran' ('Saviour'). 'Let's call ourselves "Ran"', Piraye suggested irreverently. From that date onwards the whimsical-sounding suffix

11. Nazım with his wife Piraye in the garden at Erenköy.

'Ran' became their registered family name (Memet Fuat, Interview, November 1988).

The tranquillity of married life was soon disrupted, partly by political factors, but also partly by personal ones. In November 1934 Nazım settled down to his career as a journalist, writing a regular column for *Akşam* and later for the more progressive *Tan* to supplement his meagre income. Since these chatty pieces were quite distinct from his serious political writings, they were published under a pseudonym – 'Orhan Selim'. Well over 600 short articles appeared under this name in the following two years, dealing in a popular but perceptive style with a wide range of ephemeral topics. Not surprisingly, more dogmatic left-wing comrades condemned such activities as a sell-out to the capitalist press. There was a grain of truth in Hikmet Kıvılcımlı's allegation that without his Marxism Nazım was merely an 'ordinary bourgeois poet in Babıali Street' (Korcan 1989, 88). But it would be more accurate to say that Nazım's popular journalism was a 'borrowed shirt' to conceal his Marxism, since his journalism, for all its lightness of tone, has a sharp social-critical edge. His dilemma is reflected in a self-critical poem satirising the wicked 'Orhan Selim', the 'man / on whose back I ride, heavy as lead, / living from the sweat of his brow' (A 2, 156). He was evidently uneasy to be writing under a pseudonym for his living. A further series of sixty articles, written after he was again arrested in December 1936, appeared in *Tan* during 1937, although to conceal his identity he adopted a new pseudonym, 'Anonymous Author' ('Adsız Yazıcı'). These journalistic writings form a substantial part of his *oeuvre*, taking up almost four volumes in his collected works.

It was one of the articles by 'Orhan Selim' in *Akşam* which led Nazım to form a brief liaison with another young woman with literary ambitions, Cahit Uçuk. Born in Istanbul in 1911, Cahit had spent her youth in Anatolia where her father, a government official, had moved at the end of the First World War in order to escape the occupation. Growing up amid the beauty of southern Turkey, she developed a sensitivity to the landscape which was to find expression in the stories she wrote for children, emphasizing the harmonious interaction between man and nature. Though without formal education, by the age of seventeen she wanted to be a poet, as she explained in a letter to her father. But her parents, ignoring her desire for an independent career, arranged for her to become engaged to a lawyer. She recalls in her memoirs that during their engagement they were introduced to Atatürk while he was on a visit to Antalya, and the great man was so impressed that he invited them to Ankara (Uçuk, 400 & 409-18). However, the marriage lasted a mere two years, and in 1931 the independent-minded young woman moved to Istanbul and began a new life.

In Istanbul she discovered that Nazım was the talk of the town. She immediately bought the gramophone recording of his poetry and began to imitate his style of reading at private gatherings (Uçuk, Interview, March 1996). In short, she began to hero-worship him well before they actually met. Towards the end of January 1935 her eye was caught by one of his 'Orhan Selim', articles in *Akşam* entitled 'The Scent of the Sun'. Using rather sensuous language, he describes how fresh the bed linen smells during sleepless nights, after his woman has put it out in the sunshine to air during the day. This scent restores his youthful energy and zest for life ('Güneş Kokusu', 22 January 1935, A 23, 14). The article struck such a chord with Cahit that she wrote to the newspaper recalling her own associations with the scent of the sun: 'I felt the scent of the sun so early', she writes, and 'you felt it so late'. In her village in Anatolia high in the mountains she used to sleep on the roof, waking with the sunrise, and the bed linen would be carefully arranged there to soak up the sun throughout the day. Here in Istanbul she missed the bright sunlight of Anatolia and the warmth of those sun-drenched beds: 'Those days are long past. Now I am no longer satisfied with beds which have been aired in the sun for only one day.' Nazım was delighted with this letter, publishing it in *Akşam* on 26 January with an appreciative commentary (A 23, 18).

They must have become friends almost immediately. Cahit recalls that when they first met – a chance encounter on the ferry crossing the Bosphorus – the poet was so bowled over that he did not even dare to inquire who she was (Uçuk, Interview, March 1996). However, when he described her appearance to his friend at Ipek Film Studios, the director Muhsin, he guessed her identity. Cahit was a striking figure on the Istanbul scene – a woman so emancipated that she sometimes even wore Western-style jacket and trousers. She and Nazım became acquainted at a party hosted by mutual friends, and the account she gave of an idyllic childhood amid the orchards and orange groves of southern Anatolia entranced him. They began to meet at a tea garden overlooking the Bosphorus, and predictably he tried to convert her to communism. But for her the most important thing in life was the harmony of nature, not the conflicts of politics.

Where Piraye offered Nazım the delights and comforts of married life, Cahit attracted him as a gifted author. Within a fortnight of the 'Scent of the Sun' episode, we find him promoting her writings in print; his first step was to arrange for one of her short stories to be published in the fortnightly magazine *Yarım Ay*. Under the bold heading 'A Story That Everyone Must Read' her contribution was introduced on 14 February 1935 by a writer who signed himself 'Anonymous' ('İmzasız'):

There are some people who are very warm. As soon as they arrive at a social gathering, they are loved more than someone you have known for forty years. There is a flowing, curvaceous, lively style of writing which is like that, like falling in love with someone at first sight.

You are going to see the signature of Cahit Uçuk printed below for the first time today. [...]

After you've read this writing, you will be able to imagine the writer of this vivid and condensed story as sensitive, profound and very creative. You are going to love her just like a warm person loved at first sight. [...]

Yarım Ay is proud to introduce this enlightened mind full of western culture and full of the scent and the feelings of our own country.
('Bir Masal Ki Herkes Okumalı', A 21, 80)

Such praise would have turned the head of any young author, especially as Nazım went on to arrange for *Yarım Ay* to serialize Cahit's novel *Dikenli Çit* (The Thorn Hedge). The magazine cover announcing it incorporated her features in a boldly stylized form (Fig. 12a).

Although Cahit was soon in love, she was clear-sighted enough to realize that their relationship had no future, since Nazım was only recently married. Piraye became suspicious when she noticed the elegant clothes that Nazım put on when he went into town. The affair only lasted a few months, but Cahit was heartbroken the following year on learning that Nazım was again in prison. She was comforted during these unhappy days by Mahmut Yesari, another contributor to *Yarım Ay* fifteen years her senior, and was so touched by his kindness that she married him. Piraye was so distressed by Nazım's affair that she threatened to leave him if

YARIM
A Y

No
20

IS KURUŞ

Bu Sayıda:
CAHİT UÇUĞUN
DİKENLİ ÇİT
Romanı Başlıyor.

12a. Cahit Uçuk, on the front cover of *Yarım Ay.*

anything like it happened again. Cahit recalls that Piraye even threatened to denounce Nazım and his friends to the police as communists if the affair continued. There were further distractions, including a flirtation with his cousin Münevver, who had returned to Istanbul with her mother in 1935 after being educated abroad. Circumstances did not permit the poet's relationship with this charming young woman to develop at that time, but a dozen years later it blossomed into a spectacular romance.

Not only this personal turmoil but also the demands of Nazım's work brought the Anatolian idyll to an end. To supplement the income from his journalistic writings he had taken a job at the Ipek Film Studio, which was in Nişantaşı on the western side of Bosphorus. Travelling to work from the Anatolian shore involved crossing by ferry from Kadıköy and then taking the bus, an arduous journey especially in winter, so in 1936 they decided to move to a house in Cihangir nearer the Film Studio. In 1937, after a further short period under arrest, Nazım moved with Piraye to a new home in Nişantaşı itself, only 100 metres from the Studio.

They were fortunate to find a flat spacious enough for the extended family, which included Piraye's two children, Nazım's stepmother Cavide and her twins, but they had hardly settled in before the poet was again arrested in January 1938. Although the marriage lasted almost fifteen years, they could never enjoy a stable domestic life.

Poetry on trial

During the decade 1929-38 Nazım was in and out of prison so often that it is difficult to keep track of all the charges against him. They formed part of a concerted campaign to suppress political dissent: it was not simply an individual but freedom of expression that was on trial. First he was taken to court for 'The City that Lost its Voice', the poem published in *Resimli Ay* in July 1929 at the height of the 'demolishing the idols' controversy. The trial began on 16 August 1929, and the poem, which had defended the taxi drivers' strike in Istanbul, was cited to substantiate the charge of 'spreading communist propaganda and inciting the workers to strike'. Since strikes were illegal, the editor received a ten-day prison sentence, but Nazım insisted on appealing (Sülker 2, 47). At the second hearing the courtroom was full of the poet's admirers, including a number of taxi drivers, and on 24 March 1930 he was acquitted.

This was an interlude of relative liberalism in Kemalist Turkey with a judiciary proud of its independence. Trials were held in public and reported by the press, which enabled defendants to publicize their positions with statements from the dock. The liberal journalist Ahmet Emin Yalman, who frequently criticized the abuses of the one-party system in his newspaper *Vatan*, stresses in his memoirs that the 'judiciary remained strong, reliable and independent'. Although publication of his paper was often suspended by the censorship, he emerged from the ensuing court cases with 'a perfect record of acquittals'. However, Yalman goes too far in claiming that Turkish justice 'proved incorruptible even under political pressure' (Yalman, 207 & 230). The anti-communist legislation, which severely restricted press freedom, led to court procedure being politicized. Nazım's acquittal in March 1930 alarmed his opponents, and rumours that he would be forced to pay for provoking so many influential people were soon circulating.

After a year of freedom he was indeed arrested again in the early hours of 1 May 1931.

The tactic of arresting communists to forestall May Day demonstrations was all too familiar, but this time the charges were more serious. During the preliminary interrogation, the public prosecutor had on his desk no less than five of collections of Nazım's poetry: *1+1=1, 835 Satır, Jokond ile Si-Ya-U, Sesini Kaybeden Şehir* and *Varan 3*. When he appeared before the judge on 6 May, the courtroom was packed with spectators and reporters, and one of them, Nazım's biographer Kemal Sülker has left a description of the ensuing drama. First the charges were read: 'By calling himself the poet of the proletariat, he is defending a political system which is against the law in this country. With his poetry he encourages the dominance of one class over the others by inciting people to break the law.' This gave Nazım an opportunity to affirm the right to freedom of political thought: 'Communism is a belief like any other political or economic theory. I cannot possibly break the law by believing in communism. I have never encouraged the dominance of one class over another.' When accused of justifying communist revolution in *Jokond ile Si-Ya-U*, he cheekily replied: 'The poem is about French and English Imperialism in China. It is those governments that should take me to court. I was only expressing my sympathy for the Chinese revolt against imperialism' (Sülker 2, 184). Since the Turkish state had itself so recently fought for its own freedom against Western imperialism, this argument struck a chord. On 10 May 1931 he was acquitted amid cheers in the crowded courtroom.

The tolerance of the courts was pushed to its limit the next year with the publication in November 1932 of *Gece Gelen Telegraf*. On 5 March 1933 the book was banned, and a fortnight later Nazım was arrested on a charge of spreading communist propaganda. The publisher, Ahmet Halit, was also put on trial (Sülker 2, 205). This time the courts, alarmed by the poet's popularity, decided to proceed in secret session, claiming that public trials endangered national security (Coşkun, 72). Journalists and other spectators were removed from the court, and on 1 June 1933, midway through the trial, Nazım was transferred to Bursa prison, so that he was not even present for the subsequent proceedings. He had good reason to complain in a letter to his sister of 17

June: 'No records are kept, statements by witnesses are taken in their absence, and normal court procedure is not being followed' (Aydemir, 1986a, 178). Since the court decided to obtain an expert opinion on whether his books actively propagated communism, there were considerable delays before Nazım finally received a six-month prison sentence (AM 1, 21). Meanwhile, a second trial opened in Istanbul on 9 May 1933, at which Nazım was charged with defaming Süreyya Pasha and his family in the poem 'An Experiment in Satire'. The trial ended on 27 August 1933 with a further twelve-month sentence, a 200 Lira fine, and an order to pay 500 Lira in compensation. For an impoverished poet these were substantial sums, and Nazım could not pay – he had scarcely enough money for postage stamps (Aydemir, 1986a, 183).

A systematic campaign to suppress Nazım's work was clearly under way, since he was also named in a mass prosecution of members of the Turkish Communist Party arrested in April 1933. On 1 June he and twenty-three Party members appeared in court in Bursa accused of membership of a communist youth organisation. They were charged under article 171 of the criminal code, with 'forming an illegal organisation in Istanbul, Bursa and Adana, and attempting to overthrow the government and the constitution and to replace it with a regime like that of the Soviet Union'. After they had spent several further months in custody, the hearings continued in Bursa in November 1933 behind closed doors, and under the draconian provisions of article 171 the public prosecutor demanded the death penalty. Nazım's response to this was – characteristically – to write a poem, 'Letter to My Wife':

> You must
> be sure, my beloved,
> that if a poor gipsy's hairy hand
>   which resembles a black spider
>   is going to put the noose
>   round my neck –
>
> well, those who are waiting to see fear in my blue eyes
>   will look at Nazım in vain [...]
> If you have any money
>   buy me a pair of flannel pants.
> The sciatica pains have started again.
> And do not forget

a prisoner's wife must always think
beautiful thoughts.
('Karıma Mektup', A 2, 168; SP 44-5)

Despite the threat of the death penalty, conditions in Bursa prison were not unduly arduous. The thirty-five political prisoners had to be kept separate from other prisoners at the top of the building, which was designed for 200 inmates. Sanitation was adequate, and they were even able to heat water for hot baths on charcoal stoves of their own construction (Bercavi, 61). The prisoners came from both main factions of the party, and included one of Nazım's closest friends, the young poet Nail Çakırhan (Nail V). Nail confessed under interrogation that he had translated an article by the anarchist Bukharin; in fact it had been translated by another friend of Nazım's, Rasih Güran, but Nazım persuaded Nail to accept responsibility. However, the friendship between Nail and Nazım soon cooled when Nail discovered from fellow prisoners who belonged to the official Turkish Communist Party (the 'Muvafakat') that Nazım's faction (the 'Muhalefet') was actually a splinter group not recognised by the Comintern. In 1934, soon after his release, Nail's loyalty to the Party was rewarded by an invitation to study in Moscow (Çakırhan, Interview, March 1996).

The experience of living in a Soviet commune helped Nazım adjust to the rough camaraderie of prison life. The prisoners were provided with plenty of bread, but beyond this they had to rely on food parcels or buy things for themselves. Since not all of them had relatives able to support them, the supplies received, including cigarettes, were pooled and shared out equally (Nazım only hoarded his pipe tobacco). In addition to the daily rota for cooking and cleaning, Nazım organised an educational programme, including classes on French, history and Dialectical Materialism, not to mention revolutionary songs and communal games. There was also a small lending library for newspapers and magazines (Bercavi, 64). These months at Bursa were also productive in literary terms: Nazım kept busy writing, dictating poems to Nail and reciting them to the other inmates. Helped by other prisoners, he even prepared a film scenario entitled 'Aysel, Bataklı Damın Kızı' ('Aysel, the Girl from the Mud Hut'), based on a story by the Swedish writer Selma Lagerlöf, the first woman awarded the Nobel Prize for literature. Certain scenes from this film were actually shot in a picturesque village near Bursa during the summer of 1934, directed by Muhsin Ertuğrul, while the author still languished behind bars. Only on 4 August was he released after sixteen months in custody, as the result of an amnesty to mark the tenth anniversary of the Turkish Republic.

Films, plays and polemics

'The Girl from the Mud Hut' was one of a series of adaptations which Nazım made for Ipek Film Studios. For political reasons his name was often omitted from the credits or replaced by a pseudonym, but he had a hand in at least twenty films produced during the 1930s and 1940s. He was thus active in the new medium at a time when the Turkish cinema was making the transition to talkies under the guidance of Muhsin Ertuğrul. Having first gained experience of film-making in Paris, Berlin and Moscow, Ertuğrul emerged as the leading Turkish director of this period, although his technique remained indebted to the theatre. He and Nazım had been close friends since their days in Moscow, sharing similar social-critical assumptions. Through this productive partnership Nazım became involved in dubbing and adapting foreign sources, in addition to writing original scenarios. He embraced the new medium enthusiastically, and even wrote scripts for several musical comedies. He also tried his hand as a director, working first as assistant to Ertuğrul and later himself directing two documentaries and a feature film. Even in prison through the 1940s he continued to write scenarios, and after his release in 1950 he resumed work with Ipek Studios.

One of the most significant of these projects was a film about the Turkish War of Liberation, *Bir Millet Uyanıyor* (A Nation Awakes), directed by Ertuğrul in 1932. Set in Istanbul under the Allied occupation, this stirring tale of resistance and sabotage was based on the memoirs of another left-winger, Nizamettin Nazif (Şener, 41-44). According to an article about Nazım's cinema work published in the newspaper *Yeni Ortam* on 3 June 1974, he acted as Ertuğrul's assistant – an experience that may well have contributed to the cinematic element in his later poetry, especially *Human Landscapes*. The two short documentaries which Nazım directed, *Istanbul Senfonisi* and *Bursa Senfonisi* (both made in 1934), dealt with everyday life in Istanbul and Bursa (Özön, 70). Even more ambitious was the feature he directed: *Güneşe Doğru*

('Towards the Sun'), based on his own script. This film explores
the history of modern Turkey through the eyes of a young man
who loses consciousness in 1918 and reawakens in 1935 to find
himself in a society that has become unrecognisable through the
achievements of the Kemalist revolution. The sets were designed
by Abidin Dino, while Ferdi Tayfur and Mediha played the leading
roles. An innovative feature was the use of amateur actors for
scenes shot on location, reflecting Nazım's concern to portray
the life of ordinary people. On its release in 1937, the film had
a mixed reception. Hasan Ali Yücel praised the naturalness of
the dialogue and milieu and the atmospheric effect of Turkish
music, but another critic faulted the film for an over-reliance on
fantasy (*Yeni Ortam*, 3 June 1974, p.7). Still, this can be seen as
a promising debut, and Nazım might have had further success as
a film-maker had he not been arrested the following year.

In addition to these experimental films of the 1930s, Nazım
was also enjoying a meteoric career as a dramatist. Once again
(as he recalls) it was Ertuğrul who provided the catalyst:

I was lying ill in bed in Istanbul. My comrades were being arrested and
tortured, with burning cigarettes on their chests, being beaten until the
skins on the soles of their feet peeled, with hot boiled eggs placed under
their armpits. They had been sent for trial to Izmir. I was pretty depressed,
angry, ill and broke. Muhsin Ertuğrul, the greatest Turkish producer and
founder of the modern Turkish theatre, came to see me. Muhsin Ertuğrul,
having visited the Soviet Union several times, brought to his work the
discipline of Soviet modern art, having been very impressed by Stanislavsky
and Meyerhold. He asked me if I had a play ready to be staged. He needed
one within a week. I said yes, even though I did not have any play ready
to be staged at the time. [...] After he had gone, I began to wonder what
to write. I then remembered a play I had written which had been
confiscated by the police (B 5, 12-13).

This play was *Kafatası* (The Skull), an earlier version of which
had been performed at the Metla Theatre in Moscow with the
title *Her Şey Mal*. Nazım rapidly rewrote the text and handed it
to Ertuğrul in August 1931. The play was announced in the
fortnightly theatre magazine *Darülbedayi* in September, and on 1
December Ertuğrul praised it in that same magazine as 'the first
indigenous Turkish play which has not been influenced by any
European writer'.

'The Skull' is set in a capitalist country called Dollaryan, where the hero, Dr Dalbanezo, is working on a cure for tuberculosis, a disease which afflicts his daughter. He is asked by the sanatorium owners to abandon his research, which threatens their profits. In return they offer him a new laboratory for work on animal research. After initially accepting, he changes his mind and attempts to produce the vaccine in secret, in a last-minute attempt to save his daughter. When his activities are discovered, he has to endure poverty and imprisonment. Almost every character in the play, including writers, poets and journalists, is shown to be in the service of money-grubbing capitalists. Even attractive young women are employed to entice wealthy men into the sanatorium. In the original version performed in Moscow the satire on profiteering was extremely outspoken, but in the revised Turkish version the scenes that challenge the values of capitalist society were heavily censored (Babayev, 307-10). This play nevertheless made a breakthrough towards a new form of socialist theatre. When 'The Skull' was staged in Istanbul in March 1932, it had a rapturous reception. The audience consising – mainly of young people, including socialists and communists – remained in the theatre for over an hour after the performance, demonstrating their enthusiasm. When Nazım tried to slip out through the stage door, he was carried through the streets by his admirers. Although the play only ran for five nights, the subsequent performances had a similar reception (Sülker 2, 181).

This successful debut gave Nazım the incentive to write a series of further plays, including *Bir Ölü Evi* (A House of Mourning), also staged by Ertuğrul in 1932, this time at the well-known Darülbedayi Theatre. The play is set in a moneylender's house in Istanbul and concerns a dispute among his children over their inheritance. The essence of capitalist morality is summed up by the father's advice to his daughter: 'Do not trust the love of anyone, mother or father, brothers or friends. The only thing that does not betray you in this world is your own money.' This tragi-comedy about the destruction of a bourgeois family would have appealed to a socialist audience, but in an attempt to avoid the attentions of the censorship, it was announced under a pseudonym rather than under Nazım's own name. It therefore attracted a conventional first-night audience, who felt so affronted by the play's message that some left the theatre after second act. The satire on mercenary values was a commercial flop and closed after only four performances (B 5, 14). However, two further productions were staged in Istanbul in 1934, *Şöhret veya Unutulan Adam* (Fame or the Forgotten Man), the tragedy of a scientist; and *Bu Bir Rüyadır* (This is only a Dream), a light-hearted operetta for which Nazım provided the libretto.

It may be surprising that a social-critical dramatist should have created a playful operetta. But Nazım wrote the libretto for 'This is Only a Dream' with a particular actress, Semiha Berksoy, in mind. Born in 1910, Semiha was a brunette with lustrous dark eyes, strong features and a compelling stage presence, later to become a celebrated contralto singer. She made her debut in the cinema playing a minor role in the first Turkish sound film, *Istanbul Sokakları* ('The Streets of Istanbul'). She and Nazım met in 1931, when Semiha, still a drama student, was given a part in his play 'The Skull'. She was deeply impressed by his work and continued to follow his fortunes, even when he was sent to Bursa prison. In July 1934, when Muhsin Ertuğrul went to Bursa to direct the film 'Aysel, the Girl from the Mud Hut', she obtained permission to accompany the film crew and took the opportunity to visit Nazım in prison. Nazım must have felt rather flattered, for by this date Semiha had become the rising star of the movement to establish Western-style opera in Turkey, having been talent-spotted by Atatürk himself. After Nazım's release in August 1934 they met on a ferry-boat in Istanbul, and Semiha was so excited that she gave him her address and invited him to the house where she lived with her parents. The invitation to tea soon led to a passionate love affair, later recalled fondly by Semiha herself (Berksoy, Interview, October 1996). Semiha's charismatic personality formed a marked contrast to the literary aspirations of Cahit Uçuk and the domesticity associated with Piraye, who seems to have coped philosophically with the situation. 'There was always another woman,' Memet Fuat recalled (Interview, March 1996); but Piraye felt 'less threatened' by Semiha than by Cahit.

It was this affair with a young singer that inspired Nazım to write an operetta. Set on a luxurious cabin cruiser, 'This is Only a Dream' is a satire on social climbers who pretend to be wealthy in order to arrange marriage with the glamorous Fatma, whose family also has delusions of grandeur. Their pretensions are exposed when they experience a collective hallucination under the influence of a gypsy's aromatic cigarettes, and Fatma finally marries her true love, an engineer named Faruk, the one person who has never made a secret of his humble origins (A 10, 183-242). Nazım was so involved with this production that he regularly attended rehearsals, becoming entranced by Semiha's performance as Fatma. In December 1934 the operetta was successfully staged by Ertuğrul at the Darülbedayi Theatre, with music by Ferdi Statzer conducted by Ferit Alnar. As author of the libretto, Nazım used the pseudonym Selma Muhtar, although it is not clear whether this was designed to protect him from the censorship or from accusations of bourgeois deviationism.

The shifting moods of the operetta reflect the ambiguities of Nazım's relationship with his leading lady. The film studio provided opportunities for them to meet without exciting too much comment. 'Is it possible to fall in love with more than one person?' a colleague inquired. 'It wouldn't be a bad idea to have others to amuse you,' Nazım replied, 'but there can be only one true love' (Özbilgen, 67-8). He evidently felt flattered without needing to commit himself, but Semiha became passionately attached to him. Even after his marriage to Piraye their contacts continued, but gradually Semiha realized that there was no future in the relationship. In 1936 she was awarded a scholarship to study singing in Berlin, and spent the next three years there, becoming a visiting member of the Berlin State Opera and specializing in Wagnerian roles. At the festival to mark the seventy-fifth birthday of Richard Strauss in 1939, she sang the title role in *Ariadne auf Naxos*. On her return to Turkey she was selected by the German emigré conductor Carl Ebert to take the lead in *Tosca*, Puccini's tragic opera about a political prisoner (Fig.12b). It was this project (as we shall see in the next chapter) that was to bring her and Nazım together again.

Nazım's high-profile involvement with the artistic avant-garde provoked hostile reactions. The granting of an amnesty in 1934 to a writer convicted of subversive activities predictably incensed the nationalists, but Nazım also found himself under attack from his former ally Peyami Safa. In 1929 it had been Safa who had encouraged him in his campaign against the literary establishment. By 1935 they found themselves in opposite camps, even though both for a time were employed by the same newspaper, *Tan*. Peyami contributed humorous stories while Nazım's articles

12b. Semiha Berksoy as Tosca.

appeared on the facing page under the pseudonym Orhan Selim. At first the tone of this confrontation was restrained. Writing in *Tan* on 7 June 1935, Nazım mocked coffee-house intellectuals who pick up ideas from abroad and present them as their own (A 2, 191). Taking this as a personal attack, Peyami retaliated on 23 June with an article entitled 'Herd Man'; without mentioning Nazım by name, it condemned the type who subscribes to a collective ideology: 'Because he has the herd instinct, he does not have a personality of his own. He is a person without personality. [...] 100,000 of them do not add up to one personality. If we want to improve our population, we must decrease the number of these people so that we have a society of individuals with personality' (Göze, 199).

This article sparked off a violent polemic. Seeing himself as the main target of this 'Herd Man' article, Nazım answered it in an article called 'Little Man' (*Tan*, 24 June 1935), attacking Peyami's concept of population control as a typical instance of fascist ideology. The rupture could not be contained within the pages of *Tan*,

and Peyami switched to a rival paper, the weekly *Hafta*, in which
he published a series of seven articles entitled 'A Little Light'
('Biraz Aydınlık') (*Hafta*, 8 July to 19 August 1935). After re-
capitulating the history of their relationship, emphasising how he
had helped Nazım in 1929 in his campaign against Yakup Kadri,
Peyami concluded with a vivid satirical pen-portrait: 'Nazım betrays
himself by the way he wears a worker's cap on his head, by the
way he carries his jacket on his shoulder, by the hair in his chest
bulging out of his unbuttoned shirts, by wearing unpressed
trousers... all this screaming out "this man is a Bolshevik"' (Göze,
205-7). Changing tack in the second week, Peyami continued:
'Nazım is seeking an easy ideology, easy art and an easy fame.
He is a fake communist, ... a fake poet, imitating Russian poets.
[...] Nazım is neither a Turk nor an intellectual, he is simply an
irresponsible man' ('Biraz Aydınlık', No. 2) (*Hafta*, 15 July). This
bitter personal attack continued in further articles implying that
Nazım was pathologically obsessed with his own fame, which he
really owed to his prison sentences. The self-styled proletarian
actually came from a privileged bourgeois family, while Peyami
was proud of his humble origins (Göze, 239 & 324).

With hindsight it is clear that the alliance between Peyami and
Nazım had always been based on a misconception, since the one
was a Nietzschean individualist with mystical tendencies and the
other a revolutionary Marxist. Ultimately, Peyami was to become
an outspoken opponent of Nazım's brand of socialism, developing
Pan-Turkish and even pro-fascist sympathies. Nazım's replies represent his opponent's individualism as a social and physiological
sickness. After a long silence Nazım settled accounts in an interview
with Naci Sadullah, published in *Yedi Gün* on 17 July, denouncing
Peyami as an opportunist who leans to the left when he thinks
he can make money from socialism, but turns anti-Marxist when
that position proves more profitable (A 26, 23). Nazım's most
provocative riposte took the form of a satirical poem, 'Attempt
at a Satire on a Provocateur', which links Peyami's reactionary
conception of art with the figure of Namık Kemal, the great
national poet of the Ottoman period:

> Remember that your hero and master, Namık Kemal,
> the one with a fake lion's mane,
> was drinking wine in golden cups from the ebony hands
>   of black slaves

intoxicated with the 'eyes of freedom'
('Bir Provocateur Üstüne Hiciv Denemeleri', A 2, 152)

This poem widened the scope of the controversy, since Namık Kemal was the hero of the Turkish nationalists and had been exiled under the Ottomans. In a patriotic article published in *Aydabir* in November 1935, 'Karl Marx and Namık Kemal', Peyami played the nationalistic card (Göze, 326). This was followed by a rally of right-wing students which took place on 2 December to commemorate the anniversary of Namık Kemal's death (Sülker 1968, 131). Later that same month Peyami gained further support from Nihal Atsız, a Turkish nationalist influenced by German racial theories, who published a pamphlet entitled 'To the Communist Don Quixote, Proletarian Bourgeois, Comrade Nazım Hikmetov' (Yücebaş, 111).

In response to the pamphlet, Nazım appealed to the Communist Party to publish one analysing the place of Namık Kemal in bourgeois culture, but this was refused. Instead, two members of Nazım's camp, Kemal Tahir and Kerim Sadi, decided to organise a questionnaire on the subject, publishing the results in January 1936. This was followed by a pamphlet entitled 'The Sad Case of Peyami and the Model Youth of 1936' (Sülker 1968, 139 & 169). Their conclusion was that Namık Kemal, far from being a defender of the people's freedom, had simply represented the interests of a bourgeois élite, even defending the Sultan. These literary disputes owed their explosive power to the ideological context in which they unfolded – the rise of totalitarian political systems in Europe and the polarisation between communism and fascism. For many nationalists, in Turkey as elsewhere, fascism was welcomed as a means of resisting the menace of bolshevism. Prominent members of Kemal's government made no secret of their admiration for Mussolini, some of whose anti-Communist legislation was even incorporated into the Turkish criminal code. Nazım was seen as a particular threat because his work held such a powerful appeal for younger readers, including students and military cadets. Thus the tirades against him in the press were accompanied by more sinister machinations in the corridors of power. As a result of these manoeuvres, the polemics of 1935-6 were brought to an abrupt conclusion on 30 December 1936, when Nazım was arrested once again. This marked the start of a systematic campaign to silence the poet by the draconian methods of martial law. It also led Nazım to abandon literary polemics for the more urgent task of campaigning against fascism.

The fight against Fascism: Taranta-Babu and Sheikh Bedreddin

Since Turkey traditionally enjoyed close ties with Germany, Hitler's seizure of power strengthened nationalistic tendencies in Ankara, especially after the plausible Franz von Papen took over as German ambassador. Mustafa Kemal, now known as Atatürk (Father of the Turks), was still committed to maintaining good relations with the Western democracies and was sceptical towards Mussolini. In 1932 he took Turkey into the League of Nations, and in 1936, after the Italian invasion of Abyssinia, Turkey voted in favour of sanctions against Italy (Kinross, 480). But there were other members of the Turkish political élite who had some sympathy for the racial policies of Nazi Germany. Turkey had its own unacknowledged history of persecution – the massacre of the Armenians in the final years of the Ottoman Empire. Historians have shown that the Armenian massacres were primarily political rather than racist in character (Katz, 7-17). But this did not prevent Hitler from invoking them as a precedent for the annihilation of the Jews. In a period when racist theories were rife, the parallels were only too plausible. Political thinking in Turkey was still influenced by the Pan-Turanists, and Kemal Atatürk himself encouraged speculations about pre-history, insisting that the Turks were 'a white Aryan race, originating in Central Asia, the cradle of human civilization' (Kinross, 468).

Speaking at a meeting of journalists at the end of 1937 to launch the new editorial policy of *Tan*, Sabiha Sertel identified a double threat:

I would like to remind you of two dangers prevailing in Turkey at the moment: one is Pan-Turanism, the other is German fascism. [...] I know that even before 1935 there were such teachers at universities in Istanbul; later, some pro-Hitler professors began to arrive. [...] This was followed by the posting of many economic consultants from Germany with very low salaries to private firms. [...] In the realm of the press, we have the *Türkische Post*, a German publication. [...] Germany is about to launch a fifth-column propaganda campaign in Turkey among the civilian population, as they did in Spain, in order to gain support for fascist unity (Sülker 4, 241).

Sabiha omits to mention that some of the newly-arrived German university teachers were Jewish refugees, including scholars who brought international renown to the University of Istanbul like the literary historian Erich Auerbach. But she was certainly right to draw attention to proto-fascist tendencies in the Turkish press. Yunus Nadi, the editor of *Cumhuriyet*, made no secret of his German sympathies. It is this context that gave Nazım's writings of the mid-1930s a new political urgency, as he exposed the insidious effects of fascism and insisted on the need for international solidarity. He achieved this in two of his finest narrative poems, *Taranta-Babu* (1935) and *Sheikh Bedreddin* (1936), which used ingenious strategies to evade the censorship.

Mussolini's invasion of Abyssinia (Ethiopia) in October 1935 was welcomed in the right-wing press, while liberal journalists expressed their reservations. Using the pretext that Turkey was an ally of Italy, the government declared a ban on all criticism of fascist foreign policy. In this climate, it was not easy to find a publisher for an anti-fascist pamphlet. Nazım was obliged to borrow money to cover the cost of having his attack on 'German Fascism' printed in 1936 (Sülker 4, 40). He had encountered similar difficulties the previous year when trying to publish a narrative poem, 'An Abyssinian in Italy' ('Italyada Habeşistanlı Genç'). Parts of this poem appeared in the weekly magazine *Yedigün* on 18 September 1935 and in *Aydabir* the following month. But a book with such a provocative title would certainly have been suppressed, so Nazım outmanoeuvred the censorship by giving this work the cryptic title *Taranta-Babu'ya Mektuplar* ('Letters to Taranta-Babu'). This slim volume, which appeared towards the end of 1935, was dedicated to Henri Barbusse, a fellow campaigner against fascism.

Taranta-Babu is both thematically and formally innovative, weaving an abrasive critique of fascism into a collage of contemporary newspaper cuttings and lyrical reflections on the lives of ordinary people in Ethiopia. Images of the oppressiveness and squalor of Rome under Mussolini are offset by the narrator's recollections of everyday life in his native Ethiopian village, which form a delicate counterpoint to the death and destruction caused by the Italian invasion. The five-page prose introduction takes the form of a letter dated 'Rome, 5 August 1935', allegedly sent to the author by an Italian friend. The friend explains that in his room in a scruffy Roman boarding-house he has discovered a pile of letters written by the previous occupant, a black Ethiopian student who left the letters unposted when he was arrested by the Italian police. Since there was no possibility of sending the letters to their intended destination in war-torn Ethiopia, the friend has translated them and sent them to Nazım to be published in Turkey.

Reading the Turkish text of these 'letters', transposed into free verse (with short sections in prose), we are drawn into the confused emotions of the art student from Africa as he attempts to convey his impressions of Rome to his wife Taranta-Babu back in Ethiopia. This imaginative structure gives the sequence of thirteen letters a refreshing informality of tone distinct from the strident denunciations of fascism by more conventional communists. Nazım's critique combines the freshness of vision of an African visitor to Rome with the burgeoning political awareness of a member of an oppressed colonial people. The tone of the letters modulates between lyrical celebration, polemical protest and elegiac lament, with a longing to share these feelings with Taranta-Babu herself, embodiment of the frustrated creative energies of Africa: 'my third wife / my eyes, my lips, my everything'. The epistolary form sustains a double perspective, lending emotional fullness to the political reflections of the letter-writer through continuous evocations of Taranta-Babu's vulnerable beauty, and hence also of the spirit of a peaceful community about to be ravaged by war.

The assertion of the primacy of feeling does not prevent the historically-minded letter-writer from contrasting Rome's artistic heritage with the brutal city of today:

> [...] in the middle of Rome
>   I searched for Rome.
> No more
>   do the great masters
> cut the marble like a silk fabric;
>
> no wind blows from Florence;
> no poems from Dante Alighieri [...]
> In these days,
>   in the long wide avenues of Rome
> there's only one dark
>   one blood-stained shadow

The opening lines of the fourth letter further extend the delicate play of irony:

> Suns in each embroidered design on silk shawls,
> the hoof-sound of black mules towards Pompeii,
> Verdi's heart beating
>   in the colourful box of a barrel-organ
> and the best macaroni in the world,
> Italy, famous for these things,
>   Taranta-Babu,
> is famous for fascism too.

The piety of a traditional African community serves as a foil to expose the insanity of capitalist Europe. In Africa people may die of famine, but only as the result of drought:

> Here in Italy it is the reverse.
> People die in time of plenty:
> people live when famine comes.
> On the outskirts of Rome
> men walk like sick, hungry wolves. [...]
> They feed people with words,
> the pigs with choice potatoes.

In short, the fascist system abuses the rhythms of nature and fecundity of the earth, associated with Taranta-Babu's ample body:

> Think of me
> while my arms embrace your wide hips
> mother to my three children [...]

Other letters satirise the ostentatious wealth of the Vatican, the tight-fisted bankers who fund Mussolini, and the 'geniuses of fascist literature', like D'Annunzio and Marinetti, who have swastikas embroidered on their silk handkerchiefs. A whole letter is devoted to Marconi, the multi-millionaire scientist who, according to a newspaper report, has invented 'some kind of death-ray, soon to be tried out in Ethiopia'. The great scientist is now 'the slave of the black-shirted Benito / about to stain his hands up to the elbow / with the blood of my brothers'. The final letters are introduced by another newspaper report explaining that the Italian forces 'are awaiting the coming of spring before they start their attack on Ethiopia', a report which provokes images of the awakening African spring and his wife's bronze-skinned beauty at the moment of death:

> How strange, Taranta-Babu,
> that death
>   shall walk through our door
> tucking a spring flower
>   into his colonial hat.

The grandiloquent Mussolini is pictured 'eating spaghetti bolognese' before sending in the air force 'to kill you, Taranta-Babu, ripping open your belly / and spilling your intestines / on the sand'.

In the final letter, a prose epilogue incorporating further press cuttings, the writer anticipates that 'the military who will shoot me here will also be making red holes in your breasts'. These disturbing images of violation and death are designed to shock the reader into an awareness of the true threat of fascism, at a time when people were still extolling Mussolini's magnificent social reforms, not to mention his civilising mission in Africa. Yet despite the precise invocations of approaching disaster, the overall effect of the poem is strangely exhilarating. It is above all a defiant commitment to life, through a multiplicity of telling detail, right down to the African goats with their 'long curly hair' and the milk running 'like two arms of light from their udders'. The threat of fascism to the lives of ordinary people is conveyed with great immediacy, while a highly imaginative form of anti-fascist diction is deployed to articulate the destructive impact of war on defenceless individuals. Just as the poet (speaking with the sceptical voice of the letter-writer) does not understate the fascist threat, so he avoids easy promises about the triumph of the revolution. Only at one point in his historical ruminations is there the hint of a challenge:

> And listen:
> in the suburbs of Rome
> the sound of the breaking chains
>   of Spartacus.
>   (A 2, 179-216; SP 47-65)

Taranta-Babu was the first of Nazım's works to win a readership in the west. Within a few months a French translation was published in the left-wing journal *Commune*, edited by Louis Aragon (March 1936). In Turkey, however, it had a chequered publication history, since it was banned after the author was once again arrested in 1938, and excerpts were cited as evidence against him in the subsequent trial. During the following decades only individual sections could be included in Turkish poetry anthologies, particularly the second letter about Rome. This gave rise to the legend that Nazım had himself visited Rome and married an Ethiopian woman, an unwitting tribute to his powers of evocation.

Nazım's productivity in these years of crisis was remarkable. In 1936 he published one of his finest historical poems, the fourteen-canto *Şeyh Bedreddin Destanı* (Epic of Sheikh Bedreddin), which endows a peasant revolt in the territories of the medieval Ottoman Empire with a new political resonance. Bedreddin was an unorthodox Islamic thinker, born in 1359 in the small town of Simavne, near Edirne (Adrianople), one of the Balkan provinces of the rapidly expanding Ottoman Empire. Like Nazım, Bedreddin came from a cosmopolitan family background, his father being an Islamic judge in Simavne, while his mother was a Christian convert to Islam. He grew up in an area of mixed Turkish and Greek population, at a time when Istanbul (Constantinople) was still the Byzantine capital. After studying in Konya, Edirne and Cairo, where he married beautiful gypsy woman, he spent many years as a religious teacher, expressing his ideas in a collection of theological aphorisms entitled *Varidat* (Inspirations). Later he returned to Edirne, becoming an influential judge and religious leader with progressive views in the service of the Ottoman court. In 1413 Bedreddin was banished by the new Sultan, Mehmet I, to Iznik, where he began to develop more radical ideas and acquired the reputation of being an anti-authoritarian thinker. His ideas were taken up by members of the Simavi sect and developed into a critique of social conditions, and his followers – especially one named Mustafa – organized a revolt in his name, which Jews and Christians as well as Muslims supported. The basic assumption of Islamic thought that all property belongs to Allah became the basis for a challenge to the system of feudal land-ownership and serfdom. In 1417, after a three-year struggle, the revolt was crushed by the Sultan's forces, and in 1420 Bedreddin himself was taken prisoner, tried and hanged. Four thousand of his followers were also killed (Eyuboğlu, 182-7).

A brief reference to Bedreddin's execution already occurs in a poem Nazım wrote in 1929, 'Kablettarih' (Prehistory; A 1, 110-1). According to Nail V, one of his fellow prisoners, Nazım started to compose an extended poem on this theme in 1933 while in Bursa prison. He even used to keep his companions awake at night reciting what he had written (Çakırhan, Interview, March 1996); some of the characters portrayed in the poem resemble them. The resulting· fifty-page poem is framed by a prose introduction recounting the poet's reactions on reading *Simavne Kadısı Oğlu Bedreddin*, a disdainful account of Bedreddin's exploits published in 1925 by the Islamic theologian Mehemmed Şerafeddin. Reading this book in prison late at night, he finds himself distracted by the clanking chains of other prisoners in nearby cells, who are under threat of execution. The poet's mood becomes anguished as he struggles to absorb the ideas of Bedreddin and his disciple Mustafa. 'I wish I had an aspirin,' he observes. 'If I didn't have this blinding headache, I would be able to hear the ceaseless clashing of swords, the neighing of horses, the cracking of whips, and I would be able to see the faces of Bedreddin and Mustafa like two shining promises of hope amid the screams of women and children' (A 2, 225).

This introduction establishes a self-reflexive narrative framework showing evocatively how the constraints of prison and its accompanying fear, frustration and insomnia may heighten the poet's imaginative powers. The main narrative takes the form of a dream – a journey through time in which a follower of Mustafa appears at the prison window, wearing a white shirt, to guide the poet back to the fifteenth century. The ensuing sequence of fifteen episodes combines poetry with prose, theatrical scenes with folkloric motifs, and culminates in the final defeat and death of Bedreddin at the hands of the Ottomans and the brutal execution of his followers. Although the poem has traditional epic qualities, Nazım does not entirely abandon the experimental techniques of the avant-garde. The originality of the work arises from the interweaving of present, past and future, linking Bedreddin's medieval crusade with the cause of modern communism. Words attributed in Nazım's source to Bedreddin and Mustafa are combined with contemporary allusions into a complex poetic montage with strong dialogue elements, incorporating traditional poetic rhythms and fragments of Turkish folksong, while evocative natural images suggest a parallel between the forces of revolution and the dialectic of nature.

The dreamlike narrative allows the poet the freedom to explore a wide range of characters and situations, from the Sultan's opulent palace, with its Bursa silks and ornamental tiles, to a scene on the malaria-ridden shores of Lake Iznik, where the children go hungry and a bare-footed woman weeps for her husband, who is in prison about to be executed for poaching a carp. Bedreddin is so horrified by this scene that he lays aside his scholarly writings and issues a passionate call to arms, proclaiming that the landowners must be put to the sword and the people freed from their sufferings. His followers Mustafa and Kemal, after kissing his hand to receive his blessings, ride off to raise the banner of revolt in other regions of Anatolia. Since Bedreddin also aims to abolish the laws discriminating against ethnic minorities, Mustafa is able to rally the support of Jewish converts and Greeks from the islands. Once the landlords of western Anatolia have been defeated, Bedreddin decides to return to the Balkans to extend the campaign, despite the news that the Sultan is marshalling the army and preparing a counter-attack.

The poem reaches its climax in the Ninth Canto, where the Sultan's army is confronted by 10,000 followers of Bedreddin led by Mustafa, including Turkish peasants, Greek sailors and Jewish merchants, all singing the same songs under their red and green flags:

> To be able to sing together,
> pulling the nets all together from the sea,
> together to forge the iron like a lace,
> all together to plough the soil,
> to be able to eat the honey-filled figs together
> > and to be able to say:
> > > everything but the cheek of the beloved
> > > > > we all share together
> > > > everywhere
> To achieve this
> > ten thousand heroes sacrificed their eight thousand ....
> > > (A 2, 246)

In the context of 1936 these lines can be read as a plea for solidarity in face of the fascist threat. So eloquent is Nazım's affirmation of 'togetherness' that Bedreddin's crusade becomes a timeless symbol of the need to transcend the divisions between different social groups, religions and races.

The outcome of the battle is that Mustafa and his followers are defeated with terrible losses. At this point the exalted epic

narrative is interrupted by the anguished reflections of the modern
poet:

> It's the necessary result
>   of historical, social and economic conditions –
>   don't tell me, I know!
> My head bows before the thing you mention.
> But my heart
>   doesn't speak that language.
>   (A 2, 247)

Here the tension between political analysis and poetic imagination
is made explicit. A footnote on the same page anticipates the
objections of more orthodox Marxists: 'He says his head accepts
the historical, social and economic conditions, but his heart still
burns. Well, just look at that Marxist!' Nazım's reply has become
justly celebrated: 'A Marxist is not a "mechanical man" or a robot,
but a concrete, historical, social human being with flesh and blood,
nerves, head and heart.'

Nazım uses the language of the heart to intensify the political
struggle. There follows a description of the execution of the rebels,
in which Mustafa's final lament becomes a paradigm for political
commitment. The spectacle of suffering – 'bare necks split like
pomegranates' – is counterbalanced in the Eleventh Canto, which
is in prose, by the defiant affirmation: 'Free man and the slave,
... oppressor and the oppressed, in a never-ending contradiction,
fighting against each other, sometimes openly sometimes discreetly,
have been involved in a continuous struggle'. Finally, in the Four-
teenth Canto, Bedreddin himself is captured and hanged from a
tree in the market place. But the text does not end here, on a
pessimistic note. The final sections, again in prose, bring us back
to Bursa prison. It is dawn and the poet, awaking from his reverie,
tells his fellow prisoners about the messenger in the white shirt
who has taken him on this epic journey. But his friend Şefik
points to an actual shirt hanging by the window, which he then
puts on with the words: 'You made your journey with my shirt.'
Yet the poet's vision is not presented merely as a fantasy; it is
confirmed by Ahmet, another prisoner, who recalls how he was
told the Bedreddin story by his grandfather during the Balkan
wars, when he was nine years old.

Nazım was not entirely satisfied with the book, which he later
described as 'hastily written, half finished' (B 1, 18), and so he

added a more explicitly political epilogue entitled 'National Pride' ('Milli Gurur'). This was published separately as a pamphlet, probably to reduce the risk of the whole book being confiscated. In it he elucidates his conception of patriotism by adding a dialogue between the poet and Ahmet. 'Yes, I do feel national pride', Ahmet declares, 'because even in feudal society the working people of my country (who form nine tenths of the population) created a movement that considered Greek sailors from Rhodes and Jewish merchants as their brothers' (A 2, 271). Nazım's own attitude to history is that of a poet committed not simply to lamenting the sufferings of the past but also to learning lessons for the future. His position is expressed in lines which have become famous:

> Do not weep friends, do not sigh,
> Connect yesterday with today,
> today with tomorrow!
> (A 2, 273)

The achievement of the poet is to rescue Ottoman history from the antiquarians and endow it with inspirational power.

The publication of *Sheikh Bedreddin*, even without the epilogue, provoked considerable controversy. It was perhaps surprising that it occurred at all, since new Penal Clauses based on Mussolini's fascist model were just being introduced into the Turkish constitution (the notorious Clauses 141 and 142) with the aim of suppressing all left-wing publications. This was indeed the last book by Nazım Hikmet to be published in Turkey for thirty years. The poem found admirers and detractors in both left-wing and right-wing camps. It was widely praised for its poetic qualities, for the vividness of detail and the musicality of its rhythm. More recently, the Turkish scholar Talat Sait Halman has suggested that it may well be Nazım's 'real masterpiece' (Halman, 28), and in 1994 Blasing and Konuk included an English version of the complete text in their edition of his poems (omitting only the epilogue on 'National Pride'). But other readers, especially from the communist camp, criticized the poem for being unduly emotional and nationalistic. It was to meet such criticisms that Nazım inserted at the end of the Ninth Canto the footnote defending his approach as that of a human being with 'flesh and blood, nerves, head and heart' (A 2, 247).

Nazım's political position is even more clearly defined in another publication of the mid-1930s attacking 'German Fascism and Racism' (*Alman Faşizmi ve Irkçılığı*, Adam, 24, 258-324). This 96-page pamphlet draws on a number of sources, analysing the function of fascism as a reactionary system designed to defend Western capitalism. Germany and Italy, he argues, are planning to gain a monopoly of natural resources in North Africa and to expand their markets in order to strengthen their economies. It is to justify their domination of Africa and other countries that they are developing racist ideologies. Hitler's foreign policy is inspired as much by the Thyssen steel company as by the theories of Alfred Rosenberg. A further, more popular contribution to the struggle against fascism was the novel *Kan Konuşmaz* (Blood Does Not Speak). On leaving Bursa prison in 1934, Nazım promised some of his fellow inmates that they would appear in a novel, although how far he actually planned this novel in prison is unclear. After his release and his marriage to Piraye, Nazım was conscious of the need to settle down and earn a regular income, as a responsible husband and as father to Piraye's children. This led him to accept his friend Naci Sadullah's suggestion that he write a novel for publication in *Son Posta*, owned by Zekeriya Sertel. Although Sertel expressed doubts about Nazım's political theme, serialisation began on 29 May 1936 under the pseudonym Orhan Selim, and the final instalment appeared in September. After animated discussions between Sertel and Nazım, the political message was toned down and the provocative final paragraph deleted. *Son Posta* published an interview with the author in which Nazım discussed the issues raised by the novel: 'Orhan Selim wants to emphasise that the relationship between people and their environment is not one way: human beings change their natural and social environment and that in itself results in changes in our own nature' (Sülker 4, 222).

The novel is set against the background of the Allied occupation of Istanbul, and deals partly with the resistance of the working class against occupying powers, partly with the theme of poverty and the oppression of the poor by the rich. Adapting a familiar romantic motif, it tells the story of the servant girl Gülizar who is seduced by Seyfi Bey, son of the wealthy family for whom she works. She loses her job after becoming pregnant, and a motherly, caring neighbour offers her a shoulder to cry on and a home where she can live, but soon gossip spreads around the

village that this woman's son Nuri Usta, a craftsman, is using her
as a prostitute. Nuri, an enlightened man, decides to marry Gülizar,
accepting responsibility for her pregnancy and adopting her child
Ömer. For a time all seems well, and indeed when Ömer grows
up he becomes a lawyer. But the fate of the poor still lies in
hands of the rich, epitomised by the unrepentant Seyfi Bey. Driving
his flashy car, Seyfi Bey runs over Nuri Usta and kills him. Ömer,
acting as a lawyer, prosecutes Seyfi for murder. Realising that his
life is at stake, Seyfi acknowledges his responsibilties for the birth
of Ömer and offers Ömer his name and inheritance, appealing
to the principle of family solidarity: 'Wouldn't your blood cry
out against you because you put your own flesh-and-blood father
in prison?' But Ömer's response is very different: 'No!...Because
against wicked human beings, it is not blood but reason that
speaks out...: *blood does not speak.*'

The clear implication, as Brecht later suggested in *The Caucasian
Chalk Circle*, is that social commitments far outweigh ties of blood.
In both works, the device of a trial scene is used to emphasize
the primacy of rational argument over inherited prejudice; literary
form is harmonized with an underlying didactic purpose. Nazım's
novel proved so popular that Suat Derviş, the woman author and
a close friend of Nazım's, was given the task of asking him to
write another novel to be serialised in *Son Posta*. But instead of
a novel Nazım offered to write a regular column for the paper,
to be published anonymously. There followed a series of articles
entitled 'The People's Ear and Voice' ('Halkın Kulağı, Halkın
Sesi'), accompanied by eye-catching illustrations, which focused
on current social and economic problems (Sülker 4, 225). During
1936-7 Nazım also wrote for several other newspapers. A major
theme was provided by the events of the Spanish Civil War,
which he was able to follow in the foreign press. Soon after its
outbreak he published an article in *Akşam* (26 July 1936) under
the pseudonym Orhan Selim setting out his own position: 'If
these extreme right-wing anarchists are successful in Spain, world
peace and the democracy which forms the basis of the world
peace will receive a severe wound. Spain will no longer be an
agent of peace but will become an agent of war. This is another
reason why all nations who are defending world peace are watching
Spain with concern' (A 24, 171). The conflicting news about the

progress of the war which he found in the foreign press provided the basis for further articles in *Akşam*.

The Spanish Civil War was notable for the international involvement of poets and intellectuals. In the summer of 1936 Nazım read in the French papers about the killing of Frederico Garcia Lorca. Since he had not heard of the Spanish poet and dramatist before, he resolved to track down as much information about him as he could, but in the Turkish libraries he could only find a few scraps of biographical information. In February 1937 events took a new turn when the International Brigade was formed to help defend Madrid. News that Ilya Ehrenburg and many European left-wing intellectuals had joined it soon reached Turkey, and Nazım's reaction in *Akşam* and *Tan* was enthusiastic. This provoked such a sceptical response in Babıali that jokes began to circulate: 'Did you hear that Nazım has joined Ilya Ehrenburg in Bilbao with the French Brigade?' – 'Where did you hear that?' –'I imagined it' (Sülker 4, 125). Although Nazım did not join the brigade, he organised a campaign in support of the Republicans in 1937 and wrote a number of poems about the war including the often reprinted 'Travelling to Barcelona with the Boat of the Ill-fated Yusuf'. This catches the mood of the moment, expressing the fantasy of joining the fight against the fascism with Yusuf, who is in prison for smuggling after being caught in a stolen boat ('Talihsiz Yusuf'un Gemisile Barselon'a Seyahat', A 4, 21).

This poem is in four parts, the most dramatic being the final section, 'Karanlıkta Kar Yağıyor' ('It is Snowing in the Dark', 1937), which again expresses the poet's longing to be in Spain with the International Brigade:

> It's snowing in the dark,
> You are at the gates of Madrid.
> Against you is an army killing
> every precious thing we have:
>   hope, longing, freedom and children
> [...]
> I can neither be with you
>   nor can I send you a case of bullets
>
>   a basket of eggs
>   or a pair of woollen socks
> Yet I know that,
> In this cold snowy night

Your feet guarding the gates of Madrid are wet,
shivering like two naked children.
(A 4, 28)

This poem appeared in *Haber-Akşam Postası* in January 1938 (A 4, 21). By then Franco's armies were making dramatic advances and civilians being evacuated from Madrid.

Spain represented the first great test for the popular front against fascism. For Nazım himself, the idea of forming an anti-fascist alliance with other political groups took a very specific form – a meeting with his former comrade Şevket Süreyya, now a head of department in the Ministry for Economic Affairs. After being released from prison in April 1937, Nazım paid one of his rare visits to Ankara, ostensibly to stay with a relative. However, the underlying purpose of the visit was political. In an extended interview recalling what took place, serialized in the weekly journal *Yön* in 1967, Süreyya starts out from the assumption that Nazım was a poet of social conscience, rather than a dogmatic Marxist. Surely it should be possible to find common ground in the struggle against fascism – after all, Atatürk himself was anti-fascist. He put it to Nazım that the most urgent political and social problems of the day could be addressed without insisting on communism as the only solution. If only he would distance himself from the Communist Party, he would no longer need to live in fear of being arrested every few months. Süreyya arranged for Nazım to meet senior representatives of the Turkish government, hoping that he could be brought to his senses and induced to change sides. Although Nazım expressed strong reservations, a dinner was arranged by Sadri Ertem, a journalist he had known since they worked together for *Resimli Ay*. Those invited included Şükrü Kaya, the Minister of the Interior, and Şükrü Sökmensüer, Chief of State Security, a veteran of the War of Liberation who had been Ismet Pasha's personal bodyguard.

The evening began on a light-hearted note with Süreyya introducing Nazım to the security chief with the words: 'The man you are after has been caught and I am handing him over to your authority.' Everyone laughed, and Nazım was soon his old familiar self, amiable, humorous and sincere. While they waited for the Minister of the Interior to arrive, an animated discussion developed between Nazım and Sökmensüer. When Nazım began holding forth about capitalism, imperialism and world revolution,

Sökmensüer politely replied: 'That's all very well, but do you mean us [the Kemalists] when you denounce the capitalists and imperialists? Wasn't it we who fought against them? Look out of the window, you will see Ankara struggling to develop. [...] Don't we all have a duty to serve this cause – scientists, ordinary people, poets, civil servants?' The atmosphere became so relaxed that Nazım was persuaded to read one of his poems. When he read the great poem about the Spanish Civil War, even the hard-bitten security chief was moved to tears. For him, however, the parallel with the Turkish War of Liberation was most significant: 'What is expressed in this poem is a popular uprising, like our own war of liberation. But, Nazım, isn't a shame that no Turkish poet has ever written our legend of liberation? The Spanish Civil War is child's play compared with the uprising and the war of liberation of the Turkish people. You should write an epic about our own war of liberation.' More poems were recited and the discussion went on into the small hours. They parted on good terms, with Süreyya quoting an anecdote from the French nineteenth century: 'Do you remember Proudhon saying that he dined with the Police Chief and campaigned for revolution at the same time?' Nazım was driven back to his relative's home in the security chief's car.

In the event Şükrü Kaya had been prevented from attending the dinner, so the following morning Sökmensuer collected Nazım and drove him to his Ministry. This time the atmosphere was less easy, and Kaya was quick to come to the point:

Europe is under a heavy black cloud. [...] We are ready to defend our country against this dangerous fire. [...] But we also need to feel secure about our rear-guard. Your group is causing us concern, Nazım. [...] We cannot ignore the fact that during the last few years there have been so many underground newspapers, illegal leaflets and pamphlets published in this country. [...] Why don't you direct your attacks against the religious fanatics instead of the government? Don't the six principles of the Republican People's Party constitute your safety and your future security too?

At this point Nazım attempted to dissociate himself from the activities of the Turkish Communist Party, pointing out that he himself had been expelled. But the Minister replied that one did not have to be a Party member to produce left-wing anti-government propaganda, which was precisely why Nazım had been arrested and imprisoned several times. Hence he did not mince his words:

'We have warned you several times, Nazım, but you pretended you did not understand. Be realistic, all the members of the Turkish Communist Party are in our hands. [...] We are hoping to rescue you from this dilemma. That is why you are here, isn't it?' The message was clear: 'Anyone who is not with us is against us.' Nazım became increasingly uneasy at the turn the conversation had taken, realizing that he was being given a final warning. He left this meeting with the Minister's final words echoing in his ears: 'I cannot be in every police station at once. [...] Phone me if you face any injustice' (*Yön*, 20 & 27 January and 3 February 1967).

Nazım returned to Istanbul without making any concessions. He was far too principled to bow to the blandishments of politicians, and he had a poet's pride in his independence. For Nazım, as for his early model Rosa Luxemburg, freedom was essentially the freedom to think differently. His Marxism was indeed humanist in inspiration, but those who believed the poetry could be detached from politics were mistaken. The poet who praised the heroic republican resistance in the Spanish Civil War was not an opportunist like W. H. Auden, author of another celebrated poem about Spain, whose enthusiasm for the revolutionary struggle evaporated when the going got tough. Nazım was a poet with a purpose, combining Auden's captivating eloquence with Luxemburg's revolutionary fervour. He had no illusions about the threat to his own freedom, and although he did not fight in Spain, he certainly made his own sacrifices in the fight against fascism. In January 1938, during a massive anti-communist purge, he was arrested again. It is clear that his Marxism was by no means a 'borrowed shirt'. For Nazım politics and poetry formed a single fabric, binding the coarse fibres of commitment with the pliant strands of the imagination – 'all together' (as he puts it in *Taranta-Babu*) 'as if weaving the most wonderful silk cloth'.

5

The Army and Navy Trials
1938–1940

The increasingly authoritarian climate in Turkey in the late 1930s meant that even the most innocent actions were liable to be misconstrued, as the following episode shows. Leaving work at the film studios on the evening of 30 December 1936, Nazım dropped in at his usual café, put his cap on the table, glanced through the newspaper and then laid it on top of his cap. He was promptly arrested by three plain-clothes police, who were convinced that this gesture was a coded signal to members of a conspiratorial group (Sülker 4, 141–3). Taken to Sansaryan Han detention centre, he was accused with thirteen others of belonging to an illegal organisation and held in prison for more than three months, only being released on bail on 17 April 1937. Since the civil courts could not be relied on to suppress political dissent, reactionary figures in parliament and the high command decided on a different course of action. Realizing that they could not convict him for communist propaganda through the civil courts, one right-wing deputy declared: 'We must have him tried by Special Emergency Military Courts' (Coşkun, 116). The ensuing campaign was evidently planned in the corridors of power even before events at the Military Academy provided a pretext.

The red scare at the Military Academy

The Turkish military academies attracted bright children from a wide range of social backgrounds, including peasants and poor urban families. Admission these institutions was highly competitive, since they provided a privileged education paid for by the state as well as access to a prestigious profession. But the aim of training intelligent young officers can produce paradoxical results, since students may develop ideas of their own at odds with the military establishment. During the late 1930s, following the example of Germany and Italy, the army high command became increasingly reactionary. The long-serving Chief of Staff, Fevzi Çakmak, even disapproved of soldiers reading newspapers, which he regarded as an un-military activity (Ahmad, 9). Çakmak, a devout Muslim with a distinguished war record, had been trained in Germany before the First World War, and his political sympathies lay with the Pan-Turanists. At both in the Kuleli Military School in Istanbul and the Ankara Military Academy there were heated debates between nationalists and progressives. In the early months of 1937 a group of students in their final year at Kuleli began reading left-wing books, even forming a group to discuss politics whose leading figures were Ömer Deniz, A. (Abdul) Kadir, Orhan Alkaya, Necati Çelik and Şadi Alkılıç. Orhan, unlike the others, came from a wealthy family, and the group would spend their week-end leaves at his home in Istanbul, discussing literature and politics and even reciting Nazım's poetry. They made no secret of their left-wing sympathies, and a leading figure from the nationalist camp, Süreyya Koç, succeeded in gaining their confidence and obtaining inside information about their activities. Süreyya fervently believed it was the duty of followers of Atatürk to crush communism, a view shared by Fuat Uluç, Saim Sonbaz and Sami Küçük, all of whom later had successful military careers. In a memoir published many years later, Fuat recalls that they were appalled by the 'yapping of Nazım's poetry' (Uluç, 65-8).

Süreyya's group also had their favourite authors, and decided to retaliate by organising recitations of nationalistic poetry. When they tried to force the leftists to listen to Sadık Aran's celebration of the heroic deeds of the Ottomans, fighting broke out between them, and Nazım's followers were beaten up. They were too intimidated to complain to the authorities and felt obliged to keep a low profile until they graduated from the military school in June 1937. In the summer holidays they were posted to different parts of Turkey for military experience, but the new academic year brought both groups together again in October, when they were admitted to the Harbiye Military Academy in Ankara. This time Süreyya and his friends were determined to gather evidence that would utterly discredit their rivals. Ömer formed a new group called the 'Populists and Peasants', which included a number of civilians. They allegedly addressed each other as 'comrade', and Ömer would circulate pamphlets about Marx and Engels or works by Maxim Gorki or André Malraux for discussion at their meetings. Among Nazım's writings they particularly admired 'Salkım Söğüt' (Weeping Willow) and *Benerci*. According to Fuat Uluç the biggest menace was 'that poisonous snake called Nazım'. If the authorities had taken precautions against him sooner, 'the red menace would not have grown out of proportion' (Uluç, 69). Fuat's uses racial terminology in an attempt to discredit Nazım, suggesting that he is not of Turkish blood: 'He is anything but a Turk. [...] He is the enemy of this country, a traitor' (Uluç, 26-9). Even Allah is invoked in this invective: 'We may wish that Allah will help them to change, in vain. [...] Only the angel of death will change them, but unfortunately he is taking such a long time' (Uluç, 134).

In the eyes of the establishment any form of reading outside the curriculum was suspect. 'There was a revolt in Military Academy', A. Kadir ironically recalls. 'Not a single hand touched a gun. But it was still considered a revolt – a revolt of a different kind: Books were being read in the academy – books other than textbooks. Nobody could understand why in a military academy people should read Balzac, Zola, Tolstoy, Anatole France, Gorki, Pirandello, Dostoyevsky. [...] We were reading books on the Spanish Civil War, the history of imperialism, Goethe's *Faust*, Gogol, Turgenev or Ibsen' (Kadir, 11). Stimulated by the books in the library of his father who was a teacher, Ömer dreamed of becoming a journalist, and such was his enthusiasm for Nazım's poetry that while still in Istanbul he hit on the idea of visiting his hero in person. In October 1937, shortly before leaving for Ankara, he visited Nazım at his workplace in Ipek Studios. 'Many friends in the military school read your books,' he explained after an initial exchange of greetings, 'and we have ideological discussions and try to enlarge our knowledge' (Sülker 4, 128). Nazım, suspecting a trap, cut him short and sent him away. Assuming that Ömer must be a provocateur, he phoned the chief of police in great indignation, asking him to stop sending such obvious informers. He had already had to cope with police agents disguised as plumbers and electricians and certainly was not going to be fooled by one in a military uniform.

Ömer seems simply to have wanted to meet his favourite author, and there is no evidence that he was a police spy. The irony is that such an innocent encounter should have led to one of the most vindictive witch-hunts in modern Turkish history. Ömer later recalled that he felt hurt at the brush-off he received from Nazım on his first visit. Three months later, on the eve of Ramadan (December 1937), he decided to try again, calling at the house Nazım shared with family. On this occasion Ömer was absent from the Academy without permission, a punishable offence which would almost certainly draw attention to him (Kadir, 26). Nazım was out shopping with his wife Piraye, but Ömer gained the confidence of his stepmother by pretending that he had an appointment (Sülker 4, 131). When Nazım returned with Piraye, he brusquely asked him what he wanted, to which Ömer (according to his subsequent testimony) replied: 'I told you that I am an admirer of yours. I have been reading some books and there are some things I don't understand.' He wanted to know all about Feuerbach, Marx and Engels, and above all what they should teach to other young soldiers when they finished military school. Nazım responded with understandable caution: 'On this subject you can find the answers in any encyclopaedia. [. . .] I am not a scientist, philosopher or teacher of economics.' Instead he recommended Ömer to teach the six principles of the Turkish constitution. Then, to every one's amazement, Nazım lost his temper and said: 'Now I am going to ask you a question: Where did you learn that I live at this address? [. . .] You got it from the police, didn't you? Now, get out of here, and I don't ever want to see you again!' (Sülker 5, 23-5). On his return to Ankara, Ömer proudly reported his conversation to his comrades, who included right-wing informers. Members of the nationalist group sent an anonymous letter to the Chief of Staff, denouncing Ömer for visiting Nazım (Uluç, 105). The authorities acted immediately, arresting a group of students whose main offence was their passion for poetry.

The Ankara trial

Since the eyes of the world were on the show trials in Moscow, Ankara's secret trials in 1938 almost passed unnoticed. It is only through the personal reminiscences of the accused that events can be reconstructed. Kadir has left a vivid description of the first wave of arrests, which began in January: 'In the middle of a lesson, the doors suddenly opened and a military judge, a duty officer, two sergeants and a corporal entered our class room. [...] The officer asked us to put our hands on the table and not to speak or move. [...] He took a paper out of his pocket and read people's names' (Kadir, 13). The students were then taken to the dormitories where their belongings were searched – even the pillow cases were stripped off. Twenty-three students were taken for questioning and then held under arrest in the school building. First, they were questioned by the public prosecutor, a military judge named Şerif Budak. Kadir had to explain how he acquired a copy of *Benerci*. When Şadi Alkılıç, another student with literary aspirations, was asked why he had books by Nazım, he replied: 'I also read other Turkish poets like Fuzuli. Why don't you ask about them?' The main purpose of the interrogation was to identify their leader and to discover who was supporting them outside the Academy, and they were repeatedly questioned about their alleged links with Nazım (Kadir, 60-5).

On the day of his arrest, 17 January 1938, Nazım was visiting his cousin Celalettin Ezine to discuss a project for a new literary magazine. His wife Piraye, who had decided to stay at home in Nişantaşı, had unexpected visitors: two groups of police, one sent to search the house, the other arriving later after raiding Ipek Studios. Nazım's house was searched and his books, manuscripts and papers were confiscated. Four policemen then arrested Nazım, and he spent the night in a cell at the police headquarters, wondering what could be the pretext for his arrest this time (Kadir, 23). He imagined he would soon be released, since he was no longer a party member and had kept his head down, intent on earning enough to support his family. But after questioning he was transferred to Ankara, travelling in a third-class carriage escorted by three policemen (Sülker 5, 42-4). Ankara's military prison was in Soğukkuyu, a bleak and isolated place outside the city. Here Nazım was held in solitary confinement and questioned about his relationship with Ömer. Why did he give his books to students at the Military Academy? What information did he give them about different political systems? He discovered that he was charged, under Article 94 of the military criminal code, with conspiring to cause soldiers to defy military discipline (Sebük, 88). Since he had himself reported the visit of Ömer Deniz to the police, he was confident that the charge would be dropped. The first person he wrote to, when on 28 January he was allowed to write letters, was naturally Piraye (AM 1, 65). His feelings during his first two months in prison are reflected in a group of poems entitled 'Letters from a Man in Solitary Confinement' ('Bir Cezaevinde Tecritteki Adamın Mektupları'). The first of them, like so many of his poems from prison, is addressed to Piraye:

> I carved your name
> on my watchband with my finger nail.
> [. . .]
> For me to talk to anyone other than myself
> is forbidden
> So I talk to myself.
> But as I find my conversation so boring
> I sing instead to my darling wife.
> (A 3, 139)

The poet acknowledges the fear that deprivation of human contact will prove both psychologically and physically debilitating. It was Piraye's letters which gave him the resilience to cope with prison conditions. One of her few surviving ones gives a vivid impression:

5 March 1938

My darling Nazım
    Please do not feel sad. When you are sad, we suffer more. [...] I was always the happiest woman in the world when I was with you, and I shall always remain so. You gave me the most beautiful works of your life, you wrote the most beautiful love poems for me, you wrote powerful works when you were with me, all your works contain part of me. [...] You even have a few lines on your forehead because of me. [...] We are not two people but one [...] (AM 1, 74)

Unfortunately, Piraye soon found herself in financial difficulties, since she now had to support a family on her own (money owed to Nazım by the newspaper *Haber* and by Ipek Film Studios was not paid at once). She thus had to give up her own home and move in with her sister in Erenköy (AM 1, 68 & 75).

    After many days in solitary confinement he was at last allowed to sit outside. It was this liberating experience which inspired 'Today is Sunday' ('Bugün Pazar'):

> Today is Sunday.
> Today, for the first time, they took me out in the sun.
> I just stood there, for the first time in my life, struck by
> how far away the sky is,

how blue
and how wide.
Then I reverently sat down on the earth,
leaning my back against the wall.
At this moment, no trap to fall into,
at this moment no struggle, no freedom, no wife.
Only the earth, the sun and me . . . .
I am happy . . . .
(A 3, 142)

This was the first of many poems which defiantly affirmed life in the shadow of the prison walls.

Since it was clear that the trials must have been orchestrated by the government, Nazım's family tried to appeal to higher authority. Both his mother and his sister paid visits to government officials attempting at least to get him released on bail. There was a possibility that Şükrü Kaya, the Interior Minister who had given Nazım a friendly warning the previous year, might intervene. Nazım himself suggested that Piraye and his mother should ask Ali Fuat Cebesoy to intervene (Kadir, 160 & 170). On 9 March 1938 Cebesoy accompanied Atatürk on a visit to a silk factory in Gemlik. During the meal the subject of Nazım's arrest was discussed, and Cebesoy tried to find an opportunity to warn Atatürk of the plot against Nazım. But according to the poet Nizamettin Nazif, who was present during this discussion, Şükrü Kaya dissuaded Cebesoy from raising the issue, pointing out that even Atatürk would not be able to overrule the Chief of Staff on a question of military discipline (Sülker 5, 64-6). Atatürk was in any case terminally ill, and power was slipping from his hands.

The trials, which began on 1 March 1938, took place at a military court in the Ankara Military Academy, where the students were still held (AM 1, 77). Nazım had hoped to be represented by an Istanbul lawyer, Irfan Emin Kösemihaloğlu, who had defended him in previous cases, but the authorities insisted that the accused should be represented by members of the Ankara bar. At last two pupils of Kösemihaloğlu, willing to risk their reputations by defending a communist, Ömer Fuat Keskinoğlu and Saffet Nezihi Bölükbaşı, came forward, but they paid their first visit to Nazım in prison only a few days before the trials began. According to protocol the five judges, even in a military court, should all have had legal qualifications, but in this trial four were army officers with no real legal training. The senior judge Kazım Yalman, the only professionally trained member of the court, was later described by one of the defence lawyers as a 'well-known sadist' (Aksoy, 31-5), and the public prosecutor Şerif Budak, who had handled the preliminary interrogations, was almost equally authoritarian. To keep the lawyers in line the court was presided over by another army officer, Lieutenant-Colonel Fahri.

For the students in the dock the atmosphere was intimidating. 'We were taken to the courtrooms by armed gendarmes,' Kadir recalled. 'Behind the first row of chairs were school desks. We all took our seats, everybody was there except Nazım.' The poet's arrival created a stir: 'He entered the room with a bright face glowing like a sunflower in the sun. His sparkling eyes scanned us, as if caressing us all; greeting us one by one, he hurried to take a chair in the front row.' Nazım was wearing an old coat and a grey trilby hat with a large brim. Once the members of court were seated, the accused heard noises outside – militant anti-communists shouting abuse that seemed to shake the whole building (Kadir, 77). Nazım found himself in the dock with no less than twenty-seven others, twenty of them students from the Academy, two high school students, one student from the Law Faculty, and four workers. On Friday 11 March he received the text of the charges. Under Article 94 of the Military Criminal Code he was accused on three main counts: conspiring with more than one person to encourage acts of military insubordination (minimum sentence five years); inciting a revolt against army discipline (minimum of ten years); and causing a mutiny (mandatory death penalty). They all sat in silence as the four-page indictment was read by the public prosecutor. It described how Ömer visited Nazım and allegedly received directives from him. One of the principal pieces of evidence was a document written by Ömer and his friends on 'How to organise oneself for good living', consisting of twenty-two precepts like getting up early, doing exercises and making new friends (Kadir, 41). Worse still was the undisputed evidence of the group's literary interests.

In addition to Nazım, the other alleged ringleaders, Ömer Deniz and Mustafa Ergun, were accused the capital offence of incitement to mutiny. At first Nazım found it hard to take the charges seriously. There was no evidence of any conspiracy apart from the fact that he had been visited by a student, so he confidently expected the

charges to be dismissed (AM 1, 79). According to Article 94, the
charge of conspiracy required evidence of contacts with at least
two other persons, whereas the evidence showed that Ömer was
his only contact. Nazım was the first to take the stand. He explained
that he had only met Ömer twice and that in both cases he was
an uninvited guest. After the first visit he had even informed the
police, suspecting him of being an informer – a suspicion which
he was never entirely able to dismiss (Dinamo, 26). Ömer's
evidence, extracted during the pre-trial interrogation, did at one
point appear to compromise him, since he allegedly claimed that
during his second visit he received from Nazım the following
guidance: 'The biggest danger Turkey is facing at the moment
is fascism. [...] Once you start serving in the army, you must
instruct the peasant soldiers first about the republic and then about
communism' (Coşkun, 124). During the trial Ömer retracted this
statement, claiming that he made it under duress. But the judges
ruled that all testimony recorded during the pre-trial interrogations
was admissible. Since the principal interrogator and the public
prosecutor were one and the same person, no objections were
raised (Sülker 5, 107 & 110).

The charge that the students had been reading subversive books
led to one of the most interesting exchanges, shedding light on
the function of imaginative writing in a society when there were
few other sources of social criticism. 'Of course I would read
books by Maxim Gorki and Nazım Hikmet,' Kadir explained.
'When anybody mentions poverty, and the gap between the poor
and the rich, they are immediately thought to be communists.
One day our rich neighbours sent us a plate of food. We couldn't
eat it because the food had gone stale and was inedible. Because
we were poor, we were not considered human. From that day
onwards I couldn't stand the sight of the rich' (Kadir, 83). This
speech brought tears to people's eyes, but the judges were convinced
that these young men had been converted to communism. As
the case continued, Nazım nervously began to twiddle his moustache. One of the military judges, a stickler for discipline, denounced
this as an act of insubordination. Noticing that this same officer
was continuously playing with his prayer-beads, Nazım replied
that in a secular state this ritual constituted a far more serious
contempt of court. In his closing statement he insisted on the
distinction between personal beliefs, which were not a crime even

under military law, and political actions: 'Yes I am a communist. [...] These are my ideas and ideals. But I do not subject anyone to communist propaganda. [...] One cannot bring about communism by converting a couple of students at military school' (Kadir, 95-7).

On 29 March, after four days devoted to statements by the defence, the prisoners took their seats in the court for the last time. Twelve fully armed soldiers entered the room, a clear sign that harsh sentences were about to be passed. Judge Kazım Yalman read out the verdict and sentences. Nazım was found guilty under Article 94 of inciting a revolt in the army and sentenced to fifteen years' imprisonment, the heavy penalty reflecting the fact that he had previous convictions for illegal political activity. Ömer Deniz was sentenced to nine years on the same count, reduced seven and a half years because he was under twenty-one. Of the remaining twenty-seven defendants, twenty-three were acquitted for lack of any plausible evidence. Four others were sentenced to between eleven and fourteen years, but those under twenty-one had their sentences reduced to five or six years. Even those acquitted lost their right to become officers (*Tan*, March 1967). Reacting to his harsh sentence in a letter to Piraye, Nazım drew the obvious parallel: 'With a decision resembling the conviction of Dreyfus, I have been given a fifteen-year prison sentence,' he writes. 'It is obvious that the people presiding over the court were out to see me buried alive.' Writing to his mother he tries to imagine what it will be like when he is finally released, 'fifty-two years old, crippled and brain-dead' (AM 1, 85). But there was still hope that justice would prevail when the case went to appeal.

The Court of Appeal and the Chief of Staff

The military prison, where Nazım was now joined by his fellow 'conspirators', became more sociable. Quarters were less confined than at the Military Academy, and the four friends Ömer, Kadir, Necati and Orhan were together again. They were even allowed out into the prison courtyard, where they would gather round the fountain under the poplars and acacias. When Ali Fuat Cebesoy visited the prison, he was surprised to see such a youthful crowd – scarcely hardened revolutionaries. At first it was felt that Nazım was too dangerous to be permitted to associate with these impressionable young men, but soon the commandant relented (Kadir, 159-60). They were allowed books and paper and the use of a table in a room next to Nazım's. Soon a new form of 'social family' was created, with the prisoners sharing cooking duties and supplementing the insipid prison diet with occasional delicacies. Smoking provided an additional diversion, although Nazım insisted on buying the cheapest brand of cigarettes so that supplies would not run out too quickly. Having a captive audience was an inspiration for the poet, and they would spend the evenings under the trees, talking and teaching each other songs. Sometimes Nazım would talk about writers and artists he admired, such as Cervantes, Balzac, Stendhal, Chekhov, Gorki, Jack London and Charlie Chaplin. In the evenings he would lie on his bed with a cigarette packet at hand, holding forth about political economy or reciting poetry. He shared with the students his enthusiasm for French literature, stressing the importance of being open to other cultures (he could recite Baudelaire by heart). After everyone had gone to bed, he would work on a novel to be entitled 'Ali ile Mustafa'; and the next morning the students would copy his drafts into a yellow book (Kadir, 156).

Nazım also had a white notebook from which he would read his latest poems, 'surging like a waterfall' (as Kadir recalls). But he was really writing for another audience – the wife he had left behind. In this notebook he had written Piraye's words: 'Buy yourself a notebook, write down what you see and what you hear. I am sure they will be as good as your letters. Signed Piraye' (Kadir, 120). In a letter of 24 May 1938 Nazım tells Piraye that when his watch stopped, he removed the hands and replaced them with a photo of her with her children (AM 1, 97). He loved talking about Piraye and telling everyone what a wonderful woman she was: 'She has suffered a lot because of me,' he explained to Kadir. 'Once there were forty of us in prison, and she wanted me to have some eggs. She knew that I would not eat them unless I was able to share with the others, so she sent forty eggs [...] Whenever I showed signs of becoming lazy, she would lock me into my room and bring me cups of coffee so that I could really work. This is how I finished 'Sheik Bedreddin' and 'German Fascism and Racism' in a small attic flat' (Kadir, 136).

During the two months spent waiting for the Appeal Court, Nazım for the first time suffered from nightmares, when he would wake up screaming. To calm his nerves he announced that he was going to take up painting and even produced a group portrait of some of the prisoners. He would also fantasize about his bright future as a writer or even as a film director. On 24 May Nazım received two visitors, his aunt Sara and his relative Ali Fuat Cebesoy (Kadir, 159-64). The decision of the Appeal Court was expected any moment, and Cebesoy was optimistic. On 28 May tension in the prison was high as they awaited the crucial telephone call (AM 1, 99). Everyone, including the prison governor, woke early, but Nazım stayed in his room reading a book. Others were discussing whether they would be travelling to Istanbul by train or by air, when the telephone rang. It was Orhan's father with the news that the appeals of his son and two others had been at least partly successful, since they were allowed a retrial. But the appeals of Nazım and Ömer were rejected (Kadir, 172-6). After hearing the news, Nazım went back to his room and lay there stunned, gazing at the ceiling.

Once again Piraye's letters helped: 'I got your letter,' Nazım wrote on the 31 May 1938. 'It did me the world of good. I am strong, at a certain level one does not feel the pain of the disaster any more. Believe me, the days I shall spend inside, shut away from the world, will be less painful, less hurtful and less worrying than your years, alone among people'. He hoped to be transferred to a civilian prison nearer home, where he could work to earn money. His worst fear was to be sent to some remote place like Diyarbakır, where there would be no prospect of work. 'They might exile me into one of those prisons. [...] That would mean that they also sentence me to starvation' (AM 1, 100). Nazım wrote to the Minister of the Interior, Şükrü Kaya, asking to be transferred to a more modern prison like that on Imralı island. He also asked his mother to influence the authorities over this. Celile responded quickly, arriving in Ankara on 8 June (AM 1, 102). She wept at the sight of so many fine young men in prison. The supplies she brought – cigarettes, olives and home-made jams to be shared among the prisoners – offered scant consolation. But since his mother was an artist, Nazım tried to make the most of her visit by picking up a few tips about how to complete the portraits he was working on. Piraye was unable to visit him, but continued to give comfort with her letters. On 10 June she wrote promising that she would follow him wherever he might be transferred

(AM 1, 103). Nazım, in a mood of despondency, had apparently written suggesting that she divorce him, fearing that his long imprisonment would put an intolerable strain on her. Piraye's answer became celebrated among their friends: 'I want you to know that even if you were sentenced for 101 years, I will stand by you' (Kadir, 181). On 13 June Nazım was transferred to a civilian prison in Ankara, and soon afterwards to Sultanahmet prison in Istanbul. Now at least he was near the wife he longed to see. However, his transfer to Istanbul meant no softening in the attitude of the authorities; on the conrary, they intended to confront him with further charges.

There can be little doubt that the long sentences imposed on Nazım and Ömer reflected the right-wing political agenda that was emerging in 1938. In Germany and Spain and with the Italian conquest of Ethiopia the advance of fascism seemed unstoppable. The Military Academy trial coincided in mid-March with one of Hitler's greatest political triumphs, the annexation of Austria. Within the next six months the weakness of the Western democracies became ever more apparent as Hitler, through a mixture of threats and diplomacy, succeeded in having the German occupation of the Sudetenland sanctioned by the Munich agreement. These events greatly boosted the faction in the Turkish army which dreamed of a dictatorship on the German model. While Nazım and his fellow political prisoners awaited news of their appeal, the struggle for power in Ankara approached its climax. Although it was İnönü, hero of the war of liberation, who would succeed Atatürk as President, he was in no position to challenge the growing predominance of right-wingers in the government. The most powerful figure behind the scenes was Fevzi Çakmak; a contemporary observer records that it was he who took the decision to launch a 'radical operation to put a stop to communist propaganda in the army' (Aksoy, 37).

Çakmak was a formidable antagonist. He belonged to a generation of Turkish officers who had been trained in imperial Germany before the First World War and particularly admired the German concept of discipline (Weisband, 250-1, fn). He had even fought alongside German units in the War against Allenby's army in Palestine. After winning further honours in the war of liberation, he was appointed Chief of Staff in 1925, a post he held till his retirement in 1944 at the age of sixty-eight. His relationship with the political leadership, especially with Inönü as Prime Minister and subsequently as President, was tense. Inönü's pro-Western tendencies and cautious neutrality formed a marked contrast to Çakmak's authoritarianism. Together with General Ali Ihsan Sabis, editor of the *Türkische Post*, Çakmak was one of the principal proponents of a pro-German realignment of Turkish foreign policy, and in private conversations denounced Inönü's caution as cowardice (Weisband, 247-9). While the outcome of Nâzım's appeal was in the balance, the right-wingers led by Çakmak were tilting it against him. Indeed the Minister of the Interior, Şükrü Kaya, who had originally shown some sympathy for Nâzım's plight, suggested to Çakmak that they might capitalise on their success by launching a similar purge in the navy. On 10 June 1938 Çakmak circulated a memorandum about the alleged activities of the Communist Party to all members of the armed forces: 'Nowadays', he claimed, 'the communist party slogan is no longer "Workers of the world unite!" [...] They are aiming to dismantle the discipline of the army by encouraging the army staff to rebel against their superiors.' This memorandum had a double aim: to extend the anti-communist witch-hunt and persuade the courts to apply the military criminal code more severely. According to Çakmak the Military Academy case highlighted the inadequacies of the laws for dealing with communist subversion in the army, and he insisted that major changes in the law were needed. On 6 July 1938, within a month of his memorandum, Articles 141 and 142 were amended to make the dissemination of communist ideas a criminal offence (Sülker 5, 70, 137 & 251).

Justice at sea

While Nâzım was still in the Ankara military prison, the communist witch-hunt was being extended to Istanbul. The leaders of the underground movement, Hikmet Kıvılcımlı and his wife Fatma Nudiye Yalçı, had been arrested on 25 April 1938 – a predictable gambit to forestall May Day demonstrations. This led to a raid on a watchmaker's shop, where the nineteen-year-old Kerim Korcan worked with his father. Kerim was in the habit of buying books and magazines from a left-wing bookstore owned by Hikmet Kıvılcımlı, and works by Nâzım were among the items confiscated. Kerim admitted under pressure that he had passed books on to his brother Haydar, who was serving as a technician on the training ship *Yavuz*, anchored near Erdek on the southren shore of the Sea of Marmara (Sülker 5, 146). Among the items confiscated at the watchmaker's shop was a photograph showing Kerim's brother Haydar with a naval petty officer, Seyfi Tekdilek. This led to the interrogation of Seyfi, who was forced to disclose the names of other contacts, which led to a wave of further arrests (Sayılgan, 219). The writer Kemal Tahir, later one of Nazım's closest friends, was among those detained, since his brother Nuri was in the navy.

Turkish justice now passed into the hands of the captain of the *Yavuz*. Under its original name *Goeben,* this German-built battle-cruiser had played a ominous role in European politics in 1914, bringing Turkey into the war on the German side (Fig. 13). Soon after his transfer to Istanbul, Nazım was ferried across the Sea of Marmara to the *Yavuz*, and there incarcered 101 steps below the main deck in a hold once used to accommodate pigs when the ship was in German hands. Since the hold was well below the water line, there was no fresh air, and the ship was so crowded that some prisoners were kept in the corridors and others in the machine rooms. Once the *Yavuz* was full, newly arrived prisoners were transferred to the *Erkin*, a mother ship for the submarines, where conditions were even more claustrophobic. The lower deck of this vessel was so crammed with naval cadets that even the lavatories were used to house them. The *Erkin*, which was originally anchored off Silivri, on the northern shore of the Sea of Marmara, now served both as prison and courtroom. Literally as well as metaphorically, justice was all at sea. The harsh conditions made the prisoners extremely vulnerable, and through the threat of torture they could be induced to sign almost anything, as one of them later recalled in a magazine article (*Medet*, 18 May 1950). These ruthless tactics might suggest that the navy was acting independently of political control, but when the fleet was stationed in Izmit harbour, it received official visits from Prime Minister Celal Bayar, the mayor of Istanbul, the commander-in-chief of the navy and the superintendent of the military courts.

The humiliations inflicted on the prisoners took many forms, as Nazım recalled many years later in conversation recorded by the Chilean poet Pablo Neruda:

13. The battle-crusier *Yavuz*, where Nazım was held prisoner.

Accused of attempting to incite the Turkish navy into rebellion, Nazım was condemned to the punishments of hell. The trial was held on a warship. He told me he was forced to walk on the ship's bridge until he was too weak to stay on his feet, then they stuck him into a section of the latrines where the excrement rose half a metre above the floor. My brother poet felt his strength failing him. The stench made him reel. Then the thought struck him: my tormentors are keeping an eye on me, they want to see me drop, they want to watch me suffer. His strength came back with pride. He began to sing, low at first, then louder, and finally at the top of his lungs. He sang all the songs, all the love poems he could remember, his own poems, the ballads of the peasants, the people's battle hymns. He sang everything he knew. And so he vanquished the filth and his torturers (Neruda 1977, 195-6)

Poetry may have strengthened Nazım's morale, but it was no defence against wrongful imprisonment.

Since the vessels kept changing their position, it was impossible for lawyers, relatives or friends to keep track of events. Nazım was among those transferred from the *Yavuz* to the *Erkin*, but he does not appear to have been tortured, perhaps because his family was so well connected. When he was at last allowed to write a letter to his wife from the ship, postmarked 16 July 1938, he merely mentions that he has had no time to pack any clothes (AM 1, 110). As soon as his mother Celile and his sister Samiye discovered that he had left Sultanahmet prison, they contacted an admiral named Şükrü Okan who lived in Erenköy. Celile introduced herself as the daughter of the former Ottoman official Enver Celalettin Pasha, whose name still carried some weight. The admiral arranged for them to visit Nazım on the *Erkin* submarine ship (Aydemir 1986, 226-30). This visit, which took place on 17 July, involved them in a complicated journey; they had to go first to Silivri by bus, and then on a naval vessel to the *Yavuz*. Here they had an appointment with the admiral, who instructed one of his aides to take the ladies to the *Erkin* for their visit. Nazım, after several days in a stirking latrine, was astonished to find himself dining on the upper deck with his mother and sister, accompanied by high-ranking officers. It was only when one of them said 'Don't let your dinner get cold' that he realised that he too was invited to the feast. The irony was that this officer was none other than Şerif Budak, now wearing a naval uniform. Being well aware of his reputation, they were not deceived by his polished manners. Nazım longed for a visit from Piraye, and wrote to her on 26 July: 'I spend my days alone, looking out of the porthole and seeing the same tiny part of the sea, wishing the night would come quickly so that I can dream about you'. She was finally allowed to visit him in August, by which time the ship was anchored at Erdek (AM 1, 111-4).

The navy trial began on 10 August in an improvised courtroom on the *Erkin* and lasted nineteen days; on 16 August, in the middle of the proceedings, the ship moved to Haydarpaşa near Istanbul (AM 1, 114-6). About thirty other people besides Nazım and Kemal Tahir were in the dock, including two women, Fatma Nudiye and Emine Alev. Presiding over the court was a brigadier named Gökdenizer, while the judge was Salih Könimen (Coşkun, 164). The accused were allowed legal representation, and Kemal Tahir's lawyer put the case for the defence, arguing that all the books read by the naval cadets were legally on sale in bookstores: 'With a world war approaching, young people want information about communism and fascism. They listen to the radio, read newspapers and discuss these things in their free time. [. . .] This does not mean that they are trying to damage the navy.' To these arguments Judge Könimen replied: 'Even if these people have not yet done anything wrong, they soon will damage the army, the navy and the country if they become so involved in politics. One has to crush the head of the snake while it is still young' (Sülker 5, 155).

When the defence asked for a professional opinion on whether such books were really so harmful, a complete list was sent to the Ministry of Justice, and three days later an official report confirmed that none of the books had been banned. This evidence was brushed aside by Şerif Budak, who once again acted as prosecutor: 'We are not so stupid as to look for evidence in this case; if they have not yet committed an offence, they will certainly do so in the future' (Sülker 5, 156). These arguments, however plausible to the authoritarian mind, did not convince everyone. Brigadier Gökdenizer, protested with some emotion: 'You are destroying these young people. They have done nothing to harm the navy, but what you are doing is harmful to the navy' (*Medet*, 18 May 1950). Gökdenizer was then replaced as president of the court by the more hawkish Admiral Ertuğrul. The mere fact that these young people were meeting to discuss books associated with communism was regarded as proof of conspiracy. In Nazım's case there was no evidence of contacts with any person in the navy, so he was accused of responsibility for a potential revolt among naval personnel. This was defined by the court as 'an offence even if it is a future action' (Sebük, 80).

There were those in high office who recognised that Nazım had not received a fair trial. The Minister of the Interior, Şükrü Kaya, apparently suggested that he should write a personal letter to Atatürk. To this Nazım responded that he wanted justice, not charity (Kadir, 182). But on 17 August, fearing that his sentence was about to be increased, he did send an appeal for clemency to the ailing President. In this letter, which addresses Atatürk in the informal second person singular, the prisoner's submissive appeal is blended with the poet's defiant pride:

I have been sentenced to fifteen years' imprisonment on the allegation of inciting the army to revolt. Now I am alleged to be inciting the navy to revolt.

I swear by the name of the Turkish revolution and by your name that I am innocent.

I have not incited the army to revolt.

I am not blind and I appreciate every giant step you take for progress. I have a heart that loves my country. [. . .]

I am a poet of the Turkish language who believes in you and your work. [. . .]

I want justice from Kemalism and from you.

I swear by the name of Turkish revolution and by your name that I am innocent.   (Sülker 5, 207)

This letter was entrusted to Haluk Şehsuvaroğlu, one of the younger prosecutors, who admired of Nazım and knew his poetry by heart (Günyol, 2). Haluk made a copy of the letter before sending it by registered mail from Beşiktaş. According to Ali Fuat Cebesoy, the letter was referred to Şükrü Kaya, Minister of the Interior. But Atatürk was so ill that the appeal never reached him. By this date the right-wing pressure groups had become all-powerful and it is doubtful whether he could have intervened even if he had received the letter. Atatürk's death on 10 November 1938 enabled these groups to consolidate their power. Çakmak insisted that people sentenced under Article 94 should be excluded from any amnesty (Sülker 5, 138). Those released in the autumn of 1938 included collaborators who had supported the occupying powers and even conspirators who had plotted to assassinate Atatürk – but not the poet whose epic about a medieval sheikh had beguiled a handful of students.

On 29 August the court reconvened to announce its verdict (Sülker 1974, 114). The evidence was so inconclusive that the majority of the defendants were acquitted, but twelve alleged ringleaders were sentenced to long terms of imprisonment. Tahir and Kıvılcımlı each received fifteen years, Kerim Korcan ten years. But the sentence imposed on Nazım was so severe that it seems the main purpose of the trial had been to silence Turkey's most gifted author: 'Nazım Hikmet Ran has been found guilty under Article 94 of the military criminal code and sentenced to twenty years imprisonment. [. . .] It is obvious from his previous convictions that he is a communist and a danger to the defence of the realm. [. .] The sentence is therefore increased to a total of twenty-eight years and four months in prison' (Coşkun, 166). The following day, while the prisoners were still confined in their cells below deck, the ship resounded to Victory Day celebrations marking the sixteenth anniversary of the triumph over the Greeks on 30 August 1922. Gloating at the fate of the communists made the celebration even more raucous.

The verdicts passed by the military court had both political and legal repercussions. Under existing Turkish law it was not clear that military judges had the authority to imprison civilians. There was thus a certain conflict of jurisdiction between the

Ministry of Justice and the Ministry of Defence. The harsh sentences imposed at the Military Academy trial in Ankara were also questioned, in the corridors of parliament as well as by the relatives of the defendants, civilian lawyers and intellectuals (Sülker 5, 251). Under a properly constituted legal system there would have been ample justification for an appeal. Instead, the government introduced retrospective legislation to criminalize propaganda activities. On 3 May 1939, an amendment to Article 148 of the Military Criminal Code was put before the National Assembly, stipulating that civilians involved with communist propaganda in the army were answerable to the military courts. At a cabinet meeting the Prime Minister declared that there was a conspiracy in the army promoted by foreign radio broadcasts. The Minister of Defence, Lieutenant-General Tinaz, objected to this attempt to redefine what he saw as an insignificant problem of military discipline into a criminal conspiracy – and was replaced by a hardliner, Saffet Arıkan. The proposed amendment was justified by the Prime Minister on the grounds that there had been 'systematic propaganda among military personnel designed to subvert the constitutionally established political, economic and social form of the state in favour of an alien regime'. He warned the National Assembly that this type of communist propaganda was being disseminated among the military all over the world. The new clauses, which came into effect on 14 July 1939, were applied retrospectively to the army and navy trials. A decision had been taken to enforce the judgement against the defendants 'at the highest level' (Sülker 5, 206, 246 & 259-60).

It is clear from this sequence of events that ultimate authority lay not with the courts or the National Assembly, but with the Chief of Staff. On 17 February 1939 Fevzi Çakmak had circulated a statement about the conviction of the communists, emphasising the exemplary significance of Nazım's case. Two key paragraphs in this statement confirm Çakmak's involvement in the affair:

Point 1: It has been proved that in June 1938 there was a campaign to spread communist propaganda among the members of the navy, and these ideas were infiltrated by some civilians led by the poet Nazım Hikmet, attempting to incite a revolt among the ranks of the navy against their superiors. [...]

Point 4: This country's freedom was won by the sweat and blood of our martyrs. Communists are trying to spread their ideologies among the military and the navy in order to take this country on a dangerous path, to suppress our freedom and to turn Turkish people into slaves. (Korcan, 175)

Clearly there could be no prospect of a successful appeal if the final verdict lay with the Chief of Staff.

Life behind bars: from Istanbul to Çankırı

On 31 August 1938 the prisoners were transferred to Sultanahmet prison in the old quarter of Istanbul. Nazım found himself sharing a cell with his fellow writer, Kemal Tahir, who had received a fifteen-year sentence. At night they would put their mattresses on the floor, read books to each other, or discuss letters received from their wives. But prison life involved conflict as well as camaraderie, since Nazım found himself rubbing shoulders with Hikmet Kıvılcımlı, an orthodox communist who had been one of his fiercest critics. In the months that followed they at least had leisure to try to resolve their differences. There were also convivial moments On 29 October, to celebrate the fifteenth anniversary of the Republic, they got hold of a gramophone and played whatever records they could find, including Chaliapin singing Song of the Volga Boatman. Kıvılcımlı and Kemal Tahir even performed Turkish and Circassian folk dances, while Nazım chimed in with a song from an operetta called the Charleston-Boston Waltz. Others sang nostalgic songs about separation and betrayal that they had learned from sailors on the *Yavuz* and *Erkin* (Tahir, 273).

Life behind bars proved to be a microcosm of life outside, with its own social hierarchy. Some prisoners recklessly gambled away their possessions, including their clothes and bedding, until they were reduced to sleeping naked on the floor. Others enjoyed unexpected affluence, taking their ease on double mattresses with carpets on the floor of their cells. There were also children in another section of the prison, some as young as thirteen, who could be seen playing football (Tahir, 228, 253 & 267). The women political prisoners, Fatma Nudiye and Emine Alev, were kept strictly segregated. On some days the prisoners simply passed the time playing cards – even a poet cannot be creative all the time. Nazım's attempts to continue his novel proved particularly frustrating: Kemal Tahir recalled that 'he rubbed out twice as much as he wrote'. However, in November 1938 he completed a poem, 'Onlar' ('Those People'), a celebration of the enduring qualities of working people, one of the germs for his epic 'Human Landscapes' (Tahir, 254, 293-7 & 357). They also collaborated in writing poetry. The sensuous imagery of ripening fruit in one of Nazım's love poems for Piraye – 'my heart, like a green branch of a plum tree / you are a golden hairy fruit / hanging from it' – is echoed in a version which Kemal sent to his wife, Fatma Irfan, also entitled 'Under the Sun' (Tahir, 298; AM 1, 117).

Atatürk's death on 10 November 1938 renewed hopes of an amnesty. Rumours even circulated that the new President, Ismet Inönü, was sympathetic to their plight. Perhaps Nazım would be released if he expressed a willingness to move to Ankara and write for *Ulus,* the newspaper of the Republican People's Party (Tahir, 370-4). Nazım and Kemal Tahir even wrote a letter to Inönü, distancing themselves from the dogmatic Marxism of the Kıvılcımlı fraction and expressing support for the state investment policies of the government. But these hopes were dashed on 29 December 1938, when they were informed that the appeal court had finally rejected their pleas (Sülker 1974, 143). Only one possibility remained. A favourite ploy among long-term prisoners was to fall sick and obtain a doctor's report. One of the more liberal provisions in the Turkish criminal code permitted prison sentences to be suspended to allow convalescence in cases of serious illness (Coşkun, 167, footnote). The aim was to control infectious diseases, but this provision none the less offered a paradoxical chink of hope. First, Kıvılcımlı was released after a medical examination, but he later made the mistake of trying to escape across the border to Syria in disguise, and was re-arrested by frontier guards (Kıvılcımlı, 206). Then Nazım obtained a medical report stating that he had a serious chest infection. According to his stepson, Memet Fuat, Nazım obtained a temporary release by using a fellow prisoner's sputum sample to suggest that he suffered from tuberculosis (Interview, February 1990). The substitution was made easier because there were sympathizers among the medical staff. In April 1939 the poet was freed on condition that he convalesced at home.

During this period of home leave Nazım considered the possibility of escaping abroad. He approached his former comrade Nail V, asking him to put him in touch with the official Turkish

Communist Party. However, a meeting of the Central Committee rejected the idea of Nazım escaping abroad on the grounds that the prisoners were likely to be released soon in any case because the evidence against them was so flimsy (Karaca 1996, 25). The fact that Nazım was no longer officially a member of the Party may also have been a factor. Since he was supposedly suffering from a life-threatening illness, he was under strict instructions to remain at home under medical supervision, but soon wearied of the enforced confinement and insisted on going out. Two naval officers spotted him and reported the matter to the Chief of Staff. As a result, he was ordered to undergo a further medical examination, and an X-ray conducted by Dr Ihsan Rifat found his lungs free of infection. He was promptly re-arrested, and by early July was back behind bars. Piraye's grief at this disastrous setback is reflected in a letter which Nazım wrote on 11 July:

This is the first time I have seen your tears through the iron bars. So I can't even ask you to be strong. It was always you who advised me to be strong whenever we faced difficult situations which required strength. It is strange that this time it is your tears that have given me the strength of steel.

I believe that our misfortune has now reached its worst point and only the news of death could have any effect on me. When a calamity reaches its height it is bound to give way to its opposite (AM 1, 122).

Their relationship was further strained by the policy of dispersing prisoners to remote locations in the provinces. Although Turkey maintained its neutrality when the Second World War broke out, a 'National Defence Law' was introduced in January 1940, giving the government emergency powers. This further reduced the prospect of clemency for political prisoners, and in February Nazım, Kıvılcımlı and Kemal Tahir were transferred to Çankırı, about 150 kilometres north-east of Ankara. 'Once again, the sea, a train journey, mountains and letters have come between us', he wrote to Piraye. The rigours of the journey were alleviated when his mother Celile joined the train at Izmit station and accompanied them as far as Ankara. Once they reached Çankırı, they began to settle in for a long stay, doing their best to transform their cheerless cell into a habitable home (AM 1, 124).

The move to Çankırı did not lessen the prisoners' sense of solidarity. A photograph dated 19 May 1940 shows the three comrades sitting side-by-side, with Kemal Tahir strumming a Turkish lute while Nazım and Kıvılcımlı put on a brave face for the camera (Fig. 14b). Better still, Piraye followed them to Çankırı, renting a place near the prison for two months so as to visit Nazım regularly. She was also permitted to meet his friends and share meals with the prisoners. The atmosphere in this remote provincial town seems to have been more relaxed than in Istanbul. Photographs of Çankırı show Nazım and Piraye sitting in the prison garden with her teenage son Memet Fuat, her elder sister Fahamet, Kemal Tahir and Hikmet Kıvılcımlı (Fig. 14a). The poet even finds words to celebrate the simple pleasures of sitting in the prison yard 'at the foot of a sunny wall' (AM 1, 127).

Nazım was acutely aware that while local people were relaxing in the afternoon sunshine in the public park, eating ice cream and drinking lemonade, the most terrible events were unfolding on the battlefields of Europe as the German army thrust into Denmark, Norway, France, Belgium and the Netherlands. This awareness is reflected in the poem 'Five Minutes', written in June 1940 ('Beş Dakika', A 4, 50). The tranquillity of the afternoon is shattered by a loudspeaker announcing (in the chilling language of news bulletins): 'The enemy lost many dead with a whole motorised division.' The poet's response to this announcement is highly original. He shows no interest in the obvious question: which enemy – the victorious German army, or the British and French, who were retreating on all fronts? Instead his imagination brings back to life four individual servicemen killed in the war: John, a stoker from Liverpool; Hans, a worker from Prussia; Mafeo, a composer from Naples; and Gilbert from Brittany. In this visionary poem the mutilated men seize the loudspeaker to give a gruesome account of how the war destroys the lives of working people, regardless of nationality. The poet's refusal to take sides reflects his general revulsion at the horrors of war, reinforced by a Marxist conception of international working-class solidarity. War is seen as an imperialist adventure, in which the workers are inevitably the first to suffer. His position in the summer of 1940 was surprisingly close to that of the government under Inönü's leadership, which remained neutral throughout the war.

At the end of June, Piraye was obliged to return to Istanbul. She herself was the prisoner of circumstances, having little money to live on and two children to look after. Few of her letters are available, but we gain occasional glimpses of her ordeal from Nazım's replies: 'You say that you are depressed and nothing

Scenes from Çankırı Prison: 14a. Nazım with Piraye, her son Memet Fuat
and her sister Fahamet.

14b. Nazım, Kemal Tahir and Hikmet Kıvılcımlı.

gives you joy. It is my fault, I wasn't able to write or to paint things to fulfil your darkest days. [...] I wish I was a genius of a poet, painter or musician, so that with one line or one song I could give you strength and hope' (AM 1, 152). In his letters and poems he redoubled his efforts to define the unique quality of their love, finding in Turkish folk tradition a symbol for his feelings. After reading the tale of Leyla and Mecnun, he reflects on the fifteenth-century poet Fuzuli's vision of love. In that earlier version Mecnun begins by falling passionately in love with Leyla, but his feelings later dissolve into a platonic ideal with intimations of divine love. Nazım feels that in his own case the process has been reversed: the longing for love started as an abstract need and became intensified through the encounter with Piraye: 'When anyone speaks of love and intimacy, what I see is Piraye ... with her movements, with her flesh, bones and soul. [....] The fact is that our mind evolves from the abstract to the material world' (AM 1, 153).

Many of Nazım's verses of this period are in an informal epistolary mode, as if what began as a letter unexpectedly changed into a poem. Precious moments spent with Piraye form the predominant theme in a sequence of seven poems, enclosed with letters written between July and October 1940 and entitled 'Letters from Çankırı Prison' ('Çankırı Hapisanesinden Mektuplar', AM 1, 127-45). Recalling the prison garden where they 'used to sit side by side', he goes on to remind her of how they read together the description of a more exotic garden in the Rubaiat by Ghazali, a mystic poet fascinated by the theme of death. He begins by citing four lines from Ghazali:

> 'Night:
>   the great azure garden.
> The glittering swirl of the dancers,
> and the dead, laid out in wooden boxes.'

Nazım, by contrast, takes up a local proverb to underscore his emphatic conviction that 'the only real thing is life':

> I keep remembering
> a local proverb
> which I first heard from you:
> 'After the poplar catkins bloom
>   the cherry blossom follows.'

> The catkins bloom in Gazali,
> but
> the master does not see
> the cherry blossom.
> That's why he worships death.
>   (AM 1, 130-1)

Other poems exemplify this commitment to life through down-to-earth images, like the Wednesday market in Çankırı with its 'eggs, cracked wheat and burnished purple aubergines' (AM 1, 133). But nature is not idealised. The heat of an August day reduces the poet to lying under a mosquito-net soaked in sweat, while the sudden chill wind at night seems to threaten the prisoners' health: 'we shiver in our skins / afraid of nature' (AM 1, 135). The sequence gains an additional resonance by charting the changing seasons, from the sunny garden of the spring to the evocation of dusk in October: 'It gets dark at five [...] / The tailors are drinking linden tea ... / This means winter's here' (AM 1, 143).

These letter-poems also reflect a quest for a new style. In mid-September 1940 he mentions the idea of writing an 'Encyclopaedia of Famous People' – the tentative first step towards *Human Landscapes*, his great panorama of modern Turkey (AM 1, 149). Since his aim is to achieve greater objectivity, he creates vivid vignettes of life in a typical Anatolian town:

> Beside the road
> in front of the white house
> at the tip of an iron post
>   a street lamp is shining.
> The street is lit.
> In the garden of the military barracks are weapons
>   and trees.
> I know:
>   mulberry, acacia, plum. [...]
> Hissing with anger
>   the Zonguldak train approaches. [...]
>   (AM 1, 137)

In the development of this new style, his correspondence with Piraye clearly played a crucial role. 'Please send me your ideas about this poem in as much detail as possible,' he wrote. 'I need your opinions and impressions.' He hopes that these efforts will lead to a breakthrough to a more realistic idiom (AM 1, 141).

However, despite the vividness of the opening lines, it can hardly be said that the poem fulfils Nazım's aims: the imagery seems static and even the train does not carry much freight. A few weeks later, in a letter of 28 November, he implicitly acknowledges his failure (AM 1, 143). The 'Letters from Çankırı Prison' have a refreshing directness, but the poet has not yet succeeded in transforming casual impressions of Anatolia into compelling human landscapes.

Although Nazım emphasizes his quest for objectivity, Piraye's imagined presence remains the strongest motif: 'your red hair, / your eyes, / sometimes green / sometimes honey-coloured' (AM 1, 144). Like every long-term prisoner, he also has nightmares. 'Sometimes', he writes in a letter from Çankırı, 'I dream that you are leaving me. I am not angry with you or offended, I even think that you are right. [...] After such a dream, I walk around for a couple days with a sorrow inside me like a cloud.' Among the presents which he is sending Piraye is a self-portrait in which he has attempted to depict the anguish experienced within the dream (AM 1, 150). While acknowledging such moments of extreme distress, he also emphasises the therapeutic value of writing these 'Letters from Çankırı Prison', which provide an outlet for his feelings. But this does not mean that he is missing Piraye and the children any less. With the approach of winter, he applied for a transfer to Bursa, where the climate was milder and he would be able to visit the spa for medical treatment (AM 1, 151).

There was a strong incentive to work both to alleviate the tedium of prison routine and to earn some money. In the quest for literary commissions, he was fortunate to have the support of his mother Celile. While Nazım was adjusting to life in prison, she was busily knocking on doors in Ankara. Her aim was not merely to protest her son's innocence, but also to promote his career, for example by getting permission for one of his plays to be staged (AM 1, 125). These efforts met with some success when the Minister of Education, Hasan Ali Yücel, commissioned Nazım to do some translations. His first commission was to produce a Turkish text for *Tosca*, the opera by Puccini based on a play by Victorien Sardou, which was to be performed in Ankara. The task must have been full of ironies for a writer languishing in prison, since the central male character is a caricature of the authoritarian personality, the lewd and sadistic police chief, Baron

Scarpia. Scarpia's adversaries are Cesare Angelotti, a political prisoner on the run, and the painter Mario Cavaradossi who is engaged to marry Tosca. Mario falls into the clutches of Scarpia while helping his friend Angelotti escape. After a complex action involving various disguises and deceptions, the scheming Scarpia finally gets his deserts as Tosca stabs him to death while resisting his advances. The tragic story reaches its climax when Tosca herself commits suicide after the failure of all her efforts to save her friends from imprisonment, torture and execution.

For any political prisoner the story of Tosca, the passionate woman prepared to risk everything for her lover's freedom, must hold a strong appeal. For Nazım the project held an additional attraction, since the lead was to be played by the singer Semiha Berksoy, with whom he had a brief liaison a few years previously. On her return to Turkey in 1939 after three years in Germany, Semiha began to send him letters and food, followed in the spring of 1940 by a parcel of books including a novel by George Sand. Her letters suggest that she helped to obtain for Nazım the commission to translate *Tosca* (Özbilgen, 129-31). In November 1940 Semiha made the journey from Ankara to visit him in Çankırı prison, and he completed the translation that same month (AM 1, 145 & 154). To conceal his involvement, it was credited to another collaborator, the conductor Ferit Alnar who, ironically, was also pursuing Semiha and was jealous of her close rapport with the poet. Out of this tangled situation a successful production of *Tosca* emerged, premiered in Ankara in April 1941 with Semiha in the title role.

Piraye's reaction to the renewal of this affair can only be surmised. 'Nazım was such a gentleman that he would never refuse a woman,' his relative Refik Erduran recalled many years later (Interview, January 1990). The most vivid impression of Piraye's reactions to her husband's infidelity can be found in a long autobiographical poem he wrote at Çankırı in the summer of 1940, 'Bir Küvet Hikayesi' ('The Tale of a Tub'). This miniature drama recreates the tensions provoked by the 'other woman' through the voices of a couple named Süleyman and Fahire, re-enacting the acrimonious exchanges that presumably took place between Nazım and Piraye. Here it is only possible to paraphrase this perceptive dialogue between anguished wife and hapless husband.

Fahire, discovering Süleyman's infidelity, calls him home from

his office and bombards him with questions: 'Is it true? Where
did you meet?' 'In a hotel.' 'How many times?' 'Maybe three or
four, I don't know.' 'The sheets must have been so dirty. I read
in an English novel that in that kind of hotel there is always a
cracked tub to wash in. Was there a tub in your room?' 'I don't
know.' 'Think hard, a cracked tub with pale pink flowers?' 'Yes.'
'Did you give her presents?' 'No.' 'Chocolate?' 'Just once.' 'Did
you really love her?' 'Love her, certainly not.' 'Were there any
others, Süleyman?' 'No.' 'That means you loved her. If there
had been others, I'd feel easier. Was she really good in bed?'
'No.' 'One more question, Süleyman: Why did you do it?' 'I
don't know...'

Next day, after a sleepless night, Fahire tells Süleyman that she
has been contemplating suicide. The thought that came to her
in the night was to throw herself down a well: the next day they
would have to follow her footprints through the snow and use
a ladder to retrieve her body. But the sight of her husband in
bed beside her, asleep as usual, prevents her from carrying out
the attempt; she walks out on to the balcony in spite of the bitter
cold and calms down, thinking of her children, the police, the
gossip. 'Betrayed wife commits suicide' – how ridiculous! We have
to fight to survive (she concludes), 'to live together, you, me,
the cracked tub'. The snow stops, the sun rises – if he'd woken
then, she'd have rushed into his arms. From now on she will
sometimes remember this episode, sometimes forget it: 'We'll live
side by side, believing that you love me.'

Six months later, returning one dark summer's night from the
seaside, with stars in the sky and fruit on the trees, Fahire stops,
looks at her husband with loving eyes and slaps him – as if spitting
in his face! (AM 1, 157-62).

Receiving this poem in a letter from Çankırı in August 1940,
Piraye must have felt it was a strange form of apology. The letters
Nazım sent her in the following months while he awaited the
transfer to Bursa are full of longing to be with her again.

6

Bursa Prison
1940-1950

'Nazım Hikmet is coming!' It was mid-December 1940 when the news reached Bursa prison, causing great excitement. 'Everyone was waiting for his arrival,' recalled Orhan Kemal, another aspiring writer convicted for political offences; he was doing secretarial work in the prison office when they brought the new arrival in. Nazım immediately started showing them portraits and photographs of the inmates from Çankırı and recounting details of their lives, and everyone, including the warders, was fascinated by his stories (Kemal, 24). Nazım was given a cell just two doors down from Orhan. After the iron gates had clanged shut behind them, they climbed the stairs and walked along corridors reeking of urine – the cans into which prisoners urinated during the night were left outside the cells in the morning (Sebük, 71). Orhan Kemal lit the charcoal burner, and soon the air was filled with the succulent smell of spicy sausages. This was not the usual prison fare, for the basic allowance was 600 grams of bread per day (Balaban 1979, 126). Wartime shortages were making conditions extremely austere, since rationing was introduced even in neutral Turkey, but there was a grocer's shop attached to the prison, where little extras could be bought at inflated prices. To welcome Nazım, Orhan prepared a feast, and the two soon became close friends. Orhan, originally named Raşid Kemal Öğütcü, and only sixteen when arrested in May 1938, was still sentenced to a full five years for allegedly spreading communist propaganda in the army – he too possessed copies of Nazım's poems! (Sülker 1988, 5 & 32).

The Stone Aeroplane

Nazım's first priority after settling in was to report his safe arrival

168

to Piraye and to Kemal Tahir, who had stayed behind in Çankırı. Writing letters became one of his principal activities, and a vivid account of prison conditions can be found in those he wrote to Kemal Tahir, who was transferred first to Malatya Prison (1941-4) and then in Çorum (1944-50). On 6 December 1940 Nazım described his first impressions:

Since 1933 Bursa prison has not changed, its walls, windows, and walkways are still the same.[...] Even some of the same prisoners are still here. [...] I described this place to you once before: it is a building like an aeroplane. My room is on the third floor in the left side of the tail. My room-mate is called Kemal, and not only is his name like yours, he also looks like you when you were younger (AM 3, 15).

The prison had been built by German engineers, and the ground plan was indeed reminiscent of an aeroplane, taking the form of a large T, with a further small cross-bar at the bottom forming the 'tail'. The building, as Nazım's friend Abidin Dino recalls in a memoir written in 1979, became jocularly known as *'taş tayyare'* – the 'stone aeroplane' (ML, 2, 5-10). It was a massive building covering 750 square metres, surrounded by high walls and holding as many as 1,000 prisoners.

Most of the prisoners were accommodated in barrack-like dormitories, but there were also thirty smaller cells which offered greater privacy (Sebük, 65). After Nazım and Orhan had obtained permission to share one of these, they decorated the walls, planted seeds in the window box, and divided the room so that one part could be used for working and the other for painting. Prison life was strictly regulated, and Nazım found the routine frustrating. 'I get up at 8,' he writes in another letter, 'wash, drink tea and walk around till 9. Then I read a little and paint till dusk, apart from the lunch break. After 8 o'clock, doors are closed, I still don't have anything to read, so I go to sleep. I am not writing poetry, I don't know why, but I know that there is some build-up of ideas and once I start writing again, it's going to be good' (AM 3, 18).

Conditions were spartan and the building was damp and cold, but the treatment of political prisoners in Turkey was comparatively humane. Nazım had obtained his transfer to Bursa on medical grounds, and the new location offered a number of advantages. It was a spa town with a milder climate and better medical facilities than Çankırı. Moreover the regime was relatively liberal as a result of the progressive outlook of Tahsin Akıncı, governor of the prison from 1940 till 1945, who encouraged artistic activities. Prisoners could also receive books and magazines sent by friends (AM 3, 100). Soon Nazım's creativity returned, and Orhan Kemal recalls how he began to walk up and down the corridor reciting poetry and scribbling verses on scraps of paper while puffing at his pipe (Kemal, 66). When Tahsin was transferred to another post in 1945, his successor as governor, Kutsi Bey, also treated Nazım with sympathy, but in 1948 he was replaced since he was regarded as too lenient. Under the subsequent harsh regime prisoners were ordered to have their heads shaved (AM 3, 256 & 340).

During the first months of 1941, when they had to endure sub-zero temperatures, Nazım and Orhan Kemal arranged a temporary transfer to the sick bay, where they made friends with Vehbi Ertuğrul, an inmate employed on medical duties. Here they enjoyed the luxury of a warm stove and a better diet (AM 3, 102). Another of the focal points of prison life was the radio set, which kept inmates in touch with events in the war. They listened every day to the news, and people would gather in Nazım's room to discuss the situation at the front. Nazım succeeded in making a map from a collage of newspaper cuttings. He drew in the front lines carefully, following the progress of the war from newspaper and radio reports day by day. The German and Italian invasion of Greece in May 1941 and the occupation of Athens and Salonika brought the war threateningly close to the Turkish frontier; and anti-fascist political prisoners began to fear for their own safety if a fascist regime were imposed on Turkey. Reports of communists being tortured and shot by the Nazis filled them with apprehension (Kemal, 73).

The sensation of 1941 was the assault on the Soviet Union by the German army in June. Its spectacular advances suggested that fascism was unstoppable and that the Soviet Union would be forced to capitulate. Influential figures in the Turkish establishment favoured an alliance with Germany, including Marshal Çakmak, and in October 1941 two Turkish generals, Ali Fuad Erden and Hüseyin Erkilet, were sent on a mission to the German military headquarters in East Prussia. They were tremendously impressed by their meeting with Hitler, and on their return they reported to President Inönü that 'all that was left of Russia was its snow' (Weisband, 125). Erkilet was a leader of the resurgent Pan-Turkist faction, which urged the government to enter the war on the German side. German advances in the Crimea culminated in July 1942 with the capture of Sebastopol, which meant that Turkey now faced a further potential threat from across the Black Sea.

There were economic as well as military reasons for co-operation with Germany. In June 1942, Hitler's ambassador Franz von Papen succeeded in negotiating a trade agreement which ensured that Turkey supplied Germany with the chrome essential for its armaments industry in return for trade credits. But the Japanese attack on Pearl Harbor in December 1942, by bringing the United States into the war, decisively changed the balance. Churchill was so determined to enlist Turkey on the Allied side that in January 1943 he himself led a delegation to Adana to put pressure on Inönü. Legend has it that when he suggested Turkey should abandon its neutrality, the partly deaf Turkish President switched off his hearing aid. The Turks certainly had difficulty in understanding Churchill's French. 'When the conversation began to veer towards anything like practical action on their part', the man from the Foreign Office noted, 'it seemed that they found more than usual difficulty in hearing what was said' (Denniston, 91-2). The Soviet military successes after Stalingrad also caused apprehension in Ankara by reviving the spectre of Russian imperialism. The pro-German agitation continued, but finally, after an illegal demonstration in May 1944, Inönü ordered the arrest of thirty Pan-Turkish leaders, including General Erkilet and Nazım's old adversary Peyami Safa (Landau, 113-17).

For Nazım being in prison during this period, helpless to influence the course of events, was intensely frustrating. Gathering in their rooms under the dimmed lights, the prisoners endlessly debated the issues. Should Turkey declare war on Germany and join the struggle against fascism? Or did Soviet imperialism pose an even greater threat? The prisoners in Bursa were as divided in their political opinions as the politicians in Ankara. To Nazım it seemed invidious to be living in relative security while such terrible battles were being fought elsewhere: 'My heart, my head are at every front in the world, but unfortunately I can only fight in my heart and mind,' he wrote to Kemal Tahir in June 1941. 'It is a fight that does not give me a chance to face death or risk my own life.' At least he was now able to define his position more clearly, since Soviet involvement in the war had transformed the ideological picture. The pacifist perspective of poems written at Çankırı, like 'Five Minutes', had reflected the Marxist view of war as a contest conducted by decadent imperial powers. In June 1941 he abandoned this perspective and unreservedly supported the Great Patriotic War of the Soviet Union. 'To the people of Turkey and to the world we are going to tell the most beautiful things possible,' he adds in this same letter, foreshadowing the heroic 'Moscow Symphony' sequence of *Human Landscapes* (AM 3, 91).

A Marxist Academy

Nazım may have been frustrated by his inability to comment on world events, but in prison he could influence hearts and minds. The majority of the inmates were petty criminals, often illiterate and the product of poverty, deprivation or family vendettas. Some of them welcomed the opportunity to improve their reading and writing, and Nazım soon set to work as a teacher. To those with a better education he was able to offer tuition in French, literary criticism, painting, philosophy and current affairs. Reciting his own poems was part of the package, and he encouraged other aspiring writers to show him their efforts in return. The young Orhan Kemal was his most promising pupil, and Nazım taught him French as well as becoming his political mentor. He also encouraged him to write short stories rather than poems. So promisingly did Orhan's narrative skills develop that after his release in 1944 he became a successful novelist.

Nazım also encouraged the talents of a young painter from a remote village, Ibrahim Balaban. For Nazım himself painting was primarily recreation, although it also acquainted him with different character types since he listened to people's life histories while he painted their portraits. He also charged people 2.5 TL for a portrait, so that he could at least cover his expenses. For Balaban, however, painting was to develop into a lifelong career. Born in 1921 in the village of Seçköy near Bursa, he had only had three years of education. Leaving school aged ten, he developed a passion for hunting, roaming the countryside on shooting expeditions. He became implicated in a tobacco-smuggling venture and illicit drug-dealing (Balaban, Interview, October 1996), and in December 1937, aged sixteen, he became involved in a shoot-out with the police, and was fined and sentenced to six months in prison, extended to three years when he failed to pay the fine. He and Nazım first met in 1941, towards the end of this term in Bursa prison; Balaban planned to marry as soon as he was released, since his family had found him a bride. However, towards the end of 1941, only few months before his release was due, he was attacked by four other prisoners, including one of his smuggling accomplices. These rivalries continued after their release, since the man who had organized the attack in prison also coveted Ibrahim's bride. In November 1942, acting in accordance with the prevailing code of honour, Balaban killed his rival, and was then sentenced to a further ten years. Blood feuds between families, arising from boundary disputes or sexual transgressions, were a feature of Turkish life in the 1930s and accounted for over half the murders committed. In these cases the death sentence was rarely imposed (New Turkey, 119), and so Balaban returned to Bursa prison, where he spent the years 1942-5 and 1948-50.

As a bright peasant boy who was good with his hands, Balaban learned various trades in prison, but he liked making sketches of other prisoners best. Shortly after their first meeting in 1941, while cutting Nazım's hair, he mentioned his drawings and was delighted when the poet asked to see them (Balaban 1979, 163). Nazım was amazed to discover such a natural talent. One day Balaban stood watching Nazım painting the portrait of a fellow prisoner. He was fascinated by the way Nazım held up a pencil to calculate the proportions of the human face, and back in his own room he began to experiment with more sophisticated forms of drawing, using fellow prisoners as models. Soon he began to receive systematic coaching from Nazım, and the two became friends, even painting each other's portraits. Balaban recalls how he proudly donned a smart suit and tie when about to be painted. When Nazım portrayed him without a tie, he felt so upset that he later painted in an elegant one himself. The resulting portrait has an implausible formality, forming a striking contrast to Nazım's sketch of another prisoner, Orhan Kemal (Fig. 15a & b). During his time in Bursa, Balaban had to endure further disasters. His wife died in childbirth, and the continuing vendetta led in 1943 to his father being killed in retaliation for Balaban's own crime (Balaban 1992, 22-8). His immediate impulse was to kill his father's murderer, but Nazım suggested that a better way of honouring

his father's memory would be by immortalising him in a painting. This made sense to Balaban, but he had no photograph of his father to guide him. Following Nazım's suggestion, he used a mirror, recreating his father's features from his own inverted image (Balaban 1979, 187).

After a while Nazım encouraged Balaban to apply for a transfer to Imralı, the progressive island penitentiary near Mudania, where long-term prisoners were able to earn a reduction of their sentence through productive work; here he spent 1945-8. Under its governor Izzet Akçal, a man with socialist sympathies, prisoners at Imralı were encouraged to learn to read and write and play musical instruments, and it was here that Balaban learnt to play the clarinet and violin (Interview, October 1996). Akçal's activities attracted the critical attention of the authorities, and he was replaced as governor by a more authoritarian figure. Two months before he was due to be released, Balaban was sent back to Bursa, after being sentenced to a further five years for spreading communist propaganda. During 1948-50 Balaban and Nazım became particularly close, since they both now lived in the political wing of the prison and for a time even shared a room. When Nazım himself was going through a particularly difficult phase, and even contemplated suicide, Balaban helped to restore his faith in life.

The third main feature of Nazım's educational activity was his correspondence with Kemal Tahir. The published edition of his 'Prison Letters to Kemal Tahir' contains over 240 items, extending from December 1940 to April 1950. This is the most important source for the understanding of the two authors' artistic development in this decade. They had great debates on aesthetic questions, especially the concept of Socialist Realism, and the mutual support between two revolutionary writers forms a model of co-operation. When one was depressed, the other would remind him of the duty to testify to a brighter future. The correspondence also reveals a strong emotional attachment: Nazım's fatherly feelings led him to send money to Kemal, who was receiving no support from his own family. In return he might ask Kemal to obtain dried apricots for Piraye, a particular delicacy in Malatya (AM 3, 195). He was very concerned about Kemal's health, and if no letter arrived at the expected time, he would send him a telegram.

These activities did not alter the fact that prison remained a harsh and potentially brutalising environment. Political prisoners

were not separated from those convicted of violent crimes, and
even the most enlightened governor could not prevent drug-taking
and physical assaults. Gambling was endemic, and new arrivals
were forced to join in. This sometimes led people to gamble
away their clothes and their daily bread ration, until they were
literally starving. Gambling disputes, exacerbated by the effect of
drugs, sometimes resulted in prisoners being killed. Nazım managed
to keep out of trouble by being courteous towards everyone,
including the warders, but he still had to endure several threats
to his life, including an attempt planned by two ruthless criminals
serving life sentences (Balaban 1979, 126, 136 & 157). Perhaps
they felt they could ingratiate themselves with the authorities by
disposing of a notorious communist. Fortunately Nazım was
forewarned, and the two murderers were reduced to assaulting
each other (Aydemir 1986b, 121-8). Associating with hardened
criminals hardly seems conducive to creativity, but several of these
encounters later found their way into his poetry. Bursa prison
provided an environment in which literary intellectuals and manual
labourers were able to pool their experiences; in the workshops
he would listen with rapt attention to the life stories of criminals,
who sometimes turned out to have fought heroically in the War
of Liberation. Consequently the workers who feature in Nazım's
poetry are not the idealised heroes of Socialist Realism, but incorporate the bitter experiences of the prison population. When
Nazım, having recast their stories in a poetic narrative, read his
text back to them, they were sometimes moved to tears. One
exclaimed: 'You have made my story even more real than the
way I told it to you' (Kemal, 95-9).

Earning a living

The fundamental problems of prison life were how to earn a
living and cope with ill-health. Money was essential to survive
in prison, since almost everything had to be paid for: nourishing
food, warm clothing and medicines, paper, paints and yarns, cigarettes and postage stamps. Nazım also felt responsible for supporting
Piraye, who at this time was living with the family of her sister
Fahamet, while the children Memet and Suzan were with their
grandfather. Some of their friends thought that it was unfair for
Piraye to accept money from Nazım. However, when he heard

that Piraye was trying to obtain a job in a bank, Nazım felt so jealous that he dissuaded her (Memet Fuat, Interview, March 1996); earning money to maintain her and the children was his duty as a family man, and even in 1947, when his health was deteriorating, he was reluctant to accept defeat. 'As an oriental bourgeois head of my family,' he wrote with a certain self-irony, 'I take pleasure in bearing this responsibility' (Nurettin 1986, 83). However, in practice, he could never be financially self-sufficient. Like most prisoners he relied on food parcels brought by visitors or sent by friends and relatives. The money due to him for the films he had helped to make for Ipek Studios did provide an initial sum for Piraye, with a residue left for Nazım himself (AM 1, 66 & 90), but in the longer term he had to find other sources of income, particularly through his writing.

The translation of *Tosca*, completed while he was still at Çankırı, had earned him a modest fee and raised his hopes of further commissions (AM 3, 60). His most ambitious project was to translate Tolstoy's *War and Peace*, another commission arranged by the Minister of Education, Hasan Ali Yücel. As he could not publish the translations under his name, he had to share the work and the fees with Zeki Baştimar, a leader of the underground Communist Party, under whose name they were actually published. When this arrangement later came to light, it aroused the ire of General Çakmak, who accused Yücel of conniving at communism (Sebük, 122). Nazım and Zeki completed their translation of *War and Peace* in two volumes in 1943, a remarkable feat under such difficult conditions (AM 1, 170). Since Zeki's knowledge of Russian was even better than Nazım's, he worked from the Russian original while Nazım relied on a French version (Memet Fuat, Interview, March 1996). Initially Nazım had to do much of his writing by hand. A poem written in 1947, 'Since I was thrown into this hole', memorably records the synergy between prisoner and pencil:

> Since I was thrown into this hole
> the Earth has gone round the sun ten times.
> If you ask the earth, it will say,
>   'Doesn't deserve mention
>   such a microscopic amount of time'.
> If you ask me, I'll say,
>   'Ten years off my life'.
>
> The day I was imprisoned

> I had a small pencil
> which I used up within a week.
> If you ask the pencil it will say,
>   'My whole lifetime'.
> If you ask me, I'll say,
>   'So what? Only a week'.
> ('Ben İçeri Düştüğümdenberi'; A 4, 153; SP, 78)

Writing in longhand was no impediment for shorter composi-
tions, but it delayed completion of major projects. However, in
1943 Nazım proudly announced to Kemal Tahir that he had
bought a secondhand typewriter, manufactured in 1913 (AM 3,
166). The new means of production increased his creativity, and
his outside commissions soon included the translation of a film
script and the writing of film scenarios (AM 3, 256). Later he
was commissioned by his publisher Ahmet Halit to produce a
verse translation of the Fables of La Fontaine. Translating was
both time-consuming and underpaid, but he had little choice.
His comments on the La Fontaine project are revealing: 'He
offered to pay 400 lira for seventy sections. I asked for 50 lira
more, but in despair I immediately started working on it. [...]
One has to be a prisoner like myself to accept such a fee for
that work. But I am enjoying it' (Nurettin 1986, 28, 159 & 165).

Nazım found an additional source of income through a weaving
co-operative, initiated by Vehbi Ertuğrul, a prisoner with rather
reactionary views whom he had met in the sick bay. The shared
ordeal of prison led them to set aside their ideological differences,
and the two became friends (Aydemir 1986b, 158). In May 1942,
Ertuğrul suggested that they should buy a weaving loom from
another prisoner who was about to be released. This not only
provided a form of occupational therapy, but also enabled them
to earn money from the fabrics they made. According to Nazım
it was Orhan Kemal who enabled them to get started by putting
up the substantial sum of 200 lira, although Orhan himself has
played down the importance of his role (AM 3, 251; Kemal,
66-8). Later they were also able to obtain the use of a second
loom, and completed the formalities required for membership of
the prison co-operative. This enabled them to receive their al-
location of cotton yarn, which was strictly rationed under wartime
austerity regulations. Nazım mentions that there were five
shareholders in the collective, but exactly how it was constituted

is not clear, since he adds that Kemal Tahir himself is to be a member (AM 3, 132).

Organising the co-operative was a complex business. Nazım would walk around the workshops, checking that everything functioned smoothly. They were weaving materials for shirts, trousers, sheets, handkerchiefs, towels, even silk cloth, which were then sent for sale to a co-operative distribution centre. Finding a market for these products was initially less of a problem than locating additional yarn for purchase on the black market (AM 3, 193-4). Sometimes Kemal Tahir was able to help find yarn, which may explain his participation in the profits. Nazım would make careful calculations to ensure that each person was properly remunerated for his work and any extra profit was shared out equitably. Both Tahir and Piraye received payments as 'shareholders', even though they were not working members of the co-operative. For two years this enterprise was quite successful. Their products were even displayed at an exhibition in Istanbul in 1944, accompanied by a painting by Balaban showing the weavers at their looms. Nazım saw himself as an innovator: 'I am the inventor of this new material, which I call Kaymacıköy cloth, named after the weaver who works with me. This is a unique material for making shirts, woven half of silk, half of cotton' (AM 3, 216). His stepson Memet Fuat has recalled how proud he was as a teenager to be given a jacket and trousers tailored by Piraye from this wonderful material (Interview, March 1996). But serious problems arose towards the end of 1944 as a result of wartime shortages, which meant that they could obtain no yarn for two whole months. The price that he had to pay on the black market became so inflated that their sales no longer covered their costs. In November 1944 the co-operative went into liquidation with debts of 249 lira (AM 3, 230 & 247).

This was not the end of their weaving activities, for the looms could not be allowed to stand idle. After various misfortunes they started in August 1946 to make lace curtains, an activity described by Nazım with a certain defiant pride:

My whole day spent weaving [...] but I am still in debt. At last I managed to produce lace curtains as good as European quality. [...] If somebody asked me what I did in the year 1946, I would say: 'I made lace curtains, and today, there isn't a single factory in Turkey that can make curtains to compare with my loom' (Nurettin 1986, 59).

For Nazım's group, as for any small enterpise, marketing proved more difficult than production. The curtains may have been of high quality, but they proved difficult to sell. The prisoners also tried their hands at woollen cloth, but in this case their timing was wrong. It took so long to complete a consignment large enough to be marketed in Istanbul that by the time it was finished the winter cloth-buying season was over. In 1947 Nazım asked his old friend Va-Nu, with whom he had resumed contact, to help with the marketing of some woollen material. A letter written in the autumn of 1947 conveys his desperate plight: 'The weather was mild and we were two weeks behind schedule, so the dealer who ordered the cloth used this as an excuse not to buy it. I am enclosing samples of the materials. [...] It cost us 7 lira per metre. But we are willing to sell at any price to pay our debts' (Nurettin 1986, 80, 132 & 144).

In 1946 Nazım also began making lampshades, once again adopting a confident tone in his letter to Tahir: 'First one has to do the watercolour pattern on paper, then one brushes it with linseed oil until it becomes like a transparent camel skin, then one ties it round the frame with a silk thread' (AM 3, 299). But in a letter to the Va-Nus he had to explain that the lampshade business had also proved a failure since they were unable to compete with factory products: 'I closed that business with a loss of 25 lira.' But Nazım soon had other ideas: 'Now I am making trays. [...] I have made great inventions, using golden glitter. You will like them when you see them – I'll make one for you' (Nurettin 1986, 59, 171, 181 & 187). His final scheme, in 1948, was to produce handbags decorated with beads, designed by the well-known painter Bedri Rahmi (AM 1, 287). These activities drained the poet's energy: 'It is sad and comical too that, even in prison, out of sixteen hours of working time I spend more than ten earning enough for just a loaf of bread.' His financial situation became so bad that in July 1947 Kemal Tahir, in a reversal of their habitual roles, actually sent him 50 lira (AM 3, 320). Other friends rallied round, and in 1948 he received some money from Piraye while Rasih Güran made an effort to organize monthly contributions (AM 1, 281 & 287). There was further support from his sister, his mother and his mother's cousin Ali Fuat Cebesoy. Nazım was keen to reciprocate, and several of his friends received lace curtains or lampshades.

Prison conditions exacerbated Nazım's health problems. At first he suffered from minor complaints, which could even be turned to advantage. Soon after he arrived at Bursa he discovered that Dr Neşati Uster, a communist who had known him since the 1920s, was working at the local hospital. Uster visited him in prison and even helped him to obtain permission to visit Bursa Spa (Aydemir 1986b, 88). This was an expensive luxury, but since Piraye stayed at the Spa Hotel during her first visit, nothing could have been more convenient (AM 3, 19). But in the longer term harsh conditions and inadequate medical care did great damage to Nazım's health. His long list of ailments included sciatica, which had troubled him intermittently since 1933, and rheumatism of the right shoulder, which developed in 1943. The damp concrete floors made things worse, even though he wore wooden clogs for protection. Towards the end of 1944 he developed an enlarged liver, of which the symptoms were shivering and general malaise. Although Nazım was blessed with a robust constitution, his liver complaint became so severe that in 1946 he had to be hospitalised and took a full month to recover. A specialist in Istanbul diagnosed the enlargement of his liver, and he was put on a diet of potatoes, carrots and yoghurt (AM 3, 163, 240 & 325).

In July 1947 he began to suffer from shortness of breath, which affected his general mobility (AM 3, 319 & 347). Since he was fond of composing his poetry while striding up and down, difficulties in walking also impaired his creativity. This time it was his mother who arranged for him to see a specialist from Istanbul, Dr Nebil Bilhan, who diagnosed a coronary disorder, angina pectoris (AM 1, 287; Aydemir 1986b, 97). Since Nazım's poetic impulse was strongly autobiographical, he was soon transposing physical symptoms into lyrical form. Anxieties about illness, ageing and death became one of the themes of his mature poetry, although he characteristically gave personal distress a political meaning. In April 1948, after learning the truth about his heart condition, he wrote 'Angina Pectoris':

> If half my heart is here, doctor,
>   the other half is in China
> with the army flowing
>   towards the Yellow River
>
> [. . .]
>
> And that, doctor, is the reason

for this angina pectoris —
not nicotine, prison or arteriosclerosis.
I look at the night through the bars,
and despite the weight on my chest
my heart still beats with the most distant stars.
(A 4, 165; P, 132)

Thoughts of death filled him with an uncharacteristic melancholy. He wrote in July 1948: 'It is a pleasant sadness, thinking of growing older, departing from this world which is so beautiful, even if I can only observe it from prison' (Kurdakul, 48).

Poems for Piraye

During the first ten years of his sentence, from 1938 to 1948, the relationship with Piraye provided a lifeline. Her occasional visits and their continuous exchange of letters kept alive his hopes of returning to a normal family life. At first he even hoped that Piraye would come to live in Bursa; and he was at least permitted to meet her at the Spa Hotel. The authorities showed a certain leniency towards their most distinguished prisoner, and the gendarme who escorted him to the hotel did not even insist on him wearing handcuffs (Aydemir 1970, 262). But Piraye's visits were infrequent, and Nazım was intensely aware of the emotional and sexual deprivation of prison life, a feeling vividly expressed in 'Lodos' ('South Wind'), a poem written in January 1941:

We are 600
         men without women
Being deprived
         of our right to procreation,
My immense capability is forbidden me:
to inject a new life,
to overcome death in a fertile womb,
to create with you:
My darling I am forbidden to touch your skin.
(A 3,181)

Although Bursa is not much more than 200 kilometres from Istanbul, the cost of travel and accommodation restricted Piraye's visits. For two months, from 10 February to 8 April 1941, she did manage to stay in Bursa, and this seems to have been the period of particular intimacy (AM 3, 38 & 56). While Nazım would be flamboyant, chatty and flirtatious, Piraye's manner was composed and rather formal (Kemal, 86). These moments of happiness with Piraye did not preclude occasional contacts with Semiha Berksoy. When Nazım was transferred from Çankırı, she promised to write to him every week. On 27 March 1941, towards the end of Piraye's visit, Nazım reported in a letter to Semiha that he was visiting the Spa regularly and seeing Piraye every day. Semiha felt so piqued by this news that she threatened to stop writing (Özbilgen, 143). Fortunately, she soon relented, since he relied on her for news of the artistic and theatrical world – she would send him photos of the latest opera productions. In December 1941 she too came to stay at the Selvinaz Hotel in Bursa, and the fact that Nazım mentions her visit in his correspondence with his wife suggests that Piraye did not feel threatened by this relationship (Özbilgen, 154; AM 1, 171).

For Piraye resettling in Istanbul after her visit to Bursa proved a complicated process, since she decided she could no longer live with her sister Fahamet, and moved instead to her aunt's villa in Altunizade on the green hills of Çamlıca. Piraye continued to rely on her family's support, but she could not keep asking for money to travel to Bursa; to pay for one visit she was even obliged to use money given to her son Memet to mark his circumcision. During the mid-1940s Piraye had other priorities, above all the responsibility of looking after her two growing children. Memet's health caused anxiety, and to complicate life further her daughter Suzan would move back in with her whenever she found living with her grandfather too trying. By 1943 she was a young woman of marriageable age, and there was some tension between mother and daughter: Suzan wanted to become engaged to a rather unsuitable young man (AM 3, 188 & 246). Piraye also felt increasingly isolated, especially as members of Nazım's family seemed to resent the way she relied on him for support.

In January 1943 Piraye visited Bursa again, staying in a chilly, run-down hotel room for five days (AM 3, 157). This time Nazım had planned for her to lodge at the house of one of the prison warders, where he hoped to meet her – under a prison escort – and enjoy some intimacy. But Piraye would not fall in with his plans, feeling that this would place her in far too compromising a situation. It was difficult for Nazım to reconcile his sexual desire with Piraye's self-esteem. The visit was ruined by twelve hours of bitter argument, and Nazım felt so humiliated that he told Piraye he did not want to see her the following day. Fortunately, when she did reappear at the prison gate the following morning, the governor succeeded in talking him out of his embittered mood (Kemal, 82-5). A letter written to Piraye after this visit clearly reflects his frustration (AM 1, 179). After this unhappy episode Piraye's visits became even less frequent – sometimes only once a year. But distance made the heart grow fonder, and in the letters and poems of this period her image becomes luminescent:

> How beautiful to think of you
> amid news of death and victory,
> in prison
> when I'm past forty...
>
> How beautiful to think of you:
> your hand resting on blue cloth
> your hair grave and soft
> like my beloved Istanbul earth...
>   (A 3, 95; P, 93)

The date of this poem is uncertain – probably 1943, but one can readily imagine the consoling effect it must have had on Piraye. This was one of more than 100 lyric poems she received through the post from Bursa.

By 1945 Piraye's health had begun to worsen: she suffered from low blood pressure, which affected her eyesight. And in the autumn of 1944 her son Memet, who was staying at his grandfather's house, had fallen ill with tuberculosis. Piraye visited him every day during his treatment, which lasted for at least a year (AM 3, 249-52 & 320). The political news brought some consolation, since the end of the war in Europe raised everybody's spirits, and Piraye visited Nazım with her family in June 1945. But hopes that peace would bring an amnesty for political prisoners were soon dashed. The Soviet Union, which had extended its power throughout Eastern Europe, now began to demand control of the Dardanelles. This provoked an anti-Soviet reaction in Turkey, which felt obliged to abandon its neutrality, align itself with the United States and become a member of NATO. Although President İnönü began to edge cautiously towards a multi-party system, there was no incentive to relax the campaign against communism. Early in December 1945, demonstrations against the left-wing press resulted in the destruction of a number of newspaper offices, putting an end to the publication of *Tan*, the daily newspaper which had been so resourcefully edited by Zekeriya and Sabiha Sertel. The Republican People's Party consolidated its position in the general election of July 1946, held at a time when there was no opposition party sufficiently well organised to mount a serious challenge (the RPP won 390 seats, the newly founded Democratic Party only sixty-five). Thus İnönü kept his grip on power and Nazım had to come to terms with the prospect of more years in prison.

He remained sane by structuring his daily routine in such a way as to sustain his poetic creativity. By this means he was able to maintain progress with his major project, the epic poem *Human Landscapes* (to be analysed in the next chapter). He also began to set aside a devotional hour every evening – between 9 and 10 o'clock to reflect on his relationship with Piraye. The result is a remarkable sequence of love poems, 'Poems from 9 to 10' ('Saat 21-22 Şiirleri'). This series of thirty-two short and unpretentious pieces endows the relationship with the aura of one of the great Turkish love stories. 'Nazım' and 'Piraye', named characters in the drama of frustrated love, acquire a mythic status comparable to the tragic lovers of traditional oriental folktales. This is achieved not by elevated diction, but through language which spells out the pain of separation in the simplest terms possible. It is characteristic of this sparse new style that the poems have no titles. Each is simply headed by a date, from 20 September to 14 December 1945. Some poems have a *haiku*-like terseness, while the longest is scarcely more than twenty lines. Although this spate of inspiration lasted only three months, these poems have moved thousands of readers, not only in Turkey, through their evocation of passionate love constrained by political oppression. There have been numerous translations, including an English version of the complete sequence by Randy Blasing and Mutlu Konuk, from which the quotations in the following pages are taken.

Nazım succeeds in endowing an individual dilemma with social significance, so that these intensely private poems reach out into a wider world:

> *21 September 1945*
> Our son is sick,
> his father is in prison

your head is heavy in your tired hands
our fate is like the world's...
[. . .]   (A 3, 98)

This connection is made even more explicit in a poem written
five days later:

26 September 1945
They've taken us prisoner,
they've locked us up:

me inside the walls
you outside.

But that's nothing.
The worst
is when people – knowingly or not –
carry prison inside themselves... .
Most people have been forced to do this,
honest, hard-working, good people
who deserve to be loved as much as I love you... .
(A 3, 101)

Like any lover in prison, the poet acknowledges attacks of jealousy
(*8 October 1945*), while sensuous longings for her moist lips visit
him in his dreams (*9 October 1945*). There are even moments
when he can hear her voice:

8 November 1945
Over the rooftops of my far-off city
under the sea of Marmara
and across the autumnal earth

your voice came
rich and liquid.

For three minutes.
Then the phone went black...
(A 3, 109)

The poet may 'lie in Bursa like an anchored freighter' (*20 November
1945*), but his mind is preoccupied with reports of poverty, suffering
and disease afflicting honest, hard-working people in Istanbul – 'the
city I hold in my heart like the loss of a child, / like your image
in my eyes...' (*13 November 1945*). The personal seems naturally
to converge with the political:

4 December 1945
Take out the dress I first saw you in,
look your best,

look like spring trees...
Wear in your hair
      the carnation I sent you in a letter from prison,
raise your kissable, lined, broad white forehead.
Today, not broken and sad –
                      no way! –
today Nazım Hikmet's woman must be beautiful
            like a rebel flag....
              (A 3, 112)

The political animus which suffuses these poems is the more effective for being disguised. The 'enemies of hope', first invoked in *6 December 1945*, are targeted not in abstraction as enemies of the working class; they are 'the enemy of Receb, the towel man from Bursa, / of the fitter Hasan in the Karabük factory [. . .] / the enemy of anyone who thinks' (*7 December 1945*) – an allusion to the widely reported attack on left-wing newspaper offices in Istanbul on 4 December.

The imagery of nature in these poems has a double quality, with the cycle of the seasons hinting at arduous processes of political renewal. Autumn must be over as the wild geese head for Iznik Lake (*12 December 1945*). The onset of winter, with which the cycle concludes, conveys an awareness of both aesthetic delight and economic hardship:

13 December 1945
Snow came on suddenly at night.
Morning was crows exploding from white branches.
Winter on the Bursa plane as far as the eye can see:
a world without end.
My love,
the season's changed
        in one great leap after labour.
And under the snow, proud
                 hard-working life
                       continues...
              (A 3, 116)

The simple language disguises the hints of a Marxist-Hegelian perspective: the dialectic of nature, the irrepressible power of labour and the qualitative leap towards a better world. This is socialist poetry which eschews rhetoric and abstraction, and un-flinchingly acknowledges the harshness of urban experience:

14 December 1945
Damn it, winter has come down hard....
You and my honest Istanbul, who knows how you are?
Do you have coal?
Could you buy wood?
Line the windows with newspaper.
Go to bed early.
Probably nothing's left in the house to sell

To be cold and half hungry:
            here, too, we're the majority
            in the world, our country, and our city....
        (A 3, 116)

These poems were all sent to Piraye through the post. She herself appears not to have had strong political convictions, although she sympathized with Nazım's outlook, but for the poetry, this is a source of strength. Far from relying on the stock categories of Marxist discourse to elicit a predictable response, Nazım appears to be wooing the reader in these poems, both emotionally and ideologically:

27 October 1945
We are one half of an apple,
            the other half is the big world.
We are one half of an apple,
            the other half is our people.
You are one half of an apple,
            the other half is me,
                us two...
        (A 3, 108)

Nazım's socialist utopia has undertones of a quest for paradise, endowing the whole sequence with an additional resonance (P, 93-108).

    These poems are all the more impressive when read in the context of Nazım's failing health. By 1946 he felt so debilitated that he could hardly summon up the energy to write (AM 3, 308), and the situation was compounded by anxieties about Piraye's health. Their relationship began to suffer under the strain, and by the late 1940s it seems to have become rather ethereal, as if it now only existed through letters and poems. Writing to Kemal Tahir in June 1946, Nazım attempted to sum up his marriage: 'Piraye and I have loved each other for years. [...] In this love

there is motherhood, brotherhood, fatherhood, comradeship, friendship and humanity, but no romance. Or rather, no melodrama'
(AM 3, 294). The poet seems to have been longing for some
more passionate form of love, but even the author of a melodrama
could hardly have imagined the events that were to follow.

Thwarted destiny with two women

'I am forty-five years old,' Nazım wrote early in 1947, 'but I am
falling more in love every day. With everything – my wife, art,
nature, people, my ideals, even my canary. [...] To me life is not
worth living unless one is in love with one person and also with
millions of people' (Nurettin 1986, 57). This was certainly a creative
outlook for the poet, but for ordinary human beings it caused
complications. In the autumn of 1948 he became entangled in a
triangular love relationship which was to change the direction of
his life. Nazım's erratic behaviour may be related not only to his
romantic temperament but also to the demoralizing effect of ten
years in prison. There seemed no hope of an early release, since
the political situation, especially the crisis caused by the Soviet
blockade of Berlin in the spring of 1948, led to a hardening of
anti-communist attitudes. His physical condition, with a weak
heart and enlarged liver, led him to fear that he would die in
prison. Even if he did survive to serve out his full twenty-eight
year term, he would be well over sixty when the final release
came in 1966. The relationship with Piraye promised continuity
in old age, but not the renewal for which he longed.

It was Va-Nu's wife Müzehher who initiated the relationship
which now unfolded. Reconciliation with Va-Nu was one of
the few heartening personal developments of the late 1940s. Although Va-Nu had been the closest companion of Nazım's youth,
he had distanced himself from communism in the 1930s, when
he worked as a journalist in Istanbul. Under the martial law introduced in January 1940, the freedom of the press had been so
severely curtailed that even the Sertels had been obliged to keep
a low profile. However, with the ending of the war a cautious
liberalisation began, and some of Nazım's former allies began to
rediscover their convictions. In December 1945, after an estrangement lasting over ten years, Va-Nu finally made contact with
Nazım again. His wife Müzehher recalls the circumstances:

Together with some close friends we met for a meal at the Sertels' house in Moda. It was our custom, whenever we gathered together, to read some of Nazım's poems. Va-Nu would read out loud, imitating Nazım's voice and style. [...] We all felt very pained about the estrangement of these two childhood friends who had once been so intimate [...] and we all began to look for an opportunity to repair this broken chain (Nurettin 1986, 7-8).

Sertel suggested that they should send Nazım a New Year food parcel. Whether from political caution or personal pride, Va-Nu was reluctant to send it under his own name, and Sertel too was unwilling to associate himself with a convicted communist, so Müzehher sent the parcel herself. Nazım was delighted, and his reply made it clear that he was willing to patch up his differences with his former friend.

The first visit to the prison by Va-Nu and Müzehher took place early in 1946. After obtaining permission from the public prosecutor, they were able to see him every day for six days, and the governor even invited them to his room and allowed them to have a meal together. When Nazım first appeared, he wore a rather formal suit and tie. The two old friends, who had not met for ten years, embraced each other and started to cry. Soon Nazım was his old self again, taking off his jacket and tie, unbuttoning his collar, and starting to read poetry in his familiar voice. He showed them how he had been able to follow the events of the war on an improvised map on the wall and he insisted on reading excerpts from work-in-progress on his poem 'Yusuf ile Zuleyha' (Joseph and Suleika) while they sat perched precariously on the bunk beds (Nurettin 1986, 9-10). After this first visit a lively correspondence followed, and the hundred-odd letters which Nazım wrote to the Va-Nus between 1946 and 1950 shed a vivid light on his feelings, particularly as Müzehher acted as his confidante while he was suffering emotional turmoil.

In the autumn of 1948 the name of Nazım's cousin Münevver Andaç began to crop up in correspondence with Va-Nu's wife. Müzehher kept emphasizing what a charming woman Münevver had become and how much she admired the poet. Nazım was rather surprised:

Lately, almost everybody has been telling me about Münevver's qualities with such praise. Also, she has started writing to me from time to time. [...] I guess she is a wonderful woman. I am pleased to hear that. I understand she is happily married too. I hear that her husband is an intelligent, educated, handsome man. So why should I be expected to appreciate her? (Nurettin 1986, 98-9).

Münevver had brown hair and green eyes, and the characteristic good looks of Nazım's mother's family. Born in Sofia on 12 February 1917, she was the younger daughter of Celile's brother Mustafa and his French wife Gabrielle Taron. Mustafa had been a close friend of Kemal Atatürk when both were attached to the embassy in Sofia at the outbreak of the First World War. He died young, and it was apparently at Atatürk's suggestion that the family adopted the name Andaç (meaning 'memento'), when surnames were introduced. After her husband's death Gabrielle moved to Paris with her daughters Leyla and Münevver, both of whom were brought up speaking French. In 1926 Gabrielle also died, and Münevver was sent to a French boarding school in Italy, before completing her education in Marseilles in 1934. The following year she returned to Istanbul with her sister and began studying law, while beginning to earn her living as a teacher of French. In 1945 she married Nurullah Berk, painter and professor at the Istanbul Academy of Fine Arts, and the next year their daughter Renan was born. But Münevver was far too independent a spirit to settle into a conventional Turkish marriage.

Nazım's first impressions of Münevver dated back to 1935, when she had fallen in love with him at the age of eighteen, after a meeting at a family gathering. In July 1996 she recalled that for three years she and Nazım had a rather turbulent relationship, which ended when he was arrested in 1938. 'He was a married man,' she observed, 'so it was very difficult' (Münevver, Interview, July 1996). During his years in prison they lost contact, and he felt puzzled when suddenly he began to receive letters from her in 1948. The renewal of contact with Münevver coincided with rumours that Nazım might be freed. In October 1948 he received a letter from Va-Nu himself saying that there would soon be an amnesty, since this had been promised by the new government; but this was merely a false rumour (AM 3, 344). Was it coincidence that Münevver made contact with him just as his release seemed likely, or were the two developments in some way connected? Münevver's own account (Interview, July 1996) suggests that the timing was fortuitous and that it was Celile who prompted the renewal of contact, suggesting she should telephone Nazım on her behalf. Was there perhaps some concerted

16. Nazım in Bursa Prison, 1948.

effort among Nazım's relatives and friends to detach him from Piraye? There may have been some jockeying for position between different ideological factions as Nazım's release became more likely; after all, considerable prestige would attach to the protectors of Turkey's most famous poet once he was rehabilitated.

Early in October 1948 Münevver visited Nazım in prison for the first time, accompanied by her cousin Ayşe Baştımar and another friend, the novelist Peride Celal (Aydemir 1986b, 91). At the age of forty-six Nazım was still a fine figure of a man, despite his ten years spent behind bars (Fig. 16). Münevver's dormant feelings for the poet were reawakened, while he for his part was dazzled by this emancipated young woman. 'It is difficult to write a love poem about anybody else but Piraye,' Nazım wrote in a letter of July 1948 (AM 3, 338), but three months later we find him writing a whole cluster of poems expressing his passionate feelings for Münevver, fluctuating between despondency and desire. In 'Sonbahar' ('Autumn', October 1948), autumnal imagery is used to convey a mood of sensuous expectation:

> The days are getting shorter,
> the rainy season is about to start,
> my doors were wide open, waiting for you,
>   what kept you so long?
> On my table are green pepper, salt and bread,
> The wine in my pot I have been keeping for you
>   I drank half of it on my own
>   waiting for you.
>   what kept you so long?
> But, now the succulent fruits are hanging
> on their branches ripe and crunchy.
> They were about to fall on the earth
> if you were delayed any longer.
>   (A 4, 176)

The imagery of autumnal fruits, hinting at his own overripe sexuality, forms a dramatic contrast to another poem sent to Piraye three years earlier, '5 November 1945', in which autumn was associated with renunciation (A 3, 109; P, 103). The poem inspired by Münevver was sent both to Kemal Tahir and to Müzehher, but not to Piraye who at this stage was unaware of Nazım's new attachment. In another poem, dated 1 November 1948, Nazım expresses his sense of guilt at betraying Piraye: he feels he has 'stabbed her in the back' (Nurettin 1986, 139).

It was Rasih Güran whom Nazım entrusted with the task of conveying to Piraye the letter announcing that their relationship was over. Nazım now suggested that their sexual relationship, which had been in abeyance for so long, could not be revived; but they would remain friends because of his gratitude to her for the most beautiful years of his life and for inspiring his most beautiful works. This letter came as a terrible shock for Piraye, since there had never previously been any suggestion of a separation. She was so distressed that she locked herself in her room for several days (AM 1, 292-3). According to her son Memet she reluctantly accepted the situation, saying she would not stand in the way of Nazım and Münevver (Memet Fuat, Interview, March 1996). Nazım's response also became more conciliatory: 'I cannot be separated either from you or from my country. [...] You and I are going to remain in the minds of our people together whether you like it or not' (AM 1, 294).

Piraye was supposed to remain the ideal woman to whom the poet could proclaim an eternal attachment, while Nazım had the freedom to take another lover. In a letter to Kemal Tahir at the end of 1948, he attempted to justify his position:

For me Piraye is such a perfect, brave and good person and woman that I could not lie to her – I owe her the most beautiful years of my life and my best works.[...] In our relationship – including that of husband and wife, which has been the least important part – I decided that I would rather let her be hurt and perhaps very badly hurt and even torment her rather than tell her lies or cheat her. I too still feel very sad and tormented. But we both have our dignity and self-respect (AM 3, 346).

During the next eighteen months we find Nazım in the grip of classic mid-life crisis, longing for a younger woman who might restore his vitality. Münevver's response must have been equally intense, since she promptly informed her husband of this new relationship. In late October, Nurullah Berk visited Nazım in prison, and asked him what were his intentions. After this visit, Nazım demanded that Münevver should leave her husband immediately and start divorce proceedings (Nurettin 1986, 116), but for her this transformation was too abrupt. She wrote to Nazım asking him to be patient, because her husband was unwilling to give her custody of their daughter. When she tried to explain the need to be patient, Nazım felt angry and rejected. His ambivalent feelings towards Münevver and his guilty conscience about Piraye are dramatically expressed in an undated letter to the Va–Nus, probably written in February 1949:

> How could she [Münevver] do this to me? She was the first woman I ever loved unconditionally. While I was stabbing my closest, best and most honest friend who never lied to me [Piraye], I felt I was discovering love as if I were discovering a totally new universe. What did the other one discover while digging a knife into me? Even after I was stabbed, why did she need to say, in a letter she wrote in Istanbul, five or six days ago: 'You must never doubt my love for you, I shall wait for you, will you wait for me too?' On the day of writing this, I expect she went for a promenade in Beyoğlu, arm-in-arm with her husband, and perhaps even went to bed with him, and in the middle of night simply got up out of her husband's arms when she wrote me that letter. What hurts me most is, as I say, not just that I feel I've been discarded like an old handkerchief. Even though that hurt my pride, part of me also says that I deserved this, but my real anguish lies elsewhere: what hurts me is not being able to explain it all (Nurettin 1986, 141).

However, in this same letter, we see him turning pain into poetry, using the motif of 'stabbing' as the pivotal image in a short five-scene sketch with Prologue and Epilogue entitled 'Melodrama' ('Melodram'), which features three characters: 'Myself', 'My Red-headed Sister' and 'You'. The Redheaded Sister is clearly Piraye, while 'You' (the rather formal 'Siz') refers to Münevver. Nazım sent this 'Melodrama' to his stepson Memet, so it was clearly intended for Piraye's eyes. The Prologue establishes the self-lacerating tone:

> The most hopeless escapade:
>   is not caused by being wounded seven times
> The most hopeless escapade:
>   is losing your hold on the tether
> and with our eyes as sorrowful as the eyes of an ox,
> putting ourselves under the knife
>   our own necks under the knife
>   tired and stretched [. . .]

Scene Two is addressed to the (unnamed) Münevver:

> You are only a rumour.
> Ceaselessly my head is turning you around,
> Ceaselessly creating you.

And without touching you with my hands
I am going to remove your green dress from your naked body.

There are undertones of self-criticism, since Scene Four, which is addressed to Piraye, dramatises the poet's guilt:

Tonight, perhaps now, this very second
          you were stabbed in the back, my sister.
    It was me too who stabbed you
with blood dripping from my fingers.
                    (A 4, 182)

The theatrical language suggests that Nazım has lost control of his art as well as his emotions, and the effect is not redeemed by his awareness that he is using the techniques of melodrama. The final section has a particularly hollow ring, as the poet appeals to 'my son Memet' to pass on to his mother the consoling news that Nanking is about to be captured by 'our people' (Mao's Red Army). It is difficult to think of any other point in Nazım's *oeuvre* where the pathos of revolutionary politics is so misplaced.

Münevver refused to be swept off her feet, and Nazım, denied the grand passion he longed for, acted as if he had been totally rejected. The feeling that she had dropped him 'like an old handkerchief' prompted him to have second thoughts about divorce and even to write to Piraye suggesting a new start. The tone of self-pity can scarcely have made much of an impression, even though he piles on the agony by suggesting that he probably has only two more years to live. Now that he has (as he claims) definitely decided to end his relationship with Münevver, the nightmare is surely over for both of them. Even those little difficulties about sex can soon be sorted out. Is it worth making themselves miserable just because he made a silly mistake?

Yes, I have poisoned you by my mistake, but I have realised my mistake now and I am holding my feeble hand out to you; our relationship is strong enough to forget this memory. [...] I would like to die holding your hands. [...] When I die, you will be able to say: he was a wonderful person but he was too weak in some areas (AM 1, 297).

The following letter is even more sentimental:

I stabbed you in the back. [...] I have no right to ask your forgiveness. [...] Come, I have to live. If my life belonged only to me, it wouldn't matter. [...] I have myself, my physical needs, the crazy and sick side of my mind.

[...] Come for the sake of our daughter, our son and honest people like them (AM 1, 299).

He evidently feels that he is entitled to sympathy for his sexual needs, while her primary duty is to the family. Not surprisingly, Piraye was unmoved by this special pleading. She simply disappeared, reportedly leaving Istanbul to stay with relatives, and Nazım had to rely on his stepson Memet for further news.

The fifty-odd letters which Nazım wrote to Memet from Bursa prison between 1943 and 1950 add a further dimension to the story. Far from acting merely as a conduit for communication with Piraye, the young man clearly gained Nazım's affection and respect in his own right. Reflecting on their relationship in a letter of 27 January 1950, Nazım writes:

Everybody is the child of two people. But you are my son, independent from your mother. [...] Your mother gave you to me, just as she did all my writings since I came to know her. [...] No father can ever love a son in the way that I love you. [...] You are not my biological continuation, but the continuation of my best qualities (AM 2, 109).

At times Nazım writes to Memet with astonishing frankness about his relationship with Piraye, even alluding to their sexual difficulties:

My Piraye loved me with pride, unconditionally, loyally, cautiously, rationally, habitually, enormously, with her mind and heart. [...] All this is the love of a friend, a mother, a wife. [...] But she never felt a physical need for me. She never desired me passionately. [...] Piraye never once lost herself, gazing into my eyes and saying: I love you (AM 2, 90).

Memet mentions in a letter that Piraye used to feel heartbroken because of his affairs, but she could not leave him because she loved him so much (AM 2, 94). Nazım finds this impossible to believe, claiming that he was pushed into having affairs by Piraye's lack of love. The poet's efforts to justify his infidelity become even more tortuous:

I did not want to be unfaithful to her again. [...] When Münevver told me that she cannot possibly be separated from her child, she needed time to think about it, she also wanted me to promise that I shall wait for her, [...] then I used the occasion to finish my relationship with Münevver, told her that I cannot wait, I have been unfair to her, to her husband and especially to my red-headed sister. [...] It may sound strange to you but it is true that ever since I got to know your mother, in every story I have read, in every film I saw, in every book I read, I could always see your mother and me as lovers. [...] When I declared love to Cahit Uçuk or others, even writing love letters to Münevver now, it was always your mother I was writing to. [...] If Piraye had not been too proud to tell me that she loved me, if she had not left me so isolated both inside and outside, no other woman could have come between us (AM 2, 96-7).

To disentangle all these confusions would have needed many hours on the analyst's couch. Nazım's mother was indeed so concerned about his state of mind that she asked Va-Nu to arrange for him to be transferred to a sanatorium (Nurettin 1986, 243). But Piraye felt that after so many passing infidelities Nazım had finally gone too far, and dealt an irredeemable blow to her self-respect. The poet could hardly claim that he had not been warned; in a letter of September 1949 to Kemal Tahir he ruefully recalled a conversation with Piraye many years earlier after his affair with Cahit Uçuk, when she admonished him: 'If you commit this kind of nonsense again, I will not remain your wife any longer' (AM 3, 353).

Piraye refused to write to him for almost a year, and when she at last relented in September 1949 it was only to ask who his lawyers were. Her tone was so formal that she even addressed him as Mr Hikmet, thus clearly implying that she would never live with him again (AM 1, 309). In a reply dated 29 October addressed to Memet, Nazım once again pleaded with her to visit him, even hinting that he would commit suicide if she did not come: 'This will be the last time I shall ask her to visit me. I want you to know that if she does not come, I will be physically and spiritually gone for you, for Suzan and for your mother' (AM 1, 314). Under pressure from relatives and friends, Piraye visited him in prison again on 30 October, accompanied by Memet and Suzan, and by Izgen, her cousin (whom Memet later married). 'I was the happiest man in the world,' Nazım later wrote to Kemal Tahir. 'Despite her suffering, Piraye hasn't lost the ability to smile' (AM 3, 355). But Memet recalls that as they left the prison Piraye said simply: 'I don't love Nazım any more' (AM 1, 315).

Nazım felt heartened when Piraye began writing to him again; according to Memet, she was under pressure from her friends as well as from members of the Turkish Communist Party to resume her relationship with Nazım. Also, his continuing dependence on her is vividly expressed in a short note written on 4 November

1949, which mentions that he has been hallucinating about her during an attack of high fever (AM 1, 316). It was at the end of December 1949 that he sent her a poem inspired by Ibrahim Balaban's painting 'The Prison Gates'. This painting, the finest produced in Bursa prison, shows a group of six women with their children clustered outside the prison gates, surrounded by the gifts they have brought for the men inside. In Balaban's composition the figures acquire an aura of heroic endurance, even though the details, as picked out in Nazım's poem, appear so mundane: 'green peppers in wooden baskets, onions / and garlic in saddlebags, sacks of coal.' The poet adapts the motif of the waiting women to his own purpose in lines directly addressed to Piraye:

> Six women wait outside the iron gates,
> and inside – well, there are five hundred men;
>
> you aren't one of the six women,
> but I am one of the five hundred men.
>   (A 4, 196-7; P, 142-3)

Fortunately, this was not his final word. In January 1950, having received two letters from Piraye after a silence of almost three months, Nazım felt so overjoyed that he wrote to her explaining how he spread the pages out on his bed to feast his eyes on her handwriting (AM 1, 322). But by this date he had accepted that she would never live with him again.

His physical health continued to get worse, his liver deficiency causing his face to be marked with blotches, and he suffered from sleeplessness. He became so depressed that he even attempted suicide by overdosing on sleeping pills; he was saved by Vehbi Ertuğrul, his friend from the weaving collective, who succeeded in waking him from a coma-like sleep (Memet Fuat, Interview, March 1996). His letters written during these months of crisis are full of agonised reflections: 'I am in a state of loneliness', he wrote to Müzehher in the spring of 1949. 'Sometimes I feel suffocated with grief. I have to defeat this feeling of loneliness' (Nurettin 1986, 160). He feels that he no longer exists as a human being:

Münevver was the last branch that I tried to clutch. [...] If Piraye did not neglect me, I would have been still be holding on to her [...] I was a baby, enchanted by colour, light, voices, people, animals, universe, and life around me. [...] Unfortunately, I have now grown up (Nurettin 1986, 171-2).

Waking in the morning and *not* remembering Piraye or Münevver may bring momentary relief, but by lunchtime he cannot stop thinking about them (Nurettin 1986, 174). Sometimes the letters show psychological insight:

Approaching the age of fifty, we may experience a hopeless love affair. Unfortunately, we take love affairs very seriously under prison conditions. Moreover our lover's betrayal, her lack of love, leaves us with the feeling of being stabbed from both sides. [...] I am going to live to be seventy-five and I will still fall in love with unworthy women, under difficult circumstances. [...] For when I fall in love, I invent a great deal of that person myself. Yet I shall fall in love even when I am seventy-five, and I shall be rejected again, and scream with heart-ache again (Nurettin 1986, 182).

The letters reveal both a capacity for detached self-observation and characteristic swings of mood: 'When I have a crisis, like a hysterical woman I watch it as if someone else were suffering from it. [...] I, the living me, watching the dead me' (Nurettin 1986, 174-5). He is aware that it is being in prison that makes him so vulnerable: 'If I were outside, I would perhaps have got over my feelings for Münevver long ago, and perhaps after a while, maybe a year, I would even have forgotten Piraye' (Nurettin 1986,187). Towards the end of the year he was still searching for words to do full justice to the pain of being rejected by Münevver: 'I am afraid that my wings will catch fire and I will turn into ashes like a moth whirling around a candle light, with already half-burned wings. It is very bizarre that a woman axing me at my roots should have felled me so completely, because it hit me at a certain passage in my life' (Nurettin 1986, 209).

The only way for Nazım to survive such a crisis was to write about it. Since he was working on a Turkish version of La Fontaine, he hit on the idea of an animal fable, 'Tabby Cat and the Poplar Tree' ('Tekir'le Kavak'). In this story an adventurous tabby cat climbs a handsome, mature poplar tree. The tree feels thrilled, its leaves rustle and its catkins start dancing in the wind. But when the night turns chill, the cat begins to miss its cosy home and decides to return to its master, leaving the tree feeling abandoned. When Nazım sent this fable to Piraye, he seems to have expected her to take it as a sign that he had learned his lesson:

middle-aged men should avoid adventurous feline creatures. But Piraye sensed that the melancholy tree was really longing for the cat to return. Responding to her comments, Nazım rather implausibly insisted that the ending of his affair with Münevver was nothing to do with the unpredictable behaviour of the cat. It was he himself who had 'woken up from a nightmare' (AM 1, 306).

A second project conceived as a means of working through difficult feelings was the play 'Blessings Upon You' ('Allah Rahatlık Versin'), on which he started work in the spring of 1949 (Nurettin 1986, 152 & 160). The title Nazım originally had in mind was even more suggestive: 'Thwarted Destiny with Two Women and Two Men' ('Kambur Felek ve İki Kadınla İki Erkek'). Although this play remained a fragment, its central figure is clearly conceived as a means of refocusing his feelings about Münevver. The heroine Zeliha, a respectable married woman with a three-year-old daughter, falls in love with a radical and bohemian painter. Her husband cannot believe that she will really leave the security of her marriage for a life of poverty. The two men agree that Zeliha must decide her own future, but the husband then exploits the situation by threatening to deprive her of all contact with her daughter, as well as denying her financial assistance. The fragment ends with a conversation about how people cope with jealousy and desire (A 12, 79). Clearly, there was nothing original about the plot. Indeed, Nazım's letters to Va-Nu's wife suggest that it was really a pretext for collecting information about Münevver's feelings by pretending to ask for comments about the heroine of the play. The play was still incomplete when, on 20 February 1950, Nazım experienced a moment of great joy: Münevver visited him again in prison and revived his hopes that she would marry him. His feelings are recorded in another letter to Müzehher: 'Despite my rage, panic, guilt and pain, I knew that she would come. [...] I sat and talked to her as if she had never gone. [...] Despite my incongruous behaviour and although at times I seem to be so weak, I get what I want once I put my mind to it' (Nurettin 1986, 221). Münevver seems to be a 'character' who has come in search of her 'author', as in the celebrated play by Pirandello. But the play could be left incomplete once the real-life drama had begun.

202 *Bursa Prison, 1940-1950*

A Turkish Dreyfus case

In the summer of 1949, a time when his personal life was in turmoil, Nazım's spirits were raised by the launching of a public campaign for his release. This did not originate among his allies on the Turkish left, since the communist party had effectively been crushed, but arose from the revival of multi-party politics. It was rumoured that there would be an amnesty before the general elections due in May 1950 – the first truly free multi-party elections. The Republican People's Party, which had held power for so long, was being challenged by the newly founded Democratic Party. A journalist from the Democratic camp, Ahmet Emin Yalman, first took up Nazım's case in a series of articles; he was alarmed by the letters of protest about Nazım's imprisonment arriving from abroad (Yalman, 186), but seems to have been motivated less by humanitarian considerations than by the fear that Turkey's international reputation was suffering. In addition, he clearly wanted to score points for the Democrats.

Yalman, a native of Salonika from a converted Jewish family, was a man of wide-ranging interests who had studied at Columbia University in New York before the First World War. He was an outspoken Turkish patriot, and during the Allied occupation of 1919 was arrested by the British and exiled to Malta for several months. The first phase of his journalistic career came to an abrupt end in 1925 as a result of prosecution by the Tribunal of Independence in the aftermath of the Kurdish revolt. After fifteen years as a businessman, he relaunched his newspaper *Vatan* in 1940. His independent stance brought him into conflict with the government after the Turkish National Assembly introduced a discriminatory tax, the *Varlık Vergisi*, that tended to penalize businessmen of Greek, Jewish and Armenian origin. Tax defaulters were publicly denounced and sent to forced labour camps, and their property was confiscated. In October 1943 Yalman began a campaign against this policy, suggesting that Turkey was succumbing to the disease of anti-Semitism. Only in March 1944 was the tax was finally abandoned under pressure from the Western powers. The racist principles underlying it were acknowledged after the war by the Istanbul Director of Finance, Faik Ökte, and historians have described this as a disgraceful episode (Weisband, 231-6).

As a journalist Yalman had a record of defending unpopular

causes, but his intervention was especially remarkable because he was an outspoken anti-communist. His memoirs, published in English in 1956, abound in references to the sinister activities of 'reddish leftists' whose only loyalty was to Moscow (Yalman, 1956, 225-6). However, he was also a cultivated man whose interest in Nazım's work dated back to 1942, when he had been so impressed by sections of the manuscript of 'Human Landscapes' that he considered publishing them in *Vatan* (AM 3, 162). In June 1949 he visited Nazım in prison, which marked the first stage in the campaign. This was evidently not his first visit, but their conversation, as described by Nazım in a letter of 10 June 1949 to Müzehher, seems to have marked a breakthrough, although it was certainly not a meeting of minds:

We talked for twenty minutes. I talked, he listened. I asked him how he can be so concerned about Bulgarian priests and Hungarian cardinals being jailed, and campaigning for the freedom of Catholics and Orthodox Christians, devoting whole columns to lamenting their plight, while he doesn't seem to remember that he is a Turk and doesn't concern himself about the innocent people rotting in Turkish prisons for twelve years. He did not answer, but nodded his head. [...] He told me that in the Soviet Union they had issued a postage stamp with my picture on it, in Bulgaria they had named a school after me. [...] I told him that I have no knowledge of these rumours. [...] If it is true, our Post Office and Ministry of Education should learn a lesson from it and do as they did. [...] The sort of comments made by Yalman get up my nose (Nurettin 1986, 189).

Yalman's own account shows that he was impressed by Nazım's undogmatic approach to Marxism. But he saw himself as a missionary whose aim was to rescue Nazım from the snare of communism and 'win him over for the Turkish nation' (Yalman, 14, 186-90).

Despite these tensions, Yalman wrote a rather sympathetic account of this interview, published on 19 August in *Vatan*. The three-month delay was due to resistance within the editorial office – two earlier articles by Yalman about Nazım's case had been spiked. In this article he argued that it was unjust to imprison Nazım for so long, since he had never been an agent of Moscow and his communism was motivated by his sensitivity to the sufferings of the Turkish people. His conclusion was notably forceful:

Responsibility for the unfair treatment of Nazım does not only rest with the two military courts, or with the political leaders who gave the orders during the single-party regime, or the jurists who hold all the files [...], or even the intellectuals of this generation. It also rests with the twenty million people Turkey ('Fikret ve Nazım Hikmet', *Vatan*, 19 August 1949).

Yalman insisted that if the Turks honoured great writers of the past like Tevfik Fikret, they should protest at Nazım's wrongful imprisonment.

Nazım remained sceptical about the attempt to play down his communism. 'Yalman wrote things that I never said,' he complained to Va-Nu's wife in a letter of 21 August 1949, 'and some of the things that I did say were distorted.' His frustration was expressed in a further letter of 29 September: 'Either Yalman & Co. believe that I have been imprisoned unjustly for twelve years and will continue to be for another sixteen, or they don't' (Nurettin 1986, 194 & 201). Yalman's article implied that Nazım should be released on compassionate grounds, rather than as a victim of injustice. And he relied too heavily on the pragmatic argument that Nazım's continued imprisonment helped the communist cause and damaged Turkey's reputation abroad. The article nevertheless made a considerable impact, and provoked a lively press debate. On 1 September *Vatan* published a letter of support from Selami Helvacıoğlu, one of the military judges involved in Nazım's case, acknowledging that the sentences imposed had been unjust. Casual contacts between communists and members of the armed forces did not constitute a crime.

In late September or early October Nazım received a further visit from Yalman, accompanied by his wife and another poet, Behçet Kemal. Yalman promised that he would be released within two years (Nurettin 1986, 206), but Nazım felt that two years was too long to wait and objected vigorously. Meanwhile, Yalman also found it necessary to defend himself against right-wing critics, who objected to him campaigning for the release of a communist. In another article in *Vatan* on 20 October, he justified his position in patriotic terms, placing less emphasis on Nazım's human rights than on Turkey's international reputation. 'It was inevitable', Yalman wrote, 'that the Nazım affair would spill over into the international arena. We are proud that we have taken the first steps as it is our family affair and the initiative should not be left to foreigners.'

Though sceptical about Yalman's methods, Nazım was persuaded to enlist the support of a lawyer, Mehmet Ali Sebük, who had studied criminology in France and was well qualified to support Yalman's campaign. He was a member of the Democratic Party, later elected to the National Assembly; he also acted as legal adviser to *Vatan* and could claim credit as a campaigner for improvements in prison conditions. A sense of justice led him to take up Nazım's case, even though he disagreed with his political opinions. Sebük has left a lively account of the ensuing ideological exchanges. 'Do you consider Moscow as your Mecca?' Yalman sarcastically inquired, and Nazım replied that his Mecca was his love of his nation. He believed in Sheikh Bedreddin, who had defended equality, brotherhood and the rights of the people long before Marx. He respected Marx as a thinker, but not in a narrowly dogmatic way: 'I believe in a system that can be reached by economic planning, in which people are no longer poor and oppressed. [...] This dream may not materialise for a thousand years. If loving this dream is a crime, then I am a criminal' (Sebük, 56-8).

Sebük recalls that he found Nazım emotionally and physically debilitated when he visited him in Bursa prison. But Nazım was impressed that such an eminent lawyer was willing to reopen his case after twelve years of silence by the legal profession. After three months spent studying the court files, Sebük wrote a series of ten articles on the case, published in *Vatan* between November 1949 and February 1950. His critique concentrated on procedural questions and ignored Nazım's politics. For the first time Turkish readers were informed of the precise nature of the case, which had never been accurately reported, because the army and navy trials had been held behind closed doors. Most people assumed that Nazım had been convicted for spreading communist propaganda, but now for the first time they learned that he had actually been charged with inciting the army to revolt. It was not difficult to demonstrate that Nazım's conviction on this charge was absurd. Sebük identified a series of procedural errors, which he attributed to the fact that of the five presiding judges at the military court in Ankara only two had any legal training. Their grasp of the rules of evidence was fundamentally flawed, since they accepted a series of uncorroborated statements extracted under interrogation as factual testimony. Ömer Deniz had denied in court that Nazım ever said to him, as was claimed, 'You must teach the soldiers first about the republic and then about communism.' In the navy trial, too, the prosecution failed to substantiate the charge that Nazım had asked a naval rating for the names of men who might be converted to communism. Both these alleged statements were retracted in court, and there were no independent witnesses to substantiate them. It is a fundamental axiom that a confession extracted from a defendant is inadmissible as evidence against a co-defendant unless corroborated by a third party.

The second plank of Sebük's argument related to the length of the sentences. He pointed out that the standard sentence for murder was fifteen years, which in practice meant twelve years in prison. But Nazım has already served thirteen years, not for murder but for casual conversations; and he had fifteen years still to serve. According to the military criminal code, the minimum sentence for inciting the army to revolt was five years and the maximum twenty. Court procedure required that cogent reasons be given for any sentence above the minimum; if those reasons were not valid, the judgement was liable to be overturned on appeal. The reason given by the Ankara military court for raising Nazım's sentence to fifteen years was that he had previous convictions under the Civil Code, but technically the Military and Civil Codes formed two distinct systems of jurisdiction. Communist propaganda was not a criminal offence under the Military Code, so that previous convictions on that count did not entitle the military court to impose a longer sentence. Similar arguments applied to the further thirteen year sentence imposed during the navy trial.

These articles in *Vatan* provoked a flood of letters. For the first time in Turkish history, the establishment found itself under pressure from media-led public opinion. However, Sebük was not content to focus on legal technicalities. In two articles published in January 1950, he spelt out the political implications under the provocative headings 'The Dreyfus Affair' and 'Dreyfus – Nazım'. First he reviewed the events leading to the victimisation of Dreyfus and the campaign which brought about his release. Then he went on to show that at almost every point the miscarriage of justice in Nazım's case was far more blatant. The French authorities had at least produced written documents, supposedly written by Dreyfus, to justify the charge of treason; in Nazım's case the evidence was mere hearsay. Under French law espionage really was a crime; under Turkish law conversations about communism were not. In France in the 1890s espionage really did threaten state security; in Turkey in 1938, the fact that military cadets were reading books by left-wing authors was of no consequence. Finally, Dreyfus was released after four years on Devil's Island, but Nazım had already spent thirteen years in Turkish jails. In short, his case could be seen as 'the worst miscarriage of justice of the twentieth century' (Sebük, 104-14).

Sebük was firmly convinced of Nazım's innocence, but he was too much of a realist to expect this to be readily acknowledged. Following the example of Zola, he hoped to provoke the Ministry of Justice or the Ministry of Defence into opening a case against himself, so that he would have a chance to justify his position in open court. Failing that, he hoped that his exposure of procedural errors would at least lead to Nazım being released under an amnesty. A further argument was that a prisoner in Nazım's condition would normally be released on grounds of ill-health. When the authorities failed to respond to his revelations, Sebük decided to give priority to the health factor. He submitted a formal application to the Bursa public prosecutor, arguing that Nazım was suffering from angina and tuberculosis, as well as serious nervous disorders – conditions which the hospitals in Bursa were not adequately equipped to treat. But his application for Nazım to be transferred to Istanbul for medical treatment was refused.

Sebük's next move was to apply to President İnönü for a special amnesty. He discussed the matter with İnönü in person, presenting him with a report of the flaws in the judicial procedure (Sebük, 142). In February 1950 Sebük made formal applications both to the Appeal Court and to the National Assembly for a review of Nazım's case, in an effort to obtain a special amnesty (Nurettin 1986, 223). But these efforts failed, and the most he was able to achieve was the promise that Nazım would be transferred to Istanbul prison because of his poor health. Nazım regarded these efforts with growing scepticism. He did not want an amnesty, he wanted justice (Sebük, 153-60). Why did İnönü reject the arguments in favour of an amnesty? This will remain a mystery until further documentation becomes available. If any individual bears ultimate responsibility for this case, it must be the Turkish President, who was in office throughout the period of Nazım's imprisonment. Admittedly, it was Fevzi Çakmak who initiated the anti-communist witch-hunt, but when it came to a test of strength, İnönü was capable of overruling Çakmak, and in January 1944 compelled him to retire as Chief of Staff (Weisband, 249). After the defeat of Germany, İnönü's strategy of maintaining a cautious neutrality was fully vindicated. And it was he who presided over the process of liberalisation after 1945, leading to the establishment of a multi-party system. Thus the responsibility for Nazım's continuing incarceration lay squarely with President İnönü. Only after his removal from power was Nazım finally released.

In the early months of 1950 rumours of an amnesty were so widespread that Nazım wrote to the Va-Nus urging them to listen to the parliamentary news every evening so that they could come to Bursa to collect him the day after the announcement (Nurettin 1986, 227). On 20 March wide-ranging amnesty proposals were put before the National Assembly, but they came up against a barrage of criticism. Communists are worse than murderers, it was argued, because murderers have only committed a crime against a single person, whereas communists have committed a crime against the whole nation. Send them and their families to the USSR! (Tutanak 1951) Meanwhile, the Va-Nus had set out for Bursa, confident that they would soon be celebrating Nazım's freedom. When they were admitted to the governor's room, they found they were in good company: a reporter from *Cumhuriyet* was also there to report his release (Nurettin 1986, 10). When the news reached them that the Assembly had gone into recess, on 22 March 1950, without approving the amnesty, they were bitterly disappointed. At the last minute the Republicans, desperate to hold on to power, had lost their nerve, fearing that the Democrats would claim credit for pushing the amnesty through. Amendments were proposed to exclude those convicted by military courts from the amnesty, and the whole issue was referred back to a special 'Justice Committee'. Thus all hope of an amnesty before the May election disappeared.

The news that the amnesty had been blocked left Nazım visibly distraught. Müzehher describes the scene when she and Va-Nu arrived in prison:

Nazım was looking very pale; [...] He just sat there drawing some traditional kilim patterns until visiting time was over, he then walked with us up to the iron door. [...] I remember Va-Nu weeping in the street as we took the empty suitcases away with us (Nurettin 1986, 10).

After this setback, there seemed only one alternative – a hunger strike. Balaban, who had nurtured Nazım during his potentially suicidal moods in 1949, once again helped to strengthen his resolve. On the day before the hunger strike was due to start, a fellow prisoner named Yakup Yıldırım prepared a meal including some of Nazım's favourite dishes (Balaban 1979, 339). He received a visit from Izzet Akçal, inspector of prisons in Bursa, who was sympathetic to his cause but urged him to think again. 'I am risking my life, but it is worth it,' Nazım replied (Sülker 1974, 217). The decision to begin the hunger strike was announced in *Vatan* on March 30 in a letter from Sebük. This was supported the following day by an open letter from Yalman, appealing to the Prime Minister to release Nazım under a special amnesty, since his health was so frail. 'Nazım Hikmet', he declared, 'one of the most distinguished writers of the modern generation who has used the Turkish language so skilfully, has been wrongly imprisoned for thirteen years, contrary to the declaration of Human Rights of which Turkey is a signatory' (Sülker 1974, 194). Nazım was upset by the tone of Sebük's article, which he found too sentimental (Nurettin 1986, 232). On 30 March he wrote to the Va-Nus: 'I am appalled [...] I am supposed to be distressed, a broken man [...] my baggage ready, waiting to be set free [...] my wife outside the prison gate waiting. [...] Why can nobody understand that it is to obtain justice that one can decide to risk one's life?' Nazım's final letter to Piraye was also written on 30 March 1950, emphasising that he faced the hunger strike with patience and hope (AM 1, 333).

These events were accompanied by continuing publicity as Sebük, supported by a second lawyer Irfan Emin, organised press conferences, even reading patriotic passages from Nazım's 'Epic of National Liberation' to gain public sympathy (Sülker 1974, 216). Once the hunger strike was announced, events gathered momentum. On 7 April Sebük travelled to Ankara to lobby members of the government, warning them of the damage to national prestige if Nazım were to die in prison. The hunger strike was due to start the very next day, and this at last concentrated the minds of the politicians. It was decided to transfer Nazım to Istanbul for improved medical care pending a further review of his case. A medical examination took place in Bursa on 8 April, and the next day Nazım sent a telegram to Sebük saying that he had decided to postpone the hunger strike, since their demands were being met and investigations were under way. The same day Nazım was moved to Üsküdar Prison on the Anatolian shore of the Bosphorus (Sebük, 128).

After the transfer to Istanbul it was hoped that the public prosecutor would use his authority to suspend the remainder of Nazım's prison sentence on health grounds. For Nazım the continuing uncertainty was extremely distressing. Between 10 April and 2 May he found himself being shunted between the infirmary of Sultanahmet prison and Cerrahpaşa hospital for medical check-ups, and finally to Paşakapı prison in Üsküdar (Sebük, 128). It was in Üsküdar prison on 16 April that Piraye visited him for the last time, accompanied by her children (Bezirci, 58). Any hope of a reconciliation quickly evaporated when Münevver and Nazım's sister Samiye arrived; by this date Münevver's support had become far more important for Nazım than that of his wife (AM 1, 335). His great fear was that once he was transferred to hospital, the amnesty would be indefinitely postponed. A hunger strike offered the only hope of success. On 2 May 1950, while still in Üsküdar prison, he again began fasting, and the hunger strike that followed involved Nazım in great physical hardship. During the first few days he was able to read books and newspapers, but on the third day he began to lose his voice and his breath began to smell. On the seventh day he was taken to Cerrahpaşa hospital, and after various examinations the doctors certified that he needed to stay in a fully equipped medical environment (Sebük, 130). But Nazım refused the offer of a hospital bed and demanded to be sent back to prison (*Vatan*, 10 May). When Yalman visited him in Üsküdar Prison, he was dismayed to find that Nazım was profoundly changed. He no longer seemed to be the gifted and open-minded poet he had so admired in Bursa the previous year (Yalman 14, 194). Feeling that he had made a mistake in supporting a committed communist, he published an open letter in *Vatan* on 11 May appealing to him to abandon the hunger strike.

On 14 May, the day of the general elections, Nazım finally agreed to be transferred to Cerrahpaşa hospital. His resolve began to weaken when he was told that he would be given a private room where he would be allowed to receive visitors, including Münevver. During the first twelve days of the hunger strike he had lost 8 kilos and had to be given a drip (Nurettin 1991, 158). According to another report he had become completely unconscious by the eighteenth day (Sülker 1975, 241). The accounts of contemporaries are inconsistent, and it is difficult to disentangle fact from myth. There was certainly an element of stage management – of insisting in public that Nazım might die at any moment, while privately ensuring that he stayed alive. The timing of the hunger strike – to coincide with the run-up to the general election – turned out to be a mistake, since the press was so preoccupied with national politics that the campaign for Nazım's release was sidelined. His supporters became concerned that, if he persisted with the hunger strike, he might die during the interregnum between the outgoing Republican People's Party and the new Democratic Party governments. Nazım's friend Abidin Dino was delegated to persuade him to suspend the hunger strike until the new government was in office. It was above all the question of political timing that led Nazım to agree to take nourishment again.

When Dino, backed by Zekeriya Sertel, put these arguments to Nazım, his response was that to give up the hunger strike might be seen as a sign of weakness. However, if a public campaign was orchestrated appealing to him to suspend it in order to give the new government a chance to respond to his demands, he was willing to consent. Dino and Sertel quickly organised a petition signed by prominent figures calling on him to end the strike (Dino, 123-5). Two separate appeals were drafted, one signed by prominent writers and artists, including Halide Edip, and the other by members of other professions including doctors, lawyers, writers and politicians. At the same time telegrams of support were arriving from abroad, since Nazım's case was attracting increasing international attention. Thus when, on 20 May, Nazım officially ended his hunger strike, this could be construed as a magnanimous response to public appeals and not as a sign that he had lost his nerve. One of his first treats was a basket of strawberries brought by Münevver.

The hunger strike marked the climax of a campaign which was having international repercussions. When Yalman published his first article in *Vatan* in August 1949, he rightly argued that Turkey should put its own house in order. Since this advice was ignored, the affair did indeed develop into a new Dreyfus case, as the government increasingly came under pressure from abroad. In September 1949 an international committee was formed in Paris, co-ordinated by the poet Tristan Tzara. Leading French artists and intellectuals supported the campaign, including Camus, Sartre, Simone de Beauvoir, Picasso and the singer Yves Montand (Sülker 1974, 219). Aragon, who had been an admirer Nazım's work since the 1930s, also played a leading role, and on 6 November 1949 Tristan Tzara sent a petition to the Turkish Prime Minister. Later that month a further appeal was issued by the Paris-based International Student Federation, which represented students from sixteen different countries (Sülker 1974,174-5). Even more significant was the cogently-argued appeal issued in February 1950 by the International Association of Lawyers. This appeal was sent to the Turkish National Assembly, the Ministry of Justice and the Ministry of Defence, as well as being released to the press (Sülker 1974, 172 & 181-6).

When a letter from Nazım, announcing his first hunger strike, was published by Va-Nu in *Akşam* on 9 April 1950, it was promptly reprinted outside Turkey, especially by socialist journals like the New York *Daily Worker* (Nurettin 1986, 234; Sülker 1974, 199). Given the growing importance for Turkey of the American alliance, demonstrations on Rockefeller Plaza in front of the Turkish Consulate in New York significantly increased the pressure. 'NAZIM HIKMET BELONGS TO ALL HUMANITY – HELP FREE HIM FROM TURKEY'S DUNGEONS', the placards proclaimed (Fig. 17a). Letters demanding Nazım's release were sent to the American Secretary of State, Dean Acheson (Aydemir 1970, 300); and the singer Paul Robeson, who had himself been victimized by the anti-communist witchhunt in the United States, added his powerful voice to the campaign. When Nazım's hunger strike began in earnest on 2 May, the international campaign was intensified. In Eastern bloc countries there had always been lively interest in his case, but there were now also protests and petitions in Britain, India, Switzerland, Egypt, Cyprus, Iraq, Iran, India, Syria and Lebanon. In several of these countries, translations of his poems appeared for the first time, their delicate cadences forming a poignant contrast to the harshness of the prison sentence. In Bulgaria, where his work was already well-known among the Turkish minority, the Writers' Union declared 15 May as a day of commemoration for Nazım's fight for freedom (Babayev, 205). These demonstrations

17b. Nazım's mother Celile demonstrating in Istanbul.

CAMPAIGN TO FREE NAZIM HIKMET
17a. Demonstration on Rockefeller Plaza, New York.

of solidarity provided a tremendous boost to Nazım's morale, reflected in the poem he wrote 'On the Fifth Day of the Hunger Strike':

> I know that
> > I am going to go on living on your side:
> in Aragon's lines
> > – that tell the story of the beautiful days to come –
> > > and in Picasso's white dove
> > > and in Robeson's songs.
> > and above all
> > > and the best of all:
> In the smile of the comrade worker in the docks of Marseille [...]
> > ('Açlık Grevinin Beşinci Gününde', A 4, 200)

Clearly there was a danger that this form of international solidarity might prove counterproductive. For right-wingers in the Turkish Assembly, expressions of support from notorious lackeys of the Kremlin like Aragon and Robeson merely confirmed their worst suspicions. Ultimately, the matter had to be resolved by the Turks themselves. It was the national campaign, launched in the run-up to the general election, that tipped the balance. The campaign was taken up by almost the whole Turkish press, with *Vatan*, *Akşam*, *Cumhuriyet* and *Tan* (which had reopened) taking the lead. Even the most stony-hearted politician could hardly remain unmoved by the spectacle Nazım's mother, the indomitable Celile, who by this time was almost blind, appealing for public support on the streets of Istanbul. On 9 May she made her way to Galata Bridge and started collecting signatures from the throngs of passers-by. A contemporary photograph shows her holding placard denouncing 'MY SON'S UNJUST IMPRISONMENT' and announcing that she too had begun fasting in protest (Fig. 17b). Three well-known Turkish poets – Orhan Veli, Melih Cevdet Anday and Oktay Rifat, who called themselves the 'Absurdists' ('Garipciler') – also joined the hunger strike on 12 May. Describing these actions as 'fasting' was designed to increase public sympathy among Muslims (Sülker 1974, 235-9). Münevver, too, succeeded in collecting hundreds of signatures for a petition, which was sent to the President and the Prime Minister. Even the actress Semiha Berksoy played her part in the campaign to secure Nazım's release. A number of small-circulation magazines gave further support. On 4 May a special weekly paper began to appear called *Nazım Hikmet*, designed to publicize his work and co-ordinate public protests. There were also large-scale demonstrations and public meetings. On 10 May the 'Organisation of Istanbul Youth in Higher Education' began distributing leaflets, undeterred by the threat of arrest. But the popular movement in support of Nazım was not uncontested. On 15 May there was a particularly turbulent meeting at Çiçek Palas Hall in Istanbul, which anti-communists disrupted. Nazım's mother Celile and his aunt Sara were present to represent the family. When Ilhan Berktay, leader of the Organisation, began a passionate speech, he was heckled from the back seats and from the balcony by nationalists shouting 'Go back to Moscow!' Fighting broke out, the police were called; the nationalists were removed but they regrouped outside the hall armed with stones, shouting anti-communist slogans and waiting for the campaigners to emerge. The windows of the building were smashed, and not until the Mayor of Istanbul appeared on the scene was the counterdemonstration brought under control (Sülker 1974, 241-53).

This incident coincided with the declaration of the election result, sweeping the Democratic Party into power. Benefiting from the bias of a first-past-the post system, the Democrats won 408 seats (53% of the vote) compared with the Republican People's Party's 39 (38% of the vote). Inönü resigned as President to be replaced by Celal Bayar, while the dynamically pro-American Adnan Menderes became Prime Minister. Although the Democratic Party was just as anti-communist as Inönü's Republicans, it was irrevocably committed to an amnesty. Nevertheless, Nazım's release remained in doubt until the very last minute. When the National Assembly reconvened, the amnesty proposals, amended by the Justice Commission, still provoked controversy. The debate began on 13 July and lasted two days. The Minister of State, Fevzi Lütfi Karaosmanoğlu, argued in favour of a comprehensive amnesty to include those convicted by military courts, which provoked impassioned reactions from right-wingers. Communists, it was argued, were not criminals but traitors. Worse still, they were hostile to Islam and opposed to private property (Tutanak, 1951). One denounced Nazım as 'a mad, red barking dog, ready to bite the Turkish nation'; those who were 'trying to lick his saliva' should be eliminated. Another newly-elected deputy used a more legalistic argument: 'It is madness to doubt that Nazım is a communist.

He is a communist, and if the charge on which he was convicted was wrong, he should be retried. If there was a judicial mistake, it is not the responsibility of the Assembly to exercise clemency.'

It is certainly ironic to find right-wing Turkish politicians defending the independence of the judiciary. But in 1950 a retrial might well have resulted in a conviction on other charges, given the anti-communist fervour which shortly afterwards led to Turkish troops being sent to fight in the Korean War. 'If we are going to let loose a person who is injecting poison into our very own sacred navy and army', another deputy demanded, 'who will defend our country in future? [...] Communists all around the world are waving their flags to claim Nazım as their own' (Sülker 1974, 253-5). The Amnesty Bill finally approved on 14 July was actually a compromise. It released all short-term prisoners (serving less than two years) and reduced the sentences of long-term prisoners by two-thirds. Since Nazım had already served almost half of his twenty-eight-year sentence, he was immediately freed, together with 110 others who had been convicted for communist propaganda or crimes against the state, including Kemal Tahir and Ibrahim Balaban. Around 2 o'clock in the afternoon on 15 July 1950 Nazım packed his bag and walked out of Cerrahpaşa hospital with Münevver and his lawyer Sebük – to face a freedom fraught with difficulties.

7

Human Landscapes

Nazım's most challenging task after his release in July 1950 was to prepare for publication the great project of his prison years, *Human Landscapes*. The difficulties which confronted him become clear when one reconstructs the poem's genesis. In the preface which he wrote in 1961 for the Russian edition, Nazım records that he began the work in Bursa prison in 1941 (B 4, 5). However, it is clear from his correspondence that it also incorporates passages composed in Istanbul and Çankırı. Since Nazım was not in a position to make the final revisions till the late 1950s, the successive phases of creativity, which added layer after layer of artistic refraction and political reference, extended intermittently over twenty years. The genesis of the poem thus provides valuable insight into the intellectual development of the poet.

The evolution of an epic, 1939-1961

Human Landscapes incorporates a series of narratives, initiated at different times and with divergent intentions. The work was not completed – if 'completed' is the right word – till the early 1960s, but its origins date back to December 1939 when, in prison in Istanbul, Nazım hit on the idea of writing an 'encyclopaedia' recording the lives of ordinary Turkish people – the workers, peasants and housewives who truly deserve the credit for shaping human history, rather than the 'great men' who feature in the conventional 'Who's Who' (Tahir, 357). Soon after his transfer to Çankırı he started work in earnest, giving it the provocative title 'Encyclopaedia of Famous People' ('Meşur Adamlar Ansiklopedisi'). In a letter to Piraye in late 1940 he explained: 'Most of the people in this book are the people we got to know together and the people we thought about when you were here. I am trying to tell about a historical period and about a section

of society with the background of people's personal life stories'
(AM 1, 149). The work continued after the move to Bursa, and
by December 1940, following an alphabetical scheme, Nazım had
produced a series of about thirty short biographical vignettes covering the initial letters A – H. Two entries under the letter A give
an idea of his approach:

> AHMET (Corporal)
> He fought in the Balkan war
> He fought during mobilisation
> He fought in the Greek war.
> 'Hang in there, brother, the end's in sight!'
>   he's famous for saying.
>
> ATIFET (1927, Sülemaniye, Istanbul.)
> Works at the stocking factory
> (Tophane Street, Galata).
> In 1940 she is thirteen years old.
>   (A 4, 55)

A further example is slightly more dramatic in conception:

> GALIP (Born in one of the cities)
>   (around 1883)
>   famous for thinking strange things
> 'If I could eat sugar wafers every day,' he thought
>   (at five)
>   'If I could go to school,' he thought
>   (at ten)

A dozen further 'strange' thoughts register the parameters of a
frustrated human life up to the age of fifty-two (A 4, 55 & 70).

At first, Nazım seems to have been satisfied with this minimalist
approach, but the letters he wrote in 1941 to Kemal Tahir reveal
that the 'search for a style' caused him much uncertainty: 'My
sultan-like laziness continues, but it is not really laziness: despite
the fact that I do not think systematically about literature, my
head is buzzing with ideas – searching for a style in poetry is
wrecking my nerves.' This new style was to be defiantly unpoetic,
since 'poetic style is a disease'. The rationale of the new realism
is to lie in 'its effectiveness, its teaching and guidance of the
audience to be more effective in life and in practice', while at
the same time not being merely 'a tool for agitation'. The debt
to Marxism is reflected in a further comment that 'modern realism

is conscious application of dialectical materialism in literature'. But Nazım also drew on literary sources. A comment by Engels identifying Diderot's novel *Le Neveu de Rameau* as a masterpiece of dialectics led Nazım to declare in April 1941 that he was 'willing to live on dry bread for a month in order to find this novel'. Within two weeks he had tracked down a copy, sharing his excitement over this discovery with Kemal Tahir (AM 3, 25, 42-8, 57 & 62).

Diderot's novel (as Hegel had pointed out in the *Phenomenology of Spirit*) shows how contrasting philosophical positions can be crystallized through vivid dialogue. But a more significant breakthrough came at the end of May 1941 when Nazım's original encyclopaedia concept began to evolve into a new formal structure, suggested to him by his reading of a history of medieval English literature by Halide Edib, *Ingiliz Edebiyatı Tarihi*. Here he read of William Langland's *Piers Ploughman*, the fourteenth-century English narrative poem in which characters from all sections of society appear in a vision. Nazım was fascinated both by Langland's social-critical focus and by his imaginative technique, which seemed to anticipate the panoramic quality of the modern cinema. This encouraged him to return to work on the 'Encyclopaedia' with renewed energy, redesigning it in a radically different style. At the same time he mentions a new project which he calls 'Onlar ve Maceraları' (They and Their Adventures), not restricted to the life of Turkey. His aim here was to make his panorama more dynamic: 'I am making my characters more active,' he explained to Kemal Tahir. 'To tell the truth, some of these people are alive and mobile, others – as you mentioned in your last letter – are like tombstones. [...] I am going to try to portray the people of my country in various historical times, using the most representative types' (AM 3, 71-5).

This exchange shows how valuable Kemal Tahir was as a sounding-board for Nazım's ideas. Both writers benefited from this critical dialogue, and when Nazım sent his friend a new poem, he would even ask him to get the feel of it by reading it out loud – 'clearly, with very little declamation, as if it were prose' (AM 3, 134). To obtain further reactions, he also regularly sent the drafts to Piraye, in addition to discussing them with friends in Bursa prison like Orhan Kemal. But whereas Piraye used to respond by saying simply 'I like it' or 'I don't like it', he could rely on Kemal Tahir for more professional comments (AM 3, 228). It was in a letter to him dated 17 June 1941 that Nazım used the title 'Human Landscapes' for the first time:

I have started writing my work which I have decided to call 'Human Landscapes in Turkey in the Year 1940'. I am writing fifty lines a day. It will take six months to write. It will contain 10,000 lines. I have stuck to the schedule up till now. I have already written 650 lines (AM 3, 81).

In the same letter Nazım claims that he has stopped searching for a new style: 'I am not wasting my time with sentence structure or choice of tenses or problems of rhyming. [...] Farewell to searching for an independent, abstract style. Content, content, content.' With this move Nazım felt re-energized 'like a boxer, a wrestler, a football player in an arena' (AM 3, 81).

At this point the encyclopaedia, redefined as a historical portrait of 'the people of my country', was still quite separate from the second major project on which Nazım was working at this time, 'The Legend of National Liberation' ('Milli Kurtuluş Destanı'). This poem too was begun in Sultanahmet prison in 1939 (AM 1, 118): could it be that the poet had been stung into action by the conversation in 1937 at which Şükrü Sökmensüer, the Chief of State Security, complained that no one had yet written a poem about the Turkish War of Liberation? Work on the first draft of the 'Legend', which was more patriotic in tone, continued intermittently in 1940-1. The patriotic note was present partly because Nazım drew on Atatürk's speeches, first published in 1938, to reconstruct details of the War of National Liberation. Certain passages, such as the description of the Turkish victory at the battle of Sakarya between 23 August and 13 September 1921, closely echo Atatürk's own diction. The archaic phrase 'Sakarya Melhamei Kübrası', used by Atatürk for 'the grandiose battle of Sakarya' (Atatürk, II, 454), recurs in the text of Nazım's poem (A 5, 195).

After receiving excerpts from this manuscript in June 1941, Tahir felt so excited that he advised Nazım to send the 'National Legend' to President İnönü himself, asking for permission to publish it. The poem also contained a section referring to the battle of İnönü at which the Turkish President, then still known as Ismet Pasha, had himself commanded the victorious Turkish forces. Nazım's mother Celile accordingly gave a copy to her relative

Ali Fuat Cebesoy, who showed it to İnönü. In September Nazım heard that both Ali Fuat and Ismet Pasha 'liked it very much' (AM 3, 78 & 97). İnönü reportedly observed that Nazım had 'won the liberation war all over again with this poem'. When this was retailed to Nazım, the poet responded that İnönü must indeed be thankful that the war was won – 'otherwise he would be here in prison with us' (Va-Nu, 372). İnönü was not the only politician to take an interest in the poet's work. We are told by Nermin Menemencioğlu, who was secretly transcribing Nazım's poems, that they were being read by members of the cabinet (Menemencioğlu, 3). She was in a position to know, since her uncle was İnönü's Foreign Minister.

The hope that the favourable impression made by this poem might expedite the author's release was overtaken by events. On 22 June 1941, five days after Nazım announced that his poem was to be called 'Human Landscapes', the German army launched its surprise attack on the Soviet Union. At first, Nazım seems to have been so stunned that he failed to see how events in the Soviet Union could be related to his poems about Turkey. A short poem written in September 1941 entitled 'Zafere Dair' (About Victory) reflects his despondency over the Soviet casualties (AM 3, 97-8). Only in September 1945, after the defeat of Nazi Germany, did the sections describing the Soviet battlefront become an integral part of the poem. During the autumn of 1941 we find Nazım still struggling to find the most effective technique for presenting his Turkish material. 'It is not a poetry book,' he explained to Kemal Tahir. 'It has an element of poetry, even technically of rhyme, etc. But equally it has elements of prose, theatre, even as you noticed of film scenario' (AM 3, 105).

In March 1942 he proudly announced that he had written 2,300 lines and that the work as a whole would consist of four Books of 3,000 lines each, making a total of 12,000 lines. This letter also recorded a radical change of focus – the introduction of the motif of the railway journey. Book One, he explained, would be called 'Haydarpaşa Station and the Third-class Carriage No. 510', while Book Two would deal with 'Haydarpaşa Station and the Express'. Book Three was to be entitled 'A Prison and a Hospital on the Steppe', and the fourth and final Book 'Journey and Istanbul'. This clearly implied a circular structure with the train finally returning to Istanbul. In the following letter, written

on 20 March, Nazım spelt out the class structure underlying the
new design, particularly the contrast between the proletarian scenes
in Book One and the bourgeois figures introduced in Book Two.
There was certainly no hint in either of these letters that the war
raging on the Russian front would feature in the poem (AM 3,
121-3). It was the railway journey that gave Nazım's epic its
dramatic momentum:

> Haydar Pasha Station
> spring 1941,
>   3 p.m.
> At the top of the steps, sun
>   fatigue
>   and confusion.
> A man
>   stops on the steps,
>   thinking. [...]
> 'If I could eat sugar wafers every day' he thought
>   when he was five.
> 'If I could go to school' he thought
>   at ten. [...]
> 'Will my wages go up?' he thought
>   at twenty. [...]
> 'What if I get laid off?' he thought
>   at twenty-two. [...]
> And out of work from time to time
> he thought 'What if I get laid off?'
>   until he was fifty. [...]

This is Galip, transformed from the colourless figure of the
'encyclopaedia' into a vivid dramatic character, come to the station
to say good-bye to his friends Fuat, Süleyman and Halil. His
friends, prisoners in handcuffs being taken under armed escort to
Anatolia, form the main focus of the action (Halil is in part a
self-portrait of Nazım). Amid the bustle of the station Galip's
attention is easily distracted, first by a war veteran and then by
a teenage girl:

> Corporal Ahmet.
> He fought in the Balkan war
> He fought during mobilisation
> He fought in the Greek War.
> 'Hang in there, brother, the end's in sight!'
>   he's famous for saying.

A girl goes up the steps.
She works at the stocking factory
in Galata – Tophane Street.
Atifet is thirteen.
Galip
looks at Atifet
and thinks:
        'If I'd married,
            I'd have a granddaughter her age.'
            (A 5, 14; HL, 25)

The alphabetically arranged character sketches from the 'encyclopaedia' had been endowed with new life. The railway terminus, with porters bent under enormous burdens and passengers weighed down by the cares of the world, provided a spectacle of alienated human relations and the narrative of a train journey made it possible to introduce a rich panorama of social types – from the prisoners in the 'Third-class carriage No. 510' to the plutocrats in the Anatolian Express.

In his letters of March 1942 Nazım announces his second brain-wave: the idea of integrating the patriotic 'Legend of National Liberation' with his dynamic new conception of 'Human Landscapes' (AM 3, 123). This idea took Kemal Tahir by surprise, since the resulting dual perspective has a disconcerting complexity. The patriotic 'Legend' is inserted in Book Two, where the focus shifts from the third-class train crawling up the hillside with its freight of peasants and prisoners to the elegant interior of the Anatolian Express. As a result of this inspired decision, the 'Legend' ceases to be a separate poem and becomes a text within a text, being read out by the waiter Mustafa, who has obtained a copy from the poet Celal (a further pseudonym for Nazım himself). As the occupants of the first-class dining car sip their wine and gloat over the military successes of Nazi Germany, the waiter recites a series of heroic exploits, culminating in the celebrated description of Turkish women bringing ox-carts laden with ammunition up to the front line in preparation for the final assault on Izmir:

    I'm reading [the voice of Mustafa begins]:
    'The ox-carts rolled under the moon.
    The ox-carts rolled beyond Akşehir toward Afyon.
    But the earth was so endless

and the mountains so far in the distance,
it seemed they'd never reach
             their destination.
The ox-carts advanced on solid oak wheels,
the first wheels that ever turned
under the moon.
The oxen belonged to a world
          in miniature,
              tiny and dwarfed
under the moon, and the light played on their sickly broken horns,
and the earth flowed
         under their feet,
              earth
                  and more earth.
The night was bright and warm,
and in their wooden beds on the ox-carts
the dark-blue bombshells were stark-naked.
And the women
hid their glances from one another
as they eyed the dead oxen
and the wheels from past convoys...
And the women,
our women
with their awesome, sacred hands,
        pointed little chins, and big eyes,
           our mothers, lovers, wives,
who die without ever having lived,
who get fed at our tables
        after the oxen,
whom we abduct and carry off to the hills
        and go to prison for,
who harvest grain, cut tobacco, chop wood and barter in the markets,
whom we harness to our ploughs,
and who with their bells and undulant heavy hips
surrender to us in sheepfolds
in the gleam of knives stuck in the ground –
               the women,
                  our women,
walked under the moon now
behind the ox-carts and shells
with the same ease
and accustomed weariness of women
hauling amber-eared sheaves to the threshing floor.
And scrawny-necked children

> slept on the steel of 15-centimetre shrapnel shells.
> And the carts advanced under the moon
> beyond Akşehir toward Afyon'.
>   (A 5, 218-20; HL, 131-2)

The passage has undoubted grandeur, and yet abounds in critical ironies. The erotic undercurrent subverts the easy equation of modern weaponry with male sexual conquest, and the implied protest against centuries of oppression suggests that women are quite capable of taking power into their own hands. This impression is enhanced through the illustrations by Abidin Dino showing women guiding the carts with the shells (Fig. 18). Technically as well as poetically, the placing of the 'Legend of National Liberation' within the framework of the train journey is remarkably effective. The patriotic discourse is given its full emotional weight, but at the same time it is ironically distanced by the constant reminder that the heroic sacrifices of the Turkish people result in a system where bloated plutocrats travel first-class, while the people of Anatolia remain oppressed.

Towards the end of 1942 Nazım asked Piraye to send the drafts of the 'Legend of National Liberation' back to him so that he could make the changes necessary for its inclusion in 'Human Landscapes'. Sections of the poem now began to circulate in manuscript, and Ahmet Emin Yalman, editor of *Vatan*, was so impressed that in December he expressed interest in buying the rights to the 'National Liberation' sections from 'Human Landscapes' and serializing them. Nazım declined the offer, since he feared that his poem would have to be politically emasculated before it could appear in a Turkish newspaper as long as wartime censorship was in force (AM 3, 161-2). However, at least one section from the manuscript was published during the war: the account from Book Two of the heroic defence of Antep in the War of Liberation, 'Hikayei Karayılan', was included by Ismail Habib in the collection *Yurddan Yazılar* in 1943 (Habib, 70f).

In the spring of 1943 Nazım mentioned the possibility of renaming the book 'My Country from the Human Landscapes' (AM 3, 173). Around this time he decided to extend the emotional range of his poem to endow the political narrative with more personal overtones:

I feel like writing poetry again, but completely different, contrasting with the human landscapes, lyrical, full of fantasies, soft, sweet and colourful.

18. *Human Landscapes*: 'Women with Ox-Carts' by Abidin Dino.

As I get older, with more courage I understand that one needs healthy, hopeful, even a little sad lyrical poetry. To avoid and despise this is a form of childish leftism (AM 3, 165-6).

The significance of this lyrical element becomes a leitmotif in this period. In a characteristic fusion of the political with the personal, he decided to use letters received from friends as the basis for these more personal motifs. In a letter to Kemal Tahir, he emphasizes that these lyrical sections ('şiirli parçalar') will be the part he will most enjoy re-reading (AM 3, 219). These lyrical passages are most prominent in Books Three and Five. Letters exchanged between Nazım and Piraye form the basis for a delicate epistolary dialogue between Halil in prison and Ayşe struggling to make ends meet with her children in Istanbul:

> Halil was depressed
> until he saw Ayşe's writing.
> He read her letter over and over.
> It wasn't enough.
> He took out her old letters.

> They were all undated.
> He had numbered them –
> Ayşe's letters over the last eight months.
> He lined them up on the table
> like cards in a game of solitaire.

Letter no. 1 from Ayşe begins:

> I'm writing this letter sick in bed.
> If you were here, what good care you'd take of me.
> Leyla just turned six.
> She's small for her age,
> and I make her take naps during the day.
> I just woke her up:
> her cheeks are rosy,
> and her hazel eyes look almost grown up.
>   (A 5, 477-8; HL, 247-8)

This creative use of Piraye's letters – as indeed of letters and stories from other friends and fellow prisoners – makes 'Human Landscapes' a collaborative work – 'your book', as he said to Piraye (C 6, 485). These sections serve to reaffirm the value of personal relations amid the dehumanizing pressures of war and prison.

During the early months of 1944 Nazım completed the more political sections of Book Three, including reminiscences of the revolt of the Young Turks in 1908-9. He also wrote the hospital episode, with its dialogue between Halil, the idealistic socialist, and Faik Bey, the nihilistic doctor. Once again he was very sensitive to his potential audience. The influence of Diderot may be discerned here – in the philosophical dialogue between the poetically inclined prisoner Halil, who is being treated for a progressive eye disease, and the hospital director Dr Faik Bey. Faik adopts a tone of condescension in discussing a peasant's wife, who has come to him for treatment: 'She's like a piece of earth [...] /she hasn't *lived*' (A 5, 353; HL, 185-6). The doctor is an enlightened representative of the Kemalist elite, more public-spirited than the cynics encountered in the dining-car of the Anatolian Express, but being alienated from the people he is supposed to serve, he is overcome by 'the loneliness / of someone thinking about his death'. Book Three ends with the disclosure that Faik has committed suicide in the night, while from the nearby maternity ward Halil hears the most beautiful sound in the world: 'the first victory cry of the new-born' (A 5, 389; HL, 215).

In November 1944 Nazım records that he is hard at work on Book Four (AM 3, 249). Up to this point 'Human Landscapes' had still been a poem written from the perspective of '*my* country', dealing with the history of the Turkish people. Early in 1945 he estimated that it would be finished before the summer (AM 3, 263), but the defeat of Nazi Germany and the dramatic extension of Soviet power led him to realize that the implications of the work reached far beyond the boundaries of Turkey itself. The poem 'is breaking out of its framework', he explains to Kemal Tahir in October 1945. 'It is impossible to write now without mentioning the war. This thought took me to the battlefront two or three times in the book. The most important characteristic of this century is revolutions, liberation movements' (AM 3, 274-5). By this date he had written 16,000 lines, including the new 'battle-front' sections describing the war on the Eastern front, which were later to become known as the 'Moscow Symphony'. And he was still planning to write a further 8000 lines.

Nazım begins the war sequence in Book Four by incorporating motifs from the poem 'Five Minutes' which he had written at Çankırı in 1940 at the time when the Nazi–Soviet pact was in force. But the tone has now subtly changed. The earlier treatment did not distinguish between the four figures representing the belligerent powers: Hans from Germany, Gilbert from France, Mafeo from Italy and John from Britain (A 5, 51-3). All are seen as members of the international working class, conscripted to fight and die in an imperialist war. In 'Human Landscapes' this motif is radically revised, setting up a dramatic contrast between Harry Thompson from Liverpool and Hans Mueller from Munich, who are fighting respectively for 'freedom' and for 'the Führer'. Thompson is proud of 'the freedom to curse Churchill if I want, even in wartime', and he anticipates that the military struggle will lead to a programme of social reform: 'we won't go hungry and jobless after the war. / One of our lords has devised a solution: / justice without revolution' – an unexpected tribute to the Beveridge reform proposals which the British Labour government implemented after 1945. Mueller, by contrast, has only three ideas in his head: saluting his superior officers, loyalty to his gun and 'to round up a minimum of three Jews a day'. As a result of a naval battle, the bodies of both men are now lying at the bottom of the Atlantic. But whereas 'the fish ate Thompson with pleasure', they 'wouldn't touch the other – scared, I guess, that Hans's flesh was poison' (A 5, 429-30; HL, 227-30).

Writing in November 1961, Nazım assigned a central significance to the German invasion of the Soviet Union. He recalled that in responding to this event he had resolved 'to start with Hitler's attack and work back to the Boer war, then to work forward again, and to keep at this history till the end of my life, was my goal. I had no doubt that Fascism would be defeated and that I would get out of prison' (B 4, 5; HL, xiii). This retrospective account does not correlate very closely with the actual text, although it is clear that certain sections of the poem have been lost. The earliest event dealt with is in fact not the Boer war but the revolt of the Young Turks in 1908. Moreover, Nazım's correspondence suggests that it was not till 1945, after the defeat of Fascism, that he decided to extend the range of Book Four of 'Human Landscapes' to include Hitler's attack on the Soviet Union and the heroic response of the Red Army. In his original plan the poem was to have a circular structure, Book Four concluding with the rail-way-borne narrative returning to the starting point in Istanbul. The whole structure of the poem was transformed by the decision to feature the Soviet resistance to Fascism. In place of an aesthetic of closure we are left with an open ending which gives the poem a stronger historical dynamic. The exploits of the Red Army, which develop into the dominant theme of Book Four, can be seen as the fulfilling of that earlier phase of the anti-imperialist struggle fought out in Turkey twenty years earlier. The transition from scenes set in a prison in Anatolia to the Soviet-German battlefront is achieved through the device of Turkish prisoners picking up radio broadcasts. This recapitulates actual experiences of listening to news of the war which had been such a feature of communal life in Bursa prison. In Book Four of 'Human Landscapes' the broadcasts link the communists in Turkish prisons and the Red Army on the Eastern front, so that a certain narrative coherence is sustained:

> The radio at the prison was a four-valve 1929 model.
> It had been sent over from the Civic Centre fifteen days ago
> and set up in the corridor.
>
> In the cold, glassy night outside
> the steppe was frozen stiff, hairs all on end.
> Inside, Halil listened to a symphony coming from Moscow

> thousands of kilometres to the north-east
> (A 5, 443; HL, 232)

The allusion is to Shostakovich's celebrated 'Leningrad Symphony', which develops a new musical language to dramatize the German attack and the heroic resistance. At the point where Nazım's poem picks up the story, in November 1941, the German army is penetrating deep into Soviet territory, and a spokesman on Radio Ankara has just announced that within ten days the German army will roll into Moscow (A 5, 447; HL, 233-4). In the following passages Soviet soldiers are no longer presented as victims, as with Thompson and Mueller; on the contrary, the prototypically named Ivan is portrayed as a man of superhuman courage, slaying five German officers in the battle for Kiev. In an even more extreme situation, twenty-eight infantrymen die fighting the advancing German tanks with their bare hands after their ammunition has run out. This 'Moscow Symphony' sequence culminates in a passage commemorating the courage of an eighteen-year-old Russian girl, hanged by the Germans for supporting the partisans:

> Her name was Zoe;
> she told them it was Tanya.
>> (Tanya,
>> I have your picture here in front of me in Bursa Prison.
>> [...]
>> It is no longer 1941 –
>>> the year is 1945.
>> Your side isn't fighting at the gates of Moscow
>> but at the gates of Berlin ...)
>> (A 5, 461; HL, 239)

The courageous Tanya is interrogated and hanged while a German officer takes a snapshot for his photo album. This was one of the first passages from 'Human Landscapes' to appear in print – a Turkish-language booklet entitled simply *Zoya*, published in Sofia in 1952 with striking illustrations (Fig. 19). The episode ends with the news that the Red Army has launched a counter-attack, three German divisions have been defeated and four hundred settlements have been liberated.

The sections on the defence of the Soviet Union are very different in tone from the preceding Turkish sequences, where pathos was always held in check by irony. Nazım responds to the news of the great Soviet victories of 1945 with purple passages

19. *Human Landscapes*: 'Zoya the Partisan'.

celebrating the defence of Moscow which result in a problematic idealization. Despite the occasional cross-cutting to Halil and the other Turkish prisoners, anxiously following developments on their map of the Eastern front pieced together from newspaper clippings, the ironic montage technique is now abandoned in favour of extravagant pro-Soviet rhetoric. There is no eulogy to Stalin, since Nazım's heroes are still the 'little people' – Ahmet from Turkestan, Yurchenko from Ukraine, Sagamanyan from Armenia. But they have mysteriously developed superhuman powers, inspired by Klotschkov, the political commissar attached to their unit.

The decision to include the Second World War in his poem seems to have inspired more far-reaching ambitions. From one of his letters to Piraye we know that Nazım even considered changing the title of the book to 'Panorama', to reflect this broader perspective (C 6, 487). Looking back on this period in his preface of 1961, he recalls that he aimed to give an overview of the history of the twentieth century, but from 1946 onwards his

worsening health prevented him from taking this project much
further. The completion of the 'Moscow Symphony' sequence
in September 1945 marked a final creative spurt. From then onwards
illness and fatigue undermined his ability to concentrate on such
an ambitious project. Book Four ends with a tribute to one of
the heroes of the French resistance, Gabriel Peri, also executed
by the Nazis. But Book Five is a ragbag of poorly integrated
fragments composed in a very different key, returning to the
personal concerns of Halil in prison and his wife Ayşe, impatiently
waiting for her husband's release. For once Nazım fails to integrate
the political with the personal, as he abandons the historical perspective and focuses instead on Ayşe's domesticity.

After his release in July 1950, Nazım was faced with a dilemma.
The priority was clearly to reassemble the various sections of
'Human Landscapes', which had been sent for safe-keeping to
different friends, and integrate them into a single narrative. But
it was obvious that the censorship precluded publication of the
book as a whole. It was at this stage that he decided to omit the
prose sections designed as a panorama of twentieth-century political
history (B 4, 5-6). The only parts that could conceivably be
published in the Cold War climate of the 1950s were those describing heroic exploits from the Turkish War of Liberation (a seven-
page section had indeed been published in 1946 in the anthology
Kurtuluşdan Sonrakiler, edited by Orhan Burian). Since Nazım was
keen to get at least part of the great work into print, he settled
to the task of editing those Turkish episodes for separate publication
under the title 'The National Militia' ('Kuvayi Milliye'). Many years
later Münevver recalled how hard he worked on it (Interview,
July 1996). In a concentrated effort he rearranged these sections
in a chronological sequence extending from the allied occupation
of Istanbul in 1918 to the final Turkish victory over the Greeks
at Izmir in August 1922. Part Five, the section on the occupation
of Istanbul by the imperial powers on 16 March 1920, was completed at the Dinos' house with the help of the poet Melih Cevdet
(A 3, 51-6; Dino, 137). But the book was not actually published
till the 1960s, and the annotated edition produced by Cevdet
Kudret in 1968 contains over fifty pages of notes documenting
the work's complex genesis (Hikmet 1968, 127-80).

Historical authenticity is gained by incorporating motifs from
an edition of Atatürk's speeches published in 1938 in the section

on the Erzurum and Sivas congresses of 1919 in Part Two (A 3, 21). Although not mentioning Atatürk by name, Nazım does cite as the outcome of the Sivas Congress his famous words 'either LIBERTY or death!' ('ya ISTIKLAL, ya ölüm!' A 3, 29). Also a short but striking passage features an unnamed but readily identifiable commander who looks 'like a blond wolf' (A 3, 83). Another version of this text, published in 1965 with the title *Kurtuluş Savaşı Destanı* (Legend of National Liberation), alludes to the Turkish Commander-in-Chief at two different points (Hikmet 1965, 69 & 73). In an early draft of the poem there was apparently a more extended section describing Atatürk's relationship with Ali Fuat Cebesoy. This section, which Nazım read out loud to the prison doctor Neşati Uster who was posted to Bursa in 1945, was subsequently deleted or lost (Aydemir 1986a, 90-91). During the revision Nazım also removed the reference to Inönü which had been in the original draft: 'the Commander of the Western Front / Ismet' (Hikmet 1968, 147) in retribution for Inönü's refusal to grant him an amnesty – poetic justice indeed!

The typescript of 'The National Militia' contains 1,729 lines – just a tenth of the total length of the version of 'Human Landscapes' which was finally published in the 1960s. The chronological arrangement, so different from the complex montage techniques of 'Human Landscapes', shows that Nazım intended this version to have a more direct popular appeal. The typescript has survived on sixty-five sheets of rather rough yellowing paper. A sample page shows that this was carefully typed, with only minor changes (mainly to punctuation); handwritten notes to the typesetter indicate page breaks and ask for 'four lines of space' to be inserted, suggesting that Nazım expected the work to be published in the immediate future. It was also during 1950 that Abidin Dino completed a series of line drawings to illustrate the text (Hikmet 1986, 134 & 139). It must have been hard to have such a powerful poem ready for the press, only to be frustrated by the fears of publishers. We are told by Müzehher that despite strenuous efforts, no Turkish publisher·was prepared to take the risk of bringing the book out (Nurettin 1986, 151). But a letter dated 9 August 1950 reveals that Garbis Fikri, the owner of Inkilap Kitabevi, purchased the 'Kuvayi Milliye' publishing rights for 3,500 Turkish Lira – a substantial sum – to be paid in instalments. Fikri had difficulties when he tried to obtain a permit, and the typescript remained unpublished

(Hulusi, 55-8). It is also possible that Nazım had last-minute doubts. The tone of 'Kuvayi Milliye' is distinctly bellicose, hardly the kind of work that a communist poet should have been publishing at the very moment when Turkish troops were being despatched to fight in Korea.

Fragmented publication and the poetics of montage

Getting *Human Landscapes* into print was almost as complicated a matter as writing the text. It certainly took much longer, and only fragments of the Turkish text were published in the poet's lifetime. Publication of the poem as a whole was hampered not only by the censorship, but also by the problem of assembling a reliable text. Nazım had left incomplete drafts with Piraye and other friends in Istanbul, and after he fled to the Soviet Union no one was in a position to establish an authorized text. Nazım himself describes in his Preface of 1961 the difficulty of reconstituting his typescript:

You may find this hard to believe, but I did not find time to make a second copy of the 66,000 lines. This single copy was divided into segments and given for safekeeping to different friends. After I arrived in Moscow I discovered that these had either been confiscated by the police or burnt. Some parts had already been sent to Paris and published while I was still in prison. Of the 66,000 lines only these survived. A number of years passed and in 1956 some parts which escaped confiscation and burning began to arrive in Moscow. Today I have 17,000 lines. Among the parts which have not reached me are the occupation of France by Hitler and the Moscow and Leningrad sieges (B 4, 6).

The poet's memory must have deceived him when he referred to a total of 66,000 lines. The highest estimate mentioned in his correspondence when he was actually writing the poem was 24,000 lines (AM 3, 275). However, he wrote in a letter to Orhan Kemal dated 19 July 1948 that when he stopped working on the poem, he had completed 'about 40,000 lines' (unpublished letter, Aziz Nesin Archive). Clearly, substantial sections must have been lost through censorship, police action and other forms of harassment or misadventure. One section was given for safe-keeping to Münevver's friend, the novelist Peride Celal, and she deposited it with her aunt Hidayet Karacan who apparently burnt it in a moment of panic, fearing it would be discovered by the police

(Celal, 378-9). The fact that substantial parts of the 1,729-line 'Kuvayi Milliye' typescript of 1950-1 are omitted from the standard Turkish edition of *Human Landscapes* may, however, be the result of a conscious decision. The naively patriotic tone of that version would have been out of place in a poem designed to highlight the endurance of the common people.

The problem with the early published editions is that they even omit substantial parts of the 17,000 lines which have survived. Highlights from Books One to Four first appeared not in Turkish but in Italian with the title *Panorama Umano*, translated by Giovanni Crino and Velso Mucci and forming pages 615-705 of Crino's edition of Nazım Hikmet, *Poesie* (Bologna: Editori Riuniti, 1960). This was based on a word-for-word French translation prepared by Münevver Andaç (Letter from Münevver to Nazım, 13 December 1959). Two years later a relatively complete Russian translation, *Çeloveçeskaya Panorama*, translated by Muza Pavlova (Moscow, 1962) appeared; this was prepared in close consultation with Nazım and includes his Preface dated November 1961. A partial French translation, *En Cette Année 1941*, appeared the same year, translated by Münevver in consultation with Nazım (Paris: Editions Maspéro, 1962). The irony is that the first – very incomplete – Turkish version did not appear till 1965, printed as the parallel text to accompany an Italian translation by Joyce Lussu, *Peaseggi Umani* (Milan: Lerici Editori, 1965). Two years later a more complete Turkish version finally appeared, in five volumes edited by Memet Fuat: *Memleketimden Insan Manzaraları* (Istanbul: De Yayınları, 1966-7). This edition was based on the original typescripts deposited with Piraye, incorporating the poet's handwritten corrections.

It is still possible that further sections of the original typescript will come to light, either from police archives or from private collections. Sections dealing with the Boer war, the Nazi occupation of France and the sieges of Moscow and Leningrad, which Nazım mentions in various places, are missing even from the standard Turkish text, edited by Memet Fuat. In one of his letters to Piraye, probably written in 1944, Nazım asked her to send him books about the German bombing of London and the anti-Nazi resistance, so it is possible that he may even have drafted passages on these themes (C 6, 487). Another defect of the available editions is that they lack a critical apparatus describing the changes that occurred as the text went through a complex series of drafts and revisions. The process, which has been analysed above, may be summarized by means of the following chronology:

'Encyclopaedia of Famous People' ('Meşhur Adamlar Ansiklopedisi', 1939)

'The Legend of National Liberation' ('Milli Kurtuluş Destanı', 1939)

'They and Their Adventures' ('Onlar ve Maceraları', May 1941)

'Human Landscapes in Turkey' ('Türkiye'den İnsan Manzaraları', June 1941)

'Haydarpaşa Station and the Railway Journey' ('Haydarpaşa Garı', 1942)

Personal Letters and Lyrical Passages (Şiirli parçalar', 1943)

'Moscow Symphony (The Battle Front)' ('cepheye', 1945)

'Panorama of 20th-Century History' ('Panorama', 1945)

'The National Militia' (the 'Kuvayı Milliye' version, 1950)

To stress this chequered history of composition and publication is not to imply that the poem is aesthetically defective. It is only in 'Book Five' that the incompleteness of *Human Landscapes* is damaging. Nazım's correspondence clearly shows that he designed the poem to be completed in Four Books, although he changed his mind about the ending, first envisaging a return to Istanbul and later opening the narrative out to reach its climax with the defeat of Fascism. The design set out in his letters to Kemal Tahir and to Piraye contains no reference to any 'Book Five', so that this appears to be an awkward expedient of his editors to accommodate a ragbag of work-in-progress which the poet failed to integrate in his main narrative. If the poem, despite its formal imperfections, may still be regarded as Nazım's masterpiece, this is because he used a flexibly modernistic technique of montage to construct a narrative with Homeric undertones. In an undated letter to Piraye enclosing further drafts, he sets out his method of composition:

I am sending you a part of your book. This is the beginning of the first section of the second part of the Third Volume. Since I am now working in this way piece by piece, it will be an easy task later to complete the montage. I have four or five further pieces ready for this kind of montage. I will make a fair copy and send them to you. Then I will let you know the sequence for montage, and you'll assemble the pieces accordingly (C 6 , 485).

This passage shows that the disconcerting breaks in continuity are part of a conscious aesthetic strategy. Moreover, the disjunction between traditional and ultramodern modes of communication is explicitly thematized, as in the charming episode near the beginning of Book Four, where a migrating stork damages the aerial of a powerful six-valve 'Telefunken', just as its owner, the radio-ham Cevdet Bey, is listening to Voice of America (A 5, 395-6; HL, 220-21). Here, as with the ox-carts trundling across Anatolia, cradling their artillery shells and sleeping children, the modern political narrative reverberates with echoes of primeval epic. Moreover, the technique of montage facilitates the use of flashbacks and makes for fluid transitions.

If *Human Landscapes* can be seen as a kind of coda to Nazım's work on *War and Peace*, it is because both works so compellingly explore the nexus between the personal and the political. It is certainly no coincidence that translating Tolstoy's novel was one of Nazım's major tasks in Bursa prison, bringing home to him the interdependence of military exploit and social memory. But reflections on political events, from the overthrow of Sultan Abdul Hamid in 1908 to the heroic defence of Moscow, constitute only the foreground theme. The poem is enriched by archetypal elements: the impassiveness of nature, the ardours of life's journey, the constraints of prison and the struggle for liberation. Nazım's success in construing these universal themes within a specific landscape and giving them compelling human voices resulted in a poem of exceptional power.

Some of the finest artistic achievements of modern Turkey originated in prison or were inspired by prison experience: Nazım's mature poetry, Balaban's early paintings, the novels of Kemal Tahir and Orhan Kemal, and the films of Yılmaz Güney, not to mention the works of other more recent authors. In their creative vision imprisonment becomes transposed into an existential theme. The human condition as a whole is exemplified by Balaban's 'Öküzler' series 'The Oxen', straining in opposite directions under the yoke of a primitive plough. The finest work by these artists reverses the relationship between workers and their chains, suggesting that under prevailing socio-economic conditions the impulses of ambition and desire, labour and love push people so far beyond the limits of endurance that the constraints of prison may actually seem liberating. Güney directed *Yol*, his film about the experiences of seven Turkish prisoners released for a week-end of home leave, while himself serving a prison sentence for manslaughter. Following Nazım's example, he used the motif of a

railway journey across Anatolia to give their experiences an epic
quality. The dialectical reversals between prison and freedom which
give this film its power reflect the conditions of its creation. From
his prison cell Güney had to mobilize a whole team of assistants
to ensure that the film was shot in accordance with his wishes.
Nazım's position was simpler. All he needed was a typewriter to
create his panorama of oppression and his dreams of freedom.

8

A Sad State of Freedom
July 1950-June 1951

Well in advance of the amnesty in July 1950, Nazım had written to the Va-Nus to ask whether he could stay at their house in Salacak, a suburb of Istanbul, after his release, and on 15 July his lawyer Mehmet Ali Sebük escorted him and Münevver there. He was greeted with tears of joy and a special meal, the first truly festive occasion he had experienced for thirteen years. Va-Nu was impressed by how well Nazım coped with life outside prison: 'He seemed to have achieved the maturity of listening to people with tolerance and patience' (Va-Nu, 394). But the great welcome he received was overshadowed by apprehension about developments outside. Those who had campaigned for Nazım's release formed a small minority in a society which was at best indifferent to the fate of political prisoners and in many cases overtly hostile, and Va-Nu had taken the precaution of fitting iron bars to the windows to protect his home against possible attacks. They had already had bricks thrown through their windows because of their public support for a notorious communist. After Nazım and Münevver arrived, the attacks were repeated although police were on duty outside the house twenty-four hours a day. Their task was not to protect the residents but to monitor Nazım's visitors (Nurettin 1986, 14). This was a clear sign that, despite the change of government, the political climate in Turkey remained hostile.

Istanbul in the Cold War

The optimistic mood which accompanied the Democratic Party's election victory in May 1950 was relatively short-lived. The new government led by Adnan Menderes promoted free market policies which at first produced results: cheap credits, improved communications and increased agricultural production, but the American alliance had military implications. On 25 June 1950 the North Korean army launched its surprise attack, and the collapse of South Korean defences drew the United States and its allies into the resulting war. To consolidate the Turkish-American alliance, Menderes successfully negotiated Turkey's admission to NATO, and in October 1950 the first Turkish brigade was despatched to fight against the communists. In the course of the war 25,000 Turkish soldiers served in Korea, suffering more than 10 per cent casualties (Zürcher, 246). To sustain this policy, the government orchestrated a systematic anti-communist campaign, which was simultaneously directed against the peace movement. A Society for Supporters of Peace (Türk Barış Severler Cemiyeti) had been formed in May 1950 under the leadership of Behice Boran, but because it opposed Turkish involvement in Korea the Society was suppressed at the end of the year. Seven of its leading members were arrested, and on 13 June 1951 their trials ended with fifteen-month prison sentences. Although Nazım was strongly opposed to the war, he was determined to avoid political involvement, concentrating on rebuilding his career as a writer and earning enough to support his family and pay his debts. Substantial legal costs had been incurred during the campaign for his release, but Sebük had to be content with a note of hand in which Nazım promised to repay him the full amount as soon as he was in a position to do so – which never happened (Sebük, 179–80). His immediate task was to collect and edit the multitude of poems he had written in prison and sent to relatives and friends. He started to work immediately on poems which formed part of his letters from prison, many of which had been buried in a tin box in Va-Nu's garden (Nurettin 1991, 151).

After enjoying the Va-Nus' hospitality for a fortnight, Nazım and Münevver decided to set up house on their own. But rents were high and they could not afford a lease on an apartment, so they had to move in with Nazım's mother in her old timber house in Cevizlik. Münevver did not find relations with Celile easy, but they could only move into a place of their own when Nazım had a job; it was not easy to find work as a journalist in the prevailing climate of anti-communist hysteria. Fortunately, his friend Ihsan Ipekci, director of the Ipek Film Studio, came to the rescue and offered him work. Nazım still had bad health, but settled down

20. Nazım working at Ipek Film Studios after his release from prison.

to a steady work routine, editing, dubbing and script-writing for the Studios and even helping with filming (Fig. 20). For political reasons his name was not included among the credits, but he made a significant contribution to several films, including romances like 'Sultan Selim III and his Lovers' and 'The Fisherman's Beauty' (Bezirci, 65).

With money received in advance from the Studios, he and Münevver were able to move to a basement flat in Kadıköy, and they worked together to redecorate it (Va-Nu, 396). Whatever financial problems they might have had, they were rich in other ways: their walls were covered with paintings and sketches, both by Balaban and by Nazım himself. Balaban, who had also been released under the amnesty, was one of their regular visitors, together with the Sertels and the Dinos. Two portrait sketches by Balaban convey something of the magic of these first months of freedom: Nazım with his penetrating eyes and flaming hair, an icon of revolutionary energy, and Münevver composed and reflective, her hair decorously pinned up (Figs 21a & b). Nazım at last had a chance to catch up on more recent cultural developments, when he was taken by the Dinos to their house in Suadiye to meet the revolutionary folk singer, Ruhi Su (Nurettin 1991,

21. Line drawings by Balaban, 1950: (*a*) Nazım Hikmet;
(*b*) Münevver Andaç.

138). Around this time Nazım composed the short poem 'Gençlik
Marşı', ('Youth Anthem'), expressing his faith in the new generation
and his gratitude to the students who had supported the campaign
for his release (A 4, 207).

The uneasy atmosphere of Istanbul during the Cold War is
reflected in a number of poems, notably the sequence 'After Getting
out of Prison', which begins by registering the post-traumatic
disorientation which follows the long-term prisoner's release: 'This
is the kind of daze / thirteen years of prison leave you in'. The
autumn of 1950 might be mild and relaxing as the poet and his
wife take an evening stroll, but their appreciation of the figs and
mulberry trees is disrupted by disturbing memories:

> The grocer Karabet's lights are on.
> This Armenian citizen won't forgive
>> his father's slaughter in the Kurdish mountains.
> But he likes you
> because you also can't forgive
>> those who blackened the Turkish people's name.
>> ('Hapisten Çıktıktan Sonra', A 4, 203; P, 144-5)

The disruption of the lyrical mood is the more daring because here Nazım broaches the great taboo of modern Turkish politics, the Armenian deportations and massacres in the First World War. At the same time the political reflection is integrated with the central theme of the poem, parenthood: 'You no sooner got out of prison / than you made your wife / pregnant,' the poet reflects with a certain self-irony.

Through the winter of 1950-1 their domestic life was shaped by Münevver's pregnancy as they prepared for the baby, buying everything they needed on hire purchase. On 26 March 1951, eight months after Nazım's release, Münevver's son was born. Since they feared that he might be branded as the son of a communist, his birth certificate gave his father's name as Yekta – a name chosen at random. They named the child Memed, using the basic spelling of the name (in this biography he is referred as 'Mehmet Nazım', the name he later chose for himself). Nazım's feelings about the approaching birth found poignant expression in passages which again interweave the personal with the political:

> My child.
> Boy or girl,
> I don't want my child to land in prison
>   at any age
> for standing up for beauty, justice, peace.

The final poem in this sequence, written after the birth, relates the event to contemporary politics:

> My wife bore me a little boy
> blond, no eyebrows
> wrapped in a blue blanket
> a ball of light weighing seven pounds.

By contrast, children born in Korea are being killed 'before they'd had their fill of their mothers milk', those born in Anatolia 'had lice the minute they were born', while the first thing seen by children born in Greek prisons 'were iron bars'. The sequence nevertheless ends on an optimistic note:

> When my son
>   reaches my age
> I won't be in this world,
> but the world will be a wonderful cradle
> rocking

all children –
black,
white,
yellow
on its globe-blue satin cushion.
(A 4, 202-6; P, 144-9,)

Even in the harsh of post-war climate of conflict, birth is seen as a symbol of hope. And there was now some prospect of stable domestic life, since Nazım's divorce from Piraye was finalized just three days before his son was born (Aydemir 1970, 343).

During the campaign to secure his release, the poet had become an international celebrity. At the 2nd Conference of the World Peace Congress in Warsaw on 22 November 1950, Nazım was awarded a peace prize together with Pablo Picasso (France), Paul Robeson (United States), Wanda Jakubowska (Poland) and Pablo Neruda (Chile). Since there was no prospect of the Turkish authorities giving Nazım a visa to attend the ceremony, Neruda accepted the prize on his behalf, paying tribute to his paradoxical achievement: 'His years in prison were useful; Nazım's lyrical work reached its greatness there. His voice has become the voice of the world. I am proud that my poems are side by side with his in this crucial time of fighting for peace' (Aksoy, 61). The interest in Nazım's work was particularly intense in eastern bloc countries, and the Czech Writers' Union even invited him to visit a spa in Bohemia to recuperate. But when this invitation was officially transmitted to Mehmet Ali Sebük, the lawyer decided not to pass it on. He feared that if Nazım were to leave the country, the public-spirited people who had signed petitions for his release would become subject to reprisals (Sebük, 221-2).

Despite the political tensions, Nazım was doing his best to lead a normal life. Photographs from this period show him relaxing with Münevver (Fig. 22), but they fail to record the systematic police surveillance to which he was subjected. Nazım was technically free, but he had good reason to describe the situation in Turkey in 1951 as 'A Sad State of Freedom':

With this great freedom of yours you slave for others,
To turn those who dominated you for generations into Croesus
[...]
Cursed hands of Wall Street grab you by the neck,
Possibly, one day, you may be sent to Korea,

22. Nazım and Münevver.

with this great freedom of yours, you may fill a hole,
to have the freedom to be an unknown soldier.
('Bir Hazin Hürriyet', A 4, 210)

Nazım's only wish was to be allowed to live in peace and to concentrate on his writing without distraction, for he still had his greatest work to complete, 'Human Landscapes'. But we have seen that in the prevailing conditions even this was unattainable.

The great escape

One of the leitmotifs of 'Human Landscapes' is Mehmet, the eternal Turkish infantryman, courageously enduring the disasters of war. It is a strange historical irony that in 1951, just as Nazım was attempting to revise this section of the poem for publication, thousands of Mehmets were again being drafted to fight in a foreign war. Nazım himself, though now forty-nine, was by no means exempt from the threat of conscription. The many years spent in prison meant that he had never formally completed the service in the armed forces required of all Turkish males of military age. Turkish bureaucracy may work slowly, but in this case it did so relentlessly. The file on Nazım's military record was reopened in the autumn of 1950 when he applied for a passport to travel abroad. The fact that he had been a naval cadet in his teens was discounted, since officially he had been discharged before completing the full term of duty. When the authorities became aware that he had not completed his military service, they seized as this as a pretext not merely to refuse him a passport but to threaten him with conscription (Sülker 6, 218).

It may seem absurd that a man approaching fifty with a serious heart condition should be drafted into the army, but some members of the military establishment were so outraged at his being amnestied that they seized on the threat of conscription as a way to settle old scores. It was Münevver who answered the door when the police called at their house in Cevizlik to serve the conscription order, instructing Nazım to prepare to join the draft without delay. Fearing the worst, he asked Münevver to pack his bag, while he went with Va-Nu to the Kadıköy military station to present the case for exemption. They left a statement claiming that Nazım's period at the naval school should count as completed years of service and that his discharge in 1920 on grounds of ill health should exempt him from further conscription. This was supplemented by another certificate issued by the medical committee when he was transferred from Bursa prison in 1950, confirming that he was unfit for military service. The officer in charge accepted these documents and allowed him to return home (Va-Nu, 397).

For several weeks there were no further developments, and Nazım was just beginning to hope that he had satisfied the authorities when he received a summons for a medical examination. The doctor must have been under pressure from his superiors not to grant Nazım exemption, for he simply sized Nazım up on the evidence of his impressive physique and ruled he was fit for service. Nazım insisted on being examined by a medical committee, and on 6 June was sent to Haydarpaşa hospital for a more systematic examination. Given the evidence of impaired health, he was confident that he would be exempted, but the medical certificate issued on 8 June disregarded most of his symptoms (Aydemir 1970, 384). He was served with conscription papers and informed that he would be posted to Zara, a small town in eastern Anatolia. It was only with difficulty that he managed to obtain a short postponement, to allow him time to put his affairs in order (Va-Nu, 399). In the absence of official clarification, there has been a great deal of speculation about the motives of the Turkish authorities. Clearly, they wanted Nazım out of the way, since his popularity made him a focal point for left-wing opposition groups, but it would have been politically embarrassing to imprison him again.

Nazım had reason to believe that if he accepted the posting to eastern Turkey, he would be unlikely to return alive. He now had little more than a week to take the most momentous decision of his career. Given that he had distanced himself from the Communist Party since his release, he could not rely on its support in organizing an escape route out of the country. If the Party with its network of international contacts had been involved, Nazım would doubtless have been issued with forged identity papers and spirited away on one of the Soviet ships which plied between Istanbul and Odessa, but fortunately he had the support of his brother-in-law Refik Erduran, a versatile young man with Marxist sympathies. Refik's role in their subsequent adventures can be reconstructed from his memoirs *Gülerek* (With a Smile). There is a tongue-in-cheek quality to his narrative, which leaves certain aspects unexplained, but the details have been verified in discussion with Refik (Interviews, January 1990 & October 1996).

Born in 1928, Refik Erduran came from a progressive Istanbul family with an international outlook; his father had a public role as legal adviser to the state shipping company. During his schooldays Refik had become fascinated by the competing ideologies of international socialism and Turkish nationalism, especially Pan Turanism. Later he found his way to Marxism not by studying the classical political texts but by reading Nazım's poetry. He had first come across some of the poems in school anthologies while Nazım was still in prison, and became more deeply immersed while studying at Robert College, an American-sponsored institute for higher education on the banks of the Bosphorus. Here, as an eighteen-year-old, he became acquainted with Nazım's half-sister Melda (Hikmet Bey's daughter by his second marriage), even though he was not at first aware of the relationship. Through this family connection he was soon enjoying the privilege of reading unpublished manuscripts, including drafts for 'Human Landscapes'. On graduating from Robert College, he went to Cornell University to take a Master's degree in literature and drama (1947-9). There he met Paul Robeson's son and went for walks with Vladimir Nabokov, one of the teachers. Having completed the degree, he visited England and France, where he became involved in the international campaign to free Nazım (Erduran, 51-3).

Just before the Turkish general elections of May 1950, Refik returned to Turkey and became engaged to Melda. This was when Nazım was on hunger strike, and Refik, who had learned to fly in the United States, began to fantasize about hiring a plane and flying him out of prison (Erduran, 56). After Nazım's release in July Refik met him for the first time while visiting Celile's house with his fiancée, and Nazım immediately drew him into a discussion about the contemporary theatre. There was little common ground at first between the American-educated graduate and the communist poet. But in the autumn of 1950 Refik and Melda were married, and Nazım enjoyed visiting them with Münevver at their home on the island of Büyük Ada in the Sea of Marmara, a short boat trip from the city. Their shared interest in the theatre soon led to a closer collaboration. They concocted a scheme to stage one of Nazım's plays, 'Humanity is not Dead' ('İnsanlık Ölmedi Ya'), under Refik's name and offered it to Istanbul City Theatre, but their stratagem was discovered and the play could not be staged (Erduran, 58-9).

During the summer of 1951, just when Nazım received his call-up papers, Refik himself began his military service, training for a commission in the artillery. At the time he was still stationed near Istanbul, though with every prospect of being drafted to Korea. With the same daredevil impulse that made him dream of rescuing Nazım from prison by air he now proposed an almost equally adventurous seaborne scheme. Refik, a keen sailor, offered to smuggle him out of Istanbul in a fishing boat and take him to the safety of Bulgaria (Erduran, 62). Nazım hesitated, saying that he must first consult his 'friends' – his former comrades in the Communist Party. According to Ekber Babayev, a Turkologist living in the Soviet Union who later edited Nazım's writings, the Party was indeed consulted (Babayev, 207). The original plan was that Nazım should be smuggled out of the country with two other left-wingers who were at risk, Mehmet Ali Aybar and Oktay Rıfat. The prominent communist Mihri Belli decided that this plan involved too many risks (Belli, 1, 340-1), and in the event the Party's role in the affair appears to have been minimal – giving its consent without providing any practical support. But Mehmet Ali Aybar, acting as link man between Refik and the Party, played an active role in planning Nazım's escape (Erduran, Interview, October 1996).

Fearing that their intentions might be betrayed to the police, Refik insisted that the final details of their plan remain a secret between Nazım and himself. The obvious strategy would have been to disguise themselves as fishermen and make their escape aboard one of the fishing boats which were such a familiar sight in the Bosphorus. Medium-sized fishing vessels frequently trawled the Black Sea off the coast of Bulgaria and were thus unlikely to arouse suspicion, but Refik felt that such a scheme would involve too many different people in the plot, with an increased risk of betrayal and the scandal of exposure. A small high-speed motor boat, capable of being piloted by a single person with one passenger, seemed to him less likely to attract the attention of the customs or naval patrols. Refik found difficulty in persuading Nazım to entrust himself to such a small boat, given the unpredictable weather on the Black Sea. Nazım must have been very conscious of how in 1921 Mustafa Suphi and his fellow communists were murdered while trying to cross it, and apart from the risk of betrayal, it clearly seemed foolhardy to place his life in the hands of such an inexperienced young man. Nazım scarcely exaggerated when ten years later, in the poem 'Autobiography', he included the line: 'In '51 I sailed with a young friend across the sea towards death' (A 7, 100).

Refik, a young man with a strong practical bent, first set out to collect all the necessary technical information: how closely the Turkish security organizations controlled the exit from the Bosphorus into the Black Sea, the maximum speed of their patrol boats, whether they were equipped to radio for the support of aircraft, and how the Bulgarians were likely to react to intruders in their territorial waters. His family connections soon gave him the information he needed. A second cousin on his mother's side, Münci Ülhan, was the naval commander for the Istanbul Northern Region. A family visit was arranged, and Refik innocently asked for Münci's help, claiming that he had to check a film scenario sent to him by a friend in the United States about smugglers off the coast of Turkey. He wanted information on the technical aspects of the coastal surveillance system in order to eliminate obvious mistakes (Erduran, 67-8). 'The smugglers are carrying goods from Istanbul to Burgaz in a speedboat', he explained, 'and they become involved in a fight among themselves. My feeling is that it would be impossible for them to escape from the hands of Turkish authorities, given all the security at the exit from the Bosphorus to the Black Sea.' Münci's reply was that the navy was not involved with security patrols and that the customs service was hopelessly ineffective.

By dint of further questioning, Refik discovered that neither the Turks nor the Bulgarians had any patrol boats capable of speeds above 30 knots, so his next task was to find a reliable boat with a maximum speed of 35 knots. He heard that a sophisticated 'Chris Craft' speedboat had been put up for sale by Malik Yolaç, a young man in the construction business who was doing his military service (later a newspaper proprietor and parliamentarian). Malik let him take the boat out, and the following Sunday, when he had week-end leave, Refik made the first trial run, taking his wife Melda with him to give the impression of an innocent family outing. Using a chart of the Istanbul region, he measured the actual speed of the boat by travelling a specific distance across the Sea of Marmara from Sivri Ada to Bozburun. The engine ran smoothly even at 35 knots, and the tank held enough fuel for a ten-hour round trip. On his return he persuaded Malik to him try out the boat again the next Sunday.

As Refik had already started his military service, the trip could only be undertaken at the weekend, when he was on home leave. Every day that week, he listened to the meteorological reports and checked the reliability of their predictions. Fortunately, the forecast for that Sunday was favourable. Meanwhile Nazım himself made his final preparations. The first step was to find a way of eluding the police guard posted outside his house day and night. For several months he had followed a regular routine of going to work and returning home at fixed times, which had the effect of lulling police suspicions. He must have had doubts whether his health would stand up to a five-hour journey in an open boat, and a week before the date set for departure he visited his doctor for an extended consultation (Sebük, 299). Shortly before he left, he arranged a gathering at a restaurant in the suburb of Mühürdar, where Va-Nu took farewell photographs of Nazım with Münevver and their baby son, her daughter Renan, and Müzehher. A parting was inevitable since it was far too risky to attempt to smuggle his wife and children out of the country and expose them to the perils of the high seas.

On Sunday 17 June at 9 a.m. Nazım was to rendezvous with Refik at Tarabya, then a quiet holiday resort on the European shore of the Bosphorus, a few miles north of the city. In the small hours Nazım slipped out of the house, easily eluding the drowsy policemen. In his anxiety to avoid detection, he did not take any luggage. Even his precious manuscripts had to be left behind, since he could not risk their being lost at sea. Meanwhile, Refik was making more practical preparations:

On Sunday I got up early, telling my family that I am meeting friends and may return late to my army quarters in Tuzla, so they should not be concerned about me. I dismantled my rifle with telescopic sights and packed it in a parcel containing a box of ammunition and my father's old binoculars. I left the house with this parcel, collected the boat, filled the petrol tank and filled a few spare cans with petrol, which I hid under a tarpaulin. Once under way I took my rifle out and loaded it. I placed the rifle and the ammunition box together with the binoculars under the tarpaulin in such a position that it would be easy to drop them into the sea. With an appropriate speed I reached Tarabya at the prearranged time. Nazım was there, walking calmly in the direction that I suggested. He was not carrying anything, nor was anyone following him. It was just as if he was an ordinary citizen taking a morning walk (Erduran, 73).

Nazım climbed aboard, and at first they cruised towards the south, so as not to arouse any suspicions, before turning north towards the Black Sea. The poet was taken aback when he saw the rifle, since it would have been impossible to fight off a naval or police patrol single-handed, but Refik explained that it was only to be used as a deterrent. They began to joke and chat, and Nazım recommended to Refik that after completing his military service he should go into publishing or the film industry.

It was a wonderful summer's day, and the waters of the Black Sea seemed blue and welcoming. The original plan was to head north-west beyond the twelve-mile limit into Bulgarian waters, but as they passed Poyrazköy, the village at the mouth of the Bosphorous, they spotted a large ship on the horizon (Erduran, 202). Nazım asked Refik to change course and head due north. Closing in on the ship, they were soon able to distinguish the name *Plekhanov* through their binoculars – a Romanian ship, named after the celebrated Marxist literary theorist. The speedboat was able to close the gap, and Nazım hailed the ship both in French and in Russian, explaining who he was and asking them to take him on board. It was a tense moment, since both vessels were travelling at speed, and the lightly-built motor boat was buffeted by turbulence from the steamer. There were angry shouts from the *Plekhanov* as they were warned to keep clear, but Refik finally managed to manoeuvre close enough for Nazım's appeal to be heard. Both the boats slowed down and there was a long nerve-racking silence. It was now midday and the heat was becoming oppressive. Refik had no experience of idling the speedboat, and the engine stalled. For ten anxious minutes the two men drifted helplessly, while Refik coaxed the engine back to life.

By time the engine restarted, they were no longer in hailing distance of the *Plekhanov*, and began to argue about their next move. Refik wanted to revert to the original plan of heading for the Bulgarian coast, even though they had already lost valuable time. Nazım wanted to try his chance again with the *Plekhanov*, particularly as the ship really had slowed down. Reluctantly, Refik agreed to try again, increasing speed until they were once more within hailing distance. This time the Romanians lowered a rope ladder and agreed to take Nazım on board. Overcome by emotion, Nazım suggested that Refik join him in exile, but his clear-thinking friend replied: 'How about the career you asked me to follow? I am going into publishing and the film industry' (Erduran, 81). After two hours of anxious waiting and painful negotiations, the moment had come for Nazım to take his leave. Kissing Refik on both cheeks, he climbed aboard the *Plekhanov*.

Once safely on board, Nazım remonstrated with the captain about the long delay. The captain explained that he had first wired the authorities in Constantza, who then had to contact the government in Bucharest, who in turn had consulted Moscow before deciding to grant Nazım political asylum. As a former naval man, Nazım reminded the Captain that a sailor's first duty is to rescue those in danger at sea: they should have taken him on board first, and then cabled for guidance on how to proceed. The Romanians looked embarrassed, and with good reason. For when Nazım was taken into the saloon, he was amazed to see pinned to the wall a newspaper featuring his own photograph under the slogan 'Free Nazım Hikmet!'. People crowded around shaking his hand, oblivious that he might have drowned because of their delays.

Three days later, confirmation of Nazım's escape reached his friends in Istanbul. On June 21 the news was broken to the general public by *Cumhuriyet*, which reported that Bucharest radio had announced Nazım's arrival (Bezirci, 68). There followed a scramble for further details by the Turkish press. On 22 June *Vatan* reported that Nazım had been to work at Ipek Studios on Monday 18 June as usual. They also printed an interview with Münevver claiming that Nazım had left home on the Tuesday morning, supposedly to go to Ankara to resolve the question of his military service, and had failed to return home that evening. By suggesting that Nazım's escape had occurred on the Tuesday, rather than the previous week-end, Münevver was able to provide Refik with an alibi. This succeeded, and it was not till twenty-five years later that Refik's role became known with the publication of his memoirs. After serving as a soldier in Korea, he did indeed become a successful playwright and journalist.

Once the news of Nazım's escape had sunk in, there was a furious reaction. As editor of *Vatan*, Ahmet Emin Yalman was in a particularly embarrassing position, since only two years earlier he had been so prominently involved in the campaign to secure the poet's release. *Vatan* now subjected Nazım to the full blast of Cold War rhetoric, denouncing him as a traitor and declaring, in an article of 25 June, that he was morally dead and had no future in the communist world. A month later, on 21 July, Yalman himself broke his silence in a polemical article denouncing communism as a sickness and implying that its adherents must be mentally unbalanced. By this date he was so fanatically anti-communist that in his memoirs, published in the United States in 1956, he omitted all reference to his involvement with Nazım. Nothing could reveal the polarized nature of Turkish politics more clearly than Yalman's evident need to eliminate all trace of his public-spirited action on behalf of political prisoners in the late 1940s for fear of being thought a fellow traveller himself. Nazım's own final judgement on Yalman in a poem of 1959, which plays on the name of Yalman's newspaper *Vatan* ('Fatherland'), was equally severe: 'First pro-German then pro-American. / "Fatherland" was for him in every era, at any time / a newspaper to be sold / and he did indeed sell the Fatherland' (A 7, 25).

On 25 July 1951 the Turkish government announced that Nazım had been stripped of his citizenship, justifing the decision in the official *Resmi Gazete* on 15 August 1951:

Since Nazım has fled to the Soviet Union via Romania without a passport, and has made a statement against Turkey at the airport, and subsequently spoken against the government of Turkey and against the individual leaders of the government with the aim of starting a communist propaganda campaign in the service of Soviet government, [...] the Ministry of the Interior has proposed that he should be deprived of his Turkish citizenship, and this proposal has been accepted by the Cabinet.

Whether the decision was constitutionally correct was later questioned by Mehmet Ali Sebük, who pointed out that leaving the country without a passport is a minor offence punishable by a small fine (Sebük, 227). Another lawyer, Halit Çelenk, argued that the Cabinet had no right to condemn Nazım for anti-Turkish propaganda, since such matters fall within the province of the judiciary and no one should be condemned without a trial. Depriving Nazım of his citizenship was a purely political act, and there has yet to be an official review of its validity.

The right-wing press began to campaign for reprisals against Nazım's associates. On 31 July 1951, *Hür Adam* wrote: 'Nazım is gone, but what will happen to his relatives, lawyers, agents?' One suggestion was that they too should be deported. Turkish nationalists organized a meeting to campaign to punish the people who helped to secure Nazım's release from prison (Sülker 6, 227-8). On 8 August 1953 *Sebilürreşad*, a right-wing magazine with racist tendencies, published a cartoon showing Nazım carrying a portrait of Stalin, assisted by Falih Rıfkı Atay, a journalist who wrote a book about the Soviet achievement. The diminutive figure of Ahmet Emin Yalman, who like Atay is portrayed with a Jewish star, can be seen supporting Nazım from behind (Fig. 23). Such journalistic campaigns, blending racism and anti-communism, were

23. Right-wing backlash: Cartoon from *Şerbilüreşad*, 1953.

not without their consequences. Not long afterwards Yalman was
shot – not fatally – by a right-wing fundamentalist in Malatya.

The reverberations of Nazım's escape continued for many years.
The police raided the homes of his family and friends, and a
number of his manuscripts were confiscated or destroyed. Those
most directly affected were Münevver and their son Mehmet
Nazım, who suffered years of social ostracism and police harassment.
They had to endure a police unit outside their house for ten full
years, although there were occasional lighter moments: 'After a
while the policemen started looking after Memo when he was

playing in the fields, or rescuing him when he got stuck in the trees', Va–Nu's wife recalled. 'They used to take him in the jeep and put him on the driving seat' (Va-Nu, 400). So strong were feelings against Münevver that she found it almost impossible to obtain commissions for the translation work on which her living depended. She repeatedly attempted to secure a visa to leave the country, only to be told that she had no right to apply to be reunited with Nazım abroad, since they were never officially married.

A number of Nazım's closest friends also left the country in this period. The Sertels had already obtained passports and left for Paris in September 1950, and the Dinos followed in 1952. Inspite of the distress which Nazım's escape caused to those left behind, he scarcely had any other option. To justify the heavy Turkish casualties in Korea, the Menderes government orchestrated a sustained anti-communist witchhunt, creating a climate of paranoia. If Nazım had remained in Turkey much longer, his life would probably have ended in prison. Moreover, the conditions he had experienced at Bursa were mild compared with the ruthless prison regimes of the following decade, when political suspects were routinely tortured as part of a strategy to destroy opposition groups. Criticism of Turkey's involvement in the Korean war was treated as a particularly serious offence. In October 1951 there was a wave of arrests, involving no less than 184 members of the Socialist Party and the Socialist Workers' and Peasants' Party, including Mihri Belli and Nazım's fellow author Nail V. The memoirs of those arrested contain graphic accounts of the brutal interrogations, especially at the Sansaryan Han detention centre in Istanbul (Karaca, 1996, 104-5; Belli, 346-9). The trials were not completed for two years, and finally 132 of those accused received prison sentences (Darendeli, 411, 417). It was indeed a 'sad state of freedom'.

9

Romantic Communism and
Real Socialism
The Soviet Union, 1951-1963

Nazım's arrival in Constantza, the chief port of Romania, aboard the *Plekhanov* created a great stir. He travelled on to Bucharest, where he was given a room in the Grand Hotel, and stayed for about eleven days. He was taken on a tour of various communities and in one village was solemnly informed that he owed his freedom to the protest meeting that had been held there in his support just a week before his escape (Roman, 28). This interlude gave the authorities in Moscow time to organize an official welcome, and on 29 June 1951, when Nazım's plane touched down at Vnukovski airport, he faced a barrage of cameras and was almost overwhelmed by the bouquets, both floral and verbal (Fig. 24). A formal speech of welcome was delivered by the representative of the Writers' Union, Konstantin Simonov, who has left the following description of the scene:

A tall handsome man with ginger hair appeared on the steps of the aeroplane. He walked with free and firm steps, holding his head high. His blue eyes were filled with curiosity and interest. It didn't take more than five minutes to understand why he chose to come here: he came here not to receive medals and recognition, but to live, to work, to fight. As he held the armful of flowers presented to him, the tips of his fingers shook with excitement and emotion (Simonov, 209).

Another eye-witness, the Turkologist Rady Fish, recalls that he walked through the sea of flowers in silence, looking at the happy faces 'with tears in his eyes'. When handed a microphone to address his admirers, Nazım declared that he was too excited to make a formal speech. He was simply happy to be breathing the

257

24. Arriving in Moscow, July 1951.

25. At the World Youth Festival in Berlin, Autumn 1951.

air of freedom in Moscow – 'the great city of life and peace' (Fish, 390-1).

Freedom in Moscow

Nazım's arrival coincided with an intensification of the Cold War, and refugees from the Soviet bloc tended to be treated as heroes who had 'chosen freedom'. For the Soviets it was now possible to celebrate an author who had gone in the other direction and found freedom in Moscow. Nazım's credentials were almost impeccable: a dedicated Russian-speaking communist, educated in Moscow in the glorious days of Leninism, repeatedly imprisoned for his beliefs, and author of an epic celebrating the Great Patriotic War of the Soviet Peoples. The fact that he came from a third world Islamic country was an added bonus. Of course, even the most welcome guest was kept under observation by the secret police, since this was no longer the informal Moscow of Nazım's student days; under the system known as 'real socialism' the movements of foreigners were closely monitored. The role of minder was initially assigned to Simonov, deputy secretary of the Writers' Union and editor of *Novy Mir*. As they drove into Moscow together, Nazım complained about the Russian translations of his works, which he felt had distorted their meaning (Simonov, 210). His thirteen years in jail had left him ignorant of the repression in Soviet society, both political and cultural. Often, when he asked if he could meet one of his artistic friends from 1920s, he received the evasive answer: 'We haven't seen him for ages.' The author Ilya Ehrenburg recalls in his memoirs that Nazım complained about Soviet literary magazines. Why were there never any references to Mayakovsky, Meyerhold, Vakhtangov or Tairov? It was as if they had never been! (Ehrenburg, 270).

Nazım had not been in Moscow since 1928, when those great artistic innovators were still alive, and he was so unaware of the effects of Stalinism that when he checked out the theatre programmes, he expected to find plays by Mayakovsky (Fevralski, 60). After embarking on a whirlwind tour of the Moscow theatres, he was soon disillusioned, and gave vent to his frustration at a dinner in his honour at the Writers' Union about a fortnight after his arrival. Nazım appeared unexpectedly gloomy, and when it was his turn to say a few words, he stood up and, speaking in

Russian, solemnly declared: 'I have seen ten plays in ten days. Actually it was the same play each time, with a different title – all of them in praise of Stalin.' It was as if a bomb had exploded in the hall. When Nazım went on to ridicule slogans like 'Stalin is our sunshine', the audience became increasingly restless until Simonov and his wife protested: 'We are not flattering Comrade Stalin, he really is our sunshine. We cannot allow you to speak like this' (Erduran, 157). This episode made such an impression that the poet Yevgeny Yevtushenko recalled it in a televised interview forty years later. According to Yevtushenko, Stalin himself was due to receive Nazım soon after this event, and Nazım was determined to raise the question of the personality cult with the great leader himself. A pretext was hastily found to prevent a potentially disastrous confrontation, and Nazım was received by Malenkov instead (GC/TV 4).

Nazım's fiftieth birthday was marked in January 1952 by an official celebration, accompanied by flowery tributes in the prestigious *Literaturnaya Gazeta* (Ehrenburg, 293). By now he was well-established in Moscow, with a spacious third-floor apartment near the Sokol metro station. Here he created a homely atmosphere, decorating his room with hand-carved ornaments, dolls, masks, cigarette boxes, plates and china from all parts of the world, as well as reproductions of paintings by Picasso. Russian icons were later added to the collection. A friend who called at the flat in 1953 was struck by the many mementos Nazım had accumulated. 'I fill this room with objects', Nazım explained, 'because I live alone' (Fevralski, 16 & 28). Financially his life was quite secure, since he was entitled to the accumulated royalties from Russian editions of his books. Through these translations he was now able to make a living from his writings – something never possible in Turkey. The 'Nazım Hikmet Bibliographical Guide', a comprehensive list of his publications in Russian issued in Moscow in 1962 to mark his sixtieth birthday, includes over 1,000 numbered items (NHBG). Large new editions of his work had appeared in 1950-1 during the campaign to secure his release, and in 1953 an edition of his Collected Poems was published. Under Soviet arrangements it was common for as many as 50,000 copies to be printed, and writers could earn up to 60 per cent of the net profit. Nazım has sometimes been denounced for accepting Moscow gold, but he was not rewarded simply for supporting the regime. His work of the 1950s is still distinguished by its imaginative vitality and independence of judgement. Questioned by a Turkish journalist in Paris about his income, he was able to reply that he earned his living from his books (Dino, 150).

Within two years Nazım was in a position to rent a dacha in Peredelkino, a writers' colony some forty minutes by train from Moscow, where his neighbours included Boris Pasternak and Alexander Fadeyev. Here he spent relaxing days writing and receiving guests in a timber house idyllically situated among the birch trees, while a nearby lake beckoned invitingly on hot summer days. Many visitors have recorded their impressions of this house at No. 1 Trenyova Street. It stood in half an acre of land, cared for by a gardener whose wife was employed as a housekeeper by the Writers' Union. The garden was full of lilac, honeysuckle, rhododendrons and roses, just like a villa on the Bosphorus (Tulyakova, 50). In the principal ground-floor room, which opened on to a terrace with cane chairs, there was a long beech table with handicrafts, candles, toys and other ornaments. Next door was Nazım's study, overlooking the pine trees, with a large table covered with books, papers and newspaper cuttings, and with two typewriters, one with Latin, the other with Cyrillic characters. On the walls were Chinese decorations, Polish posters, a Turkish flag, and photos of Marx, Lenin, and the fifteen members of Turkish the Communist Party murdered on the Black Sea. A wooden staircase led to the upper floor of the dacha, which had two spacious rooms, one decorated in oriental style with a divan by the window. The house was lit by oil lamps, and there were straw mats, sheepskin rugs and kilims on the floor. In the corner was a chest from Turkey, copper and silver trays, wooden spoons, a hookah, a charcoal stove and wooden clogs. Hanging on the walls were the traditional shadow-puppet figures Karagöz and Hacivat made of camel skin (Erdinç, 49-53).

Here Nazım would compose poetry, striding up and down in his study dictating to Ekber Babayev, a student of oriental languages who acted as his secretary. During the last dozen years of Nazım's life Babayev was to become a close collaborator and loyal friend. The rustic mood was enhanced when Nazım acquired a handsome collie dog named Şeytan (in English, Satan) of which he grew very fond, feeling guilty when it fell sick and died. His poem 'Elegy for Satan', written in 1956, expresses his sadness at waking early, listening and suddenly realizing he could hear 'no one scratching at my door'. It ends with a muted celebration of those summer days at Peredelkino:

> Today it's thirty-eight degrees in the shade.
> I gaze at the forest from the balcony:
> tall slender pines rise deep red
> against the steel-blue sky.
> The people sweating,
> the dogs' tongues hanging out,
> they're all headed for the lake to swim.
> Leaving their heavy bodies on the shore,
> they'll know the happiness of fish.
> ('Şeytan'a Mersiye', A 6, 77-8; P, 165)

Throughout the 1950s he was able to withdraw to the tranquillity at Peredelkino, and photographs taken at the dacha show him relaxed (Fig. 26). These interludes were the more welcome because of his increasing involvement in public life.

Nazım's first official mission was to the Berlin Youth Festival of August 1951, accompanied by Fadeyev. Here he was reunited with his old friend Sabiha Sertel and her daughter Yıldız. The optimistic mood in the newly founded German Democratic Republic is reflected in contemporary photographs showing the enthusiastic faces surrounding him on the platform (see Fig. 25, p. 258). But thoughts of Turkey were never far from the poet's mind, and he was aware that the Menderes regime was becoming increasingly oppressive. Among the Turkish representatives at the Berlin Festival was a physician, Sevim Tarı, who was arrested and imprisoned on her return to Istanbul during the October 1951 crackdown on communists.

Nazım's second mission in the autumn of 1951 took him to Bulgaria, where the large minority population of Turkish-speaking Muslims were unhappy with the new regime. The Bulgarian Turks who had hitherto worked as rural labourers or small farmers were resisting pressure to join agricultural co-operatives or work in factories as part of the communist production drive. The government for its part gave low priority to the Turkish communities in infrastructural projects like road-building and extending electricity supplies (Sertel 1978, 42). At first the authorities adopted the relatively liberal policy of allowing emigration to Turkey, hoping to be rid of a minority of malcontents, but when they

26. Peredelkino: relaxing at the dacha.

realized that about 60,000 Turks (10% of the Turkish-speaking population) intended to leave, they panicked at the prospect of losing such a large labour force and decided to halt emigration (Tata, 6-9).

This was the situation when Nazım arrived in Sofia in September 1951. He must have seemed ideally qualified for this mission, since his work was already widely known in Bulgaria. Here was not some faceless party official, but a poet who could address the people in their own language. Nazım was met by Fahri Erdinç, an exiled Turkish author who worked for the state publishing company, but he was even more gratified to be welcomed to Sofia by 'Beethoven' Hasan, the music-loving fellow inmate from Bursa prison who figures in *Human Landscapes*. Hasan had escaped by walking across the Bulgarian frontier and now worked in a factory while studying music at the Conservatoire. On the day of his arrival Nazım laid a wreath on the grave of Georgy Dimitrov, a founder of the Bulgarian People's Republic, who had played a leading role in the struggle against Fascism as general secretary of the Comintern. Equipped with a dossier of information about the achievements of the communist government, including statistics about new Turkish-speaking schools, he set out on his tour. At his first stop he made a speech warning his audience not to be seduced by agents of American imperialism who were trying to undermine the regime. After the official meeting in the town hall he invited people to meet him informally to air their grievances, especially their fears about the suppression of their religion and culture. Listening carefully to their complaints, he warned them that life in Turkey might prove even worse. His arguments proved persuasive, and some of those who had already been issued with exit visas decided to remain in Bulgaria. Blaga Dimitrova, the interpreter who accompanied him on this tour, records that these were not conventional political meetings, but emotionally charged encounters which made a tremendous impact (Dimitrova, 4, 9, 18, 23 & 88).

Since the Turkish population of Bulgaria was so dispersed, Nazım found himself visiting twenty villages in four days, addressing an estimated total of 150,000 people in the whole tour (Dimitrova, 130). The villagers welcomed him with traditional Turkish music and folk dances, and in his speeches he emphasised the importance of education and co-operatives. These activities were reported by the Turkish news agency, and an article appeared in *Cumhuriyet* on 10 Oct. 1951 describing his efforts to discourage emigration and to explain the ideals of socialism to Turkish-speaking peasants. However, Nazım returned to Moscow with mixed feelings. Later in 1951, while attending a conference in Vienna, he described to Zekeriya Sertel how he had urged the Bulgarian authorities to allow the Turks greater cultural autonomy and provide new schools and radio broadcasts in Turkish. Only thus could they be convinced of the benefits of remaining in Bulgaria (Sertel 1978, 47). Nazım was aware that his position in Bulgaria was equivocal, as a Party spokesman but one who sympathized with the needs of the Turkish people (Erdinç, 38). He was also conscious that his movements were being monitored by state security, and once when a young woman sitting next to him collapsed with food poisoning, he suspected that he had been the intended victim of a murder attempt (GC/TV 4). He did not return to Bulgaria till 1957, so possibly the Party had doubts about the propaganda value of his tour.

Ambassador for peace

During his years in the Soviet Union Nazım became active in the international peace movement and attended numerous congresses abroad. These trips, organized by the Writers' Union, brought him into personal contact with the socialist intellectual élite, including Anna Seghers, Pablo Neruda, Louis Aragon, Paul Robeson and Jean-Paul Sartre. At an early meeting in Stockholm, he received guidance from a shy, bespectacled member of the Soviet delegation whom he had never met before. He only discovered later that his mentor was Dimitri Shostakovich, the composer whose heroic Leningrad Symphony had reached him over the radio waves in Bursa prison, helping to inspire the Fourth Book of 'Human Landscapes' (Tulyakova, 367). The eminence of the peace campaigners ensured that disarmament and détente remained high on the international agenda.

The intensification of the Cold War had led in the spring of 1949 to the holding of the first World Congress of Partisans for Peace in Paris, organized by French pacifists and communists, and attended by some 2,000 delegates. Picasso's dove was its evocative symbol (Ehrenburg, 136-7). This organization – later renamed the World Peace Council – drew up the influential Stockholm Peace Appeal, a petition against atomic weapons which attracted world-wide support (Treadgold, 434). The Soviet authorities were keen to exploit the peace movement, and in 1950 established a Stalin Peace Prize to reward activity in this field, co-ordinated by an international committee that included Louis Aragon, Pablo Neruda and J. D. Bernal as well as Ilya Ehrenburg and Alexander Fadeyev (Ehrenburg, 249). The Soviet-sponsored peace movement has often been derided as no more than a front for the subversion of the liberal democracies. But it succeeded in mobilizing genuine anxieties about weapons of mass destruction. During 1950 the advance of the communist forces in Korea, who by September seemed on the verge of driving the Americans and their allies into the sea, provoked the fear that President Truman might once again authorize the use of atomic weapons. In December, after a meeting in Washington with the British Prime Minister Clement Attlee, Truman finally announced that atomic weapons would not be used, but by this date he had lost the propaganda initiative. With memories of Hiroshima still fresh, it was not difficult to brand the Americans as war criminals and present the acquisition of atomic weapons by the Soviet Union as legitimate self-defence (Ehrenburg, 227).

For Nazım, as for so many of his generation, Hiroshima came to symbolize an era of unprecedented danger. From 1-6 November 1951, shortly after his visit to Bulgaria, he attended the World Peace Congress in Vienna, again accompanied by Fadeyev. The delegates he met included Louis Aragon, J. D. Bernal, Eugene Cotton and the scientist Frédéric Joliot-Curie. Most memorable of all was his encounter with Emi Siao, the Chinese revolutionary he had immortalized in *Gioconda and Si-Ya-U*. It was like meeting a ghost from the past, since Nazım had not met him since 1924 and had assumed that he had died in the revolutionary struggle against the army of Chiang Kai-shek. In fact, Siao had escaped to Vladivostok in 1927, returning to China to join Mao's revolutionary army in 1936, together with his wife Eva, a refugee from Nazi Germany (Siao, 6). Nazım's visit to Vienna was followed by a trip to Prague, where he received an international peace prize. There followed a series of World Peace Council meetings, in which he played an increasingly prominent role. He travelled to Peking to attend a meeting of Asiatic members of the Council on 25 June 1952. A note in Siao's diary, published in *Cumhuriyet* (Book Section) on 23 July 1992, records that they visited the Great Wall. A week later Nazım was in Berlin for another meeting from 1-5 July, at which the main subject was the Korean war. The military stalemate on the ground had led the Americans to intensify their use of air power, and bombing raids on targets like the ancient north Korean city of Suan had provoked an international outcry. At this meeting Nazım spoke twice about the war, condemning the government of Turkey for sacrificing workers' lives in the interests of American imperialism and reciting a song lamenting the fate of Turkish soldiers in Korea.

On 5 October 1952, Nazım and Siao met again at a Council meeting in Vienna, where Nazım made the opening speech. This was followed by a major congress in Vienna from 12-19 December, attended by 1700 delegates from eighty-three countries. The opening speech was made by Joliot-Curie, and the list of international delegates included Sartre, Aragon, Neruda, Diego Rivera, Arnold Zweig and J.D. Bernal (Siao, 193). In the Russian–occupied zone of Vienna a crowd of over two thousand people joined the delegates

on a march from the Soviet war memorial on the Schwarzen-
bergplatz along the Ringstrasse, singing songs and chanting slogans.
By the end of 1952 Nazım had become a member of the Bureau
of the World Peace Council, and in this capacity he attended
further meetings in Stockholm, Prague, Berlin, Budapest, Warsaw,
Vienna and Helsinki. It was at this time that he obtained a Polish
passport, since his efforts to obtain full Soviet citizenship had
failed (Tulyakova, 140). He officially altered his name to Hikmet-Borzenski, and used the name subsequently in formal documents. His visit to Poland in 1954 was particularly memorable,
since it was when he met members of the Borzenski family, from
which his grandfather was descended (Sertel 1978, 100).

Nazım's activities in the peace movement reached a climax in
1955. The year began with another meeting of the Bureau in
Vienna from 17-19 January, at which Nazım spoke about the
destructive powers of atomic weapons (SPA 7, 421). Here for
the first time, he was permitted to travel without an official escort
from the Communist Party. Although Vienna was still divided
into four occupation zones, economic recovery was well under
way, and Nazım was impressed by the consumer goods in the
shop windows. But he also visited the Karl Marx-Hof, the celebrated
bloc of workers' dwellings constructed by the socialist administration of Vienna around 1930, and was also impressed by the priority
given in Vienna to working-class people. Even more memorable
was the Helsinki World Assembly of Peace of 22-29 June 1955,
attended by 2,000 delegates from ninety countries. Nazım attended
as a delegate representing Turkey, emphasizing in his speech that
'we are strong because we rely on what unites people, not what
separates them' (Helsinki, 38). Although in poor health, with
circulation problems which needed medical treatment, he also
contributed to an international poetry reading (Fevralski, 65). At
the end of the conference he was re-elected to the Bureau of
the Peace Council.

The peace campaign gathered momentum especially in Japan,
and a World Conference was held in Hiroshima on 6 August
1955 to mark the tenth anniversary of the city's destruction – by
then Nazım was sufficiently recovered from his illness to fly to
Japan for the occasion. At the congress it was announced that a
petition against nuclear testing had been signed by 33 million
people worldwide (Bezirci, 208). Since it had been organized not

by the communist party but by Japanese students and housewives, the peace movement could not simply be dismissed as a Soviet plot. Nazım's role at these congresses not only involved speech-making: his early association with Mayakovsky had initiated him into the potential of poetry on the political platform, and in the mid-1950s he composed a number of poems for public performance with musical settings. He became something akin to a poet laureate of the peace movement, and translations of his texts were published with eye-catching illustrations designed to reach the largest possible audience. Recognizing the importance of appealing to liberal opinion in America, he wrote to Ernest Hemingway and Paul Robeson, asking them to help with the translation and populariza-tion of his poems about nuclear weapons (Sertel 1978, 143-8). Hemingway did not respond, but Robeson readily agreed to include songs by Nazım in his recitals.

   Others besides Robeson now began to popularize Nazım's work in the United States. One of his texts, 'Kızçocuğu' ('Girl Child', A 6, 81), was set to music by the folk-singer Pete Seeger under the title 'I Come and Stand at Every Door'. In this role-poem Nazım identifies with a seven-year Japanese girl killed at Hiroshima. The poignancy of the child's perspective is enhanced by the haunt-ing ballad tune 'The Great Silkie', which Seeger used in his musical setting. His adaptation is cited here:

> I come and stand at every door
> but none can hear my silent tread.
> I knock and yet remain unseen,
> for I am dead, for I am dead.
>
> I'm only seven although I died
> in Hiroshima long ago.
> I'm seven now as I was then.
> When children die, they do not grow.
>
> My hair was scorched by swirling flames,
> my eyes grew dim, my eyes grew blind.
> Death came and turned my bones to dust,
> and that was scattered by the wind.
>
> I need no fruit, I need no rice,
> I need no sweets nor even bread,
> I ask for nothing for myself,
> for I am dead, for I am dead.

> All that I ask is that for peace
> you fight today, you fight today,
> so that the children of this world
> may live and grow and laugh and play.

This song repeatedly featured in Seeger's concerts, and was issued on disk by Columbia in the early 1960s (CBS Mono BPG 62462).

One of the focal points for anti-nuclear protests was the radio-activity caused by atmospheric testing of atomic weapons. The American government was reluctant to acknowledge any risks to human life, but the fraudulent nature of this claim was exposed when the Japanese fishing boat *Lucky Dragon* strayed into the path of radioactive fall-out after the first hydrogen bomb tests at the Bikini atoll in March 1954. The episode provoked outrage in Japan and made headlines around the world. Since the 15-megaton Bikini bomb was 1,000 times more powerful than the atom bomb which destroyed Hiroshima, it is hardly surprising that it provoked international protests. Nazım added his voice through the poignant poem 'Japanese Fisherman' ('Japon Balıkçısı'), using the voice of the victims to express the impact of radioactivity:

> We have caught fish that's deadly to eat,
> and our flesh is deadly to touch.
> This ship is a black coffin
> and its deck is deadly to board
> [. . .]
>
> My almond-eyed darling, you must forget me.
> This ship is a black coffin
> and its deck is deadly to board.
> Over our heads passed the clouds
> [. . .]
>
> This ship is a black coffin.
> My almond-eyed darling, you must forget me.
> The child that you will get from me
> will be as rotten as a rotten egg.
>   (A 6, 79-80)

The sparse language and resonant rhymes suggest that this text too was conceived as a song. Indeed it was later set to music by a number of Turkish folk singers, including Zülfü Livaneli. Nazım's message is summed up in the title of another poem of this period, 'Don't Let the Clouds Kill' ('Bulutlar Adam Öldürmesin', A 6,

54), written in February 1955. Nazım wrote two further anti-nuclear poems in 1958 in anticipation of World Peace Council meetings at Stockholm in July: 'Strontium 90' ('Stronsium 90', A 7, 132) and 'Hope' ('Umut', A 6, 135). In 1959 he was again in Stockholm for the tenth anniversary of the founding of the Peace Council.

How should Nazım's sustained involvement with the peace movement be summarized? Although clearly designed to advance Soviet interests in the Cold War, the movement had a wider significance. Subjectively, the peace conferences gave substance to Nazım's lifelong commitment to international co-operation. He was received with honour and affection in Africa and China, as well as in many parts of Europe and Central Asia, and made a host of new friends. These international gatherings could be convivial occasions. The poet Charles Dobzynski, one of Nazım's French translators, recalls an exhilarating encounter in Warsaw in the summer of 1955, when he and Nazım would spend the day discussing linguistic nuances, followed by a long evening listening to Simonov's reminiscences at the Crocodile bar (*Anka*, 20/21, 187-9). Such contacts gave a new impetus to Nazım's literary reputation, more than counterbalancing the suppression of his work in Turkey. 'My writings are published in thirty or forty languages,' he wrote with justifiable pride. 'In my own Turkish they are banned' ('Autobiography', A 7, 99). Objectively, too, the peace movement produced substantial results. By 1955 the bitterness of the Cold War which prevailed at the time when Nazım first joined the movement had given way to a spirit of détente. In May of that year the Kremlin put forward a package of disarmament proposals, and at the 20th Congress in 1956 Khrushchev embarked on a policy of peaceful coexistence, repudiating the theory of the inevitability of war between the capitalist and communist systems. There followed a period of détente which survived the Hungarian and Suez conflicts of the autumn of 1956 and even the Cuban missile crisis of 1962.

Nazım did not only devote his diplomatic and literary skills to the cause of peace. His mission was also to strengthen the international commitment to communism, not least in other Warsaw Pact countries. He frequently visited the German Democratic Republic, where his work was becoming well known through translations by Alfred Kurella and Stephan Hermlin. His role as a propagandist was tempered by an underlying humanism, aptly illustrated by an episode in January 1956, when he was invited to a meeting of the East German Writers' Union, attended by Walter Ulbricht. Here he found himself drawn into the debate between Ulbricht's hardliners and the more liberal movement led by the novelist Stefan Heym. Heym recalls his moment of panic after being denounced by the doctrinaire Willy Bredel for criticizing the achievements of the German Democratic Republic:

There followed a coffee break. Outside the realm of real socialism it is virtually impossible to imagine a more lethal isolation than that in which I and my wife Gertrude found ourselves during this half-hour amid the turmoil of the crowd thronging the rooms adjacent to the congress hall; only in this context is the human instinct for the dangerous rays which emanate from an individual targeted by official denunciations so acutely developed. Only one person breaks through the invisible wall that surrounds us, not a German but a Turk, Nazım Hikmet.

The poet Nazım Hikmet, tall, blond, blue-eyed, sits down at my table, takes me by the hand and says: 'You must defend yourself. You must reply. You are lost if you allow the accusations to go unanswered. Believe me, I've been in the game long enough, I know.'

Heartened by Nazım's words, Heym returned to the platform to deliver a speech refuting the accusations against him. Even Ulbricht was impressed, and by the end of the evening Heym and his wife were being lionized like film stars (Heym, 596–600).

In the early and mid-1950s Nazım made no less than five visits to Hungary, a country caught up in an even more extreme conflict between the hardliners, led by Mátyás Rákosi, who was appointed premier in August 1952, and the reformists, led by his successor Imre Nagy, premier from July 1953 to April 1955. The struggle reached its climax when Rákosi, who had remained secretary-general of the Party with strong Soviet support, forced Nagy out of office in the spring of 1955 and attempted to crush the liberalization process. Since writers and intellectuals played a significant role in the developments which finally led to the Hungarian revolution of October 1956, Nazım could hardly avoid taking sides, although his position was ultimately rather evasive. On his first visit in July 1952, he was the guest of the Hungarian government, staying for several weeks at a hostel for Party officials in the 7th District of Budapest. In a series of articles and interviews he took an orthodox line, expressing his thanks for the support he had received during his hunger strike and his admiration for Hungary's socialist democracy (article in *Független Magyarország*, 14 July 1952; interview in *Magyar Nemzet*, 20 July 1952). A thirty-year-old called Klari, the daughter of a French diplomat, was assigned to him as interpreter, and they enjoyed relaxing strolls together on Margaret Island (Fig. 27). He was also welcomed by the poet György Somlyó, who had campaigned for Nazım's release from prison and was translating his poems. With the help of Klari, the two poets set to work. Nazım would recite a poem in Turkish and then prepare a version in French, which Somlyó would translate and read out in Hungarian. Within two weeks they had produced an attractive volume for the '20th Century Poetry' series, and it was published later that year (Somlyó, Interview, Summer 1989).

Nazım's later visits to Hungary illustrate his difficulty in reconciling party discipline with the pressure for liberalization which gained momentum after Stalin's death. When he visited Budapest for a meeting of the Peace Council in June 1953, he paid his respects to Rákosi, even though this ardent Stalinist was about to be displaced by Nagy. The tense atmosphere at this meeting with Rákosi has been described by Sertel, who adds that Nazım felt more at ease when giving a poetry reading in Pest (Sertel 1978, 86). He also enjoyed visiting a pioneer camp run by children in the Buda hills – an experience which inspired him to write the poem 'Hungarian Notes' idealising the experiences of Hungarian children and contrasting their innocent pleasures with the fate of children in Turkey. At the end of November, Nazım visited Budapest again after attending a Peace Council meeting in Vienna. In an article for the Communist Party newspaper, *Szabad Nép* (13 December 1953) we still find him toeing the official line, emphasizing how depressing he had found Vienna by comparison with Budapest.

In the spring of 1954, after Peace Council engagements in Prague, Bratislava and Vienna, he visited Budapest for the third time (Fevralski, 48). By then his sympathies were swinging towards the reformists, and there are hints of a critique of Rákosi's hard line in a scenario he wrote during this visit entitled 'The Greatest Danger – the Greatest Doctor' ('En Büyük Tehlike, En Büyük Hekim', Fevralski, 70). A year later, Nazım was in Czechoslovakia for the staging of his plays *Legend of Love* and *The First Day of the Feast*. The latter play was also being broadcast by Hungarian

27. Budapest: with Klari on Margaret Island, 1952.

radio, and this gave him the pretext for a further visit to Budapest. But he also had personal reasons for his repeated visits to Hungary: his wish to consult Dr István Kúnos, a specialist who was developing new techniques of heart surgery. Nazım's circulation problems, as the doctor later explained, were due to the valves and not the muscles of his heart. 'If Nazım had been a few years younger', he added, 'we might have been able to help him' (Kúnos, Interview, summer 1989). Despite this disappointment, Nazım struck up a friendship with Kúnos, whose father was a collector of Turkish folk songs. In October 1955 he invited Kúnos and his wife to Moscow to undertake a further medical examination.

Nazım paid his final visit to Hungary in May 1956 as guest of the Communist Party, staying at a house belonging to the Writers' Association in Visegrád, 40 km. down the Danube from Budapest (Fevralski, 72). This time a more substantial volume of poems by Nazım was published in Hungarian, with an introduction by Somlyó. Nazım also had meetings with composers who wished to set his poems to music, but these projects were overtaken by events. Budapest was buzzing with rumours of political change, since news of Khrushchev's 'secret speech' denouncing Stalin's crimes had already filtered through. The release from prison of the Polish liberalizer Wladyslaw Gomulka in mid-April increased the pressure on Stalinists in other countries. When Nazım attended a meeting at the Writers' Association in Budapest, he encouraged critics of the regime to speak out (Sertel 1978, 149 & 158-60); but he had to play his cards carefully, since he himself risked arrest if he became directly involved. At a meeting organized by the Petöfi Circle early in June, the philosopher György Lukács publicly denounced the 'bankruptcy of Marxism in Hungary' (Zinner, 209). Rákosi was dismissed on 18 July due to direct intervention by the Soviet emissary Anastas Mikoyan, and as a result Nagy re-emerged as leader of the reform movement. Just five months after Nazım's visit to Budapest, the rumbling discontent erupted in the Hungarian uprising of 18 October, brutally crushed by Soviet tanks the following month. In the spring of 1957 the Hungarian Writers' Association was disbanded (Vali, 394). The execution of Nagy in June 1958 signalled the end of liberalization.

Nazım did not publicly question the Soviet invasion, and avoided any reference to Hungary in his poetry. He may even have shared the Kremlin's fear that allowing the Hungarians to choose their own road to socialism would lead to the collapse of the Soviet bloc. But he clearly did identify with the more cautious programme of liberalization being promoted by Gomulka in Poland. On 3 November 1956, just a few days before the Soviet tanks entered Budapest, he moved to Warsaw, where he spent several months away from the eye of the storm. During this period he also visited a number of other Eastern bloc countries, including Czechoslovakia, East Germany, Romania and Bulgaria, as well as Georgia. Perhaps the Party felt that Nazım's humanistic form of communism would help to counteract the development of anti-Soviet sentiment in other Warsaw Pact countries. He was in Prague in December 1956, when reprisals against Hungarian dissidents were at their height and refugees were flooding across the border into Austria. Not surprisingly, the poems he wrote are uncharacteristically sombre. 'This Place Called Prague', written early in 1957, presents a nightmarish vision, hinting at political disillusionment as well as personal depression: 'Lenin lies sick in a snowy forest: / brows knitted, he thinks of certain people, / stares into the white darkness, / and sees the days to come' ('Pıraǧ Dedikleri', A 6, 98-99; P, 172).

Surviving Stalinism

For Nazım, as for Brecht, it was not 'great men' who make history. Both poets were sceptical about the cult of the great leader, and the fact that Brecht, towards the end of his life, sponsored a German edition of Nazım's poems suggests that he was aware of an underlying affinity (Brecht, 555). For both poets the heroes of the revolution were the working people – ordinary men and women capable of great courage and endurance in defence of their convictions. In *Human Landscapes* it is not Atatürk or Stalin who are celebrated for leading struggle against the invaders, but Corporal Ali and his comrades in the 12th Infantry Division, fighting to liberate Izmir from the Greeks in 1922, or Zoya Kosmodemianskaya, the eighteen year-old partisan executed by the Nazis in 1941. On several occasions the cult of the great leader attracted his irony, as in his poem mocking the statues of Stalin which dominated the communist world:

> He was made of stone, steel, plaster and paper, from one centimetre to seven metres long
>   his boots made of stone, steel, plaster and paper, crushed us
> in every square of the city
>   in the parks on the tops of the trees, his shadow made of stone, steel, plaster, paper
>   his moustache, made of stone, steel, plaster, paper
> was inside our soup in the restaurants
>   in our rooms we were under his eyes
> made of stone, steel, plaster, paper
>   one morning he disappeared
>   his boots vanished out of our squares
>   his shadow from the tops of the trees,
>   his moustache out of our soup,
>   his eyes from our rooms
> and the weight of the thousands of tons of stone, steel, plaster
>   and paper
>   was lifted off our chests
>   (A 7, 102)

If this poem had been written in 1951 when Nazım was criticizing the 'Stalin is our sunshine' school of poetry, he would have been showing exceptional courage – not to say foolhardiness, but after twelve years in Turkish jails he was far too shrewd to risk a further prison term for incautious public statements. The poem 'Made of stone, steel, plaster, paper' was only written in December 1961, and remained unpublished in Nazım's lifetime. It forms an epitaph to Stalinism, written after the removal of Stalin's body from the mausoleum in Red Square in late October. It should certainly not be taken as expressing the poet's position in the previous decade, for he had every reason to be grateful for his welcome in 1951 and the privileges he enjoyed. This is reflected on the inside title page of *Moskova Senfonisi*, published in Turkish in Sofia in 1952, where he pays tribute not only to the people of the Soviet Union, but more specifically to Stalin: 'it is Stalin's hand that holds the banner of life and peace.'

In private, his comments were more critical: 'I have a great respect for Comrade Stalin,' Nazım confessed to Ilya Ehrenburg in 1951, 'but I can't bear to read poems which compare him to the sun; it's not just bad poetry, it's bad sentiment' (Ehrenburg, 271). He made similar critical comments in conversations with the young Russian poet Yevtushenko, who was so impressed by Nazım's work that he placed him in the same category as Pasternak or even Pushkin (GC/TV4). However, public criticism of Stalin was inconceivable, since it could be a capital offence even to tell a joke about the great leader. Further problems arose from Stalin's claim to be infallible in literary as well as political matters. His unpredictable pronouncements about a novel or poem which happened to catch his eye could have disastrous consequences for the author. It was a sign of his paranoia that in January 1953, when suffering from a serious heart condition, he ordered the arrest of nine prominent doctors, accusing them of involvement in a so-called Zionist 'doctors' plot' to poison members of the central committee. Nazım himself, after the food poisoning episode in Bulgaria, was apprehensive about the machinations of Beria's secret police, one of whose favourite methods for eliminating their victims was by staging 'car accidents'. According to Yevtushenko, Nazım was later told by his driver that such an 'accident' had been planned in his own case (GC/TV 4).

Nazım had reason to avoid comments that could be construed

as hostile to his hosts. One advantage of his involvement with the international peace movement was that it directed the focus of his work outside the Soviet Union itself. By making politically 'correct' pronouncements in public, he consolidated his position in the eyes of the literary establishment, particularly the secretary general of the Writers' Union, Alexander Fadeyev, a leading Stalinist. In propaganda terms his accounts of the way the communist movement was repressed in Turkey were particularly welcome, since they directed attention away from the repressiveness of the Soviet system. One of his most tendentious plays, *Fatma Ali ve Başkaları* (Fatma Ali and the Others), was given alternative titles like 'A Tale from Turkey' or 'A Cell with a Thousand-Watt Lamp' when adapted for performance in communist countries. Set in Turkey around 1950, it deals with the repression of protests against Turkish conscripts being sent to fight in the Korea. The central character, Satılmış, a left-wing folk singer from Erzincan in eastern Turkey, is imprisoned and tortured by the Turkish police at the instigation of an American agent, the villainous Mr Smith. When this play was translated into Czech and staged in Prague in 1952, a Hungarian reviewer recorded that it culminated in an explicitly pro-Stalinist message. Undeterred by his captors, the heroic Satılmış (we are told) defiantly sang a revolutionary song, culminating in the words: 'He creates a new world and loves us, so we have to sing for Stalin.' However, it would be misleading to take these words as a direct expression of Nazım's own views. The source quoted is a report in the Hungarian newspaper *Beke es Szabadsag*, dated 27 July 1952, reviewing a production of the play in Prague, and the accompanying photograph shows Satılmış defiantly strumming his lute under the scrutiny of Mr Smith. But Nazım was hardly in position to supervise the ways in which his work was adapted for performance in other languages, and possibly the praise of Stalin was accentuated in the Czech translation. The Turkish text, published in the 1960s, contains a straightforward critique of the Korean war – but no tribute to Stalin (B 6, 315).

Like so many other loyal communists, Nazım was deeply moved by the announcement of Stalin's death. Lying in state in the Hall of Columns in March 1953, Stalin appeared to symbolize the sufferings and achievements of the whole communist movement. A Russian memoir of this period recalls that 'the whole country

shuddered with an almost fanatical sense of grief and a sudden
boundless hope for change in the future'. But there was also an
atmosphere of insecurity and fear, since 'everyone anticipated fresh
persecution and show trials' (Zabolotsky, 303). Leading authors
were summoned to a memorial meeting at the Writers' Union
and instructed to write poems to mark the momentous event.
Pablo Neruda recalls this moment – the sole occasion when he
wrote a poem about Stalin: 'The death of the Cyclops of the
Kremlin had world-wide impact. The human jungle shattered.
My poem captured the feeling of that panic on earth' (Neruda
1977, 319). For Nazım the death of Stalin awoke memories of
the death of Lenin; in 1924 he had written a poem celebrating
Lenin's inspiring example, and now, in a fifty-line poem entitled
'5 March 1953', he composed a similar tribute to Stalin:

> I love him
> as I love Marx, Engels, Lenin,
>> as you love him
>>> with the same affection,
>>> with the same reverence.
>
> [. . .]
> Comrades,
>> Soviet people
> these are heavy days.
> Without him these heavy days will pass
>> without turmoil, without cracks
> if we stand together with him and with Lenin
>>>> (*2000'e Doğru*, 10 January 1988, p.12)

This call to close ranks and maintain party unity avoids mentioning
Stalin by name – an indication of Nazım's detachment from the
dominant personality cult. He pays tribute to the whole tradition
of Marxist-Leninism, not merely to one individual. Far from compromising his integrity, this poem commemorates Stalin's death
in a language which subordinates the emotions of the moment
to a larger historical continuum. The poem first appeared in Russian
in the edition of his Collected Poems published later in 1953
(NHBG, No. 395). The original was apparently first published
in Sofia in 1954, although it has not been included in any subsequent
Turkish edition. In January 1988 the poem was republished in
the magazine *2000'e Doğru* with a commentary by Nedim Gürsel,
a researcher who discovered the original in Moscow. An excerpt

had been published twenty years earlier by Ergun Göze, a right-wing critic who claimed that Nazım broadcast the poem on Budapest Radio on 5 March 1955 to mark the second anniversary of Stalin's death (Göze, 351).

During the three years between Stalin's death and the denunciation of his crimes at the 20th Congress in March 1956, the first halting steps were taken towards liberalization. In the ensuing struggle for power, the crimes of the Stalinist regime were initially pinned on the Director of the KGB, Lavrenti Beria, who was arrested in June 1953 and later executed after a secret trial. There was also a purge of the Politburo and at least 7,000 Stalinist officials were removed from office. But until Khrushchev succeeded in asserting his authority over Bulganin and Malenkov, the reform process was tortuously slow; the political class was far too deeply compromised to make a clean break with the past, and the system of gulags, in which several million people died during Stalin's reign of terror, was still maintained, even though some dissidents were now released and rehabilitated. For writers a premature bid for intellectual freedom might still have disastrous consequences.

In the painful process of readjustment two of Nazım's friends played decisive roles: Alexander Fadeyev, representing the political establishment, and Ilya Ehrenburg as spokesman for a cautious liberalization (Fig. 28a & b). The contrast between them epitomizes the conflict within Nazım's own position between party loyalty and individual self-expression. Fadeyev was a hero of the revolution, having fought on the Bolshevik side in the civil war. Through the darkest years of Stalinism he remained a loyal supporter of the system, becoming a member of the Central Committee as well as the dominant figure in the Writers' Union. The full extent of his involvement in the purges only came to light after 1989 (Garrard, 51-2 and 70). But he also earned credit for using his influence to help rehabilitate authors who had been arrested and sent to labour camps (Zabolotsky, 299). Some people regarded Fadeyev as a 'man of iron', but those like Ehrenburg who knew him well were aware of a more vulnerable side (Ehrenburg, 159). Although Fadeyev's novels are now virtually forgotten, he was for thirty years one of the dominant figures in Soviet literature. His novel *The Young Guard* (1945) tells the romantic story a group of teenagers resisting the German army of occupation, based

28. Allies in the Soviet Writers' Union: (*a*) Nazım and Alexander Fadeyev.

(*b*) Nazım and Ilya Ehrenburg.

on actual events in Krasnodon in 1942-3. Fadeyev's subservience
to the party line was revealed by his response to the criticism
this novel attracted from Stalin for failing to give a more positive
picture of communist organizations during the war (Ehrenburg,
160). In a revised edition which he issued in 1951 the heroes
are not courageous teenagers but exemplary apparatchiks.

Nazım certainly admired Fadeyev's work, and throughout the
debates that followed Stalin's death the two remained friends. On
23 October 1953, Nazım was invited by Fadeyev to address a
general meeting of the Writers' Union. He prepared a short speech,
but at the last moment decided to play safe and shelter behind
the opinions of others. After listening to a report delivered by
another hardliner, Konstantin Simonov, he diplomatically said: 'I
agree with the points in the report and I have nothing else to
add' (Fevralski, 35). Whether Nazım really accepted the view of
Fadeyev and Simonov that literary policy should be subjected to
centralized party control remains unclear, but in the autumn of
1953 he evidently still felt too dependent on the approval of the
cultural establishment to express sympathy with the reformers.
However, as the process of de-Stalinization gathered momentum,
Fadeyev found himself under pressure. He lost his position as a
full member of the Central Committee, and soon became depressed
and started to drink heavily. At the time of the 20th Party Congress
he was subjected to a humiliating public attack in a speech by
Mikhail Sholokhov, the celebrated author of *Quiet Flows the Don*.
The last twenty years, Sholokhov argued, had produced only a
handful of good, intelligent books but huge piles of grey trash,
and under Fadeyev's leadership the Writers' Union had degenerated
into a sterile apparatus controlled by a power-hungry bureaucrat.
This tirade appeared in *Pravda* on 21 February 1956, and Fadeyev's
humiliation was complete; less than three months later he committed suicide. 'The official version', Marc Slonim concludes in
his history of *Soviet Russian Literature*, 'attributed his death to
alcoholism', but the underlying cause may have been 'the feeling
that all his activities under Stalin, and perhaps his whole life,
constituted a tragic, useless error' (Slonim, 181 & 326).

Nazım was deeply distressed by these events. Fadeyev had been
a friend and mentor, and his death was all the more poignant
for him because it reawakened memories of the suicide of
Mayakovsky twenty-five years earlier; one had signalled the onset

of Stalinism and the other its demise. In each case Nazım seems
to have felt that a committed revolutionary had no right to take
his own life, however adverse the circumstances (Fevralski, 74).
His response was to write a play, provisionally entitled 'Olmak
veya Olmamak' (To Be Or Not To Be), inspired – as he later
said in a recorded interview – by 'the fate of my intimate friend
Alexander Fadeyev'. This play was never staged, although it was
reportedly published in translation in 1988 in the Russian magazine
Teatr (Tulyakova, 335). In Nazım's collected works a revised version, dealing with the problem of individual responsibility, appears
entitled *Herşeye Rağmen* (Despite Everything, A 14, 181-246).
The action of this Pirandello-type 'play within a play' is set in a
theatre controlled by a director named Enver, whose policy is so
authoritarian that he sacks anyone who challenges his views. The
leading actor Orhan is aware that the Director's policies are mis-
guided, but lacks the courage to raise any objections, especially
as he does not wish to jeopardize his own privileged position.
However, when he hears that one of the sacked actors has died
in poverty, he finally reports the director to the authorities. After
the director has been replaced, Orhan experiences a crisis of conscience in which he becomes aware of his own shortcomings.
On the evening of a production of *Hamlet* in which Orhan, no
longer the great star, has been demoted to the role of Fortinbras,
the news comes that he has killed himself. Although the plot
involves further complications, the basic message is clear:
Enver/Stalin was only able to abuse his powers because of the
weakness of subordinates like Orhan/Fadeyev.

Although Nazım grieved for the loss of Fadeyev, he found
another ally in Ilya Ehrenburg, who survived the Stalinist period
through a mixture of good luck and opportunism. Born in Kiev
of Jewish parents, he spent some years in Paris before the First
World War, acquiring a sophisticated grasp of modernism. Back
in the Soviet Union, he adapted to the demands of socialist realism,
and his novel *The Fall of Paris* (1942) gives a classic account of
a corrupt and decadent society collapsing before the German
onslaught. During the Second World War his journalistic gifts
enabled him to play a leading role as a propagandist, denouncing
Nazi atrocities and extolling the leadership of Stalin. Thus it was
ironic that he became a target in the campaign against 'Zionists'
and 'cosmopolitans' which Stalin initiated in 1949. Ehrenburg's

prominence in the international peace movement may have saved him from arrest, and after Stalin's death he became a leading reformer, publishing the novel *The Thaw* in May 1954, which signalled the onset of a milder climate (Rubenstein, 279-82). The turning-point came with the Second Congress of Soviet Writers in December 1954, which Nazım himself attended. Although the authority of the Party could not be directly challenged, the ten days of discussion created a new intellectual climate and it became clear that artistic innovations no longer needed to be denounced as crimes against the state (Slonim, 324-5). Nazım shared the excitement of the thaw. In the paper he prepared for this occasion, he argued that artistic style is not determined by ideological position – a clear indication that he supported the campaign for freedom of expression. In the event, ill health prevented him from speaking, and his paper had to be read for him (Fevralski, 54).

Nazım undoubtedly welcomed the demise of the crude socialist realism that had dominated Soviet writing for so long. In an affectionate memoir published after Nazım's death, Ehrenburg recalled a number of their private conversations. For Nazım the discovery that heroes of his youth like Meyerhold had been sent to die in Soviet concentration camps came as a terrible shock, but so strong was his commitment to communism that it survived even the most appalling disclosures. 'Some people really are extraordinary,' he remarked after Stalin's crimes were exposed. 'When tongues were silent, they had faith, when the truth was told, they began to waver' (Ehrenburg, 273). For Nazım communism still made sense in the context of his own experience of oppression and liberation, even though he too was chastened by Khrushchev's revelations. A public debate began in Soviet literary journals on how writers should respond to the new opportunities, and Nazım's flat became the scene of intense discussions (Erdinç, 68). He welcomed the rehabilitation of writers banned, persecuted and liquidated under Stalin, including Babel, Bulgakov and Meyerhold. In February 1956 Alexander Solzhenitsyn was released from prison, although it was only in 1962, with the publication of *A Day in the Life of Ivan Denisovich*, that the horrors of the gulags at last became known.

Khrushchev's denunciation of Stalin's crimes at a special Trade Union session of 20th Party Congress in March 1956 provided the reformers with their greatest opportunity. Nazım captured the mood in his characteristic style, writing a thirteen-line poem entitled 'The Twentieth Congress' ('Yirminci Kongre'). Avoiding all reference to the discredited Stalinist regime, he imagines Lenin entering the congress hall, 'his almond-shaped blue eyes smiling':

> What a relief to be under the same roof as Lenin,
> feeling in our hands
> the humanity of his wise hands.
> Lenin arrived at the Twentieth Congress.
> Over the Soviet Union
> an abundance of hope is building up
> like white clouds in the twilight.
> (B 2, 79)

In private conversation Nazım made no secret of his relief. 'After the 20th Party Congress', Ehrenburg recalls, 'when some were shocked and filled with doubt, he said: "I believe we all feel a stone has been lifted from our hearts"' (Ehrenburg, 272-3). Ehrenburg's memoir tends to simplify what was doubtless a painful process of readjustment. Other friends recall that during 1956-7 Nazım felt so disoriented that he because seriously depressed (Erdinç, 46, 55 & 66-8). However, this may have been due more to personal than political factors. In September 1956 he had a severe attack of pneumonia. In the aftermath of Khrushchev's revelations, he also spent long periods outside the Soviet Union, first in Poland and then in Czechoslovakia, convalescing at the Yasenik sanatorium from 3 November 1956 to 27 July 1957.

As a representative of the Writers' Union, Nazım found himself in a dilemma. From 1957 onwards he made a number of visits to eastern regions of the Soviet Union, including Turkish-speaking areas systematically persecuted under Stalin. His official role was to defend the achievements of Soviet system and the authority of the Communist Party. But on all sides he was confronted by evidence that the party he supported had played a tyrannical and oppressive role. Millions of people, including large segments of the Turkic populations of Azerbaijan, Uzbekistan, Kazakhstan and Turkmenistan, had been deported to Siberia. Nazım accepted that campaigns to purge bourgeois tendencies within the Party were justified in the interests of creating a socialist society. There was good reason to fear a resurgence of nationalism in the regions if the Kremlin relaxed its hold on power. But the sheer scale of the crimes now revealed left him stunned. He naturally welcomed the fact that a number of Turkish communists were among those released from labour camps in 1956, and was able to give newly released prisoners financial help. But the situation was complicated by disputes within the Turkish Party, especially with Ismail Bilen, the comrade with whom Nazım had shared a cell at Hopa in 1928. Bilen was a Stalinist who had spent the war in the Soviet Union and collaborated in the purges of other Party members. He was thus indirectly responsible for the deaths of a number of other Turkish communists, including those sent to Soviet labour camps in the purges of 1949 (Ihmalyan, 246). Nazım attempted to challenge Bilen's dominant position in the Foreign Bureau of the Turkish Communist Party, then in Leipzig (Ihmalyan, 249-50).

Nazım was particularly distressed by the case of Hacıoğlu Salih, a veterinary surgeon and one of the founding members of the Turkish Communist Party. They had first met in May 1926 at the Party conference in Vienna, and the poet was impressed by Salih's idealism. Like Nazım, Salih soon came into conflict with the Party leadership, being denounced in 1927 as a Menshevik and expelled (Harris, 145). After fleeing to the Soviet Union, Salih dedicated his veterinary skills to the service of rural communities. However, in the purge of 1949 he was denounced, probably by Ismail Bilen, and deported with his wife to a Soviet labour camp, where conditions were so harsh that he died within five years. This tragic episode haunted Nazım's memory. 'I often think about N. [Salih]', he observed in a conversation recorded by Ehrenburg. 'I was lucky. I was gaoled, but by the enemy' (Ehrenburg, 272). Clearly, the greatest horror was to be imprisoned by one's own comrades. At least Nazım was able to provide financial support for Salih's wife, Sabiha Sümbül, after her release (Ihmalyan, 248).

In one of his most outspoken poems of this period, 'Hacıoğlu Salih', written in 1956 in the aftermath of the 20th Congress, Nazım tries to reconcile Salih's sufferings with a defiant commitment to communism. Imprisoned for his beliefs in Turkey, Salih made the Soviet Union 'his second homeland':

> Then, in 1949, in Moscow, one evening in March,
> they came and fetched him,
> exiled him to the Altay region.
> He was not swept away by a landslide,
>   nor even by a slippery piece of earth.

But he had a stroke on his right side
at the age of sixty-seven.
For six years Hacıoğlu Salih
      celebrated the anniversary of the revolution
      surrounded by barbed wire and wolf hounds.
And he died one day in the spring
     in a barracks for fifty people.
Tonight in Moscow we celebrated
the anniversary of the revolution,
reciting Marx
     Engels
      Lenin as we walk through the streets
     and Salih's certificate of rehabilitation.
          (B 2, 81-2)

Despite the sobriety of the narrative, the poem culminates in a
wilful piece of wishful thinking – romantic communism, rather
than a realistic view of the Soviet system. Sketching the kind of
tragedy that Arthur Koestler classically described in *Darkness at
Noon*, Nazım still suggests that Marxism itself can be rehabilitated,
but inspite of this he had difficulty at first in getting the poem
into print – the references to barbed wire and wolfhounds were
too explicit. However, it appeared in 1962 in a Turkish edition
of his 'New Poems', dedicated to 'Comrade Khrushchev' (*Yeni
Şiirler*, Sofia, 1962, 18-19).

    Nazım's most daring attempt to reassess the Stalin period took
the form of a three-act play, *Ivan Ivanoviç Var Mıydı Yok Muydu?*
(Did Ivan Ivanovich Exist or Didn't He?). On 2 July 1956 a
resolution of the Central Committee was published with the title
'On Overcoming the Cult of the Individual and its Consequences,'
which raised the question why the party leadership had not spoken
out against Stalin sooner (Ehrenburg, 307). Nazım's play suggests
a possible answer, exploring the double-bind which develops between a political leader and those who fawn on him. The play
is a satirical comedy in the tradition of Mayakovsky's *The Bedbug*,
which is actually mentioned in the opening scene. It is set in a
remote town in the Soviet Union, although (as one of the characters
observes in the opening scene) it could be any country in the
communist bloc. In the opening scenes the audience is introduced
to Petrov, chairman of the Central Committee, an approachable,
hard-working socialist who is helpful to members of the community, treats people well and gets things done; he represents

the altruistic values of early communism which became corrupted by the personality cult, and he is on friendly terms with working-class comrades like Kasketli (the Man in a Cloth Cap).

Petrov's antagonist is Ivan Ivanovich, a devious manipulator who claims to represent 'democratic centralism'. He sets about the task of corrupting Petrov by flattery, telling him that the Party needs a strong leader who keeps his distance from the common people. His most insidious suggestion is that portraits and statues of Petrov should be displayed in every corner of the office building. Under Ivan's influence Petrov becomes increasingly remote and authoritarian. His speeches are collected and published in book form, which increases the adulation surrounding him. The flattery goes to Petrov's head, and the result is a psychological drama of considerable subtlety, abounding in ironic dialogues and farcical episodes. In Act Two the dramatic illusion is broken in the manner of Brecht or Pirandello, as Ivan becomes aware that Nazım Hikmet, the dramatist, is presenting his activities in a very unfavourable light. He appeals to the author to stop criticising the Soviet people, as he is only a guest. To this Nazım's Voice replies: 'If I am a guest in the Soviet Union, then I'm a good guest who crushes the head of the snake that is about to bite. [...] The play is not going to end the way you want' (A 12, 294). Through this interlude Nazım asserts the right of the author to have the final word, despite the blustering of politicians.

In Act Three, Petrov is called to the Central Committee, where he meets an old woman who knew him as a humane socialist in his earlier days. Petrov is stunned by the realization of how alienated he has become. In a surrealistic scene which forms the climax of the play, he enters the office of a colleague whose name sounds suspiciously like his own, sitting, with his head bowed over his desk, beneath a huge gold-framed portrait. Petrov is amazed to discover that the portrait is almost identical to the one hanging in his own office back home, but twice as large. When the colleague looks up, Petrov finds himself confronted by his *Doppelgänger*, equally cut off from the people and spouting empty slogans. This is the moment of truth as he realizes that the personality cult has come to dominate the whole communist system. There must be some great conspiracy which is turning party officials into petty tyrants, as Ivan has succeeded in doing in his own case. Returning home, he finds it is impossible to pin the blame on any particular person, since all the staff at Party headquarters deny their involvement in the personality cult. The Man in a Cloth Cap suddenly notices that Ivan is standing there, and tries to grapple with him. But Ivan simply vanishes like a ghost, and the play ends with the question: 'Did Ivan exist or didn't he?'

In this play Nazım obviously lets Stalin himself off far too lightly. He not only omits all reference to purges and labour camps, but even implies that the personality cult was due to the misplaced zeal of underlings and not to the great man himself. However, we know that the 'deification of Stalin', as Ehrenburg emphasizes, 'did not come about suddenly nor did it stem from an explosion of popular feeling. Stalin organized it himself, systematically and over a long period. On his instructions currency was given to a fictitious version of history' (Ehrenburg, 303). Nazım's failure to acknowledge this is the fundamental defect of his play. The early Soviet leadership, as represented by Petrov, is credited with the best of intentions, rather than a ruthless appetite for power. In an introduction written for the Russian edition of his works published in 1957, Nazım even suggested that 'bourgeois' influences were to blame for the personality cult, once again avoiding a direct critique of communism (Babayev, 315). However, the play succeeds in illuminating another, less tangible dimension of Stalinism – popular collusion in the personality cult and the problem of collective responsibility. In her memoirs Stalin's daughter Svetlana Alliluyeva emphasizes that Nazım's 'wonderful satirical play' was particularly directed against abuses in the Soviet satellite states 'most obviously of Hungary and Rákosi' (Alliluyeva, 215). It was certainly theatrically effective to reduce the activities of Party bosses and their obsequious henchmen to the level of farce. There is a parallel with Brecht's *The Stoppable Rise of Arturo Ui*, where Hitler's seizure of power is represented as a bid by a group of gangsters to control the cauliflower market. The problem with both plays is that the comic mode is inadequate to the task of conveying the crimes of ruthless dictators.

Ivan Ivanovich had its premiere on 11 May 1957 at the Moscow Satire Theatre. Perhaps the censorship was misled into thinking that the satire was directed at petty tyrants in the satellite states rather than at Stalin. But members of the audience could hardly fail to make the connection: the larger-than-life painting which dominates the action shows Petrov with the unmistakable moustache (Fig. 29a). In the event the play was banned after the première, even though the poster had announced that there would be seven further performances that same month. 'The play was so unbearably real and witty', Svetlana recalls, 'that the Central Committee instantly forbade it, after its very first showing' (Alliluyeva, 215). Its controversial stage history shows that Nazım touched the nerve of the multitude of corruptible Petrovs and manipulative Ivanoviches. The critique of the personality cult may have been too close to the mark to be tolerated in Moscow, but the play was later staged in Riga, and a number of productions were put on in other countries, including Czechoslovakia and Bulgaria. When Nazım attended the Prague production with his comrade Vartan Ihmalyan, the audience was so excited that he had to take a curtain call, saying a few words of thanks in Russian (Ihmalyan, 148). The use of ironic techniques reminiscent of the epic theatre enhanced the impact of the play in East Germany, where it was translated by Alfred Kurella (Spuler, 128-32). In 1957 Nazım had the satisfaction of attending a production at the municipal theatre in Senftenberg, which he found particularly congenial (Fevralski, 79). By then he had become a significant force in the communist theatre, and audiences could no longer complain that every time they went to the theatre they saw 'the same play with a different title – all of them in praise of Stalin'.

Thaw in the theatre: the legacy of Meyerhold

The years 1946-53 have been described as 'among the bleakest and most sterile in Soviet literature'. The dearth of imaginative writing for the theatre was even acknowledged by *Pravda* in an article of 4 March 1952 to mark the centenary of the death of Gogol (Hayward, 99 & 118). Theatre policy was strictly regulated, and although the dictatorial Andrei Zhdanov had died in 1948, his denunciations of bourgeois tendencies still had a crippling effect. Critics who complained about the provinciality of Soviet drama were denounced as 'cosmopolitans', and Konstantin Simonov led a new crusade to reimpose 'Bolshevik principles'. Ideologically this implied the portrayal of exemplary Soviet heroes, while aesthetically it gave precedence to the Stanislavsky system of naturalistic representation devoid of artistic fantasy. Even more inhibiting for

29. Political theatre: (*a*) A. Talanov in the role of Petrov in the Moscow
Satire Theatre production of *Ivan Ivanovich*.

aspiring dramatists was the so-called 'no-conflict' theory. In a
classless society governed by principles of co-operative production,
it was self-evident that traditional class conflicts or personal dilemmas
could no longer occur. Moreover, from 1949 onwards the repertoire
of each theatre was regulated by a 'chief producer', usually a
Party bureaucrat with little knowledge of cultural affairs. Every
theatre was required to stage at least two new plays each year
dealing with contemporary life in a politically uplifting way. At
the same time state subsidies were reduced, so that theatre managers
found themselves in the almost impossible position of having to
entertain the public without offending the Party (Hayward, 150-69).

   This situation provided Nazım with unexpected opportunities.
Drawing on his knowledge of Turkish society, with its rich tradition
of folk literature, he offered frustrated theatre directors a way out
of their dilemma: a style of theatre uncontaminated by Western

decadence, and yet more inventive than the formulaic dramas of
Stalinist orthodoxy. In these projects he was encouraged by
Alexander Fevralski, whose memoirs offer valuable insights into
Nazım's evolving conception of the theatre. After his return to
Moscow, Nazım resumed contact with Nikola Ekk, the pupil of
Meyerhold with whom he had collaborated during the 1920s.
Ekk had survived the anti-modernist purges of the Stalinist regime,
adapting his style to the demands of socialist realism. But Nazım,
although influenced by Stanislavsky's style of realism, still identified
himself with the more imaginative approach of the avant-garde.
Even before the death of Stalin we find him reintroducing elements
of fantasy and folklore which had been banished from the Soviet
theatre since the disgrace of Meyerhold, who had perished in a
Soviet labour camp in 1941.

The most successful of his plays was *A Legend of Love*, based
on the story of Ferhad, the Turkish folk hero who labours ten
long years for the love of Şirin. The play's first draft, written in
prison in 1948, had autobiographical undertones, with the labours
of Ferhad symbolizing the poet's long years in prison. 'There is
an aspect of Ferhad and Şirin that resembles you and me,' Nazım
had written to Piraye, in a letter explaining his decision to modify
the original story, which traditionally ended with Ferhad dying
in Şirin's arms (AM 1, 285). When it came to be adapted for
the Moscow Drama Theatre in October 1953, this poignant fairy
tale acquired an austere socialist moral. The production was a
great success and Nazım, who attended the première with Zekeriya
Sertel, took six curtain calls. However, he was not entirely satisfied
with the production, feeling that the element of fantasy was un-
derplayed. He also resented being pressurised into adding an extra
scene to make the political message more explicit (Fevralski, 22-3
& 47).

Nazım chose the story of Ferhad, in preference to other oriental
love tales like Leyla and Mecnun, because Ferhad has to earn the
love of Şirin by the work of his hands. The main obstacle to
their love is Şirin's dominating elder sister Mehmene, who is
herself in love with Ferhad. Mehmene requires Ferhad to prove
himself by bringing water from the other side of the Iron Mountain
to a region where the people are suffering a severe drought. To
achieve this, Ferhad begins to dig a tunnel. For ten years he
labours valiantly until Mehmene releases him from his task, allowing

him to marry Şirin. But Ferhad is so committed to bringing water to his long-suffering people that he places duty above self-fulfilment. Şirin appeals to him to abandon his task and find happiness in marriage, but Ferhad remains resolute. In place of the traditional romantic finale, the play ends with Nazım's hero still fighting for his ideals, while the People cheer him on: 'Dig, Master Ferhad, dig, so that the water from the Iron Mountain will gush forth to fill our buckets' (B 6, 146). *A Legend of Love* had great success in Georgia, Czechoslovakia, Bulgaria and East Germany as well as the Soviet Union (Fevralski, 70). It received the final acolade when the scenario was set to music by Arif Melikov and performed as a ballet in Leningrad in March 1961 by the Bolshoi Ballet (Fig. 29b).

Turkish local colour also adds distinction to *The First Day of the Festival* (*Bayramın ilk günü*), a social drama based on a Turkish original entitled *Bir Ölü Evi* (The House of the Mourning), originally staged in Istanbul in 1932. After returning from his stay in a sanatorium in July 1953, Nazım teamed up with the director Nikolai Ekk to produce a new version suitable for the Soviet stage (Fevralski, 16, 19-20). The task proved time-consuming, and Nazım had to draw sketches of certain scenes to clarify his intentions. In the original version the main focus was on the fratricidal struggle between the two sons of a wealthy Istanbul moneylender to gain control of their father's fortune after his death. In the Russian adaptation, completed in November 1953, this satire on bourgeois morality gained a more positive dimension through additional scenes portraying the aspirations of working-class people (Babayev, 314). *The First Day of the Festival* also achieved considerable success, being translated into Czech, Polish, Hungarian and Ukrainian. The first recorded performance was in Budapest in April 1954, and the play was also broadcast over Hungarian radio (Fevralski, 46-8). In December 1954 Nazım attended the first Russian production at the Leningrad Drama Theatre, which transferred in May 1955 to the Moscow Arts Theatre. Two years later it was again staged in Moscow as a student production (Fevralski, 61 & 95).

Even more significant was Nazım's reworking of the Joseph legend, *Yusuf ile Menofis*. Reading the Torah in prison, Nazım had been fascinated by the story of Abraham and his family: 'It is difficult to meet another family whose members are so ambitious,

29. Political theatre:
(*b*) *Legend of Love*: scene from a production by the Bolshoi Ballet.

so clever, so cowardly, so rebellious, so cunning, so cruel and so victimised,' he wrote at the time to Kemal Tahir (AM 3, 359). In Nazım's hands the exploits of Yusuf (Joseph) are redefined to reflect the origins of class struggle, while his relationship with Potiphar's wife, Zeliha, is also given a new twist. Yusuf ceases to be the centre of sympathy – the man whose resourcefulness and skill in interpreting dreams earns him the favour of Pharaoh. He is portrayed instead as manipulative and self-centred, someone who has made himself the most powerful man in Egypt by hoarding scarce resources during the seven years of drought. He even reduces his brothers to slaves and cynically sacrifices his love for Zeliha to preserve his position at the palace. Nazım was also concerned to find ways of conveying Zeliha's inner turmoil, experimenting with new techniques for giving voice to inner feelings. In *Yusuf and Menofis* 'three different monologues from Zeliha's inner world are conveyed in three different tones of voice'. His idea is to make gramophone recordings of the three voices, to be played back in the theatre as an alternative to the conventional form of inner monologue (A 21, 276). This technique is effectively deployed in Act 1, Scene 2 of the play, where Zeliha, sitting alone before a mirror, is haunted by disembodied voices that express her conflicting desires. Far from being simply a scheming seductress, she emerges from the love scenes with Yusuf as by far the more admirable personality.

However, it is not Zeliha who emerges as Yusuf's principal adversary but Menofis, the worker whose sense of social responsibility is juxtaposed with Yusuf's individualism. Beginning as a stonemason labouring in the Egyptian construction industry, Menofis develops into a working-class hero. From his study of historical sources, Nazım discovered that there had been a strike of craftsmen in Egypt in 1170 BC (Babayev, 325). Menofis becomes the militant who leads the strike and organises raids on food storage depots, until he is finally stabbed by Yusuf's armed guards. As Menofis is dying, he confronts Yusuf with words which break the dramatic illusion in order to drive home the political message: 'We shall both live on for thousands of years. But after thousands of years, you will have died for ever, but I shall go on living [...] Pharaoh and God may be with you, but life is with me' (B 6, 226). *Yusuf and Menofis* was staged in Russian early in 1956 (a review of the Soviet premiere was published in *Rude Pravo* on 26 June of that year). Translated into German by Kurella under the title *Joseph in Ägypten*, it was staged in 1961/2 in East Germany. The play was also translated into Czech, and during 1956 Nazım visited the Moravian town of Olmutz to see one of the Czech productions (Fevralski, 73).

Nazım's visits to Czechoslovakia, where he spent several months recuperating during the winter of 1956-7, inspired another short play, *The Clocks of Prague* (*Prag Saatleri*). This imaginative work was written – rather, dictated – at the Iasenik sanatorium between December 1956 and April 1957. The inspiration came from his friendship with the Czech actress Sonja Danielova, who asked Nazım why he introduced no elements of pantomime into his dramatized folk tales. At her suggestion he set this play, based on a Czech folktale, in medieval Prague. The heroine is a profoundly deaf girl (hence the importance of mime), and her experiences are both comic and tragic. Because he was not fit enough to wield a pen, he dictated the play to Sonja in Russian, and she translated it into Czech. The task was completed in five days. 'I always create in my head before I write,' he proudly explained in an interview with the Romanian writer Sanda Faur. 'One does not need pen or paper to be creative – I got used to that in prison' (Roman, 35). The text of this play is not included in any Turkish edition of Nazım's writings, although according a newspaper cutting in the Hungarian Theatre Archives it was staged by the Romanian State Jewish Theatre in 1960.

Nazım's plays of this period owe their success to his way of adapting traditional folk motifs to the 'New Humanism' emerging in the 1950s. Soviet writing had tended to celebrate 'the romanticism of creative labour', the 'effort to overcome the hostile forces of nature' (Slonim, 244-5). His folkloristic themes enabled him to create more imaginative heroes and to steer clear of the personality cult. Through his use of fantasy he began to undermine the dogmas of socialist realism, even before the death of Stalin opened up the possibility of a more sustained thaw in the Soviet theatre. The scandal provoked by the Moscow production of *Ivan Ivanovich* shows that he overestimated the scope for new developments. Nevertheless a cautious liberalisation was under way, reflected in the revival in 1954 of Mayakovsky's previously banned satirical comedies *The Bathhouse* and *The Bedbug*. For Nazım these developments were an incentive to write plays that did not simply hammer home a political message but also explored people's individual strengths and weaknesses.

A further successful adaptation was *The Railway Station* (*Istasyon*, 1957), originally written in Turkish as *Yolcu* (The Traveller). The early versions, dating from 1942, are set in an isolated railway station during the Turkish War of Liberation. Trapped in this claustrophobic environment, the telegrapher has fallen passionately in love with the stationmaster's wife, and violence seems certain to follow. But a liberation fighter arrives with news of the heroic defence of the fatherland, and patriotism enables them to overcome their petty personal desires (Babayev, 317; cf. A 11, 11-57). Given such a simple moral scheme, it was easy for Nazım to adapt his fable to Soviet circumstances. In the Russian version the station is threatened by skirmishes in the war between Bolsheviks and counter-revolutionaries. At first the group at the station, which includes a Turkish prisoner-of-war, Osman, are tempted to side with the counterrevolution, but finally they overcome their prejudices, repair the telegraph system and help the Bolsheviks beat off the attack. Osman is wounded, but the play ends with a visionary scene in which Marx and Lenin rise before his eyes, proclaiming the need for international solidarity.

Dramatic fables like *The Railway Station* provided little scope for psychological subtlety, and even communist reviewers tended to criticize the schematic characterization, but in one late play, *The Sword of Damocles* (*Demoklesin Kılıcı*, 1957), Nazım aims at greater psychological complexity, linking the oppressiveness of bourgeois society with the nightmarish threat of nuclear destruction. The action is framed by the apartment of an affluent professional couple, the Architect and the Architect's Wife, in an unidentified capital city. The period is overshadowed by the threat of war. As the Wife tinkles away at the piano, the steady ticking of a wall-clock marks the passage of time. Their complacent lives are disrupted by the arrival of a letter from A. B., a young man from a peasant family who attended the same primary school as the Architect but whose subsequent life has been a series of disasters. A. B. is a social drop-out whose bitter experiences have turned a sensitive youth into a paranoid adult. His only achievement has been to train as a bomber pilot, and it is this that provides him with the opportunity to destroy a society which has humiliated him since his childhood. In the letter to the Architect he announces that at eight o'clock his plane will fly over the city and drop an atom bomb as an act of divine retribution. This is the 'Sword of Damocles' hanging over the play.

Technically the play owes its effect to the disconcerting switches of scene between the affluent apartment and the primitive settings where A. B.'s humiliating experiences are re-enacted. At first, the Architect and his Wife dismiss his threats as the rantings of a lunatic, but the dramatic irony intensifies as the audience becomes aware that the clock is ticking relentlessly towards zero hour. The play ends with the roar of the bomber's engines overhead and the panic of the Architect and Wife who realise too late that their doom is sealed. A. B. has become a fanatical Doctor Strangelove intent on destroying the world (Fig. 29c). The ethical challenge of the play arises from its satire on the affluent professional classes, who self-righteously deny all responsibility for social injustice. Since the characters are representative figures (the Architect, the Judge, the Chemist's Son), Nazım's critique gains a certain universality. In place of the denunciations of American warmonger-

29. Political theatre: (c) K. Kadochnikov in the role of A.B.
in a Leningrad production of *Sword of Damocles*.

ing to which Soviet audiences were accustomed, the satire is
aimed at attitudes that might be encountered among the élite of
almost any modern city. When the play had its première at the
Moscow Satire Theatre in 1959, no doubt the author intended
members of the audience to recognise themselves.

Some critics have tended to dismiss Nazım's later work for
the theatre, arguing that artistically there is 'scarcely any significant
development' (Gronau, 110). This echoes the poet's own self-
assessment. 'When I returned to Moscow', he recalled in 1962,
'I wrote many plays. [...] It was good that most of them were
not staged. All my life I was influenced by the theatre, but I
remained a third-rate playwright' (A 21, 277). Certainly, he
produced a number of pot-boilers, including *İnsanlık Ölmedi Ya*
(Kindness is not Dead, 1955), a morality play based on an earlier
Turkish draft; *İnek* (The Cow, 1957), a satirical comedy about
the obsessions of a petty-bourgeois family; a modern version of

Tartuffe (1959), satirizing a twentieth-century demagogue; and *Kadınların İsyanı* (1961), an adaptation of the Lysistrata theme. In 1957 Nazım also adapted his own 'Legend of Sheikh Bedreddin' for the stage, but his self-assessment was far too modest, for a significant number of his works were staged, and in plays like *Legend of Love, Yusuf and Menofis, Ivan Ivanovich* and *The Sword of Damocles* he used innovative artistic techniques to explore compelling social themes. Inspired by the legacy of Meyerhold he adapted Turkish folklore to modern politics.

Nazım also contributed to the renewal of the Soviet theatre on a theoretical level, drawing on insights dating back to the avant-garde experiments of the 1920s to justify a pluralistic approach to the arts. 'What is Socialist Realism?' he asked in the course of a speech delivered at Leipzig University in 1958, and he paradoxically claimed Picasso as a socialist realist – a committed communist who nevertheless had the right to paint how he liked. 'As long as the message is communist, let there be thousands of different forms. In this way we shall be able to make better propaganda for our very complicated ideals, which are communist and humanist.' The essential point is that technique and subject matter should be proportionate. He developed his ideas further the next year: 'I want my poems to address all my readers' problems. If a young man falls in love with a girl, he should be able to read my poems to his sweetheart, an old man in the grip of sadness about dying should read my poems, people on the way to a May Day demonstration should read my poems. When a bureaucrat is giving you a hard time, read my poems. A communist writer has to reflect all human feelings.' In this defence of the imagination Meyerhold emerges as the key figure: in a talk about his own work on 1 March 1956 he was warmly applauded when he wove a defence of Meyerhold into his own reminiscences. In May 1959 a further lecture was organised at the Museum of Literature, scene of the great cultural events of the Soviet avant-garde in the 1920s. Speaking impromptu in Russian, he insisted that the time was ripe to rediscover Meyerhold, repudiating the persistent criticisms of the director's work. 'It looks as though people who admire Meyerhold still have a lot more fighting to do,' he concluded (Fevralski, 70 & 81-4).

Nazım's position is set out more systematically in 'Memories of Meyerhold' ('Erinnerungen an Meyerhold'), an article of about

4,000 words published in *Sinn und Form* at the end of 1959. First he acknowledges the plurality of styles that have influenced his approach to the theatre, including Stanislavsky, Tairov and more recently Brecht. But it is Meyerhold to whom he is most indebted, especially because of his use of fantasy and folklore, ballet and pantomime. Nazım recalls how, as a student in the 1920s he approached Meyerhold for advice on how to stage his dramatic sketch 'The Pyramid'. Meyerhold's response was to suggest the use of music and mime. In an unmistakable dig at the rigidity of the Stanislavsky system, Nazım then points out that Meyerhold admired the Japanese and Chinese theatre precisely because it was opposed to the theatre of naturalism. 'Meyerhold displayed his artistic techniques, he exposed their scaffolding, but his productions contained the truth of ideas, of feelings, images and actions.' For Nazım the most powerful of Meyerhold's effects was the surrealistic final scene of his staging of Gogol's *The Government Inspector* in 1926. When it is announced that the real inspector has arrived, the corrupt members of the ruling class are swept off the stage like a pile of dust (SF, 921-5).

Subversion by radio: the programme of national liberation

Nazım's work for the theatre brought him into contact with the main broadcasting centres of the communist world. His play 'The Skull' was transmitted several times by Moscow Radio, and a Hungarian version of 'The First Day of the Festival' was broadcast by Radio Budapest (Lontay, 176-7). In this phase of the propaganda war, when television was still in its infancy, the battle for hearts and minds was conducted by radio and Nazım enthusiastically embraced it, making a series of broadcasts to listeners in Turkey. Voice of America began broadcasting to the Soviet Union in 1947, supplementing the well-established overseas services of the BBC. Early in the 1950s Radio Free Europe and the more militantly anti-communist Radio Liberty were established with covert funding from the Central Intelligence Agency. The Soviets responded by jamming these stations and expanding their own external radio services, which by 1960 broadcast in thirty-eight languages, including Turkish (Paulu, 206-12). Turkish-language programmes also went out from a number of other communist countries,

including Hungary, Bulgaria and East Germany. These developments gave Nazım his opportunity.

Between 1954 and 1963 Nazım made numerous broadcasts in
Turkish, including poetry readings and subjects that ranged from
literary appreciations to current affairs. Only a fraction of this
material has ever found its way into print. Transcripts of the
political commentaries he broadcast from Leipzig between 1958
and 1963, recently located in the archives of the International
Institute for Social History in Amsterdam, represent a particularly
rich find. Like the broadcasts made by George Orwell for the
BBC in the Second World War, they shed new light on the
interaction between literature and politics. Radio gave Nazım
access to a large audience at a time when the future of Turkish
democracy hung in the balance. In the late 1950s the government
of Adnan Menderes was becoming increasingly authoritarian, im-
posing strict controls on the Turkish media. As a broadcaster,
Nazım actively supported the campaign for greater democracy in
Turkey, and the transcripts show how he adapted his conception
of communism to changing political circumstances. Although he
never renounced his faith in the organized working class as the
agent of historical transformation, Nazım now gave priority to a
more broadly-based programme of national liberation.

It was in January 1955, when the Turkish Service of Radio
Budapest invited him to begin a series of broadcasts on literary
and political themes, that Nazım truly began to make his mark
as a broadcaster. The texts of eighteen of these programmes are
included in his Collected Works, and a number of other broadcasts
survive in recorded form. The main focus is on modern Turkish
literature, and Nazım reviews a range of recent publications, praising
the social realism of Orhan Kemal, Yashar Kemal and Mahmut
Makal. To illustrate the vitality of Turkish writing, he also reads
verses by Orhan Veli and Oktay Rıfat which express social-critical
insights in vividly epigrammatic form (A 26, 51-7). Very few of
the authors reviewed were communists, but Nazım did single out
a forthcoming novel by S. Üstüngel for special praise, reading
excerpts from the manuscript (A 26, 59 & 108-9). What he failed
to mention is that Üstüngel was the pseudonym of Ismail Bilen
(Laz Ismail), leader of the foreign section of the Turkish Communist
Party. Nazım also answered questions about his own work-
in-progress and recited some of his poems. The list of broadcasts

from Budapest, now in the Amsterdam archive, though containing no reference to his poem on the death of Stalin reportedly broadcast in March 1955, features some of his best known poems, including a passage from his epic about the War of Liberation which he read on 30 August 1955 to mark the anniversary of Turkish victory. This apparently included a reference to 'the blue-eyed commander-in-chief' – Kemal Atatürk (Bijlage, 10). This was as far as Nazım was prepared to go in making concessions to the personality cult. In his poetic tributes neither Atatürk nor Stalin was mentioned by name, and when *Human Landscapes* was revised for publication in book form the reference to the commander with blue eyes was omitted (A 5, 228).

In these broadcasts from Hungary, Nazım claimed to speak 'with the voice of a friend of the Turkish people' (Transcripts, August 1955), and this perspective shaped his approach to political themes like the peace movement and the arms race, American imperialism and the effects of capitalist investment. At the World Peace Congress in Berlin in May 1954, he had criticized the military alliance between Turkey and the United States, and the text of that speech was broadcast from Budapest in January 1955. Since the Second World War, he claimed, Turkey had become an 'American colony', and as a consequence 60 per cent of the national budget was being spent on preparations for war, but only 5 per cent on public health. He fiercely criticized the reactionaries ('*gericiler*') who had sold out to America and were exploiting Islamic religious sentiment to justify their anti-communist crusade. This 'black peril' ('*kara tehlike*') was the real danger. The reactionaries, of course, were Adnan Menderes and the Democrat Party, which was tightening its grip on power.

The elections of 1957 had enabled the Democrat Party to consolidate its position, but as the Turkish economic situation deteriorated Menderes introduced a series of repressive measures. Opposition politicians were denied access to the radio, which was entirely under state control, and both the press laws and election procedures were made more restrictive. In defiance of the secularist principles enshrined in the Turkish constitution, Menderes also sought to consolidate his popular base by mobilizing Islam as a political force. The laws on public religious practices were relaxed and the budget for the Department of Religious Affairs expanded, with the result that a total of 15,000 new mosques were built between 1950 and 1960 (Heper, 126-8). In superstitious minds the prestige of Menderes was also enhanced by his apparently miraculous escape from an air crash. Meanwhile Turkey was becoming ever more dependent on the United States, economically and militarily. American bases were established in various parts of the country, and nuclear weapons targeted on the Soviet Union were stationed on Turkish soil. These measures not only attracted criticism from the left, but they also alienated the secular élite, including leading figures in the army, the bureaucracy and the Republican People's Party, still led by former President Ismet İnönü, who had defended Turkey's independence so jealously during the Second World War. There was also growing social discontent, as a small group of entrepreneurs became extremely wealthy while the mass of the Turkish population struggled to cope with food shortages and runaway inflation.

The first phase of Nazım's activity as a broadcaster was brought to an end by the Hungarian rising in autumn of 1956. However, in March 1958 a new Turkish-language station was established in Leipzig: 'Bizim Radyo' (Our Radio), run by the foreign section of the Turkish Communist Party, whose leader was Ismail Bilen. Although Bizim Radyo existed for thirty years, up till the closure of the Turkish Communist Party in the late 1980s, its history is not well documented. But an unpublished memoir by Hayk Açıkgöz, an Armenian comrade transferred to Leipzig after working for the Turkish service of Warsaw Radio, helps to clarify its strategy. In Warsaw the Turkish newsreaders had been restricted to reading short bulletins prepared by the Polish government, which lacked any relevance to Turkey. But at the new station in Leipzig they were free to prepare their own material: hence the name 'Our Radio'. At a meeting to plan strategy in January 1958, Ismail Bilen emphasized three main aims: to promote an anti-imperialist united front in Turkey, to build up the Turkish Communist Party, and to inform listeners of developments in socialist countries. When Nazım began broadcasting from Leipzig in May 1958, he became an eloquent supporter of the united front strategy.

The staff of Bizim Radyo included long-standing party members like Sabiha Sertel and her daughter Yıldız. Sabiha's husband Zekeriya, who was not a party member, was also a leading contributor for several years, and they were soon joined by Fahri

Erdinç from Sofia (Alper, 200-1). On his visits to Leipzig, Nazım was delighted to be reunited with the Sertels, who had worked with him on the avant-garde magazine *Resimli Ay* thirty years earlier. In June 1958 he and his colleagues celebrated their new venture with a meal at the Sertels' flat. Nazım, just back from Paris, read his most recent poems, including his tribute to the demonstrators against the officers' coup in Algeria, 'In Paris, 28 May 1958'. However, he had kitted himself out so elegantly in the Paris boutiques that he was teased for bourgeois tendencies. In a characteristic gesture he began to give away items of apparel, even presenting Ismail Bilen with his new salamander shoes (Erdinç 1987, 94-8). On this visit to Leipzig there was a meeting of the foreign section of the Turkish Communist Party, at which broadcasting strategy was more formally discussed.

The transcripts of Bizim Radyo broadcasts in the Amsterdam archive relate to talks and other short features, not news bulletins. Of the total of ninety-six surviving transcripts, twenty-seven identify Nazım as author by name or initials. A further seventeen broadcasts are identified by the pseudonym Üstat (master), a sobriquet acquired by Nazım in conversation with fellow broadcasters (Erdinç 1987, 102). Some of these talks may have been pre-recorded, but the aim was to be as topical as possible, coming to grips with recent items of political news. Nazım made repeated visits to Leipzig, and his contributions are characteristically short and succinct, lasting for three to five minutes – a maximum of four typescript pages. At first, speaking from Budapest, he showed a certain nervousness in front of the microphone, but soon developed more confidence and a rapport with his listeners, whom he addressed in short, punchy sentences designed to deflate the pretentions of the Menderes-controlled media. This is not the strident voice of communist propaganda, but a more subtle form of radio journalism appealing to the listeners' sense of humour as well as their desire for social justice.

This series of broadcasts began soon after Khrushchev consolidated his power, having ousted Bulganin in March 1958 from the Soviet premiership. Taking his lead from the new foreign policy initiatives, Nazım spoke out in support of Khrushchev's conciliatory approaches to Eisenhower (Transcripts, 13 August 1959) – East-West relations had entered a phase of détente, and now was the time for a determined effort to end the arms race

and develop international cooperation through the peace movement. Hence the importance Nazım attached to meetings of the
World Peace Congress. Immediately after attending the Congress
in Stockholm on 16-21 July 1958, he had reported on the proceedings from Leipzig in glowing terms. A declaration against nuclear
testing had been endorsed by 1,700 delegates from seventy different
countries, ranging from Polish communists and Buddhist monks
to Catholic priests and Islamic mullahs. But the Congress coincided
with an army coup in Iraq, which led the United States to send
troops to Lebanon and the Turkish government to mobilize its
forces on the Iraqi border. 'Our leaders may be taking us to the
brink of atomic war,' Nazım warned. 'Are we as a Turkish nation
going to turn a blind eye to this threat of total annihilation?'
(Transcripts, 24 July 1958).

Bizim Radyo appealed to listeners increasingly resentful at the
policies of the Turkish government. It denounced the 'lies' of
Menderes, claiming to broadcast 'the news that's been hidden
from our people' (Transcripts, 6 July 1958 & 7 August 1959). A
broadcast on 16 July 1959 was even more outspoken: 'As you
know, dear listeners, the Nato organization is an American barracks',
we are told. But 'we want to have a voice not within an American
barracks but throughout the whole world as a free nation, peace-
loving and independent.' There is a striking continuity in Nazım's
critique of imperialism. In the early 1920s he had attacked the
Sultan who 'sold out' to the Western powers. Now the target
was American imperialism. In a broadcast of 26 August 1959 he
compared Menderes to the mad Sultan Mustapha, who threw
gold coins into a pond to feed the fish. Under Menderes it was
American predators who were devouring the nation's wealth.
Nazım's anti-imperialism was not simply an opportunistic tactic
adopted in the Soviet interest during the Cold War. It was a
lifelong conviction dating back to his student days, grounded in
the historical experience of his own country, which acquired a
new focus during the 1950s in response to the perceived threat
of American domination.

Framed by this critique of foreign policy, Nazım's commentaries
on Turkish domestic affairs explored a series of topical themes,
appealing to the everyday concerns of ordinary people. He was
eloquent about petrol shortages, inflation and the price of postage
stamps, and particularly scathing about the pervasive American

influence on public life. Not only had specialists from the United States been brought in to advise the Turkish police on torture techniques, but even the newly appointed director of the Press and Communictions Office had been trained by the American propaganda service (Transcripts, 7 August 1959). From this series of commentaries it is possible to begin to reconstruct his political position, at least in outline. National liberation had become the key concept, and Bizim Radyo endorsed the strategy of forming a 'united front' ('Tek Cephe', the theme of two broadcasts in July 1959).

Nazım had been associated with the united front policy from an early stage, even encouraging his young comrade Sevim Tarı to set up a magazine, *Tek cephe*, to campaign for it (STMA, 6, 1960). Since national liberation and not proletarian revolution, was the immediate objective, he addressed his arguments to the Turkish 'people' ('*halk*'). As he intensified his campaign against Menderes, denounced in July 1958 as the 'little dictator', he made it clear that the regime could only be overthrown by cooperation between different classes. The contradictions underlying this strategy can be seen most clearly in a fictional dialogue between a tobacco worker and a textile worker, broadcast on 29 July 1959 with the title 'Should a Worker Join a Trade Union?' The textile worker blames everything on the Menderes government, which has created a handful of millionaires while nine-tenths of the population suffer deprivation. However, the tobacco worker argues that things would be no different under Inönü. The only solution was to form a coalition of workers and peasants, artisans and intellectuals, traders and industrialists who had not sold out to the Americans, and army officers who still possessed some honour. The textile worker asks how this is to be done? The tobacco worker explains that such National Liberation Committees ('*Milli Kurtuluş Komiteleri*') are already being created. What remains unclear is how this alliance with the progressive bourgeoisie would maintain a revolutionary momentum.

One of the most remarkable features of this campaign for national liberation was the implied reassessment of recent Turkish history. The repeated references of Atatürk are not merely a rhetorical device to discredit Menderes, but amount to an affirmation of fundamental Kemalist principles. It was Atatürk who first demonstrated that a whole nation could be mobilized against foreign domination. On 4 August 1959 Nazım warned against narrow-minded forms of nationalism, but he went on to describe Turkish independence as Atatürk's most precious legacy, concluding with the eloquent appeal: 'Did not Atatürk bequeath to you our independence as a country, a republic and a nation as the most precious thing of all?' Two days later he again revived memories of the Kemalist period, calling for a mobilization of public opinion under the banner of a second 'National Militia' ('Kuvayı Milliye'). On 26 August 1960 Bizim Radyo reminded its listeners that Atatürk came from a humble family background, which was seen as one of the sources of his progressive outlook. A month later there followed a talk entitled 'Are We Following Atatürk's Foreign Policy?', which endorsed the struggle for self-determination in other oppressed countries, notably Algeria: 'If Atatürk were alive, he would have defended the right to self-determination. [...] Atatürk would have supported Third World countries in the United Nations' (Transcripts, 28 September 1960). Although this broadcast was anonymous, it is likely to have been by Nazım, since he was in Leipzig that month, staying at the Astoria Hotel. Perhaps he was also the author of the broadcast about Atatürk's foreign policy on 30 August 1961, which included the memorable phrase: 'If Atatürk were to put his head out of his mausoleum, he would think he was back in 1919. Everything is under the control of foreigners' (Transcripts, 30 August 1961).

One further factor underlay this reassessment of Atatürk's legacy – a heightened awareness of the dangers of religious fundamentalism. In his early poem 'The Book with the Leather Cover', Nazım ridiculed the legends recorded in religious tomes, disdainfully suggesting that they be dropped down a well. The implication was that religion could be discounted as a political force. Although no communist is ever likely to forget Marx's critique of religion as an opium of the people, Nazım seems to have assumed that such superstitions would gradually wither away. Hence Islam only has a marginal place in his major writings. The Turkey portrayed in *Human Landscapes* is dominated by railway stations and radio masts, hospitals, army barracks and prison buildings, but there is scarcely a minaret in sight. However, the mobilization of Islam by the Menderes government opened the poet's eyes to a new danger, and in June 1959 Bizim Radyo broadcast a series of four successive programmes denouncing the 'black peril' (*kara kuvvet*).

Although these talks were not explicitly attributed to Nazım, they echoed the arguments he set out four years earlier from Budapest. The attack was not directed against religious belief in itself, but against the cynical manipulation of Islam for political purposes.

In the years 1958-60 the primary aim of Bizim Radyo was to incite public opinion against Menderes as the agent of American imperialism and religious revivalism. The impact of radio propaganda on public opinion is notoriously difficult to assess – whether the Hungarian revolt of 1956 was partly inspired by Radio Liberty broadcasts is still disputed – but it has been plausibly argued that audiences for external progammes 'are likely to be in inverse ratio to the attractiveness of the receiving country's domestic communications media' (Paulu, 219 & 363). The news bulletins of state-controlled Turkish Radio were oppressively partisan, endlessly lauding the achievements of the government and reciting long lists of Turkish patriots whose love for Menderes impelled them to join the 'Fatherland Front'. The suppression of alternative viewpoints had the contrary effect of making Turkish broadcasts from London, Moscow or Leipzig all the more attractive, and circumstantial evidence suggests that these stations had a significant effect. Bizim Radyo broadcast for several hours every day, sending out a strong and clearly audible signal which was not jammed. It was certainly taken seriously by the Turkish authorities, and its output was also monitored by the BBC in Caversham (Mango, Interview, August 1997). The Turkish population at this time was becoming increasingly well-educated, and even the illiterate could follow the news by radio. By 1960 there were 1,341,000 licensed radio sets in Turkey, compared with 362,000 ten years earlier (UNESCO, 53). Radio was the most important factor in shaping public opinion, and dissenting voices from abroad may have had a disproportionate influence.

However we assess the impact of Bizim Radyo, its campaign against the Menderes regime was rewarded. On 27 May 1960, after a series of anti-government demonstrations in Ankara and Istanbul, Menderes was deposed by a military junta led by General Cemal Gürsel. The leaders of the coup were admirers of Ismet İnönü, and were determined to reaffirm the Kemalist principles of secularism and westernization while protecting political freedoms through a reformed constitution. Menderes himself and his closest political associates were arrested and put on trial. When news of the coup was announced, Nazım was in Moscow, and his immediate impulse was to write a poem commemorating the student killed by the security forces during the demonstrations in Istanbul. His sympathy clearly lay not with the coup leaders but with the new generation of student radicals (A 7, 48). However, further divisions of opinion at Bizim Radyo now opened up. Ismail Bilen, taking an orthodox Marxist line, argued that the officers' coup was fascist in character (Ihmalyan, 246); but other broadcasters were heartened by the release of left-wing political prisoners and welcomed the proposed new constitution, which offered legal protection to organizations of the left like the Turkish Workers' Party (TIP) and guaranteed the right to strike. However, Bizim Radyo remained sceptical about the prospect of more radical reforms, particularly the redistribution of land ownership. In an unsigned broadcast of 26 August 1960, the officers of 27 May were compared to Enver Pasha and the Young Turks, who quickly abandoned their progressive programme and sold out to German imperialism.

It is notable that none of the surviving transcripts from 1960 and 1961 is specifically attributed to Nazım – which may be fortuitious, since the series is obviously incomplete. We know that the poet visited Leipzig early in September 1961 for a performance of 'Legend of Love'. Possibly he was caught up in the ideological dispute at Bizim Radyo between Ismail Bilen, who tried to impose the Soviet party line, and the Sertels, who pleaded for a wider popular appeal (Ihmalyan, 238). Perhaps for a time Bilen succeeded in restricting Nazım's access to the microphone. The dispute was certainly not resolved until Zeki Baştımar, who had been arrested in 1951 and spent ten years in a Turkish gaol, arrived in the Soviet Union. He was given the task of reorganizing Bizim Radyo (STMA, 6, 1960 & 2040). At a general meeting of the Turkish Communist Party in Leipzig in April 1962, it was agreed that Nazım should be given a more prominent role to increase the programme's popular appeal. Thus Nazım was able to make a further series of broadcasts during the summer of 1962 and spring of 1963.

It took well over a year to complete the court proceedings against the leaders of the Democrat Party. Finally, Menderes was sentenced to death for offences against the constitution, and hanged in September 1961 together with two associates. Daily reports of the court proceedings were broadcast by the military government over Turkish Radio (there was not yet any television coverage). A vivid account of these events, as seen by an impressionable teenager, can be found in an autobiographical novel by Emine Sevgi Özdamar. The narrator recalls that the whole family followed events by radio. However, her aunt, listening to broadcasts on the third-floor of a block of flats in Ankara, was passionately pro-Menderes, while her brother on the floor above was deep in discussion with a communist friend about the crimes of the Democrat Party and the inadequacies of the junta (Özdamar, 345-9). Such accounts reflect both the penetration of radio propaganda and its limitations. The Turkish army was no more successful than the Menderes government in creating a national consensus.

The surviving Bizim Radyo transcripts contain no references to the execution of Menderes. However, during 1962 the tone of Nazım's commentaries changed significantly. He now insisted that the movement for national liberation, which led to the over-throw of the Democrat Party dictatorship, had been only the first step. More fundamental changes were now needed: land reform, trade union rights, working class participation in politics and the lifting of the ban on the Communist Party. Whereas his earlier broadcasts had appealed to the whole Turkish people, he now explicitly invoked the working class as the agent of change, arguing that it had no reason to fear being tarred with the brush of communism. He ridiculed the attempts of the Turkish political establishment to block social reforms by labelling such measures as subversive. However, Nazım's definition of communism was now more flexible: 'People are branded as communists when they are progressive and love their people and their rights and freedoms. There is some truth in that.' He insisted on 30 July 1962: 'Communism is a progressive, patriotic and populist movement, committed to justice.' These broadcasts provoked such a strong reaction that one Ankara newspaper denounced Nazım as a 'traitor to his country' ('vatan haini'). The poet replied that he was indeed hostile to a country dominated by poverty and exploitation ('Vatan Haini', A 7, 145).

These radio broadcasts offer new insight into Nazım's political thinking, showing that he did not remain stranded in a Leninist time-warp, dreaming of some impossible alliance of workers and peasants to create a communist Turkey. Far from arguing that Turkey was ripe for revolution, Bizim Radyo took the line that the country should detach itself from Nato and join the group of non-aligned states led by Tito and Nehru. However, this did not imply that it should stand aside from international affairs. Kemalist Turkey provided the outstanding example of an armed national liberation struggle, achieved by the combined efforts of the whole people. Thus a government dedicated to Atatürk's principles should actively support national liberation campaigns in other countries like Algeria, Cyprus and Lebanon, Laos and Vietnam, Egypt and Cuba, not to mention anti-colonialist movements in African countries like Tanganyika. Working as a radio journalist enabled Nazım's to develop an informed view of international events like the French withdrawal from Algeria. He was also in touch with the political thinking of a new generation of Euro-Communists like Régis Debray, whom he met on his visit to Paris in 1958.

Of course, the broadcasts of Bizim Radyo were politically slanted. In the transcripts of Nazım's talks there is no reference to Soviet imperialism, let alone to popular aspirations in satellite states like Hungary, Poland and Czechoslovakia; according to official doctrine they had already been liberated by the Red Army. Given his contacts with reformers in Budapest around 1955, his silence over the suppression of the Hungarian uprising is particularly compromising. Equally problematic are the arguments be advanced in August 1961 to justify the building of the Berlin Wall, describing it as a legitimate measure to control an international frontier. This is blatant propaganda, lacking the subversive irony that distinguishes Nazım's best political commentaries. But although these were communist-sponsored propaganda broadcasts, there was no single party line. When further documentation becomes available, we may find that Nazım's deviations from party dogma led to conflicts within the broadcasting service comparable to those between Orwell and the Overseas Services Controller of the BBC (Orwell, 52-8).

By the spring of 1963 it had become clear that the Turkish military coup had not achieved the hoped-for radical reforms. Bilen overstated the case in describing its leaders as fascists, but it was legitimate to see them as representatives of a ruling class that would not willingly surrender its privileges. The Turkish Workers' Party, which Bizim Radyo supported, proved rather ineffective. Also, there was no fundamental change in the terms of the American alliance, at least until the Cuban missile crisis resulted in the removal of nuclear warheads from Turkish bases. In his final broadcasts in March 1963 we find Nazım ruefully reflecting that the reactionaries seemed to be poised to regain power under the aegis of the Justice Party, successor to the Democrats. He still expressed confidence in the 1961 Constitution, but went on to argue that if the workers failed to fight for their rights, they would lose them (Transcripts, 30 March 1963). However, he and his colleagues could look back with considerable pride on the tactics of their campaign against the Menderes regime. In another of these final broadcasts, transmitted from Leipzig to mark the fifth anniversary of the founding of Bizim Radyo, Nazım declared with a defiant pride: 'Bizim Radyo was the voice that Menderes most feared' (Transcripts, 23 March 1963).

Nazım's work for theatre and radio not only gave fresh stimulus to his career, but also enriched his personal life. He made friends among actors, broadcasters and film makers throughout Eastern Europe, including Czechoslovakia and Bulgaria. In 1958, the year when his work for Bizim Radyo began, his emotional life also entered a new phase – the result of a chance encounter with a young woman from a Moscow film studio. When he visited Leipzig in June that year, he announced to his friends at Bizim Radyo that he had fallen in love again. Moreover, as he ruefully acknowledged, he did not have 'just two but three loves in his heart' (Erdinç 1978, 98). The ramifications of Nazım's emotional life in exile were to prove quite as complex as his political and cultural activities.

10

'Leaving the cities and women I love'

Nazım's political commitment seems hardly to have wavered for forty years, from the first encounter with the Spartacists in 1920 to his final visit to Cuba in 1961. But his love-life was a switchback of compelling passions and painful separations. His volatile temperament, added to the experience of persecution and imprisonment, ensured that periods of stable domesticity rarely lasted longer than two or three years. The pattern may be traced back to the first separation experienced by the impressionable teenager, when his mother abruptly left the family for Paris. The impossible quest for a woman who would simultaneously provide both erotic excitement, poetic inspiration and maternal reassurance continued until the end of his life. 'Some people know all about plants and some about fish', he wrote in a late poem, 'I know about separation' (A 7, 99). To compensate for enforced separations he would write long series of letters, but with Münevver left behind in Istanbul, even this was difficult. They had to devise a clandestine method of corresponding through third parties, sending letters via Paris or Rome. However, from 1956 onwards they could correspond more openly, as a result of an intervention from abroad. At the 1955 Vienna Peace conference Nazım had met a Belgian socialist, Isabelle Blume, who was extremely sympathetic when told of the ban on their correspondence. Blume contacted the Belgian Foreign Minister Paul-Henri Spaak, who was due to pay a visit to Turkey, and he successfully interceded on their behalf with the Turkish prime minister (Sertel 1978, 152). Münevver actually wrote more than 700 letters to Nazım during their ten-year separation – most of them are now in a restricted section of the Nazım Hikmet Archive in Moscow.

After receiving one of her letters in May 1955, Nazım wrote a poem, 'Letter from Istanbul', expressing the difficulties of Münevver's life in her own voice:

312

My darling,
I am writing from far away,
I am very tired,
I saw my face in the mirror, a greenish
colour,
It is cold here, summer will never come
We need logs costing thirty Lira a week
            we cannot possibly manage.
[. . .]
Write back immediately,
Don't bother remembering my problems,
            forget them
        don't forget me...
            ('Istanbul'dan Mektup', A 6, 69)

This poem, full of practical matters and snippets of world news, has a strikingly different tone from those inspired by letters from Piraye ten years earlier. There the poetry confirmed the intimacy, whereas here it accentuates the separation. Nazım did his best to alleviate Münevver's plight, sending her money by circuitous routes, but the difficulties of communication eroded the emotional bond.

Two loves in one heart

The longing to be reunited with Münevver did not prevent the poet from forming new attachments. The complications began in 1952 when Nazım met Galina Grigoryevna Kolesnikova, a young physician, while under treatment for his heart condition. In a television interview recorded when she was a sprightly woman in her seventies, Galina recalled: 'I was a doctor at the Barvikha sanatorium, working as a deputy director in the internal diseases section. Nazım stayed there for three months. All the girls aged from sixteen to twenty were falling in love with him, so why shouldn't I fall in love? [...] We were very much in love with one another' (GC/TV, 4). She became his mistress, housekeeper and medical adviser all in one, supervising his diet and exercise, his sleeping patterns and even his bath times, and accompanying him on trips abroad as a kind of personal physician, with the approval of the Writers' Union (Bezirci, 89 & 71). When he collapsed in September 1956 with pneumonia and blood poisoning, she recognized that he was not responding to treatment because of a penicillin allergy and altered his medication. Nazım is quoted as saying that Galina saved his life four times (Fevralski, 77).

In November 1956 she accompanied Nazım to Poland, which they made their base for nine months while he visited other socialist countries. Gomulka's Poland, as Svetlana Alliluyeva explains, held a particular attraction for Nazım because it 'seemed like a stronghold of liberal Communism' (Alliluyeva, 215). Life in Moscow was becoming too much of a strain: 'When *Ivan Ivanovich* was banned, Nazım was going through a depression', Galina explains. 'He was contemplating suicide.' Conscious that Nazım still longed for Münevver, Galina was quite ready to renounce him if his family succeed in escaping to the Soviet Union (GC/TV 4). Although there are no love poems addressed to Galina, they spent almost eight years together, longer than Nazım ever lived with any other woman. Photographs of them together suggest genuine emotional compatibility (Fig. 30a). They enjoyed leisurely weeks at the dacha in Peredelkino, which they transformed into a comfortable home, with pictures of Mehmet Nazım on the wall to remind the poet of the loved ones left behind (Fig. 30b).

Living with Galina and longing for Münevver, Nazım now embarked on the last great romance of his life. It all started with an Albanian folktale. Folk theatre featured prominently in the communist conception of popular culture, and towards the end of 1955 the Soyuz Multifilm Institute decided to make a cartoon film based on an Albanian legend. But the design team felt handicapped by their lack of information about Albanian costumes until someone suggested contacting Nazım. After all, the Ottomans had ruled Albania for three centuries, and his apartment was decorated with figures from the Turkish puppet theatre. So the director of the Institute, Valentina Brumberg, arranged to visit him, accompanied by Vera Tulyakova, a young woman from the design department. They were introduced by Ekber Babayev, who was working on the Russian text of *Ivan Ivanovich* at this time. Nazım found Vera so attractive that he could not resist making a personal comment to Ekber, speaking in a Tatar dialect so that no one else would understand: 'She's interesting, not bad-looking, but flat-chested.' Little did he know that during the war when only nine years old Vera had been evacuated to a Tatar village, and spent two years there with her mother. She remembered

30. Scenes from Peredelkino: (*a*) Nazım relaxing with Galina.

(*b*) Nazım with photos of his son.

enough of this language from her childhood to understand Nazım's comments (Tulyakova, 19–22).

To cover up this embarrassment, Nazım showed the visitors around, and when they admired the paintings and drawings on his wall, he insisted on presenting one to Vera. The conversation then switched to more serious topics. They showed him their designs for Albanian folk costumes, and Nazım made a lightning sketch showing how the costumes should really look. After an animated discussion he agreed to visit them for further discussions at the film studio, and the very next day he came up with a whole set of new suggestions about folktales that might make interesting films. He quickly drafted a new scenario and phoned Vera to explain his ideas and arrange to meet her again. Although Nazım did not realize it at the time, Vera was married: her husband was the head of another department at the studio, and they had a daughter, Anyuta. The pattern of falling in love with a young married woman, prefigured in his relationships with Piraye and Münevver, now repeated itself. If psychoanalysis had not been prohibited in the Soviet Union, the Freudians would have had a field day.

In the summer of 1956 Nazım was supposed to be nursing his health at Peredelkino in the care of Galina (Fevralski, 77), but for the poet in love a heart tremor was no deterrent. Contacts with a charming young woman helped to restore his zest for life. He kept phoning Vera at the film studio and inventing a pretext to send his driver to fetch her and Valentina out to the dacha. These first tentative contacts were followed by a nine-month separation from November 1956 until July 1957. In her memoirs Vera recalls that on the eve of his departure his distress was such that he sat sobbing in the corridor of the studios for two hours. She made it clear that she did not return his feelings and insisted that while he was away he should try to forget her. But separation had the effect of intensifying the emotional bond, not only on his side: 'Gentler feelings towards him began to take over,' Vera recalls. 'During those nine months I was longing for the moment when he would phone to tell me he was back' (Tulyakova, 33, 47 & 67).

In 1957 their relationship entered a new phase resulting from a film scenario, 'The Cloud in Love' ('Sevdalı Bulut'). Vera recalls how much they enjoyed working together on this project, which

Nazım originally suggested soon after they first met (Tulyakova, 26). The story, designed as a puppet play, deals with the love affair between a cloud and girl named Ayşe. The cloud is so attracted to her that it ensures that her garden always has just the right mixture of sunshine and rain and everything ripens beautifully. But the course of true love does not run smooth: Ayşe has a persistent admirer – the landlord who envies her fertile garden. The rivalry between the sensitive cloud and the powerful landlord leads to many adventures, but finally true love triumphs over greed and envy. Working with a beautiful young woman on such a poignant love story had a predictable effect on Nazım, although for some time it remained unclear whether the scenario which they were sketching out together would actually be performed.

The turning point came while Nazım was staying in Poland with Galina. Early in the summer of 1957 they received a phone call from Vera saying that the scenario for 'A Cloud in Love' had been accepted for filming. Nazım became so excited that they returned to Moscow as soon as possible. 'They started working together', Galina recalls, 'and that is when their love really took off.' Nazım, who had been going through a depression, evidently wanted to prove himself with a glamorous young woman. 'If he had stayed with me', Galina continues, 'he could have lived for another twenty years, writing plays and other things, but not poetry, because as Nazım used to say he wrote poetry with the blood of his heart. [...] It was a tragedy for me, but I am very pleased that he started writing poetry again after falling in love with Vera' (GC/TV4). It may seem surprising that Vera should have become attached to a man in such frail health, thirty years older than herself (she was born in 1932). She was doubtless attracted by the privileges enjoyed by an internationally celebrated author, but it may also be relevant that Vera's father was killed fighting with the Red Army during the war. If Nazım longed for a younger woman to inspire him, Vera succumbed to the attentions of a fatherly man. 'How old would your father be,' Nazım once asked her, 'if he were alive today?' 'Six years younger than you,' she replied (Tulyakova, 107).

When he returned to Moscow on 27 July 1957, Nazım arranged for Vera to be picked up by his chauffeur and brought to Peredelkino, ostensibly to check through the scenario. She arrived with a film director named Karanovich, which immediately aroused

Nazım's jealousy. Although Vera enjoyed seeing him, she was reluctant to become emotionally involved. In November 1957, a year after they first met, Vera finally told Nazım that she was married and had a child (Tulyakova, 66 & 77-8). He then invited her and her husband to visit Peredelkino to celebrate New Year's Eve, but Nazım was withdrawn and the evening seemed tense and joyless (Tulyakova, 304). However, the discovery that she was married merely intensified Nazım's infatuation, and he sometimes phoned her at the studio ten times a day. He began to advise her about clothes and coiffure, saying he liked her hair best when she wore it long and loose. He would even check whether she arrived home in good time, and phoned her neighbours if there was no answer. His visits to the studio were a great event, since he would arrive with armfuls of chocolates and flowers (Tulyakova, 83-4).

Their relationship was interrupted by a series of further separations. In the autumn of 1957 Nazım spent a month in Baku, and in January 1958 he again left Moscow with Galina, staying in Warsaw till April, visiting Paris in May, and not returning to Moscow again till 31 August. The fact that for almost two years, from November 1956 until September 1958, he spent so much of his time outside the Soviet Union suggests that he may have been politically under a cloud. It is even possible that during his visit to Paris in May 1958 he considered emigrating to France, the country where Münevver had spent her childhood. This visit to Paris was the more liberating because Nazım had obtained permission to travel privately rather than as a member of a delegation. Galina had to remain behind, since she had not been successful in her application for a visa (Sertel 1978, 201-2). She awaited his return in Czechoslovakia, after giving Nazım precise instructions about his diet, how long he should rest and how many stairs he was permitted to climb. Arriving at the Gare du Nord, he found a delegation waiting to welcome him, including the writers Tristan Tzara and Charles Dobzynski, the composer Philippe Gérard, and the artist Abidin Dino and his wife Güzin. Details of his stay in Paris are vividly recalled in a memoir published by Güzin thirty years later. This was the opportunity to thank Tzara for initiating the international campaign for his release in 1950. They went to Philippe's house, which was full of visitors waiting to meet Nazım and hear him reciting his poems (Dino, 139-41). The Dinos then found him a room at the Hôtel de Suède in the Boulevard Saint-Michel, not far from their own apartment.

At Abidin's suggestion Nazım consulted two French doctors about his heart condition, and they advised him to rest. But this was like telling a kite to stay still in a storm. During his three weeks in Paris, France was convulsed by the crisis triggered by the revolt of General Salan and the French nationalists in Algeria. There were mass demonstrations against the nationalists, and Nazım insisted on joining the marchers, even if only for a few minutes, watching the rest of the march from a friend's balcony (Dino, 141-4). It was thrilling to take part in a public demonstration for the first time in thirty years, an experience reflected in the poem 'In Paris, 28 May 1958' (A 6, 155-6). This kind of spontaneous expression of workers' power was inconceivable in the Soviet Union. The crisis was brought under control at the end of May when General de Gaulle returned to power with a mandate to strengthen the constitution. Meanwhile, the French Communist Party was caught up in internal disputes over the expulsion and rehabilitation of certain comrades, which involved Nazım in heated arguments with Louis Aragon (Caute, 145). At the same time he tried to persuade Abidin to become a member of the foreign section of the Turkish Communist Party to counteract the influence of Stalinists like Ismail Bilen. He was taken on a tour of working-class districts of Paris in the '*Ceinture Rouge*' (the communist-controlled red belt of Paris) and on a visit to the state-owned Renault car factory. He even made time to go to a fairground and take rides, like a child. His busy schedule included signing books for throngs of students, and he sat for hours in boulevard cafés discussing politics with young left-wing intellectuals like Régis Debray (Dino, 148-54). He particularly enjoyed his visits to the Turkish painter Avni Arbaş, climbing three flights of stairs to the artist's studio. He was impressed by Avni's paintings of horses, symbolizing the revolutionary spirit of the Turkish people, a motif reflected in the poem 'Avni's Horses' ('Avninin Atları', A 6, 160).

The poems Nazım wrote during these weeks in Paris throw light on his emotional state. His longing for Vera is reflected in the poem 'Paris Without You', written on 8 May shortly after his arrival. Although she is not mentioned by name, the poet's sadness at being in Paris without 'my rose' clearly hints at this new young love ('Sensiz Paris', A 6, 148). But Paris was also permeated by other associations, as is clear from the more complex poem 'Questions About Paris', written eight days later. Here Nazım recalls earlier Turkish writers who found refuge in Paris – the romantic nationalist Namık Kemal and the communist leader Mustafa Suphi. Paris also reminds him of 'my mother's youth / doing her painting / speaking French / the most beautiful woman in the world, / and Mimi as a young girl' (A 6, 152). Here memory blends separation with desire as Mimi (Münevver) becomes intimately associated with Nazım's mother Celile, who had recently died. However, thoughts of Vera dominated his mind. In her memoirs she recalls how flattered she felt to receive phone calls as well as cards, letters and love poems from Paris, and he returned laden with presents of clothes and jewellery (Tulyakova, 277-8).

In the autumn of 1958 the relationship with Vera entered a new phase. Since they had already completed work on 'A Cloud in Love', they had to find a new pretext for their meetings, and Nazım hit on the idea that they should jointly write a play. They were soon hard at work, Nazım writing the parts for the older characters and Vera for the younger ones, using Russian as their medium (she did not speak Turkish). The piece has strong autobiographical undertones and was given the title 'Two Obstinate People', derived from a traditional wooden toy consisting of two goats which furiously butt each other when the handles are manipulated at opposite ends. The play features an elderly professor with a weak heart and a married nurse called Dasha with whom he falls in love. Sensing that he is jealous of her husband, she gives him the toy as a present – a multilayered symbol hinting at the tensions of love. A visit from an American scientist, the professor's cousin who has emigrated to the United States, sets up a further conflict between communism and capitalism. The professor has such a strong sense of social responsibility that he disregards medical advice and travels to the north-east to obtain titanium, which is essential to his work. When news comes that he has suffered a fatal heart attack, the toy falls to the floor, but Dasha picks it up saying 'I don't believe he is dead.' Finally, a recording of the professor's voice is heard, prophesying the creation of an ideal society based on love and free from exploitation, where men will live till the age of 150 and marry young girls! Although there is no Turkish version, the Russian text was published in 1960 in the magazine *Teatr* (No. 4, 77-108) and included in the 1962 Moscow edition of Nazım Hikmet's selected plays.

Writing a play on such a personal theme proved a tense experience. Not for the first time, Nazım was intent on detaching a young woman from her partner. He flattered her by suggesting that she could become an author in her own right, not simply editing other people's work (Tulyakova, 281). He also held out the prospect of glamorous foreign travel, including a trip to Paris. For most Soviet citizens travel to the capitalist world was an impossible dream, but Vera nevertheless felt that Nazım was becoming too possessive. To escape the emotional pressure, she decided in September 1958 to take a holiday with her husband at Arhipo Osipovka, a village on the Black Sea, but within days Nazım had traced her and joined them there. For Vera his attentions scarcely made for a relaxed holiday (Tulyakova, 128-9), but the poems he wrote express a sense of exhilaration: 'I steep myself in the sea, sand, and sun, / in trees, in apples like honey' (A 6, 167). His feelings for Vera are conveyed through an ecstatic self-immersion in nature – 'the sea, flat on its back, naked and warm' (A 6, 169). Yet he is still haunted by memories of Münevver, his Istanbul 'rose', with her grief and laughter returning to him like 'repetitions' in a Bach melody (A 6, 129-31).

Work on 'Two Obstinate People' continued through 1959, interrupted by trips abroad. On a visit to Germany in July Nazım wrote the poem 'Two Loves', acknowledging his divided loyalties. 'There can't be two loves in one heart', the poem begins. 'What a lie – / it happens all the time'. The poet tries to resolve his dilemma by imagining his two lovers, Münevver in Istanbul and Vera in Moscow, enjoying each other's company:

> The women I love are laughing and crying
> > in two languages.
> Friends, how did you get together?
> You don't know each other.
> Where are you waiting for me –
> at the Sycamore Café in Beyazit or in Gorki Park?
> > ('Iki Sevda', A 7; P, 205)

On his return to Moscow he intensified his pursuit of Vera until finally the stress became too much and in September she fell ill, suffering from fatigue, insomnia and depression. She spent her sick leave resting at home, and Nazım visited her every day, chaperoned by Ekber Babayev. Looking back on this episode, Vera feels that this was the moment when she began to return his love. But in November, before she had completely recovered, Nazım went down with pneumonia and could not leave his room for two months. To keep in touch with Vera he insisted on having a telephone installed by his bedside, claiming that he needed it for his work in the peace movement (Tulyakova, 337, 342 & 361).

In January 1960 they were finally united. The year began auspiciously with the rehearsals for 'Two Obstinate People', which was to have its première at the Yermalova Theatre. At Nazım's insistence, the printed programme featured a photograph of the two of them together. After attending a rehearsal they repaired to Nazım's favourite coffee house, persuading the management to stay open late so that they could celebrate their success and discuss their next move (Tulyakova, 361-3). He wanted her to commit herself to moving in with him. In return he would formally separate from Galina and give up the dacha in Peredelkino. The separation was formalized on 7 January 1960 by a notarized document in which Nazım made over to Galina the possessions they had accumulated together. The inventory included household goods, a 1957 Volga limousine, 1,500 books, thirteen paintings, two television sets, a radio, record player and tape recorder, a typewriter, an aquarium, a silver cutlery set, china and a sewing machine, valued in total at 89,975 roubles. The same day, he wrote her a farewell letter, entrusting its delivery to Ekber Babayev:

I am leaving you as a man, but I will remain as your friend whether you like it or not. As long as I live I will take responsibility for you, just as I will for Münevver and my son. When I return, I'll stay in Pesenkaya [the flat in Moscow]. If you like, don't get rid of the dacha. The instalments on the car and the dacha have been paid in advance for nine months. After that, if I am still alive, I will still pay for these things.

In his covering note, he apologizes to Ekber for keeping secret his plan to separate from Galina (Aziz Nesin Archive).

Vera now took the plunge and separated from her husband. She and Nazım travelled by train to Baku and enjoyed a blissful three-month holiday in Kislovodsk, a resort on the northern foothills of the Caucusus (Tulyakova, 441). Here, in February 1960, Nazım again began to write love poetry, as in 'Early Light':

I am recklessly happy
and a bit embarrassed
but just a little bit.
In the early morning the light in our room
is like a sail
spread for a voyage.
My rose gets out of bed naked like an apricot
('Sabah Karanlığı'; A 7, 40-1; P, 209)

As so often, personal exhilaration is fused with politics. Waiting for his 'rose' to awake, the poet turns on the radio and hears the news of Sputnik III circling the earth. But intimacy with Vera did not exclude memories of Münevver, to whom Nazım wrote several letters and cards from Kislovodsk, giving her the impression that he was recuperating from overwork and fatigue. From the tone of her reply it is clear that he had not referred to Vera (Münevver to Nazım, 9 February 1960). Further complications were in store when Nazım and Vera returned to Moscow. Their spirits were lifted by the success of 'Two Obstinate People', which they celebrated by spending an evening with Fevralski at the house of the director, L. V. Varpahovski (Fevralski, 85). But when they visited the dacha they found that Galina had carted off Nazım's favourite possessions, leaving the simple message 'Damn you two!' (Vera, Interview, January 1992).

For Nazım intimacy remained elusive. After he and Vera started living together in March 1960, he still felt insecure – Vera was reluctant to forfeit her independence, not least when he tried to insist on her joining the Communist Party. There were frequent separations, as his duties took him on extended trips abroad, but when they were together he would hardly let Vera out of his sight and grew impatient when she made long phone calls. He would proudly show off his glamorous partner at social gatherings, only to become resentful when she attracted admiring glances from other men. Vera began to wonder if she really wanted to go ahead with marriage to someone so demanding. She was in no hurry to divorce her husband, being concerned about the welfare of her daughter, whom she visited at her husband's house. Nazım tried to justify his possessiveness by arguing that he would no longer feel jealous and insecure once they were married. Moreover a marriage certificate would provide her with security after his death. On 18 November 1960 they were finally married.

It was a quiet occasion the only witness being Vera's friend Tosya
–the Turkologist Antonina Sverçevskaya (Tulyakova, 396-403).

Penelope – the woman on the horizon

Nazım had not yet resolved his attachment to Münevver, let
alone his guilt at leaving her and their son behind. He was also
grieving for his mother Celile, who had died in February 1956
at a time when political circumstances made his return to Istanbul
for the funeral impossible. Feelings of separation and loss are
reflected in some of his most resonant verses, permeated with
images of transience, dreamlike cityscapes and journeys towards
an unknown destination. 'Drive on, engineer' – the poet exclaims
in the final lines of the poem 'Two Loves' – 'take me there', only
to receive the enigmatic response: 'Where?' (A 7, 17). During
this final decade Nazım was so continuously on the move that
one cannot easily keep track of all his journeys. It is as if, after
the enforced immobility of prison, he was trying to cram the
travels of a lifetime into just a few years. Medically these activities
were ill-advised, but poetically they were highly productive,
stimulating a spate of poems inspired by the people he met and
places he visited. Many of these poems testify to the circumstances
of their origin by concluding with a specific date and place – Paris,
Warsaw, Leipzig, Berlin, Baku, Leningrad, Stockholm, Havana.
The poem 'My Woman', with the dateline 'March 1960, Mediter-
ranean Sea', was composed during a long and arduous journey.
After travelling by train from Moscow via Poland to Italy, Nazım
then continued by boat by way of Alexandria to attend a conference
in Beirut (A 25, 134). He and Vera apparently travelled together
as far as Brest, the Russian frontier town on the Polish border.
Hence the poignant opening lines:

> My woman came with me as far as Brest,
> she got off the train and stayed on the platform,
> she grew smaller and smaller [...]

The starting point for this poem may be a temporary separation
from Vera, but it opens out to express more complex feelings of
attachment, guilt and longing. Physical separation from Vera gives
way to a dream sequence in which the poet is haunted by other

voices and memories of other women – Münevver, perhaps even Piraye:

> 'Come', she said, but I couldn't reach her,
> the train was going like it would never stop,
> I was choking with grief.
>
> Then patches of snow were rotting on sandy earth,
> and suddenly I knew my woman was watching:
> 'Did you forget me', she asked, 'did you forget me?'
> [. . .]
>
> Then suddenly I knew I'd been on that train for years
> – I'm still amazed at how or why I knew it –
> and always singing the same great song of hope,
> I'm forever leaving the cities and women I love,
> and carrying my losses like wounds opening inside me,
> I'm getting closer, closer to somewhere.
>
> (A 7, 45; P, 213)

In this poem the women he has loved merge into a single composite figure, growing smaller and smaller as the poet's pounding heart is carried into the night. A temporary separation becomes a matter of life and death, and the song of hope is constrained by grief at some inescapable bereavement, hinting perhaps at the loss of the original maternal bond.

The most poignant tribute to Münevver is in the poem 'Hasret' (Longing, 1959), in which the figure of the individual woman again acquires an archetypal resonance:

> For a hundred years I have not seen your face
> I have not put my arms around you. [...]
> I have not touched the warmth of your belly.
> For a hundred years a woman has been
>   waiting for me in a city.
>
> We were of the same branch, on the same branch,
> falling from the same branch we are separated.
> There is a hundred years between us
>   and a hundred years distance.
> For a hundred years in the twilight
>   I have been running after you.
>
> (A 7, 12)

Münevver and Nazım did indeed come 'from the same branch' (they were cousins). In his imagination the poet may be 'running after' his lost love, but emotionally he was already distancing himself from Münevver, just as he had from Piraye. In these years Nazım frequently sent Münevver manuscript poems to be translated into French, and since they included 'Two Loves' she was left in no doubt about the poet's divided loyalties (Münevver, Interview, July 1996).

In April 1961 Nazım paid a further visit to Paris which was to bring a meeting with Münevver a decisive stage nearer. Vera accompanied him on what was in effect their honeymoon, and photographs show him standing proudly beside his bride. They spent forty days in Paris, after which Nazım travelled on to Cuba on his own. Fidel Castro's victory in January 1959 after two years of guerrilla warfare against the American-backed regime of Battista created new opportunities for communism in Latin America. When the United States imposed a trade embargo in an attempt to strangle the Cuban economy, the Soviet Union stepped into the breach with a systematic programme of economic and political aid. Nazım became involved as a representative of the Soviet-sponsored World Peace Committee, and his visit to Cuba in May 1961 proved the most exciting of all his missions. Its primary purpose was to present a Peace Prize to Castro, but he soon got caught up in the revolutionary fevour. 'Perhaps I made a mistake in leaving my own country,' he mused. 'One should have stayed there and started a guerrilla campaign in the mountains' (Tulyakova, 133). He was also impressed by the racial harmony in Cuba, celebrated in his poem 'Straw-Blond': 'In the space that is Cuba six million people whites blacks yellows mulattos are planting a bright seed' (A 7, 77; P, 225). In the poem 'Havana Reportage' he celebrates the heroic achievements of the Cuban revolution, in which he feels the spirit of Lenin has been reborn (A 7, 80-91).

Shortly before he left Paris to fly to Havana, Nazım had a meeting with a member of the Italian peace movement, Joyce Salvadori Lussu, which was to have important consequences for his relationship with Münevver. He had first met Joyce, an author married to the Italian socialist Emilio Lussu, at the Stockholm peace conference of June 1958. Translations of Nazım's poems were on display at the conference, and she overheard another delegate saying: 'This is the world's greatest living poet.' They soon became friends, communicating in French, he suggested that she should translate his work into Italian. In a memoir published thirty years later, she recalls their early exchanges:

> We went to the foyer of the hotel and he read a short poem to me. It was written on a small, tattered piece of paper in a childlike hand. I didn't then know that he had learned to read and write in Arabic script at the time of the Ottoman Empire, changing to the Latin alphabet as an adult during the Atatürk revolutionary period.
>
> He read poetry beautifully. His voice was resonant and effective. Turkish is a beautiful language, rich in voiced and unvoiced consonants. Then he started explaining. He knew how to clarify things for me very well. He was precise about words. Sometimes if he could not find a way of expressing the meaning in French, he would try to explain using other words and expressions from other languages, knowing how to find beautiful and flexible equivalents, even using hand gestures. I never had the feeling that I didn't understand or only partly understood. 'Use only concrete and everyday words,' he said, 'so that a simple peasant can understand the language' (Lussu, 17).

Joyce felt an intuitive affinity with his work, and their shared revolutionary commitment compensated for her lack of Turkish. 'Nazım and I really understood each other,' she affirms. A photograph of them together in Stockholm conveys their close rapport (Fig. 31). Nazım then began to talk about his wife and child in Istanbul, and she was deeply moved by their sufferings (Lussu, 18-19). Since he made no reference either to Piraye or to Vera, she assumed that his love poems expressed his feelings for Münevver. He tried to enlist her help in negotiations with the Turkish authorities, and she agreed to visit Münevver at the earliest opportunity.

At their first meeting in Istanbul in June 1960 Joyce and Münevver became very fond of each other: 'It was as if Münevver was one of my closest relatives' (Lussu, 20). In a letter to Nazım dated 25 June, Münevver described how much they enjoyed an invitation to dinner in Kemal Tahir's house. Münevver lived with her two children in a flat in Kadıköy, with a police unit still stationed outside which subjected visitors to questioning. Since she was struggling to earn a living from translation work and giving private lessons, she was pleased to receive some money which Nazım had sent with Joyce. She was in poor health and suffering from emotional stress, but she still impressed Joyce as proud and resilient, and determined to give her children a good

31. At the Stockholm Peace Conference with Joyce Lussu, 1958.

education. The walls of the flat were covered with pictures of
Nazım, and she was obviously still devoted to him. The poignancy
of her situation led Joyce to reflect on its archetypal associations:
'Münevver was a Penelope waiting for the return of a Ulysses
who, after seventeen years in prison, was voyaging from one port
to another, acquiring new friends, admirers and experiences and
even finding here and there a Nausicaa or a Calypso' (Lussu, 22).
She experienced a powerful urge to help, feeling that a Penelope
in this world always receives less attention than a Ulysses, and
has to endure social prejudice and economic exploitation.
Münevver's life in Turkey had certainly not been easy. Her hopes
that she might be permitted to leave the country had been dashed
when a cabinet minister, Samet Ağaoğlu, said to her in 1952: 'As
long as I live, you will never see Nazım again' (letter of 29 June
1960 from Münevver to Nazım).

As a result of Joyce Lussu's intervention the situation was transformed. At her next meeting with Nazım she was not content

merely to discuss the progress of her Italian translations. 'I am going to get your wife out of Turkey,' she declared. She imagined leading Münevver with one hand and Mehmet Nazım with the other so that they could be 'a family again' (Lussu, 23). He warned her how difficult it would be to outwit the Turkish security system, but Joyce was determined. Returning to Istanbul, she put the idea to Münevver, who was so enthusiastic that they immediately started discussing practical questions. Where could they find a boat in which to escape? On her return to Italy Joyce approached the Italian Communist Party, but they refused to become involved in such a hazardous escapade. Fortunately her husband Emilio, a veteran of the anti-fascist resistance in Italy, provided enthusiastic support. Another friend put her in touch with a businessman from northern Italy, Carlo Giullini, one of whose relatives had died in a concentration camp. Joyce appealed to Giullini by reading him some translations of Nazım's poetry. She then launched into an impassioned appeal: 'You spend all your time making money. Why not for once do something honourable and courageous which you will be able to talk about to your children, showing that you are a creative and humane person?' (Lussu, 24-5). Giullini consented, and in April 1961 Joyce was able to share her plans with Nazım and Vera during their visit to Paris. Nazım gave the plan a cautious welcome but did not want to become directly involved (Vera, Interview, January 1992).

In July, Joyce embarked with Giullini from Piraeus on his Triton yacht, captained by an experienced sailor named Armando. They took an ample supply of dollar bills, pretending to be a wealthy family from Milan touring the archaeological sites of the Aegean. First they anchored off the Greek island of Chios, a few miles off the Turkish coast, staying at the best hotel and ordering champagne and caviar. The next morning, because of rough weather, it took them eight hours to reach Turkish waters. As they approached Izmir, they inadvertently entered a military zone and were boarded by a Turkish naval patrol, but they were allowed to land and escorted to a hotel, where they were kept under surveillance. Smuggling Münevver and her family out through the tight security in Izmir was clearly impracticable, so they decided that Giullini should sail up the coast to the tourist resort of Ayvalık, while Joyce took the plane to Istanbul to fetch Münevver and the children. They were to meet again three days later in a café on the main square in Ayvalık. In Istanbul, Joyce discovered that Münevver was visiting her cousins in a house on the Bosphorus, so it was some time before the group was ready for departure, but they finally were able to elude the police and even to take their most precious belongings with them.

They first had to cross the Sea of Marmara, taking the ferry to Bandırma and travelling at night in the third-class saloon to escape detection. They then took a train crowded with Turkish peasants to Balıkesir, but on arrival discovered that there were no taxis – only by pretending to be an American journalist did Joyce manage to hire a vintage Buick. Their driver took them along the bumpy road to Ayvalık, where they were attracted by a crowd in the main square. Giullini was offering the locals a visit to his yacht, and this provided a pretext for taking Münevver and her children on board. Under cover of darkness they set sail for the Greek island of Lesbos, only a dozen kilometres from the coast. But just off Lesbos they ran into difficulties and had to fire signal flares to attract assistance. The Greek fishermen on the shore thought they were celebrating with fireworks, but shouts of 'We have dollars' galvanized them into action. A boat was launched, and they were all safely taken on board, although some of their precious belongings, including Münevver's documents, slipped overboard and sank to the bottom of the Aegean.

Although it was 3 o'clock in the morning, Münevver kept her wits about her. Turning the shipwreck to their advantage, she was able to persuade the Greek authorities that she was a Polish citizen whose passport had been lost overboard. Once she was in Athens, she explained, she would be able to obtain the necessary documents. At 11 o'clock that same morning they caught a plane to Athens, where Giullini treated them to a champagne dinner. He then flew back to Milan, while they contacted the Polish embassy to make arrangements to travel to Warsaw. To obtain a formal invitation from Nazım to join him in Warsaw, they had to send him a cable, and spent a further anxious week in Athens waiting for the necessary documents. According to Joyce's recollections, they had to sell her gold watch and Münevver's gold chain when they ran out of money (Lussu, 35). Finally Münevver and the children flew to Warsaw, while Joyce returned to Italy.

On 3 August Joyce was delighted to receive a telegram from Münevver in Warsaw saying that all was well. Nazım, who had just returned from Cuba, approached the meeting with mixed feelings, since he now had to unravel the tangled skein of his double life. Münevver was well aware that he had another woman in Moscow, although she only discovered after arriving in Warsaw that they were married. The romantic communist could be extremely ruthless, and the reunion was certainly not the blissful one Joyce had imagined. When they arrived at the airport, there was no Nazım there to welcome them. Instead he arranged to meet them the next day in the hotel restaurant, where an orchestra was playing sentimental music. He had to explain that Vera now formed the centre of his life, but he seems to have done his best to avoid personal subjects. 'We just talked about poetry,' Münevver recalled (Interview, July 1996). Nazım soon turned to practical matters. He had to organize a flat for the new arrivals and buy the necessary furnishings, and this involved a journey to Leipzig to raise funds from his contacts at Bizim Radyo (Vera, Interview, January 1992). He also inquired about the possibility of Münevver finding employment with the radio station, emphasizing her linguistic qualifications (Erdinç, 103). However, Münevver herself preferred to stay in Warsaw, and she later obtained a teaching post in the Oriental Languages Faculty. Their finances were barely adequate to their needs, but it must have been some consolation to know that she and her son had been named as the main beneficiaries in Nazım's will, which he had drawn up in September 1959. The fact that she continued to translate his writings into French shows that there was still a strong bond between them, but emotionally she had to come to terms with a profound sense of loss. Like Piraye, Nazım's first Penelope, she had waited patiently for ten years, only to find herself usurped by a younger woman.

In a brief memoir, Mehmet Nazım has recorded his own memories of that first meeting in a Warsaw restaurant. To judge from his comments, Nazım's conduct was extremely insensitive. He began by reciting poems he had just written about the Cuban revolution – presumably, excerpts from his exuberantly optimistic 'Havana Reportage' ('Havana Röportajı', A 8, 80-91) – which would scarcely endear him to listeners still suffering the trauma of their escape from Turkey. Mehmet then recalls Nazım speaking of his fear of death, and even exchanging glances with young women at nearby tables to prove that he was still youthful and attractive while he made desultory conversation. The situation is poignantly summed up in Mehmet Nazım's comment that he had a father 'for fifteen days' (Mehmet, 12). It is ironic to recall the poem Nazım addressed to 'Mehmet' only four years earlier on a visit to Bulgaria. Desperate with longing, the poet gazes out across the Black Sea, exclaiming: 'My son, I am calling you, / can you hear me? / Mehmet! Mehmet!' (A 6, 109). In 1957 Nazım even made a broadcast from Varna on the Turkish-language radio expressing his sadness at being separated from his son (Petrov, 22), but when it came down to practicalities he did not manage to reconcile his poetic dreams with his parental responsibilities.

Münevver's feelings during this extraordinary episode are reflected in a selection of her letters now in the Aziz Nesin Archive. Writing to Nazım from Istanbul on 29 June 1960, she had been full of optimism, since she had just heard that travel restrictions were being relaxed due to the overthrow of the Menderes regime. At this stage she seems to have hoped to get a passport and to meet Nazım in Naples. All she needed from him was a written invitation certifying that they were related. But a fortnight later, in her letters of 12 and 13 July, the tone had changed: she now addressed him not as 'My Darling' (Canım), but simply as 'Nazım'. He had evidently reproached her for her friendship with Kemal Tahir – presumably as a way of salving his own conscience. Münevver replied that Kemal had been a good friend to her when she felt most isolated, and helped her to find translation work. How could Nazım of all people blame her for having a friendship with Kemal, merely because he was a man? In some accounts this episode has been cited to justify Nazım's heartless conduct by suggesting that Münevver herself was unfaithful (Bezirci, 72), but she was emphatic that she 'never had an affair with anyone'. Quite the opposite, it was he who had dishonoured her: several years earlier she had received an anonymous letter saying that he was living with a woman doctor (Letter of 12 July 1960) – thus apparently he had never even told her about Galina.

Reading between the lines, it is clear that in the summer of 1960 Nazım was trying to create a pretext for breaking with Münevver. His tactics seem to have had the desired effect, since her letter of 9 October expressed real anger. She could not believe that it was really Nazım writing to her: somebody else must be dictating his letters! Although she thanked him for sending money, she complained that he had still failed to send a legal declaration that Mehmet was his son. Nâzım had apparently mentioned that he would like to see his son for 'just a few days', but she found this unacceptable since it would inevitably have been damaging to the child. She was resentful that Nâzım only seemed concerned about his own future plans, which (she declared) no longer interested her. In earlier days he had written such sentimental poems about the 'woman on the horizon' (*uzaktaki kadın*) for whom he felt such longing. Now that he had lost interested in this theme, he waxed lyrical about his son instead, which Münevver saw as 'emotional blackmail'. She asked him not to include any references to herself in his autobiographical novel, since she did not want anything more to do with him. Her instruction to him to give the 754 letters she had written him to Joyce Lussu was a clear sign that they had passed the point of no return. It is not surprising that the poems Nâzım wrote in the autumn of 1960 are full of self-doubt. 'The things I wrote about us are all lies' is the opening line of an untitled poem where he reflects on the element of projection in love (A 7, 61). It was best for Münevver to be warned in advance that his affections now lay elsewhere, and by October 1960, nine months before her escape, she clearly knew of Nâzım's attachment to another woman and realized there would be no loving reunion. However, her situation had become so oppressive that she could not continue to live in Turkey.

Even Joyce Lussu now had to recognize that her rescue scheme had created as many problems as it resolved. The 'thank you' letter she received from Nâzım after Münevver's arrival in Warsaw expressed an extraordinary ambivalence:

Dear Joyce,
The blessings of Allah be upon you. You have already qualified for heaven. Even though the Pope might not agree. I'd like to tell you a story. A poor Kurdish peasant is visiting a wealthy landlord, and the landlord slaughters a sheep in his honour and orders delicious pastries. He provides seven layers of mattresses for him to sleep on. But despite the seven layers of mattresses the peasant cannot sleep. 'I'm a poor pathetic Kurd', he says to himself. 'How can I ever repay the generosity of my host? I have no sheep, no mattresses, no honey, no flour. I'm going to be suffocated by this feeling of gratitude. My host will think that I'm an ungrateful person and don't deserve all these things. He too will suffer for the rest of his life. The best thing is to cut his throat. This will save everybody from embarrassment.'

Dear Joyce, now I feel like this Kurd. I shall never be able to repay what you have done for me. To save us both from embarrassment, maybe the best thing is to cut your throat? (Lussu, 36)

The letter she received from Münevver was even more poignant, describing how at the end of a nine-hour flight they were warmly welcomed by Polish people at Warsaw airport – but Nazım was not there. Next day they met, and he informed her that he was married to Vera. 'He became a Pasha with two wives', she wrote, 'and I felt so foolish' (Lussu, 36). Summing up this whole episode, Joyce wryly observed: 'Nazım has left, and the story about the beloved wife and son whom he has scarcely seen, which used to break people's hearts, has sunk to the bottom of a well' (Lussu, 37). Münevver remained for Nazım the 'woman on the horizon', living with his son at a safe distance. But it was not simply that the prospect of having to fulfil his family responsibilities was too much for him. The poet 'forever leaving' the cities and women he loved was guided by a more fundamental impulse. The element of separation seems to have been essential to his creative temperament, and in his late poetry it became fraught with intimations of death.

Stepping through thoughts of death

Nazım remained extraordinarily active in his final years despite his failing health. In September 1961, after helping Münevver settle in Warsaw, he visited Berlin, where he wrote the celebrated poem 'Autobiography', reviewing the paradoxical career of a poet who has 'slept in prisons and grand hotels' and 'fallen in love at almost sixty'. Despite its sweeping range of reference, the poem does not refer either to Münevver or to his son (A 7, 99–101). He returned to Moscow a few weeks later and resumed his public role, promoting the liberalization in the arts which had become possible under Khrushchev. On 18 November he gave a reading from his poems at the Mayakovsky Museum. First he recited his poem 'Caspian Sea' in Turkish, and then his translator Muza Pavlova read excerpts from *Human Landscapes*, which was about to be published in Russian. Another translator, David Samoylov, read some of his more recent poems, including 'Leipzig Letters' and 'Straw-Blond', and then Simonov read the poem 'Autobiography'. In the second half of the evening Nazım gave a talk about the changing role of the theatre in Soviet Society, mentioning the hurt he felt when *Ivan Ivanovich* was banned. This led him to touch on the sensitive topic of censorship, particularly the ban on Bulgakov's *The Master and Margarita*, and when he suggested that such writers deserved the same admiration as Pushkin and Dostoyevsky, he was warmly applauded (Tulyakova, 326-36). These ideas were further developed in an interview with his Italian translator Giovanni Crino. Responding to Crino's questions about the position of artists and writers in the Soviet Union, Nazım emphasized how important it was that Meyerhold and Mayakovsky had been rehabilitated. He praised the work of Yevtushenko and stressed how important it was that Tsvetayeva, Pasternak and Khlebnikov were available as models for younger writers (A 26, 160-5).

Nazım particularly admired the work of Pasternak. The two had been neighbours at Peredelkino, and the poet Gennady Aygi recalls one occasion when the two spent the whole evening together, reading poetry out loud and weeping with emotion. In Pasternak's eyes Nazım was a great 'freedom fighter' (Aygi, Interview, April 1997). When Pasternak was awarded the Nobel Prize for literature in 1958, after *Doctor Zhivago* was published abroad, he was ostracized by the Soviet authorities, who were scandalized by a novel which so overtly challenged the dogmas of Marxism. When Nazım was in Stockholm in 1958, he made a point of obtaining a copy and reading it there, although he did not venture to smuggle it back to Moscow. But he did attempt to persuade more liberal-minded members of the Central Committee to treat Pasternak with greater tolerance. 'Real poets', he declared, 'are always right, so we should thank them rather than punish them' (Tulyakova, 194).

Nazım's growing international stature meant that he could afford to deviate from the party line without incurring official censure. The year 1962 began auspiciously with a celebration at the Polytechnic Institute in Moscow to mark his sixtieth birthday, with the genial Ilya Ehrenburg presiding. The hall was packed, and the poet received a rapturous reception (Ehrenburg, 275). According to Vera, it was also in January 1962 that Nazım at last obtained a full Soviet passport, which simplified subsequent arrangements for foreign travel (Tulyakova, 140). He had previously needed to rely on Polish travel documents. This episode is significant for the light it throws on Nazım's cordial relations with Khrushchev, who by this date dominated Soviet politics. According to Abidin Dino, Nazım had just suffered the indignity of one of his articles being censored before publication in *Izvestia*. When he phoned the editorial office to complain, he was told by the editor, who happened to be Khrushchev's son-in-law, that as a foreigner he had no right to tell the Soviet authorities how to run their own affairs. In frustration he contacted Khrushchev himself, explained his dilemma and asked for a Soviet passport – which he then received within a matter of days. Yevtushenko reports that Nazım was delighted that at last he could write as a Soviet citizen, even though he added: 'I know I've got it right when the authorities don't like what I've written' (GC/TV 4).

The following month Nazım and Vera travelled to Egypt for a congress of the Asian and African Writers' Union, held at a time when the Sino-Soviet conflict was causing great tension between Peking and Moscow. Since Nazım supported the Soviet position, the Chinese tried to marginalize him by refusing him recognition as a Turkish delegate because he did not hold a Turkish passport. Nazım responded with considerable eloquence: 'I am entitled to represent Turkey', he began in his speech to the congress, 'because any writer who writes in the language of his people is entitled to represent them. [...] Unfortunately, at this moment there is no better poet than myself in my country' (Tulyakova, 259-63). He received a standing ovation, and the congress elected him chairman. The irony is that a poet who had always supported the revolutionary movement in China now heard that during the Cultural Revolution his books had been burned along with works by other pro-Soviet writers like Brecht and Neruda (Bezirci, 77). During the congress the ballet version of Nazım's *Legend of Love* was performed in Cairo by the Novosibirsk Opera Company, and Nazım and Vera were guests of honour. A day before the end of the congress, there was a reception at the Faruk Palace attended by the Egyptian president, Gamal Abdel Nasser. Later Nazım and Vera had a private meeting with Nasser, who invited Nazım to re-visit Cairo to support socialist developments in Egypt. During this visit he heard that two volumes of his poetry were to be published in Arabic (Tulyakova, 267-8).

Nazım's physical weakness did not deter him from attending further official functions in Prague, Berlin, Leipzig and Bucharest in the spring and early summer of 1962. His relationship with

Vera gave him emotional support, although it was never entirely harmonious. Her sense of frustration is illustrated by an episode in July, when they were back in Moscow for a ten-day congress of the World Council for Disarmament and Peace. Vera was employed by a Soviet news agency to interview the delegates; Nazım chaired the opening session, and Vera interviewed him too. However, he could not tolerate her spending time with other prominent figures, so he decided to invite about thirty delegates for an evening meal at their apartment so that she could finish the job in one evening. This put Vera in an impossible situation – how could she conduct the interviews in the available time when she was also expected to prepare supper? Nazım solved the problem by taking over the meeting himself. 'Comrades', he began, 'during the congress we learned that all the countries in the world are spending more than $120 billion on armaments. If each of you had to decide how this money should be spent, what would you decide?' All Vera was expected to do was write down their answers, and the task continued into the small hours. She expressed her resentment by refusing to let the final report appear under her name (Tulyakova, 187-91).

Through his marriage with Vera, Nazım experienced extremes of exhilaration and disillusionment, and these are reflected in his finest poems. The image of the railway journey, one of leitmotifs of his work, structures his most ambitious late poem, 'Straw-Blond' ('Saman Sarısı'), a 300-line elegy dedicated 'to Vera Tulyakova with my deep respect'. It was written at intervals during the most ambitious of his official tours, which took him in 1961 to Warsaw, Cracow, Prague, Moscow, Paris, Havana and back to Moscow. It is held together by the rhythm of the train and the recurrent motif of the sleeping compartment with a young woman lying in the lower berth. In a phantasmagoria reminiscent of Blaise Cendrars' *Prose of the Trans-Siberian*, political aspiration becomes intertwined with erotic desire. And time and space are transcended as Nazım recalls a conversation with Abidin Dino in Paris in which modern science and medieval mysticism become blended:

> My nineteenth year crosses Beyazit Square comes out on Red Square
> and goes down to Concorde I meet Abidin and we talk squares
> the day before yesterday Gagarin circles the biggest square of all [. . .]
> and a young woman sleeps in my attic room
> mixed with the chimneys of the Paris roofs

she hasn't slept so soundly in years
her straw-blond hair curled her blue eye-lashes like clouds on her face
with Abidin I discuss the space and the shape of the atom's seed
we speak of Rumi whirling in space [. . .]

The poem conveys a magnificent sense of the indivisibility of the
modern world, linking Havana with Warsaw, Paris with Prague,
the Turkish student revolt in Beyazit Square with the factory
workers of Nowa Huta. Yet the word which occurs most often
is 'separation' (*aynlık*) – an intense awareness that time is running
out. At the Caprice Bar in Cracow 'separation was on the table
between the coffee cup and my glass'. A similar mood undercuts
memories of homecoming to Moscow:

> [. . .] a young woman met me at the station
> her waist narrower than an ant's
> her hair straw-blond eyelashes blue
> I took her hand [. . .]
> Moscow was happy I was happy we were happy
> suddenly I lost you in Mayakovsky Square I lost you suddenly no not
> suddenly because I first lost the warmth of your hand in mine then
> the soft weight of your hand in my palm and then your hand and
> separation had set in long ago at the first touch of our fingers ...
> (A 7, 66-79; P, 215-28)

The Whitmanesque celebration of the dynamics of modern life
is infused with a sense of bereavement almost as poignant as in
'Poem of an End' by Maria Tsvetayeva, another poet whom
Nazım admired.

Nazım and Vera had their conflicts. He resented her visits to
her daughter, while her lack of Turkish created difficulties in
their social life. Turkish was part of the air Nazım breathed, and
his marriage led to friction with his Turkish-speaking friends,
especially the Turkologist Rady Fish, a close acquaintance at this
time. Fish gives a rather negative picture of the marriage, emphasizing that Nazım found the demands of keeping up with a
young wife extremely stressful (*Nokta*, 20 Nov. 1988). He evidently
felt that there was something contrived about the relationship,
with Nazım displaying his bride as if she were a work of art he
had created. He even suggests that Nazım would have been happier
if he had stayed with Galina. It was certainly a disadvantage that
he no longer had a doctor by his side to ensure that he took the
correct medication to counteract his angina: disregarding medical

advice, he started smoking again, a sure sign that he was finding
life difficult. In a poem of April 1962 he concedes that smoking
is a short cut to death (A 7, 123).

For a time Vera adapted to the demands of Nazım's life-style,
although having such an open house meant that she never knew
how many people to expect for dinner (Tulyakova, 315). She
needed some privacy, and it was around this time that they decided
to sleep in separate bedrooms. Nazım was subject to depressive
moods, insomnia and nightmares. Once again he found an outlet
for his frustrations in writing poetry – a series of epigrams dated
'Moscow, May 1962':

> I am living like dried beans lately
> like dry beans
> with dried beans one can make a stew
> from me one can't even make that.
> (A 7, 136)

'Vera's heart has doors which open and close quickly', he reflected
in an image which links their relationship with his own angina
(A 7, 125). The difficulties of their relationship are reflected in
a whole sequence of short, untitled poems, expressing anxiety:

> You are tired of carrying my weight
> [. . .]
> but the most unbearable weight will be
> when you feel inside you the weight of my footsteps
> fading into the distance.
> ('Yoruldun...', A 7, 137)

Another poem, dated 31 May 1962, sounds an even more disillusioned note:

> All the doors are closed, all the curtains are drawn
> [. . .]
> I am tired of running after the unattainable,
> I must have a cigarette.
> ('Bütün Kapılar', A 7, 137)

In November 1962, to relieve the stresses of their relationship,
he and Vera embarked on a tour of Western Europe, visiting
Milan, Florence and Rome before travelling on to Paris to celebrate
the new year (Tulyakova, 171, 367 & 407). Photographs taken
during this trip catch the liberated mood, and they particularly enjoyed
again being with Abidin and Güzin Dino in Paris (Fig. 32). They

32. Paris: Nazım and Vera with Hıfzı Topuz, Abidin and Güzin Dino.

had a surprise for them, since they had just received a food parcel
from Turkey sent by Şakir Eczacıbaşı, a businessman with an
interest in the arts. Nazım missed Turkish food, so the Dinos
prepared a feast using authentic ingredients. Among those who
joined them was the young novelist Yaşar Kemal, who had been
imprisoned in 1951 for campaigning for Nazım's release (Dino,
154). They enjoyed a New Year's Eve party at the apartment of
American communist friends, the heart specialist Hershel and his
wife Dora, a poet. There was also a pancake party with Aragon
and his wife Elsa, and at one of these Paris gatherings they met
Picasso. Apart from visiting theatres and attending literary discussions, Nazım went on a spending spree. He insisted on buying
expensive shoes and clothes for his glamorous young wife, including
an eye-catching scarlet dress that made Vera feel self-conscious.
Nazım's wife had to look elegant at soirées attended by Aragon,
Dobzynski and other left-wing intellectuals and their partners.
The glamour of Paris did not tempt Nazım to defect, and on 4

January 1963 he and Vera returned to Moscow (Tulyakova, 34, 119, 143-5, 358-9, 376, 388 & 410).

Nazım's journeys continued into the last months of his life. In February 1963 he attended a conference of African and Asian writers in Tanzania and his long poem 'Report from Tanzania' in the form of letters addressed to Vera describes his experiences day by day, including the life he imagines Vera living without him. The tone recalls the panegyrics of Whitman and Mayakovsky, but the poem also incorporates more realistic details like a leaking roof that needs repairing and the water and electricity supplies that are still not connected. It ends with hopeful images of an Africa, where the anti-imperialist struggles in Angola, Mozambique, Uganda and South Africa still continued; at the same time the continent is at a cross-roads between slavery and freedom (A 157-71).

These final journeys brought emotional renewal. A poem written in May 1962 reflects this life-affirming mood: 'I stepped through my thoughts of death / and put on the June leaves of the boulevards [...]' (A 7, 134). His late poetry, particularly 'Autobiography', celebrates the life of a poet who has experienced the full Faustian range of joy and suffering: 'Even if today in Berlin I'm croaking with grief / I can say I've lived like a human being' ('Otobiyografi', A 7, 99; P, 229). Memories of childhood come flooding back, especially in the poem 'Things I Didn't Know I Loved'. Again the poet is on a train, aware of merging with a great poetic tradition as haunting images flicker past the darkening window:

> Wading through a dark muddy street I'm going to the shadow play
> Ramazan night
> a paper lantern leading the way
> maybe nothing like this ever happened
> maybe I read somewhere an eight-year-old boy
> > going to the shadow play
> Ramazan night in Istanbul holding his grandfather's hand
> > his grandfather has on a fez and is wearing the fur coat
> > > with a sable collar over his robe
> > and there's a lantern in the servant's hand
> > and I can't contain myself for joy
> > > ('Severmişim Meğer', A 7, 119-23; P, 231)

But memory cannot entirely counteract the advance of years:

> I'm getting used to growing old
> the hardest art in the world –

knocking on doors for the last time
endless separation ...
[...]
death has sent me its loneliness first.
                    ('Kocalmağa Alışıyorum'; A 7, 156; P, 236)

Some critics have dismissed Nazım's late poetry as over-effusive, suggesting that he let his feelings run away with him. 'Because of you my life is like a succulent slice of melon,' he wrote in August 1960 in a poem addressed to Vera. 'Because of you I don't let death come in' (A 7, 53). Ekber Babayev warned Vera that Nazım's infatuation was making him a laughing-stock. She recalled people saying: 'Nazım has fallen madly in love with Vera. He's started dedicating his poetry to her. [...] Please gently warn him about it.' When Vera passed this advice on to Nazım, he reacted furiously: 'It is because we love each other that we are able to live proudly and honestly. [...] It would be ridiculous only if we did not love each other' (Tulyakova, 239-44). He remained a romantic communist till the end, making no secret of the personal values that inspired his public commitments.

The most daring of Nazım's achievements in these years is his autobiographical novel *Yaşamak Güzel Şey Be Kardeşim* (The Romantics). Discussing this project with one of his comrades in 1958, he remarked on the impossibility of writing a factual record of the Turkish Communist Party because of the need to maintain confidentiality about illegal activities. However, the use of semi-fictional disguises enabled him to reconstruct his experiences in a compelling narrative form, juxtaposing the exhilarating early years in Moscow with the grim ordeals of arrest and imprisonment in Turkey. He takes as his starting point the anguish of a man on the run who has been bitten by a stray dog and is in hiding in Izmir in daily fear of developing rabies. This account of the sufferings of left-wing activists, with its complex treatment of time and memory, is a disconcerting blend of fact and fiction. Biographers who have tried to mine the novel for facts about Nazım's early life have been baffled by the allusive narrative, but the book is now recognized as one of his most original literary achievements. It was Louis Aragon who suggested the title *Les Romantiques* for the French edition, translated by Münevver, which appeared in 1964 – two years before it could be published in Turkish.

Few exiled writers can have had such a late flowering. While intellectual freedom in Turkey was stifled in the Menderes years, the language of Turkish poetry attained an unprecedented vitality in exile through poems jotted down by a hand still shaped by the Ottoman heritage, in railway carriages, hotel rooms and conference halls throughout the socialist world. Between 1958 and 1963 Nazım wrote over 150 poems, ranging from poignant lyrical reflections to rhapsodic travelogues. His pride in Soviet achievements is expressed rather predictably in a tribute to the cosmonaut Yuri Gararin, written in Paris in April 1961 (A 7, 64-5). But even in the most political poems Nazım retains an individual voice. In one of his prison letters to Kemal Tahir, he had suggested that in some ways his poetry was better than Mayakovsky's – 'even if only slightly better' (AM 3, 69-70). With the passage of time and the maturing of Nazım's lyrical gifts, the difference became even more marked. Where even Mayakovsky's most personal poetry has a declamatory element, Nazım achieves intimacy of tone even when his subject matter is political. Two poems written on successive days in the spring of 1958 display his imaginative spectrum. The first, 'Strontium 90', written on 6 March in Warsaw, is a sombre warning of the effects of radioactive fall-out from atmospheric nuclear tests, which may bring 'death to the world' (A 6, 132). The next day he wrote his celebrated 'Fable', which places individual consciousness within an ontological framework:

> Resting by the water-side
> the plane tree, I, the cat, the sun and our life.
> Our reflections are thrown on the water,
> the plane tree's, mine, the cat's, the sun's and our life's
> The sparkle of the water hits us
> the plane tree, me, the cat, the sun and our life.

Like most of Nazım's late poems, this 'Fable' is written in free verse, but the vowel harmonies which govern Turkish word-formation enable him to maintain melodic control through patterns of assonance and counterpoint. Melody and meaning converge in a hypnotic drift towards eternity:

> First the cat will go
> its reflection will be lost on the water.
> Then I will go

> my reflection will be lost on the water.
> Then the plane tree will go
> its reflection will be lost on the water.
> Then the water will go
> the sun will remain
> then it will go too.
> (A 6, 133; T 214-15)

Using the simplest Turkish words, the poet succeeds in re-animating a tradition of meditations on transience traceable to the *Rubaiyat* of Omar Khayyam; but he does so within the framework of a modern cosmology.

Nazım's late poetry owes its resonance to intimations of death, although his feelings for Vera helped him to face that final separation with courage. Even while actively involved in international politics, he remained conscious of his precarious physical condition. Before leaving for Tanganyika in February 1963 he wrote a letter asking the Central Committee to provide financial support for Vera and for his son Mehmet Nazım if the income from his copyrights was insufficient. This does not mean that he contemplated death with equanimity. At the beginning of 1963, Vera records, Nazım suffered from nightmares and insomnia (Tulyakova, 121 & 136); he would wake up screaming from recurrent nightmares about being attacked by dogs with rabies – the fate which befell his father. In May 1963 they went to stay at a dacha in Staraya Ruza, 100 kilometres from Moscow, while their apartment was being repaired, and on long walks through the woods they were able to talk about death with more detachment. As they contemplated the beauty of the landscape, they heard in the distance the music of a funeral procession. Of his own funeral arrangements Nazım said: 'The Writers Union will know what to do. Just phone them' (Tulyakova, 91, 419 & 422).

This same detached attitude inspired the poem 'My Funeral Service'. In April 1963 Ekber Babayev was surprised to receive a phone call from Nazım saying that he had written something rather special (Erdinç, 32). He was taken aback by what seemed an inescapably morbid theme, only to be captivated by the life-affirming tone of the poem:

> Will my funeral start out from our courtyard?
> How will you get me down from the third floor?

The coffin won't fit in the elevator,
and the stairs are awfully narrow.

Maybe there'll be sun knee-deep in the yard, and pigeons,
maybe snow filled with the cries of children,
maybe rain with its wet asphalt.
And the trash can will stand in the courtyard as always.

[. . .]

Our kitchen window will watch me leave.
Our balcony will see me off with the wash on the line.
In this yard I was happier than you'll ever know.
Neighbours, I wish you all long lives.

(A 7, 177; P, 239)

The poem effectively refutes the platitude that 'we die alone'.
The place of death is not the cemetery but a courtyard filled
with the cries of children. For Nazım working out feelings through
poetry served as a therapy, reconciling him with the harshest
aspects of existence.

Vera has left a poignant description of the last day of Nazım's
life: 'On the Sunday, the day before you died, I woke up early
and brought you a cup of Turkish coffee and other things. You
drank your coffee and lay there with all the newspapers around
you. I went to the study and started working quite fast.' After a
while Nazım asked her to work in his bedroom so that he could
keep her within his field of vision. A conversation began, and
Nazım talked for two hours about his life, not in snippets but
conveying a sense of the whole. He remembered his mother,
which was unusual since he still found her death distressing. Even
though she was so much in love with his father, Nazım explained,
she had to leave him because separation was more bearable than
jealousy. But after their divorce they remained friends and would
talk in an affectionate but melancholy way about their experience
'as if life had passed through their fingers like a river, flowing
nearby, and they could never find the source' (Tulyakova, 425-7).
That evening, on 2 June 1963, they went for a walk in the park
and sat on a bench under a chestnut tree. Then they went back
home, took their sleeping pills and went to bed. Nazım woke
the following morning as usual, around 7.20, and went to the
front door when the post arrived (Tulyakova, 434-5). After a
while she began to wonder why he had not returned and went
to look for him. He was collapsed and unconscious, slumped

against the door. She phoned her friend Tosya, who alerted the hospital, and a first-aid team arrived with a doctor from Kremlin Hospital, but Nazım was already dead.

Looking for his passport in the pocket of his jacket, Vera found a photograph of herself, with an eight-line poem written on the back (Tulyakova, 438):

Come she said to me	*Gelsene dedi bana*
stay she said to me	*Kalsana dedi bana*
smile she said to me	*Gülsene dedi bana*
die she said to me	*Ölsene dedi bana*
I came	*Geldim*
I stayed	*Kaldım*
I smiled	*Güldüm*
I died	*Öldüm*

(A 7, 185)

Nazım's poetic gift enable of him to 'step through thoughts of death', transposing profound anxieties into simple words. The poem blends the lapidary utterance of final words with the language of lovers *in extremis* and the baby-talk of mother and child.

Ten years earlier, in the poem 'Vasiyet' (Testament), written while recovering from his first serious heart attack at the Barvikha sanatorium, he had expressed the wish to be buried in an Anatolian cemetery under a plane tree (A 6, 21). But in the event he was accorded something like a state funeral, with eulogies by representatives of the Party and the Writers' Union. His body was laid out in the stone courtyard of Writers' Union, where Vera and Galina were joined many Russian friends and members of Turkish Communist Party. Yıldız Sertel arrived from Baku, and other friends came from as far away as Paris. On the day of the burial, 5 June, Münevver arrived from Poland with Mehmet Nazım. The body was taken from the Writers' Union to the cemetery outside the Novodevichy convent, where the most celebrated Russian poets and politicians are buried. Tributes in Russian were given by Simonov and other members of the Writers' Union, but there were no speeches in Turkish, as Münevver reported in a letter 20 June to Aziz Nesin (now in the Nesin Archives). None of the three women spoke, but Vera, in tears, threw a handkerchief on the coffin as it was lowered into the grave. Galina, Münevver and Mehmet Nazım stood in silence. For the twelve-year-old boy the experience, of seeing his father's body laid out at the Writers' Union was traumatic: 'There I saw my father', he later recalled in an interview, 'stretched out... just like that on a table. A woman was holding his body and wailing. This was the wife he married late in life.... At first I was very frightened.... It was the first time I saw a dead body... and the dead man was my father...' (Mehmet, 14). Münevver, wrote of her pride in her son in a letter of 18 June 1963 to Nazım's sister Samiye:

I went to Moscow with Memo. It was an impressive and very moving ceremony. The boy was very brave. He stood up for hours like a man. But at the last moment, before they closed the coffin, they asked him to kiss his father, he did and burst into tears. Memo has been such an unlucky child. He never experienced what it is to have a father! I put flowers on his coffin on your behalf. [...] The fact that he lies next to Chekhov, Turgenev, Gogol and Mayakovsky is perhaps a comfort (Özbilgen, 182).

A block of black granite now marks Nazım's grave, with a bas-relief inspired by his early poem 'The Man Walking Against the Wind'. When a bystander at the funeral was asked the cause of death, she replied: 'He died of a burst heart' (Ehrenburg, 270-5).

After the funeral, the question of Nazım's estate had to be resolved. In a will written in Russian, dated 10 September 1959, he had divided the most valuable item, the copyright in his literary work, between two beneficiaries, leaving three-quarters to 'my wife Münevver and my son' and the remaining quarter to the Turkish Communist Party. He had deposited this will, with the Writers' Union, and it was accepted for probate. Vera, who had been his wife under Russian law, was not mentioned in this will, but she was able to retain the apartment in Moscow and some of Nazım's personal possessions. A plaque on the wall outside the house says: 'The Turkish poet Nazım Hikmet, holder of the International Peace Prize, lived and worked here 1952-1963'.

The news of Nazım's death was followed by the publication of many tributes from admirers, who included Anna Seghers, Louis Aragon, Jean-Paul Sartre and Philippe Soupault. Sartre singled out the 'melancholy and ironic clarity of his spirit' as Nazım's most distinctive gift (Aksoy, 182). At Aragon's suggestion, the text of *Les Romantiques* was published in Paris as a tribute to his memory. A poem by Pablo Neruda, published in *El Siglio* on 9 July 1963 (Neruda 1982, 48-9), ends with the lines:

Gracias por lo que fuiste y por el fuego
que tu canción dejó para siempre encendido.

Thanks for what you were and for the fire
which your song has left forever burning.

Epilogue

The history of the communist movement since Nazım's death has clearly not fulfilled his expectations. In the Soviet Union the thaw of the late 1950s did not lead to the more open and tolerant form of communist society which he envisaged. After the stagnation of the Brezhnev era, the Gorbachev reforms came too late to save the communist bloc from disintegration. The Turkish Communist Party suffered a similar fate. Initially, the Turkish left benefited from the reforms introduced by the Constitution of 1961, which heralded a period of liberalization and of dynamic political debate. For the first time Nazım's writings became widely available, even though he himself did not live to see his major works published in his native language. But this brief period of liberalization was followed by a renewed persecution of socialists and intellectuals. Parliamentary government was suspended for substantial periods as a result of military coups in 1971 and 1980, and once again it became a criminal offence to be caught in possession of an edition of Nazım's poetry.

Since 1980s the revival of Islam as political force has cast a further shadow over the future of the Turkish Republic. Repeated physical assaults on progressive Turkish writers culminated in the Sivas disaster of July 1993. During a conference to commemorate the sixteenth-century mystic poet Pir Sultan Abdal, thirty-seven people were burned to death in a hotel fire started by right-wing religious fundamentalists. Those who perished included Asım Bezirci, a literary scholar noted for his fine edition of Nazım's writings. These developments confirm the validity of Nazım's warning against the political exploitation of Islam. This debate has intensified as a result of the proposal that the poet's remains should be reburied in Turkey, in fulfilment of his own wishes. A report by Stephen Kinzer in the *New York Times* of 27 February 1997 emphasized the crucial importance which this proposal acquired in the context of the struggle between secular and religious ideologies.

During the thirty-five years since his death, Nazım has come to epitomize the principles of political courage and radical dissent.

A whole generation of Turkish writers, from Aziz Nesin to Yaşar Kemal, has been inspired by his example, and his international admirers range from Harold Pinter to Yevgeny Yevtushenko. It is not simply Nazım's personal courage but the imaginative power of his writings that gives his work its enduring value. He was by no means simply the prophet of a new dawn. The struggle against oppression, imprisonment and exile forms his most poignant theme. In his finest work the experience of prison intensifies the longing for freedom, just as the light shines most brightly in the darkness. Persecution and exile, even ill health and the approach of death, reinforce the spirit of resistance and the longing for liberation. In prison Nazım became aware that his mission was to provide a voice for those whom society had silenced, and in *Human Landscapes* he succeeded in expressing the sufferings and aspirations of a whole generation. Despite the controversies associated with his name, Nazım has become a kind of Turkish national poet. In 1996 an adaptation of his epic of the War of Liberation was performed at the State Theatre in Ankara.

Nazım's poetry speaks to a wider world through translations into many different languages. In the United States the Persea Press translations by Randy Blasing and Mutlu Konuk have greatly enhanced his reputation, while in Britain a new translation of poems and letters is being prepared by Ruth Christy and Richard McKane for Anvil Press. In France a further selection of Nazım's poems, translated by Münevver Andaç, is due to be published by Gallimard, while in Germany the early translations produced in East Berlin have been superseded by the bilingual editions of Dağyeli Verlag. Nazım's career has also been featured in a series of television programmes, including a Hessischer Rundfunk production by Elisabeth Weyer (1987) and a four-part Turkish documentary by Koray Düzgören and Güneri Civaoğlu (1991). An American documentary is also due to be completed by Substantial Films Inc in New York produced by Stephanie Capparell and Niyazi Dalyancı.

Nazım has ceased to be a cult figure of the communist world and become a poet of universal significance. 'I want my poems to address all my readers' problems' he remarked towards the end of his life. 'If a young man falls in love with girl, he should be able to read my poems to his sweetheart. An old man in the grip of sadness about the approach of death should read my poems.

When a bureaucrat is giving you a hard time, read my poems.
A communist writer has to reflect all human feelings.' The first
appreciation of Nazım's work to appear in English, published in
The Bookman in 1932, compared his work with that of Byron:
'As Byron, with his dark beauty and romantic pessimism, was
the symbol of the nineteenth century poet, so is Nazım Hikmet,
with his flashing blue eyes and his positive outlook on the world
and the people living in it, that of the twentieth century'. The
achievements recorded in this biography show how those prophetic
words were fulfilled through the poet's creative engagement with
the political events and ideologies of his age. Nazım's poetry and
plays, his letters and autobiographical writings, provide a compelling
testimony to the resilience of the human spirit under pressure:

> Being imprisoned is not the problem
> The problem is how to avoid surrender.

Bibliography

PRIMARY

References to the published writings of Nazım Hikmet are identified by abbreviations (followed by volume and page number):

Collected works

A: the Adam Yayınları edition of Nazım Hikmet's Collected Works (ed. Memet Fuat), 27 vols, 1st edn, Istanbul, 1988-1991.
B: *Bütün Eserleri*, ed. E. Babayev, 8 vols, Sophia: Narodna Prosveta, 1967-68.
C: *Tüm Eserleri*, ed. Asım Bezirci and Şerif Hulusi, 8 vols, Cem, 1975-80.

Letters

AM 1: Nazım Hikmet, *Nazım ile Piraye* (Mektuplar 1), ed. Memet Fuat, Adam, 1988.
AM 2: Nazım Hikmet, *Cezaevinden Memet Fuat'a* (Mektuplar 2), Adam, 1988.
AM 3: Nazım Hikmet, *Kemal Tahire Mapusaneden* (Mektuplar 3), Adam, 1990.
Hikmet M: Nazım Hikmet, *Kemal Tahir'e Maphusaneden Mektuplar*, Ankara: Bilgi, 1968

Individual works

Hikmet 1965: Nazım Hikmet, *Kurtuluş Savaşı Destanı*, Yön Yayınları, 1965.
Hikmet 1986: Nazım Hikmet, *Kuvay-i-Milliye*, ed. Cevdet Kudret, Ankara: Bilgi, 3rd edn 1986.

Translations

HL: *Human Landscapes*, tr. Randy Blasing and Mutlu Konuk, New York: Persea, 1983.
ML: *Menschenlandschaften*, tr. Ümit Güney and Norbert Ney, with illustrations by Abidin Dino, 4 vols, Hamburg: Buntbuch Verlag, 1978.

MS: *The Moscow Symphony*, tr. Taner Baybars, London: Rapp and Whiting, 1970.

P: *Poems of Nazım Hikmet*, tr. Randy Blasing and Mutlu Konuk, New York: Persea, 1994.

SF: Nazım Hikmet, 'Erinnerungen an Meyerhold' in *Sinn und Form* (1959), 5/6, pp.916-26.

SP: *Selected Poems*, tr. Taner Baybars, London: Cape, 1967.

SPP: *Selected Poetry*, tr. Randy Blasing and Mutlu Konuk, New York: Persea, 1986.

T: *Penguin Book of Turkish Verse*, ed. Nermin Menemencioğlu, Harmondsworth: Penguin, 1978.

Where no English source is given, the translation is by Saime Göksu and Edward Timms.

SECONDARY

References to secondary literature are normally identified by author and page number (in brackets). Where several books are cited by a single author, or by authors with the same name, the page reference may be preceded by name and publication date (followed by 'a' and 'b' for two books published in the same year); by name and initial; or by volume number. The name of the publisher is given wherever possible. The place of publication of Turkish books is Istanbul unless otherwise indicated.

Adıvar, Halide Edib, *Türkün Ateşle Imtihanı*, Çan, 1962.

Ahmad, Feroz, *The Making of Modern Turkey*, London and New York, 1993.

Aksoy, Mehmet et al. eds, *Nazım Hikmet, Türkülerimizden Korkuyorlar*, ed. Mehmet Aksoy and others, Berlin: Türkiye Akademikerler ve Sanatçılar, 1977.

Alliluyeva, Svetlana, *Only One Year*, Harmondsworth: Penguin, 1971.

Alper, Osman Rauf, *Mülteci Komunist*, Timaş, 1995.

Anka, Revue d'art et de littérature de Turquie, ed. Paul Dumont, Paris, 1986.

Ataöv, Türkkaya, *Nazım Hikmetin Hasreti*, May, 1976.

Atatürk: Gazi M. Kemal, *Söylev (Nutuk)*, Ankara Universitesi, 1966 (revised reprint of 1938 edn.)

Aydemir 1986a: Aydın Aydemir, *Nazım, Gençlik ve Mahpusane Yılları*, Broy, 1986.

Aydemir 1986b: Aydın Aydemir, *Nazım Nazım*, Broy, 1986.

Aydemir 1970: Aydın Aydemir, *Nazım*, Tisa, 1970.

Babayev, Ekber, *Yaşamı ve Yapıtlanyle Nazım Hikmet*, Cem, 1976.

Balaban 1979: Ibrahim Balaban, *Şair Baba ve Damdakiler*, Aydınlık, 1979.

354 *Bibliography*

Balaban 1992: *Ibrahim Balaban:Yaşamı, Sanatı, Anılar, Yankılar*, ed. Ahmet Köksak, Bilim, 1992.

Belli, Mihri, *Insanlar Tanıdım* (2 vols), Milliyet, 1989.

Bercavi, A. Faik, *Nazımla 1933-1938 Yılları*, Cem, 1992.

Berkes, Niyazi, *The Development of Secularism in Turkey*, Montreal: McGill University Press, 1964; reprint London: Hurst, 1998.

Bezirci, Asım, *Nazım Hikmet: Yaşamı, Eseri, Sanatı*, Berbes Amaç, 1989.

Braun, Edward, *The Theatre of Meyerhold*, London: Eyre Methuen, 1979.

Brecht, Bertolt, *Letters*, tr. Ralph Manheim, London: Methuen, 1990.

Bursalı: *Türkiye Komunist ve Işçi Hareketi*, ed. Fatma Bursalı, Aydınlık Yayınları, 1979.

Carr, Bernard Hallett, *The Bolshevik Revolution, 1917-1923*, Harmondsworth: Penguin, 1966.

Caute, David, *The Fellow Travellers: Intellectual Friends of Communism*, New Haven and London: Yale University Press, 1988.

Celal, Peride, *Kurtlar*, Can, 1991.

CER: *Cambridge Encylopedia of Russia and the Soviet Union*, ed. A. Brown et al., Cambridge University Press, 1982.

Charters, Ann and Samuel, *I Love: The Story of Vladimir Mayakovsky and Lili Brik*, London: André Deutsch, 1979.

Coşkun: Atilla Coşkun, *Siyasal Yaşamından Kesitlerle Nazım'ın Davaları*, Cem 1989.

Coşkun K 1988: Kıymet Coşkun, *Nazım Hikmetin Yurtdaşlık Hakkı*, Cem, 1988.

Coşkun K 1990: Kıymet Coşkun, *Fotoğraflarla Nazım Hikmet*, Cem, 1990.

Darendeli, Ilhan, *Türkiyede Komünist Hareketleri*, Toker, 1979.

Denniston, Robin, *Churchill's Secret War*, Stroud, England: Sutton Publishing, 1997.

Dinamo, Hasan Izettin, *TKP ve Aydınlar*, Yalçın, 1989.

Dino, Güzin, *Gel Zaman, Git Zaman*, Can, 1991.

Dimitrova, Blaga, *Nazım Hikmet Bulgaristanda: Yolculuk Notları*, Sofia: Narodno Proseta, 1955.

Duberman, Martin, *Paul Robeson*, Ballantine, 1990.

Ehrenburg, Ilya, *The Post War Years*, London: MacGibbon & Kee, 1966.

Erdinç, Fahri, *Kalkın Nazım'a Gidelim*, Varlık, 1987.

Erduran, Refik, *Gülerek*, Cem, 1987.

Ertuğrul, Muhsin, *Anılar: Benden Sonra Tufan Olmasın*, Eczacıbaşı Vakfı, 1989.

Eyuboğlu, Ismet Zeki, *Şeyh Bedrettin: Varidat*, Der, 4th edn, 1995.

Fevralski, Alexander, *Nazımdan Anılar*, Cem, 1979.

Fish, Rady, *Nazım'ın Çilesi*, Gün, 1969.

Garrard, John and Carol, *Inside the Writers' Union*, London: I.B. Tauris, 1990.

Bibliography 355

Gronau, Dietrich, *Nazım Hikmet,* Reinbek: Rowohlt, 1991.

Gövsa, Ibrahim Alaettin, *Meşhur Adamlar Ansiklopedisi,* vol 3.

Göze, Ergun, *Peyami Nazım Hikmet Kavgası,* Yağmur, 1975.

GSE: *Great Soviet Encyclopedia,* vol. 5, p. 575 (Peace); vol. 17, p. 27 (Nazım Hikmet Ran).

Günçıkan, Berat, *Gölgenin Kadınlan,* Yapı Kredi Bankası, 1995.

Günyol, Vedat, 'Benim Nazım Hikmet'im' in *Yeni Ufuklar,* 1976, no. 273.

Habib, Ismail (ed.), *Yurddan Yazılar,* anthology, Cumhuriyet, 1943.

Halman, Talat Sait (ed.), *Contemporary Turkish Literature: Fiction and Poetry,* East Brunswick, NJ: Associated University Presses, 1982.

Harris, George S., *Origins of Communism in Turkey,* Stanford: Hoover Institution, 1967.

Hayward, Max, and Leopold Labedz (eds). *Literature and Revolution in Soviet Russia 1917-62,* Oxford University Press, 1963; esp. the articles 'Zhdanovism' by Walter N. Vickery (pp. 99-124) and 'The Repertoire of the Fifties' by Franois de Liencourt (pp. 150-69).

Helsinki: *Helsinki World Peace Assembly Report,* 1955.

Heper: *Political Parties and Democracy in Turkey,* ed. Metin Heper and Jacob M. Landau, London: I. B. Tauris, 1991.

Heuss, Theodor, *Schattenbeschwörung. Randfiguren der Geschichte,* Stuttgart–Tübingen: Rainer Wunderlich, 1947.

Heym, Stefan, *Nachruf,* Munich: Bertelsmann, 1988.

Hulusi, Şerif, 'Kurtuluş Savaşı ve Nazım Hikmet'in Kuvayi Millliye Destanı' in *Eylem,* vol. 2 (1965), no. 17, pp. 55-8.

Hüsnü, Şefik, *Yaşamı Yazılan Yoldaşlan,* Sosyalist, 1994.

Ihmalyan, Vartan, *Bir Yaşam Öyküsü,* Cem, 1989.

İleri, Rahsi Nuri, *Atatürk ve Kommunizm,* Sarmal, 1995.

Kadir, A., *1938 Harbokulu Olayı ve Nazım Hikmet,* Istanbul Matbaası, 1967.

Karaca 1992: Emin Karaca, *Nazım Hikmetin Şiirinde Gizli Tarih,* Belge, 1992.

Karaca 1995a: Emin Karaca, *Nazım'ın Aşklan,* Milliyet, 1995.

Karaca 1995b: Emin Karaca, *Yeraltı Dünyadan Başka Bir Yıldız Değildi,* Yön, 1995.

Karaca 1996: Emin Karaca, *Eski Tüfekler'in Sonbahan,* Toplumsal Dönüşüm, 1996.

Karal, Enver Ziya, *Osmanlı Tarihi,* Ankara, 1956, vol. 7.

Karaosmanoğlu, Yakup Kadri, *Gençlik ve Edebiyat Hatıralan,* Ankara: Bilgi, 1969.

Katz, Steven T., *The Holocaust and Comparative History,* New York: Leo Baeck Institute, 1993.

Kemal, Orhan, *Nazım Hikmetle 3,5 yıl,* Tekin, 1976.

356 Bibliography

Kinross, Lord, *Atatürk: Rebirth of a Nation*, London: Weidenfeld & Nicolson, 1964.

Kıvılcımlı 1994: Hikmet Kıvılcımlı, *Günlük Anılar*, Diyalektik, 1994.

Kıvılcımlı 1979: Hikmet Kıvılcımlı, *Kim Suçlamış, Breznev'e Mektup*, Yol, 1979.

Korcan: 1988: Kerim Korcan, *Ateşten Köprü*, Bibliotek, 1988.

Korcan 1989: Kerim Korcan, *Harbiye kazanı*, E-Yayınları, 1989.

Kurdakul, Şükran, *Nazım'ın Bilinmeyen Mektupları*, Broy, 1986.

Landau, Jacob M., *Pan-Turkism: From Irredentism to Cooperation*, London: Hurst, 1995.

Lewis, Bernard, *The Emergence of Modern Turkey*, Oxford University Press, 1968.

Lontay, László, 'Beszélgetés Nazim Hikmettel' (Conversation with Nazım Hikmet) in *Szinház és Filmmüvészet*, March 1955.

Loti, Pierre, *Aziyade*, Paris: Flammarion, 1989.

Lussu, Joyce Salvatori, *Buluşma*, Açılım, 1992.

Mehmet: *Mehmet Nazım'ı Anlatıyor*, Ankara: Kardeş, 1970.

Menemencioğlu, Nermin, 'Nazım Hikmet', 5-page typewritten reminiscence, 1979 (Saime Göksu collection).

Mouvafac, Nermine (= Nermin Menemencioğlu), 'A Poet of the New Turkey' in *The Bookman*, New York, January–February 1932, pp. 508–15.

Neruda 1977: Pablo Neruda, *Memoirs*, tr. Hardie St Martin, Harmondsworth: Penguin, 1977.

Neruda 1982: Pablo Neruda, *El Fino del Viaje*, Seix Barral, 1982.

Nesimi, Abidin, *Yıllann içinden*, Gözlem, 1977.

New Turkey: *The New Turkey: Articles Reprinted from the Turkish Number of 'The Times'*, London, 1938.

NHBG: Nazım Hikmet Bibliographical Guide of Publications in Russian, Moscow, 1962 (numbered list of 1,067 works in Russian by or about Nazım).

Nurettin 1986: Müzehher Vala Nurettin, *Va Nu'lara Mektuplar*, Cem, 1986.

Nurettin 1991: Müzehher Vala Nurettin, *Bir Dönemin Tanıklığı*, Cem, 1991.

Orwell: *Orwell: The War Broadcasts*, ed. W. J. West, London: Duckworth, 1985.

Özdamar, Emine Sevgi, *Das Leben ist eine Karawanserei*, Cologne: Kiepenheuer, 1992.

Özbilgen, Füsun, *Sana Tütün ve Tesbih Yolluyorum: Semiha Berksoy*, Broy, 1985.

Özön, Nijat, *Türk Sineması Kronoljisi*, Ankara: Bilgi, 1968.

Paulu, Burton, *Radio and Television Broadcasting in Eastern Europe*, Minneapolis: University of Minnesota Press, 1974.

Petrov, Angel, 'Söylenen Sözlerin Büyük Değeri', in *Yeni Düşün* (June 1987), pp. 219-23.

Riddell, John (ed), *To See The Dawn: Baku 1920 – First Congress of the Poples of the East*, New York: Pathfinder, 1993.

Roman, Erem Melike, *Nazım Hikmet Romanyada*, Broy, 1987.

Rubenstein, Joshua, *Tangled Loyalties: The Life and Times of Ilya Ehrenburg*, London: I.B. Tauris, 1996.

Rudnitsky, Konstantin, *Russian and Soviet Theatre Tradition and the Avant-garde*, London: Thames and Hudson, 1988.

Sadi, Kerim, *Nazım Hikmetin Ilk Şiirleri*, May, 1969.

Sayılgan, Aclan, *Türk Solunun 94 Yılı*, Arık, 1968.

Sebük, Mehmet Ali, *Korkunc Adli Hata ve Nazım'ın Özgürlük Savaşı*, Cem, 1978.

Seghers, Anna, *Aufsätze, Ansprachen, Essays 1954-1979*, Berlin: Aufbau, 1980.

Sertel 1977: Zekeriya Sertel, *Hatırladıklarım*, Gözlem, 1977.

Sertel 1978: Zekeriya Sertel, *Nazım Hikmet'in Son Yılları*, Milliyet, 1978.

Sertel 1991: Zekeriya Sertel, *Mavi Gözlü Dev*, Belge, 1991.

Sertel S: Sabiha Sertel, *Roman Gibi*, Ant, 1969.

Sertel Y: Yıldız Sertel, *Ardımdaki Yıllar*, Milliyet, 1990.

Siao, Eva, *Çin Hayallerim, Hayatım*, AFA, 1994.

Simonov, Konstantin, *Bugün ve Yıllar Önce*, Ankara: Söylem.

Slonim, Marc, *Soviet Russian Literature*, 2nd edn, Oxford University Press, 1977.

Spuler, Christa-Ursula, *Das türkische Drama der Gegenwart: Eine literar-historische Studie*, Leiden: Brill, 1968.

Stalin: Joseph V., *Works*, Moscow: Foreign Languages Publishing House, 1954.

STMA: *Sosyalizm ve Toplumsal Mücadeleler Ansiklopedisi*, 6 vols, İletişim, 1989.

Sülker 1-5: Kemal Sülker, *Nazım Hikmetin Gerçek Yaşamı*, Yalçın, 5 vols 1987.

Sülker 1968: Kemal Sülker, *Nazım Hikmetin Polemikleri*, Ant, 1968.

Sülker 1974: Kemal Sülker, *Nazım Hikmet Dosyası*, May, 1974.

Sülker 1976: Kemal Sülker, *Şair Nazım Hikmet*, May, 1976.

Sülker 1980: Kemal Sülker, *Nazım Hikmetin Bilinmeyen Iki Şiir Defteri*, Yazko, 1980.

Sülker 1988: Kemal Sülker, *Nazım Hikmet Orhan Kemal Dostluğu*, Amaç, 1988.

Süreyya, Şevket, *Suyu Arayan Adam*, Remzi, 1993.

Şener, Erman, *Kurtuluş Savaşı ve Sinemamız*, Dizi, 1970.

Tahir, Kemal, *Kemal Tahirden Fatma Irfana Mektuplar*, Sander, 1979.

Tata, Sabri, *Türk Komünistlerinin Bulgaristan Macerası*, Boğaziçi, 1993.

Tansel, Fevziye Abdullah, *Nazım Paşanın Anıları*, Arba, 1992.

Tevetoğlu, Fethi, *Türkiyede Sosyalist ve Komunist Faaliyetleri*, Ankara, 1967.

358   Bibliography

TKP: *TKP 65 Yaşında: Türkiye Komünist Partisinin Savaş Tarihinden Sayfalar*, Essen: Ermis, 1986.

Topcuoğlu, Ibrahim, *TKP Kuruluşu ve Mücadelesinin Tarihi*, Eser, 1976.

Treadgold, Donald W., *Twentieth Century Russia*, Boulder, CO: Westview Press, 1990.

Tulyakova: Vera Tulyakova Hikmet, *Nazım'la Söyleşi*, Cem, 1989.

Tunçay, Mete, *Türkiyede Sol Akımlar*, vol. 1, Ankara: Bilgi, 1967; vol. 2, Ankara: BDS, 1992.

Tutanak: Turkish Parlamentary Proceedings, 1951, D9, V1, 331.

Uçuk, Cahit, *Bir Imparatorluk Çökerken*, Yapı Kredi, 1995.

Uluç, Fuat, *Nazım Hikmet ve 1938 Harbokulu Olayının Gerçek Yüzü*, Ayyıldız, 1967.

UNESCO: *Statistics on Radio and Television 1950-1960*, Paris: UNESCO, 1963.

Vali, Ferenc A., *Rift and Revolt in Hungary: Nationalism versus Communism*, Cambridge, MA: Harvard University Press, 1961.

Va-Nu: Vala Nurettin, *Bu Dünyadan Nazım Geçti*, Cem, 1988.

Weisband, Edward, *Turkish Foreign Policy, 1943-1945*, Princeton University Press, 1973.

Yalman, Ahmet Emin, *Yakın Tarihte Gördüklerim ve Geçirdiklerim*, 14 vols, 1945-70.

Yalman 1956: Ahmet Emin Yalman, *Turkey in My Time*, Oklahoma University Press, 1956.

Yücebaş, Hilmi, *Nazım Hikmet Türk Basınında: Kavgalar, Hatıralar, Şiirler*, Tekin, 1967.

Zabolotsky Nitika, *The Life of Zabolotsky*, tr. R. R. Milner-Gulland and C. G. Bearne, Cardiff: University of Wales Press, 1994.

Zenkovsky, Serge A., *Pan-Turkism and Islam in Russia*, Cambridge MA: Harvard University Press, 1960.

Zinner, Paul E., *Revolution in Hungary*, New York: Columbia University Press, 1962.

Zürcher, Erik J., *Turkey: A Modern History*, London: I. B. Tauris, 1993.

Other Sources

Archives

ANVA: Aziz Nesin Vakfı Archive.

Bijlage: 10-page typewritten list of Nazım's broadcasts from Budapest, now in the IISH Archive in Amsterdam, catalogue number 'Bijlage bij Gb 205 t/m 212'.

HTA: Hungarian Theatre Archives, Madyar Szinhazi Intezet, Budapest.

IISH: International Institute of Social History, Amsterdam: Comintern Archives.

NHA: Nazım Hikmet Archive in Moscow, Centrali Archive Literatiru i Iskusstva.

SPA: Soviet Archives of Peace and Mutual Understanding, Moscow.

Transcripts: Transcripts of Bizim Radyo broadcasts from Leipzig, International Institute for Social History, Amsterdam.

Newspapers and magazines

References to short reports or articles in newspapers and magazines are normally identified in the text by means of the date and/or number concerned.

Television

GC/TV 4 = Güneri Civaoğlu (presenter), 'Rüzgara Karşı Yürüyen Adam', Part 4 of a television series devoted to Nazım's career, 1995.

Interviews

Andaç, Münevver, July 1996.
Aybars, Mehmet Ali, January 1990.
Aydemir, Aydın, January 1990.
Aygi, Gennady, April 1997.
Balaban, Ibrahim, January 1989, October 1996.
Berksoy, Semiha, October 1996.
Bozışık, Mehmet, January 1990.
Coşkun, Atila, October 1988, January 1990.
Çakırhan, Nail V, January 1992, October 1995, March 1996.
Çambel, Halet, October 1995 (London).
Dino, Abidin, 1987 (London).
Dino, Güzin, March 1994, July 1996 (Paris).
Ekmekci, Mustafa, October 1988.
Erduran, Refik, October 1988, January 1990, October 1996.
Fish, Rady, 1989 (London), November 1990 (Moscow), October 1991, (Moscow).
Günyol, Vedat, October 1996.
Ileri, Rasih Nuri, March 1996.
Kalyoncu, Melda, January 1990, October 1996.
Karaosmanoğlu, Leman, September 1988.
Korca, Kerim, January 1990.
Kúnos, István, August 1989 (Budapest).
Mango, Andrew, August 1997 (London).
Melikov, Tofik, October 1991 (Moscow).

Nesin, Aziz, January 1992.

Memet Fuat, November 1988, February 1990, March 1996.

Nurettin, Müzehher Vala, September 1988, January 1990, March and October 1996.

Sayılgan, Aclan, September 1988.

Sebük, Mehmet Ali, January 1990.

Sertel, Yıldız, April 1995.

Sülker, Kemal, September 1988.

Sömlyó, György, August 1989 (Budapest).

Şen, Bilal, (Telephone) August 1997 (Bulgaria).

Tulyakova-Hikmet, Vera, January 1992.

Türkali, Vedat, August 1997 (London).

Uçuk, Cahit, March 1996 and October 1996.

Yaltırım, Samiye, January 1990.

Index of Personal Names

Wherever possible, this index is arranged alphabetically by surname. Since surnames were only introduced in Turkey in 1935, members of earlier generations may be listed by their first names; a surname adopted later in life may follow in brackets. Authors of sources cited in the text are not included.

362   *Index*